Doing Comparative Education:

Three Decades of Collaboration

Who would have
believed it !

Max.
Cohrain   July 2003

CERC Studies in Comparative Education 5

Doing Comparative Education:
Three Decades of Collaboration

Harold J. Noah & Max A. Eckstein

with a foreword by

Philip Foster

Comparative Education Research Centre
The University of Hong Kong

Comparative Education Research Centre
Faculty of Education
The University of Hong Kong
Pokfulam Road, Hong Kong, China

© Comparative Education Research Centre 1998
First published 1998

ISBN 962 8093 87 8

Cover design by Leung May Shan, Sue
Printed by The Central Printing Press Ltd, Hong Kong

The authors acknowledge permission to use material from work previously published by: Academic Press; Butterworth Publishers; Canadian Society for the Study of Higher Education: Carfax Publishing Company: Evans Brothers Ltd.; The Free Press; Georgia State University; Kluwer Academic Publishers; Peter Lang Publishers; OECD; Peacock Publishers; Teachers College Press; UNESCO; University of Chicago Press; University of North Carolina Press; University of Pennsylvania Press; University of Wisconsin Press; The World Bank; John Wiley and Sons; Yale University Press.

Harold J. Noah and Max A. Eckstein have asserted the moral right to be identified as the authors of this work.

Contents

Part IV: Educational Policy   287

Notes on the authors   353

Index of authors   355

Foreword

Philip Foster

Just a few years before the more celebrated 'British Invasion' of the Beatles and the Rolling Stones in the early 1960s, Max Eckstein and Harold Noah arrived in the United States and began graduate studies at Columbia University's Teachers College, in New York. One hopes that this less publicized event will be just as enduring in its influence. Some years before, both Eckstein and Noah had completed their undergraduate studies at London University, and each had taught for a lengthy period in English secondary grammar schools. It is worth noting that their earlier differences in disciplinary background seem, to me at least, to have created a fruitful synthesis between the humanities and the social sciences that characterizes most of their written work. The more austere elements of economic and sociological analysis need to be enriched by humanistic traditions that give us a deeper understanding of the historical and cultural traditions within which national systems of education have evolved.

Perhaps it is time that we gave more formal recognition to the contribution that so many migrant scholars have made to the field of comparative education. Many, like Noah and Eckstein, first traveled to the USA as graduate students while others, like Isaac Kandel and Robert Ulich, had already had distinguished careers elsewhere. While in no sense diminishing the major contribution of the 'home-grown', it is apparent that these intellectual emigrés were able to provide insights into educational issues that stemmed from their earlier training and experience. For example, it is likely that Eckstein and Noah's concern with the content and selective and allocative functions of external examinations in a variety of national contexts was, in part, a result of their teaching stint in English secondary schools where 'teaching to the examination' was so crucial to subsequent student success. Likewise, Noah's early emphasis on Soviet education stemmed, as he once told me, from familial roots in Odessa, which was at one time the locus of one of the most lively cultural traditions in pre-Soviet Russia. I feel that there must be a graduate student somewhere who could undertake some analysis of the various paths by which scholars have entered the field and what experience has determined their subsequent research agendas. In the case of Noah and Eckstein, the word cross-national or comparative appears frequently in their writings but they have, very wisely, largely confined their studies to the analysis of educational issues in a cluster of Western nations. They have been content to focus their work on the societies with which they feel most comfortable and thus have avoided becoming that bane of the field, the universal expert. At the same time they have taken the word 'comparative' seriously and have avoided the danger of narrow overspecialization. A good deal of their work in fact provides the kinds of observation that can lead to research in very different cultural contexts.

Both arrived in the United States at a time when the outlook for international studies of any kind was propitious. American alarm at the triumphs of Soviet science and technology culminating in Sputnik had led to a spate of rather superficial literature praising the supposed superiority of the Soviet educational system particularly in the hard sciences.   The fact that formal curricula did not in fact measure what was necessarily taught nor, indeed, learned in Soviet schools escaped many authors. However, the anxiety that the Soviet achievements created had one salutary effect.   The passing of the National Defense Education Acts in the early 1960s initiated a massive expansion of federal support for higher education, particularly at the graduate level. This federal largesse emphasized not only the hard sciences but led to growth in a host of area-studies programs concentrating on the language, history and cultural traditions of a wide range of societies.

This support undergirded the quantitative and qualitative growth of international studies in education; support that it most certainly needed!   In the United States, Kandel's writing in the 1930s had given the field greater salience and respectability in academe, but the post-war years had shown little advance. With a number of notable exceptions, most published work eschewed the explicitly comparative route and more often than not consisted of a descriptive catalogue of the features of education in one nation. The treatment was usually historical in thrust and while I should be the last to underestimate the importance of historical studies, I find it difficult to applaud many efforts that were frequently based on limited documentary sources and which were written by authors with inadequate training in historical research. Moreover, in the USA many graduate dissertations in particular concluded with an almost mandatory chapter entitled 'Suggestions for Reform' or something like it. These effusions usually added up to the suggestion that the system of education under review would do well to emulate the characteristics of the US system supplemented not infrequently with commendatory quotations from the then icon of American education, John Dewey.   The fact that American educational practices bore no relation to any that Dewey had envisioned (except at the rhetorical level) seemed to escape most writers. All in all, it was a rather depressing scene that often confronted our authors: a mixture of rather superficial historical description conjoined with a hopeless confusion of fact and hortatory judgement.

The intellectual frailty of comparative educational studies was paralleled by the relative lack of any institutionalized, professional setting within which scholars could function.   The image of the lone scholar valiantly pursuing a line of research is misleading. In fact, most scholars require and benefit hugely from dialogue with others in the field through the meetings of scholarly societies and the publication of reputable journals.   In the early 1960s, this crucial dimension was embryonic.   The US Comparative Education Society was established in 1956, although its title was later changed to the Comparative and International Education Society (CIES) in deference to members whose concerns largely focused on policy and practice rather than more formal research. That the society survived at all was due to the efforts of small band of scholars supplemented by the administrative and financial acuity of Gerald Read of Kent State University. The *Comparative Education Review* likewise owed its continued existence to the untiring efforts of its first editor, George Bereday at Teachers College. It was not until 1971 that the Society was able to hold its first entirely independent Annual Meeting. Until then such meetings had consisted of tiny gatherings usually of 50 or so individuals held in one hotel conference room for a single plenary session and organized under the auspices of the Association of Colleges of Teacher Education. The Presidency was a largely ceremonial office with election by show of hands of those members present.

Compare this with the situation today. The CIES is a flourishing organization with a substantial individual and institutional membership and the whole academic paraphernalia of Presidents, Vice Presidents, Presidents Elect and Standing Committees. Above all, we note the existence of an internationally prestigious journal whose pages document the progress of the field and reflect the salient and changing intellectual agendas of the decades. Indeed, the aspiring graduate student could usefully compare essays in the early numbers of the *Review* with current titles to realize what an immense distance we have come in terms of scope and intellectual sophistication. That we have come thus far is in significant measure due to the continuing efforts of scholars like Eckstein and Noah on the Society's and the Journal's behalf. They have been frequent contributors to the *Review* over the years, and, Noah was editor of that journal in some of its crucial years of qualitative transition. Moreover, both scholars are distinguished Past Presidents and Honorary Fellows of the Society. They have served on the editorial boards and special committees of the organization while providing sensible advice concerning its administrative structures and financial status over the years. These kinds of sometimes unrewarding but essential activities often get overlooked in scholarly encomia, but we are bound to recognize how much the field owes to their contributions at the institutional level. They have been committed academics as well as scholars (the two are not quite the same thing) and the present book amounts to considerably more than the republication of excerpts from a formidable number of books, articles, and reviews: it subsumes 30 years of service to the field in general.

This is not the place to undertake a detailed critique of the essays that follow, so I propose to emphasize just a few elements in the substantive intellectual contribution of the pair. Having already noted the early rather precarious state of the field, we can thoroughly agree with their observation that a self-conscious preoccupation with epistemology and methodology typically characterizes weaker intellectual traditions. Not surprisingly, the 1960s witnessed a continuing examination of the scope and nature of the field. However, it must be recognized that over the last 30 years or so, impetus to change almost invariably arose from controversies that began in *other* disciplinary areas. In other words, comparative education has borrowed extensively from other fields, although I sometimes feel that in the process of borrowing some intellectual traditions have been diluted or even distorted as in the case, for example, of Marxist or neo-Marxist traditions of analysis.

Some early attempts to establish comparative education as a distinctive "discipline" were short lived, and I think that Noah and Eckstein are correct in viewing the field as multidisciplinary but not interdisciplinary in nature. Indeed, the number of truly interdisciplinary endeavors in the social sciences, for example, could be counted on the fingers of one hand. In the case of comparative education, the largely historical traditions which had dominated the field hitherto were forced to move over to accommodate "some new boys on the block" namely anthropology, sociology and, a little later, economics.

This was because sociology, in particular, was itself undergoing some transformation. The nineteenth century had witnessed a number of large scale attempts at comparative analysis within a substantially evolutionary framework. However, these were later eschewed as being conceptually flawed and methodologically suspect, and were replaced by more in-depth studies usually conducted within one national or societal context. Comparative studies once more became fashionable in the late 1950s partly as a result of interest in what were then termed the "New Nations" and events in the Soviet-dominated parts of the world.

I would link the development of a more hospitable view toward the pretensions of the social sciences with the foundation of the Comparative Education Center at the

University of Chicago in the late 1950s. Faculty at that Center were pre-occupied with types of cross-national research that did *not* involve earlier evolutionary theories, and thus the pages of the *Comparative Education Review* and other journals witnessed a succession of early articles written by the staff of the Center concerning the creation of cross-societal typologies, the necessity for 'controlled' comparison, and, where appropriate, the use of more quantitative modes of enquiry based on survey rather than just documentary-based materials. At the same time, doubts began to be raised, for example, concerning the utility of the concept of national character that had been emphasized in some of Kandel's writings. Some of these critiques received a rather hostile reception and I recall with some amusement that Kandel himself was moved to write a rather acerbic rejoinder in the *Review* criticizing with some justification the pretensions of the then 'Young Turks'.

Nonetheless, debate continued throughout the 1960s, and methodological controversy was supplemented by new substantive issues such as the relationship between education and economic development, the methodologies of educational planning, and enquiry into the nexus between educational development and social inequality in both more-developed and less-developed nations. The publication of Noah and Eckstein's *Toward a Science of Comparative Education* in 1969 was particularly timely, since it provided a general overview of many of these issues within the context of a particular approach to the logic of enquiry. A companion edited volume entitled *Scientific Investigations in Comparative Education* provided examples of what were then perceived as successful attempts at explicitly cross-national research that might be emulated.

These volumes introduced scholars in the field to types of investigation that were quite new to many of them, though in all fairness some of the discussion would have hardly seemed startling to many social scientists. Indeed, the whole intent of Noah and Eckstein was to show comparative educators that the social sciences could constitute a fruitful alternative approach to enquiry that could supplement but *not* replace older traditions of historically-based research.

The first volume in my view (some parts of the second edited volume now seem rather dated) still constitutes a valuable introduction to 'scientific method' in comparative education, and I suppose that for those who enjoy classificatory exercises Noah and Eckstein would be placed in the 'positivist' camp. Yet their work is distinguished by its eclecticism and receptivity to alternative approaches (with one exception as will be shown later). Although supportive of those types of cross-national quantitative investigation best exemplified in the series on International Educational Achievement, both were very conscious of the limitations of such kinds of research; and Noah's lively rejoinder in the later pages of this volume to the critics of these endeavors is everywhere sustained by a clear understanding of just how far we can go in that direction. Thus, as we attempt to explain the amount of variance in a particular dependent variable (for example, level of tertiary educational attendance in a range of western nations characterized by similar levels of economic development), we may find that the explanatory power of a whole set of selected quantitative independent variables is so limited that we are then obliged to look at 'unique' historical and cultural traditions as the major causative factor in tertiary education expansion. Moreover, as Eckstein and Noah point out, the most appropriate kinds of units for the investigation of many educational phenomena lie not at the national, but at the sub-national level whether we are looking at geographic regions, ethnic or cultural minorities and so on. In fact, in comparative educational studies, the amount of variation in any particular educational phenomenon is often greater *within* nation states than it is as between them.

However, the careful reader will discern that in earlier works, some of Noah and Eckstein's own enquiries fall rather short of their own stricter methodological prescriptions. Note, for example, the discussion on prefects, monitors and ultimate deterrents in English and American schools. Here parallel qualitative descriptions of divergent behavioral patterns of control are attributed to the value systems or cultural traditions that obtain in the two societies as a result of their different historical experience. Surely, in this case are we not far from ascribing educational practices to differences in "National character"? I still believe that the whole question of the degree of symmetry between social structures and personality systems is still important; but these essays might raise the eyebrows of hard-nosed sociologists who would regard the conclusions as little more than very plausible hypotheses hardly susceptible to controlled investigation.

In short, there is plenty of evidence in the following pages that our authors are sometimes less concerned with the actual testing of hypotheses in a cross-national or cross-cultural context than in providing solid, descriptive accounts of educational practice. In parts of their other writing, the creation of typologies for the investigation of educational phenomena constitutes only a prologmenon to possible lines of research which others might usefully build upon. Above all, both recognize that methods of enquiry depend very much on the way that the research problem is initially formulated.

As I noted earlier, nearly all of Eckstein and Noah's writing has been concerned with education in a cluster of Western nations. Their only major departure in this regard so far as I am aware consists of their highly critical essay on dependency theory, which drew them a little closer to educational issues in less developed nations. They note themselves that they have little sympathy with a body of writing that appeared in the late 1960s and 1970s which we might refer to as the 'radical critique' of which dependency theory constituted one element. To my mind, their commentary on that theory is quite damning; but it is only fair to note that the positivist tradition was far from being 'the only game in town' at that time.

Some, but not all, of the radical critique had its roots in orthodox or neo-Marxist theory. It is hardly surprising that Eckstein and Noah were not only critical of these intellectual developments but were hardly impressed by the claim that they represented new paradigms in comparative educational research. For anyone reared in essentially European educational traditions, they were in fact exhumations of controversies that had flourished in the more radical salons of Europe in the late nineteenth century. To be sure, an ostensibly new vocabulary emerged in comparative education such as 'cultural imperialism', 'social reproduction', 'intellectual hegemony', 'dependency theory', and so on; but in the United States a good deal of rather old intellectual mutton was being served up as lamb in the late 1960s and early 1970s, reflecting the hitherto serious neglect of Marxist and neo-Marxist traditions in American higher education.

In comparative education, the radical critique still survives in numerous forms, though the latest fashions in deconstructionism and post-modernism (once again borrowed from outside the field) have tended to usurp some of its earlier manifestations. This is not the place to examine these traditions in detail, except to note that outside lively debate in scholarly journals they have had little influence on the policy and practice of education. Indeed, they point to a research agenda very different from that proposed by Eckstein and Noah – one which, in their view and mine, makes the development of policy-oriented research, in particular, a largely futile exercise.

There is one thing however, on which we *all* agree: What are often conceived as 'educational' problems have their origins outside the educational systems. This is a valuable corrective to the historically powerful American belief (in contrast to much

European thought) in the transformatory power of schooling. Insofar as educational institutions are functionally linked to other major societal sub-systems, we can always anticipate that educational reforms, for example, will have unanticipated and indeed sometimes undesirable consequences. But surely this is nothing but a reformulation of the cautionary observations of many shrewd nineteenth century observers who were quite aware of the dangers of uninformed educational borrowing! To paraphrase a Mertonian dictum, the successful transfer of educational institutions and practices presupposes an understanding of their latent functions in their place of origin.

Yet for all the risks involved, we may be sure that educational borrowing will continue, and thus one task of the comparative educator is to enlighten educational policy makers as to what these risks might be. The gathering of sound descriptive data on educational policies and practices that have arisen elsewhere in response to perceived education 'problems' is an essential first step. Eckstein and Noah provide extensive and detailed information on the different educational strategies that a number of Western nations have followed with respect to the relationship between education and the workplace. What is less obvious to many is that some of the 'solutions', such as the German apprenticeship model would be quite non-viable in another labor market; and what is less frequently recognized is that trends in the German economy itself are making the apprenticeship solution increasingly dysfunctional in Germany. If it is often unwise to import non-viable models, it is equally short-sighted not to recognize already obsolescent ones.

Yet the gathering of descriptive data, however well organized, is for some of us only a first step which may lead to the more sophisticated examinations of more specific hypotheses suggested. Thus the IEA studies were designed to examine the differential *determinants* of educational performance in a number of nations. Note, however, how policy makers in some countries have perverted the tentative findings of this research to justify types of educational change often already determined. Indeed, the whole nexus between cross-national research and educational policy is far more complex than we suppose: it is not simply that research findings are quoted out of context, but there is also a misunderstanding of the limitations of any kind of inquiry. I shudder when I hear the statement that "comparative research proves…". No inquiry, however sophisticated, *proves* anything: it merely points to relationships that occur under various conditions, and such relationships are often compatible with a number of alternative explanatory theories. We often envisage that policy formation is based on rational planning models that derive from research; but even if the latter is appropriate and well designed and not the kind of policy-oriented investigation undertaken to provide slap-dash conclusions to false problems, it cannot provide 'answers'. For example, over the last couple of decades, a formidable body of comparative work on social and private rates of return to educational investment has shown that social returns to investment in higher education are generally lower than those at the primary and secondary level. However, this in itself says nothing about desirable levels of investment in such education except upon the basis of an implicit set of *a priori* assumptions that we make about the nature of the 'social good'. Moreover, even if it were decided on the basis of maximizing measured social returns to education to diminish levels of public expenditure to the tertiary sector, it is the institutional and contextual environment in the nation state that determines what out of a number of policy strategies available is the one that may prove most politically viable. Everywhere the political process itself modifies what the planner may regard as an optimal solution, but we are also the prisoners of history in terms of our perception of what options may be conceived of as even possible. Thus a knowledge of 'how things came to be' in some measure always determines how things will be; and at the risk of annoying professional historians, I think we can with due caution learn from the history of other societies and nation states.

I trust that Eckstein and Noah approve of some of these remarks, but I would first stress that any comparative educator who is concerned with the policy implications of research needs some grasp of history, because without it we are blind to the institutional framework within which policy decisions will be made. Second, although we know a great deal more about the *performance* of educational systems than we did three decades ago, thanks to a vast increase in the volume and quality of research, I am not convinced that the level of discussion on the *ends* of educational policy has become more sophisticated. Research may tell policy makers what is sociologically possible, but it cannot inform them about what is desirable. Moreover, as we enhance the quality of comparative research, we need to remember that what 'knowledge is of most worth' presupposes that we have some conception of the kind of society we aspire to. Sometimes I think a little more social philosophy, occasionally at the expense of technical expertise, might serve us better in the policy arena.

These issues are important insofar as we can expect that perceived educational problems which have implications for *policy* will drive most of the research agenda in comparative education in the future as much as they have done in the past. Whether we like it or not, the availability of resources, rather than simple intellectual curiosity, primarily shapes the pattern of much current research. Nevertheless, I still hope that there is room in the field for those scholars whose work is driven by intellectual curiosity and playfulness, because as in the natural sciences, the serendipitous outcomes of such endeavors may have substantial long term policy implications. Nonetheless, if we review the decades of work covered in this book, it is very evident that pressure from policy oriented agencies or popular concern has determined so much of what we do. Thus interest in Soviet education led ultimately to the IEA studies and subsequently to a focus on manpower planning and education. As the manpower approach began to be questioned, the claims of neo-classical economics led to a new cross-societal emphasis on rates of return analysis in both the developed and less developed world. Parallel with these developments the whole issue of "equality" in education, in all its various shades of meaning, generated a new emphasis on access to schooling which in turn merged with growing interest in problems of class, ethnicity, gender, and so on. Rather than amplify this catalogue, and at the risk of some oversimplification, I think that the first half of Eckstein and Noah's professional involvement saw a massive increase in the level of research sophistication in the field conjoined with a major emphasis on the link between education and other major societal sub-systems. In terms of its policy implications, this approach concerned itself with the 'external efficiency' of educational systems, and very little of the literature dealt with what went on in classrooms.

In the last decade or so, however, for North American scholars the 'Japanese challenge' has replaced the 'Soviet challenge' of 40 years ago as an object of concern, and the question why Japanese children ostensibly perform so well in school has merged with an already growing interest in examining the culture of schools and classrooms. This ironically enough, brings us back full circle to those early nineteenth century travelers and scholars whose writings were largely focused upon in-classroom phenomena. Thus, ethnography and culture are the current buzzwords, and greater interest in qualitative types of investigation reflects scepticism concerning the merits of quantitative enquiry. Policy increasingly concerns itself with issues of internal rather than external efficiency; but there is little doubt that before too long we shall see new methodological controversies over the kind of qualitative enquiry that often undergirds it since the latter makes cross-national research exceedingly difficult to pursue in terms of research design.

Interestingly, Eckstein and Noah's later comparative research on examinations merges with some of these new developments. In this work they were less concerned with the selective and allocative functions of examinations *per se*, but rather with the various cultural traditions that determine their content: what knowledge do different societies consider so important that it must be enshrined and embodied in their examinations systems? As usual, Eckstein and Noah's work rests on both work humanistic and social science traditions, and provides an enlightening synthesis between qualitative and quantitative methods of enquiry.

Let me make two final comments on Eckstein and Noah's endeavors as they pass from the status of Young Turks to that of Grand Old Men. First, they have invariably written with clarity, felicity, and economy; and at the risk of being ethnocentric, I would like to think that the English educational system had something to do with it. Whatever its defects, the English secondary grammar school obliged students to write well; and I often feel that in comparative education we suffer from too many pieces that read like bad translations from originals in other languages.

Second, Eckstein and Noah write with a degree of humor and dry wit so significantly lacking in the typical article in the field. I am told that they once were advised by a senior colleague that scholars would not be amused or enlightened by the quotations from Lewis Carroll that preface their chapters in *Toward a Science of Comparative Education*. I trust that the senior colleague was wrong. Moreover, I cannot think of a better description of the limitations of quantitative enquiry than that contained in a quotation from the *Mikado* that concludes Chapter 19 in this volume. Perhaps we can sometimes learn more from the sociology and economics of W.S. Gilbert than that of Karl Marx; and it would be a sad world indeed if successful scholarship invariably required that we abandon our sense of humor on the way!

Preface

We feel extraordinarily fortunate to have had the opportunity to collaborate over a long period of time, developing ideas and publishing on topics in comparative education that were of interest to us both. We offer here a selection of our individual and joint writings over the past thirty-five years as a celebration of that good fortune.

There was a time when individuals such as Sadler, Arnold, Kandel, Hans, or Rossello, working in comparative education, could hope to comprehend and explain the whole of education, its origins, present aspects, and future prospects in a host of countries. For the present-day single researcher this is hardly possible. The sheer volume of data from more and more countries, the way in which education and training have become central to national policies, and the need to master or at least understand many different modes of analysis have all conspired to make the example of the renaissance men of our immediate past simply unachievable today. On the macro-level, international organizations wishing to profit from comparative investigations in education have recognized the need to deploy and coordinate teams of specialists in several disciplines. On our small micro-level, as individual researchers, we have had occasion to appreciate more and more the benefit of long-term collaboration in the face of this ever-growing complexity of comparative education.

The early 1960s were years when comparative studies in education, as indeed comparative studies in many other fields, were changing rapidly. Until that time the field had been dominated by historical approaches and descriptive works, most of them taking the form of studies of school systems in individual countries. Although there were numerous examples of excellent reporting, based on intimate knowledge of the foreign systems described and evaluated, we were concerned by the subjective nature of the accounts of even the best works we read and the absence of any overt rules or guidelines for the judgements made. By the end of the 1960s, though, social science methods had gained a permanent, if still disputed, place in comparative studies of education.

We were wholly in sympathy with this trend, even though we by no means wished to cast out historical, philosophical, and generally normative approaches. But we did want to boost the social science approach. As we observed in the Preface to *Toward a Science of Comparative Education*: We are conscious .... that we have sung a single tune ..., the theme of empirical, quantitative research, and that the problems of education and society also encompass phenomena that are more amenable to treatment in other ways. Hence, we would not want the complete comparative educator to discard .... The concerns and techniques of the humanist, the philosopher, and the artist. The selection of pieces included here will, we believe, be evidence of our long-term commitment to both types of work.

In any event, one immediate result of our concern for greater attention to social science approaches was to introduce into our teaching an effort to instruct students about empirical research and to turn away from the strange lands and friendly people approach that characterized most comparative education courses at the time. In particular, we tried to show how it was both possible and enlightening to use comparative data to test hypotheses about the relation between education and social phenomena. We asked our students to assemble evidence sufficient to test the cross-national validity of such statements as: The greater the concern for political (or religious) orthodoxy, the more centralized the school system; or, educational revolutions are consequences, not causes of political revolutions; and, the longer the average length of schooling of the population, the fewer the external marks of class difference, and so forth. Eventually this led to our writing *Toward a Science of Comparative Education*, as well as editing a companion collection of studies broadly exemplifying this approach (*Scientific Investigations in Comparative Education*).

Shortly after the publication of *Toward a Science of Comparative Education* we were invited by the International Association for the Evaluation of Educational Achievement to join the group established in Stockholm to analyze the data from the six-subject IEA study. In collaboration with A. Harry Passow, we were charged to consider how far and in what ways national social and school system characteristics were related to student performance in 21 nations – a formidable task, if ever there was one! We emerged from this exercise with only at best a set of tentative conclusions. In no way could we say that any particular social or educational feature (or even combination of features) was unambiguously associated with higher or lower school achievement. But we learned a great deal from the IEA work, not least that the techniques being developed during IEA investigations could eventually lead to more confident statements about what works and what doesn't (in terms of producing school achievement) at different grade levels in different schools in different countries.

Meanwhile, the Comparative and International Education Society (USA) was growing and responding to changes in the kind of work that comparativists were doing. Its journal, the *Comparative Education Review*, developed into a leading publication, its contents frequently cited by authors within and outside the field of comparative education. Over the years we contributed a fair number of articles to the pages of the *CER*, and one of us had a spell editing the journal. We also paid our dues to our professional organization serving at different times as its president. Membership in the Society grew rapidly, drawing in a wide variety of practitioners, some of whom went beyond whatever point we had reached in extending the methodological scope of the field. These scholars sought to promote work relying on micro-observations of school processes, deconstructionist critiques of school systems and educational activities, reproduction theory, and so on. We chose not to follow these novel paths, being generally out of sympathy with them. In particular, while participating in some of the common intellectual and academic developments of the time, we somehow succeeded in avoiding the contemporary fashion of viewing the schools as oppressive instruments for maintaining an intellectual and political status quo.

During the 1970s and 1980s some of the official international organizations vastly increased their comparative education activities. UNESCO expanded its global collection of educational statistics, its promotion of literacy programs, and its journals in comparative education *(International Review of Education* and *Prospects)*. We made substantial use of UNESCO's statistical collections and we published in its journals. The Organisation for Economic Cooperation and Development (OECD) in Paris undertook a series of National Education Policy Studies. One of us was engaged in four of these, as well as in a comparative study of the financing of elementary schools. The World Bank increasingly saw a role for itself in lending money and providing advice for the development of education and training in lower-income countries. It found itself doing comparative education, without necessarily acknowledging that that was what it was doing. Agencies of the U.S. government (the Department of Education, the Office of Technology Assessment, and the National Endowment for the Humanities) and the American Federation of Teachers exhibited interest in foreign education systems, focussing on standards and assessment in education, and we were individually as well as jointly enlisted as consultants in this effort.

Our work can be characterized under a few main topics: our early and abiding interest in the way research in comparative education is undertaken; the social context of school systems and practice, in particular in metropolitan areas; the outcomes of schooling as reflected in student achievement; and the ways in which education policy is made in different countries. Although much of our work was deliberately not locked into events in particular countries, we nevertheless also paid special attention to educational policies and practices in the former Soviet Union, as well as the changes taking place since the end of World War II in Western Europe.

What to put in and what to leave out of this collection was governed by a few rules. We wanted to make sure that there was at least one piece for each type of comparative work we had done, for each issue or problem we had considered, and for each area of the world that we had studied. We were willing to include articles and book chapters in their entirety, but we wanted to be strictly economical in the sampling of our books, on the ground that an interested reader would probably have an easier job locating a copy of an out-of-print book than a fairly ancient journal article. Thus we include in this collection several book reviews, which afforded us the opportunity to comment on broader issues of comparative interest, especially changing approaches to the field, both methodological and substantive. Above all, we wanted only pieces of work we still felt happy with – translated, that meant pieces which did not make us cringe when we read them again with the full benefit of two, three, or even four decades of hindsight!

Within these broad categories, the choice of topics was largely influenced by the issues which from time to time came to the top of the list of educational policy concerns in the United States, such issues as: the training and qualifications of teachers; the financing of education; the special nature of schooling in large cities; the involvement of business and industry in the work of the schools; and educational standards, national examinations, and the measurement of educational achievement. Each of these topics is represented in the present selection from our work.

Harold J. Noah & Max A. Eckstein

PART I: COMPARATIVE ORIENTATIONS

1

Toward a Science of Comparative Education*

[From Part One: The Development of Comparative Education]

Introduction

The purpose of reviewing the development of comparative education is not simply to trace through materials that have been examined many times before,[1] but rather to search out in the predecessors of modern comparative education those elements of their thought pertinent to understanding their motives for undertaking comparative work, the types of data they used, the ways they handled the data, and their interpretations of them. The analysis reveals the gradual, unsteady emergence of an empirically based, social scientific approach in comparative education, the history of which begins with simple narrative sometimes naive, but often astute, and ends, for the present, with the application of the sophisticated methods now being employed in the social sciences.

The development of comparative education has been marked by five identifiable stages, each characterized by a different motive for comparative study and each producing a different genre of work. The earliest stage, the period of travelers' tales, was prompted by simple curiosity. Second came a period of educational borrowing, when the desire to learn useful lessons from foreign practices was the major motivation. In the third stage, international educational cooperation was stressed in the interests of world harmony and mutual improvement among nations. Since the beginning of the twentieth century, two more stages have appeared, both concerned with seeking explanations for the wide variety of educational and social phenomena observed around the globe. The first of these attempted to identify the forces and factors shaping national educational systems. The second, and the latest, may be termed the stage of social science explanation, which uses the empirical, quantitative methods of economics, political science, and sociology to clarify relationships between education and society.

These stages are far from being discrete in time: each of these types of work in comparative education has persisted down to the present and may be observed in the contemporary literature, and rarely can any contributor to the field be confined within a single category. But the categorization suggested, loose though it is, provides a convenient, unforced framework within which to review the development of the field.

STAGE 1. The first and most primitive comparative education observations were the tales brought home by travelers to foreign parts. Such reports were essentially the work of amateurs who included in more general descriptions of institutions and practices abroad details of foreign ways of raising children.   These rapporteurs tended to emphasize exotic information simply because it threw into sharp contrast the familiar practices and institutions of their homelands.   Curiosity was the mainspring of their voyages, and local color the attraction of their descriptions.   Only the rare observer could extract systematic conclusions with explanatory value from a mass of indiscriminately reported impressions. In the form of superior journalism, this style of work remains a prominent feature of writing on foreign countries today.

STAGE 2.   From the beginning of the nineteenth century, coincident with the rise of national systems of education in Europe, journeys abroad were made by travelers with a specialized interest in educational matters.   No longer motivated by general curiosity, they went the rounds of foreign countries to discover information useful for charting the course of education in their own countries.   This group of precursors of modern comparative education were predominantly educational politicians, experts, and activists.   Often they traveled not at their own expense, or following their private interest, but as emissaries, sometimes self-appointed, of their national governments. They concerned themselves with educational theory, methodology, finance, and organization.   Teacher training, instructional methods, and alternatives to traditionally accepted curricula were matters of major importance for them.   Though their reports now focused sharply upon the schools, characteristics associated with travelers' tales persisted: many of the reports took the form of encyclopedic descriptions of foreign school systems, perhaps enlivened here and there with anecdotes, but rarely explanatory.   Of necessity, objectivity and detachment were lacking, for these educational emissaries, committed as they were to the cause of education in their own countries, mostly saw and reported from abroad merely what they judged would advance their domestic enterprises.

STAGE 3.   This was a period, too, when exchange of information about foreign countries and particularly about foreign education was considered desirable simply to break down the barriers of ignorance that divided nation from nation.   Encyclopedic work was still the fashion, but it was argued that the very process of systematically amassing and publishing information on foreign countries would require extensive exchanges of scholars, students, and publications.   The resulting network of international contacts would of itself help promote international understanding, as well as the improvement of social and, in particular, educational institutions around the world.

STAGE 4.   Coincident with the rise of the social sciences towards the end of the nineteenth century there came a recognition of the importance of the dynamic relationships knitting education and society.   Education was seen as the mirror of society; but society, in turn, was molded partly by the schools. Changes in one were revealed in the other. The concern now was to understand the interaction of education and society by analyzing the historical forces and contemporary factors that had shaped both. Moreover, exponents of this approach were interested in more than laying bare the nature of these relationships. They began to consider the possibility of using their conclusions to steer educational reform and so engineer the future shape of society.

    In this phase of comparative education, studies of foreign schooling became to a considerable extent studies of national character and the institutions that help form it. They relied heavily on history and tended to strike a deterministic note. Problems of cause and effect preoccupied comparative educators, but inevitably their discussion quickly descended into a familiar circularity: national character determines education, and education determines national character. Where to break in to this perplexing circle was a question not easily answered.

STAGE 5. A significant strengthening of the explanatory powers of the social sciences took place after World War 1. Many governments improved the quantity and quality of their statistical series, and statistical techniques became much more sophisticated. Partly in response to these new possibilities, the social sciences came to rely more and more upon quantitative methods; and the demands of researchers stimulated the production of yet more statistical material. This was particularly true in economics and sociology, and in later years this trend extended to political science and even to anthropology. Quantitative methods were adopted not only in the social sciences, per se, but also in some branches of education, particularly in psychology and psychometrics. In this manner, the humanistic origins of the social sciences, which accounted for their early philosophical and historical emphases, were gradually overlaid by new concerns and methods of an empirical and quantitative nature. Comparative education slowly followed the same path.

Since World War II these trends have accelerated and the empirical orientation of the social sciences has begun to reshape comparative education. Contemporary cross-national study in education is thus founded upon the twin bases of vastly increased bodies of data and improved techniques in social science research. Empirical, quantitative methods in comparative education are still beset with serious difficulties, but there can be little doubt that their potential contribution to the field is so great that they will have to be reckoned with.

Conclusion

It is now possible to review a century and a half of development and progress since the proposals of Marc-Antoine Jullien de Paris in 1817. This was the period when "pantometry" held sway, indiscriminate measuring was a fad, and hopes were strong that a science of education could emerge from massive collections of data, expressed wherever possible in numerical form.[2] The early quantitative approaches in comparative education failed (as did pantometry in general) partly because they were inappropriately applied, partly because the sources of data and the means of their collection were even more limited than they are today, and finally because the dangers arising from personal and cultural bias were barely recognized.

At that time the failure of primitive quantitative approaches was not crucial since comparative education was directed mainly toward selective cultural borrowing and was little concerned with the problems of explanation. However, suspicion of statistics persisted even as comparative education moved toward the search for explanation. The qualitative interpretations of Sadler, Kandel, and Hans were magnificent attempts to explain the dynamics of education and society, largely without reference to statistical and quantitative data. From Sadler on, the common approach relied on the identification of forces and factors *(Triebkräfte)* in the search for explanation. Initially, the emphasis was historical; later, sociological, political, and even anthropological factors were introduced. However, the most recent stage in comparative education and cognate fields reverses the classic post-Sadlerian approach: the forces and factors that previously had been the bases for explanation have now themselves become objects of inquiry.

At the same time as the social sciences were developing increasing sophistication in quantification, nonquantitative explanations tended to be ignored. If comparative education was to fulfill its potential as a tool for educational planning, it had to offer a means of reliable prediction. Without a quantitative base, it appeared, this could not be adequately achieved.

In summary, then, during a century and a half comparative education has moved from the stage of curiosity to the stage of analysis. This movement may be discerned along three dimensions: from indiscriminate data gathering to vastly greater precision; from philanthropy in international educational cooperation to professionalism; and from analysis based on intuition toward scientific explanation.

First, comparative education has advanced from the stage of curiosity exemplified by Bache's enormous and indiscriminate collections of pedagogical material to the equally vast but now highly structured collections of data of the IEA project. Second, the early workers in the last century were imbued with humanitarian and philanthropic intentions. They saw the international exchange of educational information as good in itself, but with the exception of Jullien they could not conceive of it as a possible object of conscious, planned, international cooperation. Since the foundation of the International Bureau of Education after World War 1, and of Unesco, OECD, and the World Bank after World War II, Jullien's dream has been partially realized. The work of these organizations is in the hands of specialists. Thus, what began with philanthropy has ended with professionalism.

The third and perhaps the most significant dimension along which comparative education has advanced concerns the search for explanation. Early workers were motivated by a vague sense of the differences among nations, an interest in what was going on abroad, and the intention of learning useful lessons. Even when the search for explanations superseded these earlier motivations and when the theories of comparative educators developed comprehensiveness and a sense of the dynamic interrelation of education and society, their approach was largely intuitive. In the most recent phase, a new order of work has appeared in which no explanation can be deemed satisfactory unless validated by rigorous scientific testing.

[From Part Two: The Method of Science]
Comparative Education as a Field of Inquiry

> *"It seems very pretty," she said when she had finished it, "but it's rather hard to understand!" (You see she didn't like to confess, even to herself, that she couldn't make it out at all.) "Somehow it seems to fill my head with ideas – only I don't exactly know what they are!"*

So far, this section has been concerned with the value of the method of science as a way of knowing and its major features as a way of investigating social reality. It is now necessary to consider the special characteristics of comparative education and the case for applying empirical methods to its study.

Comparative education began with observations about foreign peoples and their education and developed into descriptions of foreign school systems. Inherent in this work was the practical aim of borrowing from abroad useful educational devices for the improvement of education at home. The descriptive phase gradually expanded to include examination of the social, political, and historical context in which school systems developed. A further dimension was added to the description of these relationships as comparative educators proceeded to consider the dynamic interaction between education and its societal setting. Most recently, comparative education has entered yet a new phase in which cross-national data are used to test propositions about the relationship of education to society.

Comparative education is thus part of the wider attempt to explain phenomena, first, within educational systems and institutions, and second, surrounding education and linking it with its social environment. Attempts to do the first lead to a concern with the technology of education: the methods, practices, and outcomes of different modes of instruction, organization, supervision, administration, and finance. Where attention is paid to the teaching-learning process in a number of countries, educational psychology and particularly psychometrics are especially relevant. Insofar as comparative education is concerned with pedagogy, the work has largely been done by teachers, administrators, and educational psychologists seeking to comprehend and possibly to improve the instructional work of the schools, and it is useful to term this branch of the subject comparative pedagogy. But to the extent that comparative education has looked outside the confines of the classroom and the school system, its concerns and its data have overlapped with the interests of social scientists, some of whom have recently undertaken systematic comparative study of education as a social phenomenon.

Comparative education has one foot firmly planted in pedagogy and the other in the wider area of the social sciences. Concern with the form and function of the school has, however, united these two aspects of the field by concentrating attention on similar kinds of data and complementary topics. A second unifying element, and possibly a more important one, has recently become apparent in a common movement toward empirical and quantitative methods of inquiry. Notably, the IEA study described in Chapter 6 has welded together the two aspects of comparative education: concern with technology of education (comparative pedagogy) and with the interaction of schooling and its social context.[3] Comparative education in its most recent phase emerges as the attempt to use cross-national data to test propositions about the relationship between education and society and between teaching practices and learning outcomes.

Characteristic Problems of Comparative Education

> *"Well, in our country,"* said Alice, still panting a little, *"you'd generally get to somewhere else – if you ran very fast for a long time as we've been doing."*
> *"A slow sort of country!"* said the Queen. *"Now, here, you see, it takes all the running you can do, to keep in the same place."*

The serious problems of the field are not hard to perceive. For the comparative educator the nagging questions persist: why do we know so little for certain in comparative education, and why does comparative education hardly figure at all in the list of recognized fields of comparative study (history, sociology, religion, literature, economics, political science)? A recent compendium of scientific findings about human behavior includes a great deal of material on education, but can report nothing that relies on cross-national research in this area.[4]   Similarly, a review article by an outstandingly well-informed scholar on the status of comparative studies in the United States makes not a single mention of comparative education.[5] A number of problems appear fundamental to comparative education and presumably must be met head on and overcome if the field is ever to realize its potential. They are the problems of bias, utility of results, and eclecticism in both methodology and data.

Bias may arise at every stage of the comparative educator's work, from the identification of problems to the collection of data, their interpretation, and the conclusions drawn from them.   Ethnocentrism is an obvious source of bias in comparative education: inevitably investigators view foreign societies through a selective and distorting screen interposed by their cultural experience.[6] But there is a vastly more important source of bias embedded in the whole field of comparative education and, indeed, in the social sciences in general.   This entire edifice of knowledge is part of the intellectual achievement of the Western world during the past two centuries and reflects the secularism, liberalism, and humanism of the modern Western tradition.   Just as the development of the physical sciences in the West has been the story of man's attempt to extend his control over his physical environment, so the development of the social sciences similarly has sought to extend man's control over his social environment.   Difficult though it may be for the observer brought up in this tradition to recognize, the instrumental view itself provides a value system that must bias perceptions.   For example, movement toward a secular, humanistic, liberal, and industrialized society is equated with progress and is endowed with positive value.   Comparative educators have fully shared this bias, as their writings reveal. Until very recently their attention was concentrated almost exclusively on Western-type societies and their consideration of other societies is still too frequently cast in terms of movement toward Western structures and processes. The tendency has been to regard non-Western nations as in some way primitive forms and to assume that their natural development will follow Western precedents. Moreover, these attitudes have not been a monopoly of comparative educators and social scientists in the West; they have been shared in good measure by their colleagues in Japan, India, and a host of contemporary developing countries.

As a result, comparative education has devoted primary attention to problems of change and progress: relating education to economic growth, social amelioration, and political development. Compared to the volumes produced on these topics, the amount of attention paid to conservation of existing institutions has been insignificant. Moreover, those who have concerned themselves with the maintenance and continuity of present social and cultural modes have been labelled traditionalist and reactionary. Yet there are clearly some very important and legitimate problems to be examined in this area.

The culturally imposed filter affects not only the topics selected for study, but also the data. It is merely trite to observe that the selection of some topics and the ignoring of others will inevitably condition the type of data collected. But the problem is compounded in comparative education, where an investigator from an alien culture often is unable to recognize the relevance of certain types of data for the solution of the problem he has chosen. When the comparative educator examines the relationship between education and economic development in, say, India, he is naturally attracted to an examination of those formal educational institutions for which statistics and data have been collected. Among these data he tends to search out just those elements he has learned are important in the models with which he is familiar. What has not already been identified for him and what has not in his past experience seemed to have much importance may not be taken into account. Thus, modernization and education in India may be examined on the basis of the number of technical school places opened and filled. This procedure simply reflects the role of formal technical education in Western societies. Yet the most important means of modernization in Indian society may be increasing availability of automobiles, bicycles, water pumps, and so forth – the Western-type machines that impose on their operators disciplines of use, maintenance, and repair. Insofar as the comparative educator is interested in examining the relationship between education and development, he would be utterly misled by giving attention just to the formal system of education and neglecting the informal educational effects of introducing Western machinery.

One stimulus to improved work in a field is the ease of movement between the research findings in the field and their practical applications. Although comparative interest sprang from a desire to improve education by studying foreign models, the difficulties involved in extensive foreign borrowing eventually became apparent. The later comparative studies of the role of education in society provided a mass of descriptive and sometimes interpretive writing that provided little practical guidance to educational policy makers, whatever may have been its value for scholarship. One of the major incentives for a reawakened interest in comparative education in recent years had been the expectation that lessons drawn from comparative study could be used to aid in the development of the new nations. However, comparative education still remains far from realizing these hopes and the findings of comparative educators as yet rarely enter into the considerations of planners of national education systems, for their predictive value has yet to be demonstrated.

Another important problem of comparative education warrants discussion. Is it possible to distinguish clearly a problem in comparative education from problems in the economics of education, sociology of education, and so on? In other words, is there a clear definition of comparative education as a field of inquiry? If at present comparative education is suffering from an identity crisis, one reason may be its eclecticism. When anthropologists, sociologists, economists, political scientists, historians, and philosophers can all make some claim to expertise in the field, it becomes extremely difficult to identify its limits with respect to both method and data. There is no consensus about the area of discourse over which comparative educators properly may range.

The ranking of a new field of inquiry in the "pecking order" of academic respectability depends on the "hardness" of its data or the rigor of its methods. As an eminent economist expressed the idea,

> ... economics is by its nature a softer and less exact science than, say, conventional physics. Now in a hard, exact science a practitioner does not really have to know much about methodology. Indeed, even if he is definitely a misguided methodologist, the subject itself has a self-cleansing property which renders harmless his aberrations. By contrast, a scholar in economics who is fundamentally confused concerning the relationship of definition, tautology, logical implication, empirical hypothesis, and factual refutation may spend a lifetime shadow-boxing with reality. In a sense, therefore, in order to earn his daily bread as a fruitful contributor to knowledge, the practitioner of an intermediately hard science like economics must come to terms with methodological problems. I stress the importance of intermediate hardness

because when one descends lower still, say to certain areas of sociology that are almost completely without substantive content, it may not matter much one way or the other what truths or errors about scientific method are involved – for the reason that nothing matters.[7]

The data used in comparative education are notoriously "soft," and consequently there is a high premium on methodological rigor. Yet comparative education cannot be regarded as an enterprise with its own *raison d'etre* so long as it has neither a well substantiated theoretical framework nor distinctive concepts of its own. Comparative education can expect no assured place in the hierarchy of academic studies until its data and methods are clarified and their relation to one another recognized.

The Potential of Comparative Education

> *"If there's no meaning in it," said the King, "that saves a world of trouble, you know, as we needn't try to find any."*

These multifarious difficulties nothwithstanding, the field undoubtedly contains considerable potential, arising from two sources: the special value of the cross-national dimension for studying educational issues and the arena for interdisciplinary collaboration that the field provides.

Not all propositions in education and society require cross-national treatment, but with respect to two types of validation, cross-national work is mandatory. First, quite obviously, some generalizations simply cannot be tested by using data from one country alone since there is not sufficient variation in the single case. For example, a test of the hypothesis that there is a relation between centralization of national educational administration and students' achievement levels inevitably requires cross-national inquiry. Second, the single case permits no more than a particular statement to be made, and it is only on the basis of cross-national research that propositions established by study of a single case can be generalized and further refined. This point merits further discussion.

Even in single-country studies, the cross-national dimension can enrich explanation. Confined to domestic data, a historical study of the expansion of higher education in the United States may be able to provide genetic explanations for its present state, but there is no doubt that such a particular study will gain by being set in the context of higher educational developments in other countries. Of course the expansion of higher education in the United States cannot be properly understood apart from such foreign developments as the flight of German intellectuals after the failure of the 1848 Revolution in Prussia, the foreign experiences of American students and professors, and the emphasis on graduate research imported from Germany. Here is the classic justification for the comparative dimension: including foreign data in a single-country study enhances explanation of domestic phenomena. But, more important, if a hypothesis is tested within the confines of only one society, there can be no certainty that the conclusions do not have merely parochial validity. Suppose that a study of the social outcomes of the expansion of higher education in the United States shows that expansion has promoted intergenerational social mobility from lower to middle socioeconomic levels, but not from middle to upper levels. Even if this result is regarded as having a high level of accuracy for the United States, it is only by investigating the same topic in other countries that the full value of the United States finding can be exploited. Suppose that in extending this study to England, similar conclusions are reached. A double bonus is derived from the broadened scope of the study: the United States findings are further validated, and the statement about the relationship between the expansion of higher education and social mobility in the United States now becomes more general.

Alternatively, it may be revealed that what was found to be true of the relationship between higher education and social mobility in the United States is not true in England. This should lead immediately to the suspicion that the relationship is much more complex than first thought. When confronted with evidence of two different sets of social outcomes as a result of similar educational expansion in the two countries, the investigator is forced to abandon any simplistic explanation of the phenomena. He must reconsider the entire problem and undertake an investigation embracing more factors and more cases in order to develop a more comprehensive theory. One of the great advantages of comparative investigation is precisely this heuristic potential.

Comparative education can provide an arena where representatives of different disciplines come together to their mutual benefit, forcing investigators out of their narrow specializations.[8] The field has often been considered a natural candidate for inter-disciplinary work by reason of the particular problems and data it treats. Indeed, many of the important topics that fall to comparative education can be handled satisfactorily only in an interdisciplinary manner. For example, no study of education and national development is conceivable solely within the confines of a single discipline; it must draw from a wide range of behavioral and social sciences. However, comparative education is multi- rather than interdisciplinary in both its origins and current state. Every branch of social science has made use of educational data from various countries; in return, comparative education has drawn data and concepts from the social sciences. As previously stressed, this has been a cause of much confusion concerning the scope and limits of the field. But its multidisciplinary character could be transformed into an interdisciplinary effort if the data, concepts, and methods of the several social sciences were systematically focused on the testing of specific socio-educational propositions. Then, what has been a constant source of difficulty might become instead an asset.

There are many topics of common interest to educational investigators and social scientists. All may share an interest in the social dimensions of education. For example, its political ramifications will interest political scientists, as much as educators. Because all aspects of the society cannot be treated together at one time, problems in comparative education cannot profitably be expressed holistically in terms of relationships between education as a whole and society as a whole. Rather, they must be expressed in terms of some specific aspect of education and some limited sector of the total societal context. Therefore it is necessary to consider the total social context as made up of several overlapping sectors: for example, the economy, the ideology (religious, political, and social), the social structure, and the political structure. Consequently, among the common problems comparative education is concerned with are the schools and economic development, the impact of different ideologies on education, education and class structure, and education and the formation of social and political elites. These categories are not entirely arbitrary, but coincide with some major approaches to the study of society, as represented by the several social sciences. At the same time it should be emphasized that they are by no means the only ways of categorizing the total area of interest in comparative education.

Because so many propositions can profitably be tested cross-nationally, it should not be surprising that the area of comparative education is occupied by educators and social scientists equally. Yet comparative education is potentially more than a congeries of data and perspectives from the social sciences applied to education in different countries. Neither the topic of education nor the cross-national dimension is central to any of the social sciences; nor are social science concerns and the cross-national dimension central to the work of educators. The field of comparative education is best defined as an intersection of the social sciences, education, and cross-national study. Consequently, a problem in comparative education is the common concern of both social scientists and educators, but the exclusive concern of neither.

There are, of course, severe problems involved in interdisciplinary studies. Commonly they have been accused of sacrificing depth and rigorousness to breadth and modishness. In addition, specialists in one discipline have difficulty in understanding the concepts, assumptions, and modes of proof of other disciplines. They often find it very difficult to appreciate the strategies, let alone the tactics, employed by other specialists to tackle a problem. But apart from the common focus of study (explanation of specific educational phenomena in their social context), there is one fundamental factor that promises to promote depth and rigor while uniting the disciplines engaged in comparative education. This is the scientific method, a mode of inquiry that is not merely a set of procedures or techniques, but an approach toward establishing belief.

Everything that has been presented in this section has pointed to the indispensable role of comparative work in social science explanation of educational phenomena. The implication that must be drawn from this is that comparative education is not just an exotic excursion from the main track of education studies, but that the comparative method provides one of the major routes for validating the most important propositions about education and society. Where controlled experimentation is impossible, controlled investigation, which inevitably calls for comparative study, is essential.

It is certainly important to identify more precisely than ever the substantive problems of education and society that demand attention and that can provide the arena for fruitful contributions from the social sciences. Moreover, not only is comparative study required for satisfactory explanation in problems of education and society, but the empirical methods of the social sciences must be embraced if the full potential of the comparative approach is to be realized. Of central importance then, will be the effort to develop in comparative education a systematic, controlled, empirical, and critical methodology. We now turn to a discussion of that practical task.

[From Part Four: Conclusion]
Toward a Science of Comparative Education

> *"Cheshire-Puss," [Alice] began . . . "Would you tell me, please, which way I ought to go from here?" "That depends a good deal on where you want to get to," said the Cat.*

When Alice went on to explain that she did not much care where she went, the Cheshire Cat interrupted her sharply to say that, in that case, it did not really matter which path she took. But then Alice continued, "...so long as I get *somewhere*." The Cheshire Cat pointed out that this was no serious problem. If only she walked long enough, she was bound to get somewhere.

Unfortunately, the Cat's logic is only apparent. Alice, like any traveler, conceivably might end up nowhere rather than somewhere. She might cover the countryside only to arrive back at her point of departure, or she might stumble upon new places without ever realizing she had done so. However, most damaging is the probability that, after having been somewhere, Alice would be quite unable to state where it was, how she got there, whether she had taken the best route, or what conceivable use the whole journey had been to her or anyone else. The analogy to research in cross-national data is obvious.

The exotic lure of foreign places, manners, and customs is overwhelming. The simple acts of going and seeing for oneself and the unpredictable joys of serendipity become their own rewards; and surely if we visit abroad enough, read diligently, and cooperate with others of like interest, comparative study must get somewhere. Yet the painful truth is that it may not get anywhere at all. It may simply go around in a circle, repeating over and over again the same stale "facts," refurbished from time to time. Or comparative study may stumble over important findings, but have no notion how they fit in to the surrounding territory, how exactly they were arrived at, or how to make the best use of them now that they have been discovered. It has been the single argument of this book that, armed with the question, "Where do I wish to go?" and intent on using and improving a map to reach his destination, the wandering scholar in cross-national data greatly betters his chances of undertaking a journey that will be valuable both to himself and to his colleagues in the field.

At some stage of development, most disciplines have had to give thought to several related questions. What material and which problems lie squarely within the purview of the discipline, and which lie outside? What, if any, are the characteristic methods of the field? And what are the criteria for determining whether a piece of work in the field is good, bad, or indifferent? Comparative education today is forced hard against these question, and twist and turn as they may, comparative educators have to try to provide answers that are satisfactory to themselves, to their colleagues in adjacent areas of education studies, and to colleagues working in the social sciences.

Much of this book has been devoted to an attempt to give some answer to the first two questions. The territory of comparative education has been defined as the intersection of the social sciences, education studies, and the cross-national dimension, so that the hallmark of work properly claiming to be comparative education is that it lies neatly within that intersection. In addition, it has been argued, the characteristic methods of the field presently can be specified no more rigorously than that they are (or should be) derived from the social sciences. But the third question, which demands the establishment of criteria for the evaluation of work in comparative education, has remained largely unanswered, both in the larger world of work in comparative education and so far in this volume.

Such criteria are most urgently needed everywhere in the field: by those who do research and write in comparative education, by journal editors who must judge whether or not to publish work submitted, by those who teach the subject and by students seeking to learn, and not least by planners wishing to base decisions for the reform and development of educational systems at least partly on the findings of comparative education. Yet it is no secret that the minimum criteria simply do not exist. Writing in the field tends to be largely descriptive, anecdotal, or hortatory. Publishing is indiscriminate, and though every genre of work is represented the factual and narrative items vastly outnumber the carefully explanatory. Courses in comparative education are characteristically haphazard and eclectic; beginning courses in comparative education offered in colleges and universities provide students with widely dissimilar treatments of the field, in both subject matter and method of approach – a phenomenon not to be found in, say, American History I, or Chemistry I. And woe to the planner, either national or international, who relies on the findings of comparative education to sustain his search for some guiding principles of educational development, for he will come away from a survey of the literature with very little of value.

This absence of generally accepted criteria against which to evaluate work in comparative education can best be explained by reference to the antecedents of the field. Until quite recently it has been dominated by simple curiosity about foreign lands and customs, or by a desire to borrow foreign practices, or by the hope of promoting international brotherhood and cooperation. These motives, while highly laudable, are inadequate bases to sustain a field of study. Only since the beginning of the century has the task of explanation moved to the center of the stage, and historical and philosophical methods been used to interpret educational and social phenomena with great perceptivity, scholarliness, and intuitive insight. But even here a consistent and defensible methodology has been largely lacking. Comparative education for the most part has not had as its goal the provision of validated explanations, nor have its results been assessed, as a matter of routine, for their predictive value. In short, the real potential of comparative study has gone largely unexploited. Instead of using cross-national data to test the validity of statements about relationships between education and society, comparative education has for too long remained simply a pleasantly exotic field in which those who happened to have some experience of foreign education can busy themselves.

The development of the social sciences along empirical lines has, however, opened up a new arena for comparative work. Many propositions already validated in individual (case-study) situations are prime candidates for cross-national testing of their wider applicability, while many other propositions simply cannot be tested at all without recourse to comparative models and data. Most important of all, perhaps, the method of work enjoined by an empirical social science approach provides the criteria needed for evaluating work in comparative education. Systematic, controlled, empirical, and (wherever possible) quantitative investigation of explicitly stated hypotheses is the hallmark of the contemporary social sciences; it needs to become a modus operandi of those who would call themselves comparative educators, too.

To the extent that the investigator in cross-national research is crystal-clear in his own mind and makes quite clear to his readers precisely which hypothetical proposition he is testing, he furnishes himself with a focus for research and his readers with a clear guide to understanding the implications of the results achieved. By contrast, to the extent that work using cross-national educational data is unsystematic, lacks explicit controls, appeals for proof to authority or intuition rather than to the facts, and ignores possibilities of quantification of variables it is poor social science and therefore poor comparative education. Unfortunately, to date, far too much of what passes for comparative education would fail on these essential tests.

Even in a single-country case study, it must be emphasized, only the most preliminary work can afford to proceed innocent of an explicitly stated hypothesis, clearly defined concepts and variables, and announcement of the minimum standards of proof to be accepted as validation of the hypothesis. Case studies that neglect these basic features of scientific work risk remaining isolated fragments of knowledge, unconnected to a wider understanding of the phenomena with which they deal. A series of separate country-by-country studies is no substitute for work that is overtly comparative from the beginning and is designed specifically to test hypotheses cross-nationally.

Although explanation is the ultimate aim of all scientific (and hence of all comparative) work in education, the process of explanation often yields some significant by-products. Important new information may be garnered about the educational and social systems of the world; concepts that previously appeared to have universal validity may be tested against the variety of global experience and shown to have validity only under certain specified conditions; and help may be provided to planners trying to improve the effectiveness of educational systems. None of these by-products of the scientific, comparative enterprise is to be despised. Indeed, frustrated by the complexities of the problems we choose to examine and the inadequacy of the tools at our command, they may turn out to be the only secure fruits of our labors, and we may need to console ourselves with the thought that half a loaf is better than none. But insofar as investigators actually prefer the by-products of quanta of information or concept-validation to the main goal of explanation, they are settling for second-best. Without doubt, there is a place for work that sets out simply to collect cross-national material, describe phenomena, and classify data. For example, in the literature of comparative education there are many studies of curricular developments, examination requirements, enrollment patterns, administrative structures, modes of financial provision, and so forth. Furthermore, the continual updating and extension of such compendia and catalogs is a necessary and valuable contribution. But devising and developing a taxonomy of comparative education items is only a preliminary of, and perhaps a concomitant to fruitful comparative work. In no sense does it penetrate to the core of the undertaking. The scholar who collects data on, say, teacher training practices for European secondary education, arranges them in convenient categories, discusses the validity of the categories and the reliability of the information, and goes no further, is stopping short just at the point where a comparative investigation begins. He can, and often does, suggest tentative explanations for some of the phenomena he has uncovered, but it is the precise formulation of hypotheses, discussion of the theoretical justifications for advancing them, and the statement and operationalizing of concepts and indicators that represents the essence of comparative work in education. It goes far beyond the business of assembling data simply for informational purposes, important and difficult though even that task may be.

A special question arises concerning the role of history in comparative education. The historian aims at providing what is called genetic explanation of events in time; that is, he endeavors to demonstrate how particular events were caused by a convergence of prior happenings, forces, and factors. Thus, the historian attempts to explain the Education Act of 1944 in Britain by referring to the variety of social, political, and education phenomena preceding the passage of the bill into law. Comparative educators, using historical approaches, have attempted to make genetic explanations of educational phenomena on a cross-national basis, and in the process have written some extraordinarily insightful and readable books. But these studies share the weakness of most traditional historical studies: their conclusions rely largely on the private insights of their authors, not only regarding which categories are valid and which data are relevant, but also on the matter of what quantity and quality of evidence constitute proof of a particular assertion. The new history recognizes these difficulties in the older style of historical work and is moving towards a more empirical and, where possible, quantified approach. As this movement succeeds in establishing in historical studies what is essentially the approach advocated throughout this volume, empirically-oriented comparative educators will acquire an additional instrument for their work. To the scholarly insights of the old historians will be added a measure of the empirical rigor of the new, to the benefit of both.

The criteria of the empirically based social sciences are not offered as a simple nostrum for all the unsolved problems of comparative education. Indeed, advocacy of the scientific approach adds a host of new difficulties to the many already evident. The problems involved in proceeding toward rigorous, scientific explanation in comparative education are not to be dismissed lightly. In education, as in the wider social context, both data and concepts are far from satisfactory. Data abound in some areas while remaining quite scanty elsewhere. Not only is the accuracy of much of the available statistical information highly questionable, but the reliability of nonquantified, descriptive material is very limited. More confusing still, the margin of error or the extent of unreliability is unpredictable, varying according to the country observed, the date of collection, and the kinds of data reported. Concepts tend to be at least as elusive. For example, the common use of such terms as democracy, socialization, or even secondary education as categories for observing, grouping and interpreting data cannot be satisfactory in the absence of agreement on operational definitions. Yet even generally acceptable, functional definitions are difficult to achieve.   Perhaps comparative education is suffering more from the imprecisions inherent in the term education than from vagueness in the term comparative, but whatever the source of the difficulty, typologies and explanatory concepts in comparative education remain crude, questionable, and largely unvalidated. Data and concepts tend to be narrowly ad hoc, and notions of causality are at best primitive. These are the hallmarks of any field of study in the first stages of its search for a distinguishing methodology and universe of discourse.

Concern with data and definition of concepts must not be allowed to obscure a more important goal, that of exploiting the full explanatory and instrumental values of comparative studies in education. Though the explanatory value of work motivated by the desire to import foreign educational practices or to develop a spirit of international harmony has not been high, there is a sense in which useful lessons can be learned from abroad. Sir Michael Sadler was right when he saw the practical value of studying foreign education and society in the chance to improve understanding of one's own country. Isaac Kandel, too, was right when he viewed each nation's educational system as a species of laboratory where a particular attempt was being made to solve a more general set of social, political and historical problems.   But realization of the instrumental and learning potential of comparative education depends upon using a method that will avoid the a priori judgments and biases that have characterized so much of the earlier work. As one observer has put it, the instrumental value of comparative study is great, provided one can avoid the three main traps of foreign observation: the Pago-Pago fallacy, which tends to say of everything, "How quaint!"; the Victorian lady-in-waiting fallacy, which leads us to wrinkle our noses in disgust and exclaim, "How wrong!"; and the Judy O'Grady fallacy, which dismisses the wild variety of human experience with the easy plea, "It's the same the whole world over!"[9] Especially in studying foreign nations and cultures, bias is a major problem, whether it stems from a conscious attempt of the investigator to prove a case for the superiority or inferiority of his own country's education, or from an unconscious imposition on data and conclusions of merely personal or parochial values implicitly assumed to be universal.

Although there are grave problems inherent in every effort to study education and society comparatively, and severe additional problems raised by attempts to apply social science techniques to comparative work, the promise both of the general field of comparative education and of the specific methods advocated here remains great. The potential of the field, as we have argued, lies first in the promise of extending the generality of propositions beyond the confines of a single society; second, in the provision of an arena where propositions, testable only in a cross-national context, can be investigated; third, as a field for interdisciplinary work; and finally, as an instrument for planners and policy makers.

These potentialities will be realized only if satisfactory criteria for assessing contributions to comparative education can be developed. This in turn is contingent upon securing convincing methods of validating research findings. Intuitive studies, even when bent on explanation and concerned with causation, provide inadequate proof; empirical investigation offers the hope of a more satisfactory system of validation. It provides an instrument for cutting through the circularities of reasoning inherent in even the best of the traditional studies. On the other hand, a purely inductive approach cannot be advocated. Simply to roam over the facts and to draw generalizations from them invites repetition of the errors of the past: encyclopedism (only now perhaps rendered more economical by the efficiency of electronic computers), observer bias and arbitrariness, and absence of criteria to guide the observer on the questions of which data are important and how much is enough.

A method that incorporates the intuitive insights and speculative reflections of the observer, but submits them to systematic, empirical testing appears to offer the best hope for the progress of comparative education. It provides teachers with something teachable and students with something eminently learnable and useful. Furthermore, it provides a criterion for evaluating research in comparative education, since each step in the process of investigation is always open to scrutiny, and conclusions and inferences are publicly arrived at. Researchers find built in to the hypothetico-inductive approach the expectation that their inquiries will be replicated and the validity of their data, methods, and conclusions subjected to the critical inspection of peers. Finally, because it is heuristic and open-ended, the social scientific method offers the researchers of one generation the hope of building securely on the work of their predecessors.

Clearer aims when doing research and more precise criteria after research has been completed are the essential requirements at the present stage of comparative study. The comparative educator needs to start with the questions: "Where do I want to go?" and "How will I know when I have arrived?" for the answers point the way toward an influential, intellectually cogent, and elegant science of comparative education.

NOTES

* Excerpts from Harold J. Noah and Max A. Eckstein, *Toward a Science of Comparative Education*. New York: Macmillan, 1969, pp. 3-7, 80-82, 112-122, 183-191.

1. For example, George Z.F. Bereday, *Comparative Method in Education*. New York: Holt, Rinehart and Winston, 1964, pp. 7-10; William W. Brickman, "A Historical Introduction to Comparative Education," *Comparative Education Review*, 3 (February 1960), 6-13. See also (by the same author) "Works of Historical Interest in Comparative Education," *ibid.*, 7 (February 1964), 324-326; and "Prehistory of Comparative Education to the End of the Eighteenth Century," *ibid.*, 10 (February 1966), 30-47; G. Hausmann, "A Century of Comparative Education, 1785-1885," *ibid.*, 11 (February 1967), 1-21; Franz Hilker, *Vergleichende Pädagogik*. Munich: Max Hueber Verlag., 1962, Part 1; Brian Holmes, *Problems in Education: A Comparative Approach*. London: Routledge and Kegan Paul, 1965, Chapter 1; Friedrich Schneider, *Vergleichende Erziehungswissenschaft: Geschichte, Forschung, Lehre*. Heidelberg: Quelle und Meyer, 1961; Stewart E. Fraser and

William W. Brickman, *A History of International and Comparative Education: Nineteenth Century Documents*. Glenville, Ill.: Scott, Foresman and Company, 1968.

2. *Pantometry* – "belief in the possibility of and zeal for extending measurement to all phenomena". See Jacob Viner, "The Economist in History," *American Economic Review*, Papers and Proceedings of the Seventy-fifth Annual Meeting of the American Economic Association 1963, 115.

3. Torsten Husén (ed.), *International Study of Achievement in Mathematics: A Comparison of Twelve Countries*. New York: John Wiley, 1967.

4. Bernard Berelson and Gary A. Steiner, *Human Behavior: An Inventory of Scientific Findings*. New York: Harcourt, Brace, and World, Inc., 1964.

5. Edward Shils, "Seeing It Whole," *The Times Literary Supplement*, July 28, 1966, pp. 647-648.

6. See, G.Z.F. Bereday, "The Significance of Cultural Bias: The United States and England," *Comparative Method in Education*. New York: Holt, Rinehart and Winston, 1964.

7. Paul Anthony Samuelson, *Foundations of Economic Analysis*. New York: Atheneum, 1965, p. ix.

8. This is not to suggest, of course, that an amateur in, say, economics is bound to be better than a professional in the investigation of a problem in comparative education which has an economic dimension, but the very lack of a vested interest in the orthodox methods of a particular field may be a stimulus to fresh and fruitful approaches, See David C. McClelland, *The Achieving Society*. Princeton, N.J.: Van Nostrand, 1961, pp. vii-xi.

9. V.R. Lorwin, *The French Labour Movement*. Cambridge, Mass.: Harvard University Press, 1955, p. xvii.

2

On Teaching a 'Scientific' Comparative Education*

A look at the complete run of the *Comparative Education Review* since its first issue in 1957 shows that it is far from being merely the thin, dry voice of arcane researchers. From the very beginning, some attention has been given to teaching the subject of comparative education. Moreover, several of the leading authorities in the field have devoted their thoughts to its pedagogical problems. For example, Bereday, King and the late Dr. Isaac Kandel have all considered problems of content and organization of courses, have discussed some of the determinants of teaching strategy, and have reviewed various approaches to these tasks.[1] Other articles on specific techniques of teaching or on appropriate materials for course work have been useful guides, especially for the beginning teacher, and have complemented the regular announcements, notes and more lengthy reviews of books in the field.[2] All of which suggests that, notwithstanding their serious efforts to gain the respect of academic colleagues for the quality of their scholarly contributions, comparative educators still retain a serious professional commitment to education in the strictly teaching sense. They ponder over such practical questions as creating coherent and logical course outlines, using effective teaching materials, and planning approaches and experiences appropriate to the motives and values of their students.

It was, in fact, out of this type of very down-to-earth teacher concern that Harold Noah and I first began to work together on our recent two volumes.[3] In a brief article some four years ago when we introduced the idea of a strictly empirical approach to research in the field, we did so in the context of teaching a general, introductory course to a heterogeneous group of graduate students.[4] At that time, we were thinking about the nature and value of published work in the field and of research methodology. But the spark was first ignited as we grappled with the problems of teachers seeking to do their everyday professional job. And from then on, as we have argued elsewhere, it appeared that the problems of research methodology and the problems of teaching were not to be considered and dealt with separately, as some have insisted, but that they are parts of the whole. Research strategy, educational content, and instructional technique seem somehow, at least for us, to have blended into one functional whole.

The distinction often made between the beginner (or tourist) in comparative education and the advanced student or scholar is a very important one. Their motives will no doubt differ; their respective levels of experience, information, study skill and analytical sophistication will certainly be different. But customarily, in comparative education as in other areas of study, this awareness had led to a heavy emphasis on description and on discussion of general or particular problems for the beginner, and an

31

often sudden and overwhelming addition of "Methodology" for the advanced student (including the professor embarking on the road to a publishing reputation). The argument is made that beginners or generalists will not care about the methodological ingredient and do not plan to be researchers, and that any attention given to this will turn them away from useful and interesting information and insights which will at the very least give them a smattering of "culture générale". But the good teacher, no matter at what level of instruction (from kindergarten to graduate school), must also be a good practitioner in his subject. To be effective as a teacher (as distinct from entertainer, propagandist, counsellor, instructor, shepherd and goad, which are only a few of the assortment of roles we are called upon to perform), one must be a model of doing science, mathematics, history – and comparative education. In whatever ways are appropriate to a particular group of students, the essential nature of the activity must be studied, revealed, conveyed, not in isolation from but as an inherent part of the subject or area of instruction. To separate methodological concerns from other kinds of content for purposes of instruction is artificial.

At the risk of even greater indiscretion, I would add that no subject can be considered as well-taught unless its characteristic modes of thinking and study are conveyed to students one way or another. If they are expected to read relevant work, for example, they must learn not only to absorb what is in print. They need hooks on which they can hang critical comment, evaluation, and interpretation. This cannot simply be done by reviewing the relevant information, no matter how fascinating, nor by exposition. Self-consciousness about what one is doing and what others have done, is essential to both teacher and taught. In practice, what this means for any subject of instruction, is that the big organizing ideas (theories), the kinds of information (the data), the interpretations and conclusions (modes of inference, systems of validation) characteristic of that subject must be part of the content of any course of study. The assumptions and the views just expressed can be restated in two associated thoughts, one of them more related to the theme of empirical methodology in comparative study, and the other more explicitly pedagogical. First, the teacher needs to have something teachable and conceptually justifiable; second, he must be the mediator between his students and the relevant information in books and in the world around him. It is obvious, therefore, that even encyclopedic description is not enough, no matter how dramatically and successfully conveyed. Explanation arrived at through random, impressionistic comment is deceptive. Analysis arrived at through awareness of the modes of analysis used is imperative.

Now to the actual experience of teaching. My general hypothesis is that teaching comparative education along the theme of the empirical mode produces certain tangible and desirable results. However, I am in no position to test this proposition empirically at the moment. I am hesitant to specify all the relevant outputs; I am not competent to identify all the pertinent inputs; I suspect that I shall always be mystified by what goes on in that little black box labelled 'the teaching process'. In short, I draw upon my own experience and insights only, with the help of observations gleaned from colleagues and students.

My colleagues and I have attempted to teach a course which is not a saunter (or a gallop) across the landscape of world education systems, but rather a series of discussions of relevant general problems in which education and aspects of its various cultural contexts are believed to interact. We begin, as does the book *Toward a Science of Comparative Education*, with a review of the ways some of our predecessors have tackled comparative work and of the difficulties involved in systematic comparison. We then offer the concepts and methods of the empirical approach as a means of achieving understanding of the problem-topics selected for each week or fortnight. What might otherwise be a ragbag of assorted topics achieves coherence via the methodological emphasis which, in one way another, constantly draws attention to such questions as: from what set of assumptions and preconceptions does one approach the question studied; what is relevant to clarifying it; when one reaches some conclusion, how does one know that it is so, and what reliance can be placed on it.

Having much of the relevant discussion and material in the compact form of the two books has been most useful. Class time and conference sessions which would otherwise be needed for developing an argument and for exposition, can now be used for discussion and debate. Student time formerly devoted to searching out materials can now be devoted to absorbing and criticizing articles in the collection. On an individual basis, students will still require help in identifying sources of descriptive information on particular countries or regions. But my impression, at least, is that they use such sources in a more sophisticated way, less overwhelmed by the encyclopedic detail of new material, more discerning of its significance, more discriminating about its possible explanatory uses.

Students who have undergone this strategy of teaching have had very specific criteria for study and evaluation of their work. They have also had very practical aids to carrying it out.

Personally, I have found that the utterly inadequate has been virtually eliminated from the written work of students, that, with the help of the specialized, methodological focus, discussions of socio-educational problems in class or conference are rarely stupid, though they are often, understandably, naive or uninformed. Moreover, on an individual basis, I have seen a considerable spillover to other areas of the understanding gleaned in a comparative education course, something which is rather new in my experience.

For the instructor, there are some serious disadvantages to eschewing the descriptive approach. He must perforce be more careful about his own errors, biases, and convictions and work much harder. He must guard against being trapped by technical details of research, especially since students are often poorly prepared in basic social science concepts and tools of even the most elementary kind. How to help them grasp fundamental ideas and general concepts, and still give a course of study which introduces students to the substantive problems in education and society in a comparative context remains the most difficult problem. Moreover, while some students have to overcome their personal distaste for this style of study, others become over-ambitious in their choices – both leading to considerable expenditure of time and psychic energy.

The pedagogical problems, in short, are by no means solved. Nor is the approach we have taken without problems and disadvantages. But with the general or beginning student in comparative education, I am satisfied that teaching the course around and on the theme of the empirical mode has both justification in theory and support in practice. I have not taken up the question of more advanced students. For them, I think the case is even stronger.

I must add another, very personal note by way of conclusion. Perhaps they are just peculiar to me, but there are two problems which continue to plague me as I teach the course along the lines described, using the two books, *Toward A Science of Comparative Education* and *Scientific Investigations in Comparative Education*. First, I have the common cultural bias of many people from Europe, against using a "book for the course." I never experienced this as a student in England. I never learned how to use a textbook properly as a teaching tool. Second, I have the problem of someone who has written down the content of lectures, symposia, classroom discussions and tutorial sessions, organized it into what seems to be the logical, efficient and clear pattern of words and ideas, and has no more to say. This raises a problem of how to fill class time. If a professor makes the error of letting his students see his sources, I've been warned, he cannot keep ahead of them. My students are more critical and challenging all the time. And I now know that I have committed the serious sartorial solecism of exposing my thinking and its sources to public gaze, leaving myself with only ascribed status and native wit as rags to cover my intellectual nakedness.

NOTES

* Max A. Eckstein, "On Teaching a 'Scientific' Comparative Education," *Comparative Education Review*, 14:3 (1970), 279-282. Reprinted by permission of the University of Chicago Press.
1. George Z.F. Bereday, "Some Methods of Teaching Comparative Education," *Comparative Education Review*, 2 (1958), 4-9; Edmund J. King, "Students, Teachers, and Researchers in Comparative Education," *Comparative Education Review*, 3 (1959), 33-36; Isaac L. Kandel, "A New Addition to Comparative Methodology," *Comparative Education Review*, 5 (1961), 4-6
2. Robert E. Belding, "Teaching by Case Method in Comparative Education," *Comparative Education Review*, 2 (1958) 31-32; Anthony Scarangelo, "The Use of Motion Pictures in Comparative Education," *Comparative Education Review*, 3 (1959) 24-27.
3. Harold J. Noah and Max A. Eckstein, *Toward A Science of Comparative Education*. New York: Macmillan, 1969, and Max A. Eckstein and Harold J. Noah (eds.), *Scientific Investigations in Comparative Education*. New York: Macmillan, 1969.
4. Harold J. Noah and Max A. Eckstein, "A Design for Teaching 'Comparative Education'," *Comparative Education Review* 10 (1966), 511-513.

3

Defining Comparative Education: Conceptions*

The last decade has witnessed not only a vast burgeoning of the literature in and about comparative education, but also a radical change in the rationales, methods, and goals of the field. Whether this change in landscape has been for the better or the worse I shall leave for colleagues to judge.

But imagine the situation of R.V. Winkle, professor of comparative education, who had fallen asleep at the end of 1959, to awaken again only in 1970. His slumbers would have commenced with his subject dominated by the works of Kandel, Hans, Lauwerys, and Rosselló. He would have been aware of only the barest intimations of a more deliberately social-scientific approach. On awakening he would have found a new style of work bidding strongly to take over the field, though without having won over by any means all of its practitioners. In any event, he would have had a formidable reading assignment awaiting his attention!

Much of the justification for undertaking comparative education studies prior to 1960 was in terms of their potential either for countering parochialism or ethnocentrism, or for assisting in the improvement of education at home. Basically, researchers and writers were asking such questions as: What is characteristically French about the French secondary school curriculum? or, What is happening in German schools that we might profit from? The theme of recent work may perhaps be seen as a progressive transfer of attention from country characteristics to problems, and from problems to the specification of relationships and the formulation and testing of theories. This is not to suggest, of course, that the new style has found universal and unquestioned acceptance, or that the previous genre of work is without merit. On the contrary, we continue to see, and shall continue to want studies with such titles as, "Higher Education Reform in Germany", "The Technical School in the Dominican Republic", "Local Initiatives in Pre-School Education in the Soviet Union", and so on. Moreover, all is not plain sailing in the new mode. The conceptual and practical problems of conducting theory-oriented comparative research are not only not immediately and obviously tractable, but are also being widely aired.[1]

In this change of emphasis comparative education is clearly following a course already charted in economics, sociology, and political science. Economics has ventured furthest, perhaps. It has now left far behind its earlier preoccupation with the identification and description of economic institutions and has become a complex endeavour to explain and predict behaviour connected with making choices among alternatives. Sociology, similarly, has moved beyond the description and classification of social units to analysis and prediction of their interaction. And, just at the present time, some of the most fruitful work of relevance for comparative education is currently appearing from political scientists pursuing a cross-national approach.[2]   Clearly, these parallel developments have not occurred simply by chance: they express a common reaction to a common set of methodological potentialities and problems. The challenge to move from the particular to the general, from identification-description-classification to hypothesis-testing, theory building and prediction is pervasive.

One test of the progress of a science is its acquisition of a terminology. In developing "technical terms", words are often borrowed from everyday use, and then more precisely defined for technical purposes. One thinks immediately of the use in physics of the term "velocity" (with its essential connotation of direction as distinct from the unvectored concept, "speed"); or, in economics our attempt to define "demand" as "ability and willingness to pay", and not simply to retain its common meaning of "need" or "desire". Indeed, on occasion the most far-reaching result of scientific study of a phenomenon appears to be the recognition of a new, more powerful, albeit more limited, definition of a term.

Consider what is happening to the term "comparative" in the title that denotes our field. I believe that we are about to move rather rapidly away from the everyday meaning of the word to a much more technical meaning. This rather radical redefinition of the term "comparative education" will involve at once a limitation and an extension of its scope. The impulse toward limitation will arise because we have come to realise that many studies that happen to use international and foreign data are not to be considered "comparative" simply by virtue of that fact; and the impulse toward extension will occur because many studies conducted on the basis of data drawn from within a single country nevertheless have a valid claim to be considered comparative, once we define the term in a way that reflects the function of comparison in systematic explanation.

Clearly, while this process is continuing we can expect a rather lively controversy on just what the term should and does mean. In part, I suppose, this is what this conference is about. The summary of our deliberations may legitimately expect to record what is happening to the nature of our field, and if we are optimistic, we can even hope to influence it.

Comparative education has mistakenly come to be identified either with the study of education in another country, or with studies using data drawn from more than one country. This view of what constitutes comparative education enjoys the sanction of both common usage and common sense. One finds out what is going on abroad and compares it with what is happening at home, often with a practical programme of amelioration in view.[3]   Certainly, many essays in comparative education are of this type. Alternatively, one uses a collection of multi-national data to identify, describe, and compare relationships (usually correlations) within education, or between education and other social phenomena.[4]   Again, I must emphasise that to call such studies "comparative" agrees with common sense and usage. But the weakness of that position is that it establishes as the criterion for classification as a comparative study the mere presence or absence of foreign or multi-national characteristics of data, and by implication ignores, or even denies, the existence of a characteristically comparative method. We are hindered from asking a set of key questions: Are all inter-, cross-, or multi-national studies *ipso facto* comparative? Are all comparative studies necessarily either inter-, cross-, or multi-national? What, indeed, are the necessary and sufficient conditions for a study to be comparative? Does there exist a characteristic comparative approach to a problem? If so, what is it?

Nations constitute one important set of systems that attract our attention, and we have employed so-called comparative studies largely to identify and describe the attributes of such national systems. We have ended up with "nominal" statements of the type: "In country A, the secondary school curriculum is such-and-such; while in country B. it is so-and-so; and in countries C, D, and E, it is something else." Or, we might say in quantitative terms: "In country A, the fraction of the GNP spent on education is high (7-8 percent); in country B, it is moderate (5 percent); in country C, it is low (2½-3 percent)."

However, as the social sciences have extended the range of questions they ask and as comparative studies (among them, comparative education) have matured, so we have begun to comprehend a fundamentally different role for comparison, whether conducted on the basis of national systems, or of other units. The key to this transformation in our thought lies in the attempt inherent in the social sciences to explain and predict, rather than merely to identify and describe. A simplified example may, perhaps, help illustrate the new emphasis in comparative work:

Let us assume that we wish to explain (and, perhaps predict) the relationship between the size of a family's income and the probability of the children in the family enrolling in full-time post-secondary education. If we find *mirabile dictu* that this relationship is the same from country to country, then we have no need to proceed further. We can immediately make a general (that is, a non-system-specific) statement defining a relationship between family income and the probability of post-secondary enrolment that is valid without including the names of any countries. But matters are more complicated if we are faced with the more likely case in which relationships differ from country to country. For example, we might find that while all countries exhibit a positive relationship between these two variables, the correlation is very strong in some countries, only moderate in others, and rather weak in a third group. Or. putting it in the language of least-squares linear regression analysis, we find that our best fitting equation explains different proportions of the observed variance in different countries. Let us assume, too, that no amount of within-system adjustment of either the independent or dependent variables alters the fundamental fact that in different countries similar levels of family income are associated with (or, "produce") different probabilities of a family's children attending post-secondary institutions.

This is the paradigm situation calling for employment of the comparative method. We now have to ask, what are the system-level factors that are at work, influencing the interaction of within-system variables? As we shift the level of analysis from consideration of within-system to system-level factors, we are engaged in trying out the effect upon these different within-system relationships of introducing additional, theoretically justifiable independent variables, in the form of system characteristics. We continue to do this until we can no longer (a) increase further the proportion of observed variance explained within each country; and, (b) reduce further the differences among countries in the proportions of observed variance explained.

To continue with our example, we might try out in turn the effect of including among our explanatory variables such system-level factors as "degree of income inequality", "ratio of the number of secondary school graduates to the size of the corresponding age-cohort", "proportion of direct costs of post-secondary education defrayed from non-tuition sources of finance", and "recency of the post-secondary institutions enrolling 5 percent (or 10 percent) of the corresponding age-cohort". We stop when the inclusion of further theoretically justifiable system variables yields insignificant returns in terms of (a) and (b) above.[5]

Only at this point do we introduce the names of countries in explanation, ascribing the remaining differences in proportions of variance explained to the unanalysed or unanalysable peculiarities of the countries. In this explanatory model, country names are used to tag bundles of unexplained variance. The object of the exercise, then, is not, as in traditional comparative studies, to extend and enrich as far as possible, the connotational content of country names; instead, we seek to extend and enrich to the limit general "law-like", cross-system statements, bringing in country (that is, system) names only when our power accurately to generalise across countries fails. A comparative study is essentially an attempt as far as possible to replace the names of systems (countries) by the names of concepts (variables).

In this style of comparative study, for the example we have taken, we might hope to make a statement of the type:

> In all countries, size of family income is positively associated with the probability of children in the family being enrolled in full-time post-secondary schooling, and differences in family income can explain at least one-half of within-country differences in the probability of enrolment. In those countries where income inequality is high and the proportion of costs defrayed from non-tuition sources is low, the explanatory power of differences in family income rises to at least three-quarters. Consideration of the fraction of the age-group graduated from secondary education, and the recency of growth of the post-secondary system does not improve explanation appreciably in any case except in the Soviet-type countries, where these factors do seem to be important.[6]

For our present purpose, the crux of all this is the necessity at some point in the analysis to stop further within-country analysis and to change the level of analysis to incorporate among-country variables. For this is the essential condition for a study to be classified as "comparative": data are collected at more than one level and analysis also proceeds at more than one level. With this criterion we can attempt answers to the questions posed above.

Q. Does there exist a characteristic comparative approach to solving a problem, testing a hypothesis, formulating a theory?

A. Yes. It involves formulating the analysis so that within-system relations are explained as fully as possible using within-system variables, comparing the characteristics and differences of such explanations across systems, and trying to explain these characteristics and differences by changing the level of analysis to take account of the operation of variables identified at the level of systems.

Q. Are all comparative studies necessarily either inter-, cross-, or multi-national?

A. No, although many are. National units commonly form the matrix for data collection and governments are willing to finance studies (either directly, or indirectly through the international agencies) as part of the international sport of competitive growthmanship. But we ought to insist that a study within, say, the United States of the relationship between family income and the probability of the family's children enrolling in post-secondary education, formulated in terms of South vs. non-South, or urban vs. rural areas, or Whites vs. Blacks, has an equal chance with an international study of employing the comparative approach, as defined above.[7]

Q. Are all inter-, cross-, or multinational studies *ipso facto* comparative?

A. No. Many studies use data from more than one country, but restrict the variables considered or the analysis employed to a single level, either within-system or whole-systems but not both. Thus, we have seen multi-national analyses of trends in educational expenditures that are restricted to juxtaposing country-level relationships (for example, percentages of GNP devoted to education), and there are multi-country studies of curriculum restricted to within-country univariates (for example, the amounts of time assigned to different school subjects). In the technical sense of the term that we have suggested above, such studies are not comparative.

NOTES

* Harold J. Noah, "Defining Comparative Education: Conceptions," in Reginald Edwards et al, eds., *Relevant Methods in Comparative Education* (Hamburg: UNESCO Institute for Education, 1973), pp. 109-117.
1. See Bruce M. Russett et al. (1964), Part B "The Analysis of Trends and Patterns", especially "Multifactor Explanations of Social Change", pp. 311-321. Also R. Merritt and S. Rokkan (1966) Bernhard Dieckmann (1970), Dieter Berstecher (1970), S. Rokkan (1968), and A. Przeworski and H. Teune (1970). Some points presented in this paper rely heavily on Part One of the latter book. Each of the volumes cited here contains important bibliographies.
2. See Przeworski and Teune (1970), D.E. Apter (1968). R.C. Macridis (1968), H.A. Scarrow (1969) and P. Shoup (1968). G.A. Almond and S. Verba (1965) remains a work of primary importance in the field of comparative political/educational analysis, although see Sheuch's contribution in Rokkan (1968) for a critique of many aspects of the Almond and Verba work.
3. The *locus classicus* is M.-A. Jullien's "Esquisse . . . " reprinted in S. Fraser (1964).
4. See, for example, Michel Debeauvais (1970).
5. Often, of course, we must stop short of this point, owing to lack of time and money.
6. Such a statement might set the stage for trying to develop a cross-nationally valid theory of the link between family income and family demand for schooling *in general*, and not just for post-secondary education.
7. Most participants at this conference are specifically concerned with the comparative study of educational phenomena based on national units. Perhaps, therefore, our field might be better termed "cross-national comparative education". This nomenclature would have the merit of implying the existence of other bases or units for undertaking comparative analysis. Not only would we want to retain links with comparative studies using other bases, but we would recognise the existence of a common logic underlying all comparative analysis, and be drawn to follow it in our work.

REFERENCES

Almond, G.A., and S. Verba. *The Civic Culture.* Boston: Little, Brown, 1965.
Apter, D.E. *Some Conceptual Approaches to the Study of Moderniz*ation. Englewood Cliffs, N.J.: Prentice Hall, 1968.

Berstecher, D. *Zur Theorie und Technik des internationalen Vergleichs: Das Beispiel der Bildungsforschung.* Stuttgart: Klett, 1970.

Debeauvais, M. *Comparative Study of Educational Expenditure and Its Trends in OECD Countries since 1950.* Paris: OECD, 1970.

Dieckmann, B. *Zur Strategie des systematischen internationalen Vergleichs: Probleme des Datenbasis und der Entwicklungsbegriffe.* Stuttgart: Klett, 1970.

Fraser, S. *Jullien's Plan for Comparative Education, 1826-1827.* New York: Teachers College, Columbia University, 1964.

Macridis, R.C. *The Comparative Study of Politics.* New York: Random House, 1968.

Merritt, R., and S. Rokkan (eds.). *Comparing Nations: The Uses of Quantitative Data in Cross-National Research.* New Haven: Yale University Press, 1966.

Przeworski, A., and H. Teune. *The Logic of Comparative Social Inquiry.* New York: Wiley, 1970.

Rokkan, S. (ed.). *Comparative Research across Cultures and Nations.* Paris/The Hague: Mouton, 1968. (Especially papers by H.R. Alker, Jr., L. Benson, A.J.F. Köbben, D. Lerner, G. Ohlin, E.K. Scheuch.)

Russett, B.M. et al. *World Handbook of Political and Social Indicators.* New Haven: Yale University Press, 1964.

Scarrow, H.A. *Comparative Political Analysis.* New York: Harper & Row, 1969.

Shoup, P. "Comparing Communist Nations: Prospects for an Empirical Approach". *American Political Science Review 62*, 1968.

4

A Comparative Study of Outlier Schools
in Metropolitan Settings*

The projected research project described in this paper is directed by the following questions, theoretical, methodological and pedagogical:

1. Are there exceptional schools, that is, do some schools do better (or worse) than most others in similar socio-economic settings in metropolitan school systems? If so, what explains this?
2. Do particular teacher behaviors or competencies make the difference?
3. How far can such explanations be generalized to the metropolitan context?
4. What is the utility of studying outlying cases rather than averages?

With the writer as a project director and Harold J. Noah as consultant and close associate, the study is an outgrowth of their earlier work on cross-national metropolitan school and social dynamics.[1]

Four successive phases are projected for this proposal. The first consists in identifying the outlier schools *within* given socio-economic communities in metropolitan areas. The second involves describing the schools, both the special characteristics of their surrounding communities and the particular features of the schools themselves, those items usually described as "school inputs". The next, and perhaps most difficult step, is to describe the classroom behavior of teachers (or a sample of them) in the outlier schools in such ways as to permit discrimination between teaching and other behaviors. It is at this point that attention can be given to the hypothesis which first provoked this line of investigation, that what differentiates the outlier schools is a particular dimension of teaching behavior. However, the final phase is crucial: to mount a series of replications in different socioeconomic communities, in different metropolitan areas in North America, and in selected large cities in Western Europe. For, without such replications, the generalizability of findings is severely restricted. When we seek to understand what the schools can or cannot do, given the social inequities of society, urban deterioration, systematic or casual discrimination, we are beset with contradictory evidence and argument. Studies seeking to explain why school achievement differs have shown that by far the largest portion of variance can be assigned to home background of the pupils or socio-economic community of the school. Coleman's contribution to the empirical base for this knowledge[2] has been complemented by the IEA work,[3] a comparative investigation of pupil achievement in seven subjects in twenty countries. The conclusion is inescapable: social background variables are a far more powerful force for variation in school achievement than are those factors amenable to changes in school policy. Though the importance of the social background variables does differ according to the kind of achievement (subject), the age of the student, and the country, the generalization holds true notwithstanding these factors, at least, within the city limits set by the range of variation in school inputs that we have so far observed.

Such research has encouraged the view that the great expectations for ameliorating society's ills by changing educational policies were merely part of a traditional American social myth. Social equity, for example, could not be achieved by reforming the schools but only after devising radical changes in income policy.[4] Resources poured into compensatory education schemes such as Headstart and Title I projects could not really improve anything; they were merely palliatives, an infusion to prevent things from becoming even worse. The optimistic myth that society would be improved through educational reform, gives way to the determinist notion that schools are passive tools of social and economic forces, and that the processes are unfathomable and uncontrollable.

Faith in the potential of reform to deal with some of the school problems in large urban areas has been eroded as much by these research findings as by the immensity of the socio-educational problems themselves. In the United States, as in many Western nations, a majority of the population is now urban, and the problems of metropolitan school systems do not seem to be diminishing.

The Coleman-type study finds that teacher characteristics, school and classroom organization, teaching styles, differential patterns of school staffing, finance, and management are all unimportant relative to the socio-economic background factors. One might argue that the wrong things have been measured, or that an incorrect explanatory model was applied, or that errors of statistical procedure were committed, and that we had better turn our attention back to the philosophers and discard the statisticians. Alternatively, one could conclude that the findings are, on the whole, true and that one can only concede that formal education is inherently a less powerful force than it has been believed to be.

However, without rejecting the results of research mentioned, we still have some logical and empirical bases for assuming that significance attaches to variations in school organization and teaching practice.

While persuaded by the research that *on average*, school policies and practices are relatively unimportant factors in measured student achievement, exceptional cases may in fact exist. When all the data are assembled for multiple regression analyses, they include some schools which are unusually effective or ineffective. But these exceptions are buried in the results which are conventionally statements of central tendency. Few studies have been made of the "exceptional" school, and fewer still contain data which are usable and free of bias.[5]

One recent study of the Philadelphia school system,[6] examining the effect of variations in a large number of inputs (measures of school resources and climate) upon growth in student achievement, has concluded that certain variables are quite significantly important for *particular groups of students*. High achievers, for example, appear to benefit from some items which do not affect average or low achievers (and vice versa); some school inputs are quite important for, say, the poor but not for students in high-income families (or vice versa). In a similar way, a study initiated over fifteen years ago in New York State (the Quality Measurement Project) showed how some local school systems did especially well by their high achieving students or their low-achievers (but rarely both) and how few, if any, systems were successful with students of different socio-economic status: if the system worked well for a wealthier population, it usually worked less well for others – if it worked well for the poor, it generally did not for the better off.[7]

The present study seeks to extend research strategies of this type and to pursue further those school features that do make a difference. The intention is to study relationships among social context, school organization, teachers, and outcomes (achievement) in those big-city schools which, considering their social contexts, exhibit unusually high or unusually low outcomes. In more technical terms, this approach will investigate "outlier" schools, that is, those schools which lie well off the regression plane, not fitting the statements of average tendency.

An important assumption of the projected study is that, while social class variables do explain much of the variation in the outcomes of schooling, they "explain" in only a limited sense. We hold to the fairly simple, but hopefully not simple-minded, view that learning (in the sense of conventionally measured school achievement) is greatly determined by teaching (incidentally one of the few generalizations emerging from the IEA studies which supports this intuitive view is that the more time spent teaching students a given subject and in student study or homework, the more learning occurs, on average). The reason why social class looms so large is that it impedes or enhances the capacity of teachers to teach (as opposed to manipulate, entertain, discipline etc.). While children, regardless of social origin, may all be equally open to learning, responsiveness to being taught, we suggest, is a function of earlier, home-based training, that is, of social origin.

We know that when children come to school well-groomed, well-fed, prepared to be taught, socialized in certain ways and with the appropriate values, their school achievement tends to be better than chance would suggest. Once selected as relatively high achieving students, they are likely to improve further still. When children are not thus prepared for schooling, the opposite obtains.[8] Teachers, too, behave differently according to whether their students are, from the beginning, more or less prepared to learn.

The hypothesis offered here is that, within a given (student) social stratum, some schools are outstanding because their teachers do more (or less) of this set of behaviors called teaching. Thus a second purpose of this study, once the existence of exceptional schools has been established, is to establish whether it is teacher behavior (or teaching competence) which distinguishes these more or less successful schools.

The third basis for this study is the view that comparative research is the foundation upon which educational generalizations may be built. Thus for this work we propose to use a case study approach, performing a series of replications in different socioeconomic settings in New York, then in different metropolitan settings in the United States, and finally in non-U.S. comparable metropolises.

NOTES

* Max A. Eckstein, "A Comparative Study of Outlier Schools in Metropolitan Settings," *Notes on Education.* New York: Institute of Philosophy and Politics of Education, Teachers College, Columbia University, 8 (1975): 3-5.

1. Max A. Eckstein and Harold J. Noah, *Metropolitanism and Education: Teachers and Schools in Amsterdam, London, Paris and New York.* New York: Institute of Philosophy and Politics of Education, Teachers College, Columbia University, 1973.

2. James S. Coleman et al., *Equality of Educational Opportunity. Washington*, DC: US Office of Education, 1966; Frederick Mosteller and Daniel P. Moynihan, eds., *On Equality of Educational Opportunity*. New York: Random House, 1972.
3. Reference is to over a decade of research by the International Association for the Evaluation of Educational Achievement.
4. Christopher Jencks et al., *Inequality: A Reassessment of the Effect of Family and Schooling in America*. New York: Basic Books, 1972.
5. George Weber, *Inner-City Children Can Be Taught to Read: Four Successful Schools*. Washington: Council for Basic Education, Oct. 1971; State of New York, Office of Performance Review, *School Factors Influencing Reading Achievement: A Case Study of Two Inner City Schools*, March 1974; Robert E. Klitgaard and George R. Hall, "Are There Unusually Effective Schools?" *Journal of Human Resources* X:1 (1975):90-106; Robert E. Klitgaard and George R. Hall, *A Statistical Search for Unusually Effective Schools*. Rand Corporation, 1973.
6. Anita A. Summers and Barbara L. Wolfe, "Which School Resources Help Learning? Efficiency and Equity in Philadelphia Public Schools," *Business Review*. Federal Reserve Bank of Philadelphia, Feb. 1975.
7. Samuel M. Goodman, *The Assessment of School Quality*. Albany, N.Y.: New York State Department of Education, 1959.
8. J.W.B. Douglas, *The Home and the School*. London: MacGibbon and Kee, 1964: 118.

5

Other Schools and Ours*

Fifteen years separate the publication of the first edition of this important book from the latest, fourth edition. The world has become a quite different place during this time, and so has this book changed. In its change, the book reflects some very marked shifts in the way we think about comparative education, do it, and use it.

The first edition contained a series of graphically detailed, freshly observed sketches of educational arrangements and socio-historical contexts in six major countries: Denmark, France, Great Britain, the United States, the Soviet Union, and India. Each chapter, while profoundly informative, was written in a lively, even chatty, style. For each country, educational processes were treated according to the principal "factors and traditions" (race, language, geography, economy, religion and ideology) that had formed the framework of Nicholas Hans' major work, *Comparative Education* (1949). Yet each country-essay skillfully concealed any hint of "apparatus," "method," "comparative system," or "approach." As Edmund King observed in his opening words to the first edition: "This book is primarily intended to be read – that is, read, rather than studied."

And read, indeed, it has been, with four exceptionally well-patronized editions having appeared in both hard and soft cover, in an academic field that is, after all, by no means at the center of educational training curricula.

As the successive editions arrived, it was evident that the author was moving further away from his original intent of providing a volume "primarily intended to be read," aiming more and more at a text to be studied. Now with the fourth edition, we have a full-fledged, rounded, yet readable textbook that makes an excellent introduction to comparative education for the beginning student. Seven country essays (Japan has been added to the original six) are preceded by four substantial chapters dealing with the context and nature of comparative studies in education today; and they are followed by a series of reflections on research, planning and development, together with discussion of strategies of comparative research into three important topics: urbanization, adminis-trative centralization, and a number of student-related phenomena.

The core of the volume still remains the set of seven national case studies, updated to include selected events and perspectives from about 1970. Each chapter is constructed in the same way: an opening section intended to set the general societal context; a description of the structure of the school system; special features, presumed to be of interest to the foreign reader; current educational issues. In the first part of each chapter, a brief historical introduction is followed by a section on recent national and/or international trends which challenge, clash with and amend traditional styles and ways of doing things, The sections dealing with schooling and with educational issues similarly provide basic information and highlights of current developments. These are selected and discussed as illustrations of contemporary societal movements and as variations upon a central theme asserted earlier and encompassed in the chapter subtitles (for example, France – "the central light of reason"; the United States of America – "a nation on wheels"; and England – "revolution with reluctance").

Case studies of this kind are a valuable and painless introduction to comparative studies. Without doubt they help teach students, as Edmund J. King intends, that educational "truths" are not self-evident and that no system is better or of more worth than any other, objectively speaking (p. 74). But there are problems with this approach, even when the writer, as in this case, follows an organized and consistent approach to each case, presents accurate and relevant information, and emphasizes in proper Sadlerian manner the relation of educational fact to societal context. They may be unsolvable problems, but they need to be stated.

The precedents for using a single key concept for "understanding" a nation are well founded. King uses some of Kandel's themes (notably for France, Britain, and the USSR) and invents his own, or borrows from general public stereotypes for others. But a pithy title, no matter how catchy, how self-evident to begin with, is a dangerous tool. Even an experienced and knowledgeable scholar, striving to encapsulate a whole nation in a few well chosen words will tend to see first those features which highlight his main theme and only second, if at all, those which do not easily fit in. And when the decision to edit must be made, it is the second features which go out first. This "key concept" approach is valid, certainly, but its effects upon beginning students are two-fold. It helps fix in their perceptions a useful "mind-set," helping them absorb, understand, and remember new material; but then it may become difficult, if not impossible, at some subsequent time to persuade these students that things are not quite that simple, that other data and other trends must be studied even though they may not neatly fit the stereotype. Emphasis upon American dynamism, mobility, and changeability, or India's quest for development and democracy tends inevitably to deemphasize conservatism and the persistence of traditional forces and practices in both places. Emphasis on the mainstream tends to ignore important sub-themes or, in the need to select, to report on some and neglect others rather arbitrarily, it seems. For instance, the Open University in Britain merits special note as "one remarkable innovation" (p. 250), which it certainly deserves. But is it the only one? The American reader will be astonished to find nothing on Open Education, and little on curricular and instructional reforms at the primary level. For the United States, Edmund King's assertion that the school system was successfully established "as one that was child-centered and 'progressive'" is certainly debatable. He underemphasizes the current critiques aimed at public education from many angles which suggest to the reviewers a wholesale loss of public faith in the power of schools to create a more perfect society. The problem here is not whether King is "right" or someone else is in the matter of reporting current events and placing certain constructions on them. The point is that, given the intent of writing an account with a particular theme, one must rely upon the sensitivity, experience, and common sense of the writer. And the reality portrayed is that of the writer, not necessarily of any other (equally capable) writer, and not necessarily that of any objective reality, if such exists. We are back again at those persistent problems of subjectivity, bias, and circularity of reasoning, endemic to comparative education and especially to those scholars who use a "national identity" approach.

With respect to the national case studies, earlier critics of King's *Other Schools and*

Ours took him to task on grounds both justified and not. He was faulted for a view of schools and societies that was non-analytic, perhaps even ethnocentric – in a phrase, a view from The Strand: pragmatic, urbane, temperate. It emphasized the unique aspects of separate societies and failed to direct the reader's attention toward anything but the most general commonalities in the human condition. Foster's comment was, "One commends Dr. King's desire to provide a pleasurable experience for the newcomer to the field, but it is questionable whether a volume of this nature can provoke, as he hopes, serious analytic thought on the part of students." [Philip J. Foster, Review of 3rd edition, *Comparative Education Review,* Vol. XII (June 1968), p. 194] What Foster and others might have noted is that the canons of social scientific study are hardly applicable to work of this genre. It must be judged in its own terms as one man's view of several educational scenes. The more justifiable criticism is that the earlier editions gave the reader the distinct impression that such anecdotal and personal descriptions of schooling-within-society were all there was to comparative study of education. This was a serious fault, more than adequately corrected in the present edition.

This is not to suggest that the debate over alternative strategies of comparative work is at an end. King is profoundly sceptical concerning the value of comparative studies based upon positivist, operational approaches. For him, the essence of a country's educational system is that it is embedded in a particular historical and cultural context. Because of this, concepts, variables, and indicators will always mean different things in different countries. The complete comparativist must not only be alert to these differences, but he must beware of being trapped into doing comparative analyses that are fundamentally invalid because they try to compare the incomparable. Thus, trying to relate, say, the strength of Catholicism to specific educational phenomena will always be a very difficult, if not impossible, enterprise, because the intellectual and social significance of Catholicism differs profoundly from country to country.

If context is important, King is even more concerned that we get our concepts right. We need to recognize that many of our concepts and measures obscure what is really going on in schools. For King, measures like "expenditures per capita," "degrees awarded," "mean achievement levels," "retention rates," and "enrollment ratios" not merely miss the heart of the educational process, but mislead us:

> We have now passed the time when so-called educational "effectiveness" could be measured simply by numbers of people enrolled or staying on, or by the length of time spent in various institutions, or even by observing examination results and supposedly objective attainment tests. No matter how abundant and reliable statistics may be on these matters, the obvious criteria of educational effectiveness are whether the person learning really identifies himself with what has been learned, is encouraged to develop himself further, and is more committed to a series of constructive choices in future than he was before the teaching-and-learning process began. (pp. 62-63)

For King, comparative study of education is justified by the contribution it can make to understanding, informing, and improving educational *decisions.* King sees each country's pattern of educational arrangements as essentially a series of implicit and explicit decisions to do this and not to do that. Comparative analysis helps us understand not only the context in which particular decisions get made, but the forces impelling countries to make often uncomfortable and unwelcome decisions to change old and familiar ways of doing things, as well as the limits imposed on free choice by each country's context. Indeed, he explicitly rejects the idea that comparative study will help us achieve general "explanations," or "predictions" based on identification of law-like regularities.

For good measure, the "problem approach" takes some hard knocks:

> ... to talk about 'a problem *approach'* to comparative education is illogical. How do *we* know it is a problem ... until after we have undertaken comparative studies? Further, how can a student know the shape, complexity, and repercussions of a problem unless he has discerned it in the real situations of a comparable kind across the world. Until he does that, he can not be sure of genuine identification – either of the local peculiarities, or of characteristically recurrent features. (p. 27)

We must be wary, King insists, that we do not inappropriately assume that disjunctures and inconsistencies that *we* may perceive as problems or difficulties in our own societies (for example, overpopulation and large family size) are necessarily problems and difficulties for other societies. Nor, according to King, are "trends" or "themes" (for example, coeducation) automatically problems. They may become problems, but only in the context of decision or implementation, when countries have to decide how far, if at all, such trends need to be accommodated. Once again, King brings us back to the centrality of the decision-situation for legitimizing and vitalizing comparative study.

In all of this, there is much that is appealing and true. Perhaps for the present reviewers, King takes the argument somewhat too far. For example, the impact of onrushing technological change (a major "general" factor, as King himself points out) on school organization and process is surely worth examining using some of the explanatory models derived from the social sciences. Or, socio-economic models of class differentiation and division of labor, for example, may help us to "explain" why academic stratification continues to persist within even the most dedicated of comprehensive secondary systems. Similarly, political science models of the distribution and structure of power and inertia within organizations can help to clarify the exceptional difficulties that educational systems face when they try to change themselves, or the unresponsiveness they exhibit when external political forces try to reshape them. Surely, too, we would like comparative analysis to help answer such questions as: "Is it true that, at the beginning, when a nation is poor, economic development helps a nation to improve its educational provision; but that there sooner or later comes a point where further economic development makes school improvement less, and not more, easy?" To answer such a question, and cognate ones, we may need more than sympathetic historical and cultural understanding of several nations' socio-educational arrangements. We may also need a good grounding in some social science theory and statistical method. If King does not directly help the student in these respects, it can only be a minor criticism of the present edition of *Other Schools and Ours,* given that King has provided us all with so lucid and cogent a statement of his own approach.

Both in education studies and in the social sciences, the range of approaches extends from an attempt to identify the regularities or "laws" of human behavior in social settings to emphasis upon the special, even unique qualities of the phenomena studied. Comparative education is no exception. At one end lies a group of works intended systematically to test particular hypotheses, replete with quantified data, minced through statistical analyses, seasoned with caveats, wrapped in inferences and finally served *("science farcie"?)* as tentative predictions. At the other, are found collations of a different kind: colorful, personal, free of the rigid conventions of methodological cookbooks. Whether a particular contribution to our feast of knowledge is more or less valuable is not simply a matter of where it stands on this particular range of alternative approaches, but also on how well it is done in its own terms. The present edition of *Other Schools and Ours* is eclectic, pragmatic, thoughtful, a positive contribution to the field. It represents a rich tradition in scholarly work. We all have our own tastes, of course, and these will influence our judgments of a particular contribution. King's work, which commenced at the more humanistic end, now seems to have moved over somewhere about the center of the scale. This movement has come gradually over the years. Indeed, the deliberate pace might have been predicted. After all, the author has done his work from Great Britain, a country that Dr. King himself has chosen to characterize by the key concept, "Revolution with Reluctance."

NOTE

* Harold J. Noah and Max A. Eckstein, review of *Other Schools and Ours: Comparative Studies for Today* by Edmund. J. King, London and New York: Holt, Rinehart and Winston, Fourth edition, 1973, in *Comparative Education Review 19* (1975): 290-295. Reprinted by permission of the University of Chicago Press.

6

Fast-Fish and Loose-Fish in
Comparative Education*

A presidential address to a scholarly society is a fit moment for some reflections on the state of a field of study. Comparative and international education has grown considerably in the last two decades, as the membership of our Society, the contents of our journal, and the literature in our field all testify. We have come a long way since a small group met at New York University in the mid-1950s just 20 years ago under W.W. Brickman's informal chairmanship to promote a more permanent association of comparativists in education.

Yet, as we also know, this is a period of perceptible slowdown in the pace of international and area studies in general, and of comparative and international education in particular. It may be a convenient time to do a little general stock-taking, to assess what we have accomplished and what we know we still have to do.

Herman Melville provides me with the title and theme of my remarks. Along the way in *Moby Dick,* Melville tells us something about the law of the sea, as it pertains to the ownership of disputed whales. He entitles the chapter "Fast-Fish and Loose-Fish." Let me quote as briefly as Melville's masterly style allows me from that chapter:

> "It frequently happens that when several ships are cruising in company, a whale may be struck by one vessel, then escape, and be finally killed and captured by another vessel.... For example, after a weary and perilous chase and capture of a whale, the body may get loose from the ship by reason of a violent storm; and drifting far away to leeward, be retaken by a second whaler, who, in a calm, snugly tows it alongside, without risk of life or line. Thus the most vexatious and violent disputes would often arise between the fishermen, were there not some written or unwritten, universal, undisputed law applicable to all cases....

> "These laws might be engraven on a Queen Anne's farthing, or the barb of a Harpoon, and worn round the neck, so small are they.

> "I. A Fast-Fish belongs to the party fast to it,

> "II. A Loose-Fish is fair game for anybody who can soonest catch it.
> "But what plays the mischief with this masterly code is the admirable brevity of it, which necessitates a vast volume of commentaries to expound it.

"First: What is a Fast-Fish? Alive or dead a fish is technically fast, when it is connected with an occupied ship or boat, by any medium at all controllable by the occupant or occupants – a mast, an oar, a nine-inch cable, a telegraph wire, or a strand of cobweb, it is all the same.

Likewise a fish is technically fast when it bears a waif, or any other recognized symbol of possession; so long as the party waifing it plainly evince their ability at any time to take it alongside, as well as their intention so to do."

Possession is thus seen as the whole of the law, and Melville proceeds to extend the argument from whaling to social arrangements in general, nations and the world of ideas. He asks:

"What are the sinews and souls of Russian serfs and Republican slaves but Fast-Fish, whereof possession is the whole of the law? What to the rapacious landlord is the widow's last mite but a Fast-Fish? What is yonder undetected villain's marble mansion with a door-plate for a waif; what is that but a Fast-Fish? ... What are the Duke of Dunder's hereditary towns and hamlets but Fast-Fish? ... And concerning all these, is not Possession the whole of the law?

"But if the doctrine of Fast-Fish be pretty generally applicable, the kindred doctrine of Loose-Fish is still more widely so. That is internationally and universally applicable.

"What was America in 1492 but a Loose-Fish, in which Columbus struck the Spanish standard by way of waifing it for his royal master and mistress? What was Poland to the Czar? What Greece to the Turk? What India to England? What at last will Mexico be to the United States? All Loose-Fish.

"What are the Rights of Man and the Liberties of the World but Loose-Fish? What all men's minds and opinions but Loose-Fish?

"What is the principle of religious belief in them but a Loose-Fish? What ... are the thoughts of thinkers but Loose-Fish? What is the great globe itself but a Loose-Fish! And what are you, reader, but a Loose-Fish and a Fast-Fish, too?"

And what, perhaps, is comparative education as an area of study but a Fast-Fish and a Loose-Fish, too? Fast in the sense that we have made the comparative and international study of education our own area of specialization. A Loose-Fish, too, because many workers from other disciplines, finding that the phenomena of education and schooling provide a host of problems of exceptional interest, often seize on comparative analyses of education to advance understanding in their own fields.

In this address, then, I shall devote attention to the questions: What does our profession have a reasonably secure hold on? What, in a word, are our Fast-Fish? And, conversely, what are the major prizes out there, available for the taking, if we have the wit, energy and skill to catch them? What are the Loose-Fish for comparative education?

Our Fast-Fish

Year by year a great and growing body of information about the educational systems of the world has been accumulated. More and more, these national sources have been systematized and standardized so that they are better adapted to comparative work. For this work, we are particularly indebted to the international organizations, in particular to UNESCO (and especially to the Paris headquarters that has produced the successive editions of the *World Surveys of Education* and the *Statistical Yearbook,* as well as to the International Bureau of Education, Geneva), to the OECD, and to the World Bank. Although we can all think of improvements that might be made in these compilations, and there are still some serious and surprising gaps, they form a basic portion of our total comparative education catch, without which we would have been poor fishermen, indeed.

Second, the pages of our society's journal, the *Comparative Education Review,* and of other scholarly journals here and abroad report the progress we are making in understanding processes at work inside education and the connections between educational and more broadly social changes. Indeed, it is this analytic work that has most attracted the attention of and contributions from an ever-increasing number of scholars within education studies and from the other disciplines. Comparative studies of curricula, textbooks, classroom practices, teacher training and teachers' attitudes, students' aspirations, achievement outcomes, modes of educational finance, planning and administration, as well as the relationships between education and social status, incomes, wealth, cultural and political forms have all figured prominently in the expanding literature of the past decades.

Nor has all this been devoted to purely abstract theoretical understanding. A great deal of attention has been paid to the problems of reforming and restructuring educational practices to fit new needs, thus lending comparative studies an especially practical hue. Here, also, are to be found some of our Fast-Fish.

Perhaps the chief idea that we have advanced and defended successfully is the assertion that comparative education understanding is an essential part of teacher training, theoretical work in education, and the practical tasks of policy-making and administration in education. While in large and small countries alike the forces making for national self-sufficiency and nationalist concentration are as powerful as ever, at the same time there is increasing acceptance of the thesis that knowledge and appreciation of other nations' problems and solutions in education are indispensable. Not only is the nation that forgets its history likely to repeat it, but the nation that forgets (or is blind to) the educational systems of its contemporaries is risking either stagnation, or the perils of burdensomely expensive experimentation. Comparative understanding can help countries break with old ways of arranging the educational systems without the danger that they indulge in foolish daydreams that there are just one or two fairly simplistic things they need do in order to set their schools aright.

In this respect, special commendation is due to OECD for its series of Country Reports on Educational Policy, to the IIEP for its comparative studies of educational financial policies, and to several of the official commissions on educational reform in Britain in the past decade, who have been careful to include informative studies of other countries' experiences in their deliberations and final reports.

In all these efforts to establish some secure bases, some Fast-Fish, for comparative education, many approaches have been used, and this is as it should be. Some workers have chosen to emphasize that schooling in each country operates within a particular historically constrained context, and that an understanding of each context is the key to the understanding of each educational system, its success and its failures, its problems and its solutions, its strengths and its weaknesses. Others have been more concerned to abstract from the "givens" of each national system of education, in order to attempt statements of a more general kind about educational development. Some scholars rely heavily upon scaling, quantification, and relatively complex statistical techniques; others prefer to avoid the many problems associated with quantification and employ qualitative data. Studies run the gamut from world-wide, global analyses to single-nation case studies, with every variety and size of sample bracketed between the two extremes.

Each of these approaches has value for particular purposes in particular situations. None may claim a monopoly of truth and virtue. The task of the scholar and wise consumer of the fruits of scholarship is to recognize which approach gives the most useful results for a given purpose and in a given situation. To pursue Melville's analogy, there is no single way of making fast our fish. We need to select techniques well-suited to the conditions set by the problem, the data, the skills of the investigator, and the use to be made of the results.

The vital thing is to avoid conflicts over method in the abstract, but to ask of each piece of work using a comparative approach: Are the questions asked significant and clear? Are the data appropriate? In particular, do the data measure well the phenomena they purport to describe? Are they handled in a way that gives us confidence in the inferences drawn?

There are likely to be many routes leading to affirmative answers. In particular, the complementarity of qualitative and quantitative approaches needs to be stressed, as we work to make more secure our catch in comparative and international education.

Our Loose-Fish

Let me now turn to our Loose-Fish – the catch that is not yet ours, but might be made so, if we are of a mind to engage in the chase. In what follows, I by no means intend to say or imply that members of our profession have not already begun the pursuit. Indeed, each of us knows of examples of the kind of work I shall mention. Rather, I should like to use this opportunity to underline the need, as I see it, for much more work along these lines.

Our field grew out of intense curiosity concerning different national systems of schooling. The great masters of the past Jullien, Arnold, Sadler, Kandel, Hans, and Rosselló) and most of us today in our turn, view the nation state and the entire national educational systems as the "natural" units for comparative study. Inquiries into "the French educational system," "education in Iran," or "higher education in England" continue to form a major part of our concerns. We have been led, not unnaturally, to this position by some very obvious advantages of viewing the nation state as our primary frame of reference. Our data, whether quantitative or qualitative, have most often been collected according to these units; socio-educational and pedagogical policies are devised and administered nationally; national units provide the levers for decision and change; our lives are conventionally set in the perspective of our national allegiances.

But, in pursuing comparative studies in terms of national aggregates, I believe we have been inclined to neglect too much the other, complementary way of approaching our task: the cross-national comparison of sub-national units. For example, it seems desirable that we should have relatively more studies that deal cross-nationally with problems of learning and school achievement in specific social settings. Where are the comparative studies of "School and the Inner-City Child"?, or "Recruitment of Teachers for Rural Schools"?, or "Financing Schools in Suburban Areas"? We even lack comparative studies of school provision for the important minority groups that nearly every nation state contains. Perhaps what I am saying is that we need much more vigorous seizing of the avenue of inquiry opened by within-nation social science research, to test the applicability to a broader universe of conclusions reached within one nation. It is here, I would judge, that comparative and international studies of education can contribute most to the total catch of knowledge.

In line with these remarks is the notion that most of us tend to concentrate our studies too much at what I might call the macro end of the conceptual and data continua, and shortchange the micro investigation. For example, we have had a number of studies of educational reform in the last few years. They are heavily weighted toward the macro end of the data scale, dealing with general, large-institutional problems of promoting change. We have few, if any, comparative studies of the attitudes, opinions, and actions of samples of teachers, school officials, parents, children, and politicians in the matter of changing school structures and processes. We need to develop the human and financial resources to support research that will dig deeper under the surface of the aggregative, macro-institutional type of work that has typified comparative and international education to date.

There is a quite natural tendency for comparativists to assert that the fact that they deal with more than one nation, combined with limitations of time and research funds, means that they must be excused from getting too close to the micro-situations of particular children in particular classrooms, or particular teachers in particular schools. That, for example, instead of gaining knowledge about the attitudes and actions of small groups of educational bureaucrats in a number of countries, we must limit ourselves to the public utterances and debates, the legislation, the regulations, the formal generalized acts governing education on the national scale. While some studies of this kind are clearly desirable and in plentiful supply, we need to press more in the other direction, too. I suspect that there are some very interesting Loose-Fish out there to be made fast.

It occurs to me, too, that it is in this direction that our hopes for making comparative and international education useful to policy-makers and administrators really lie. Conclusions based on cross-national aggregative studies often make valuable background reading for decision-makers, but they too seldom illumine the actual decisions that have to be made. It is easy to see why this is so. Our aggregative studies normally proceed in terms of national average tendencies, with regard to both data and conclusions. National and local decision-makers in education, however, are typically concerned with the likely outcomes of taking particular steps in *highly particular,* rather than in average, circumstances. For example, to be able to say that, on average, across the entirety of most educational systems, higher levels of parental participation in school decisions are associated with higher rates of student retention is, no doubt, of general interest to educational administrators. But, if this kind of result is to be of practical use, it needs to be expressed in substantially more differentiated fashion. Does the assertion hold at all income levels? among minority as well as majority groups? in urban as well as in suburban, or rural areas? in non-state as much as in state schools? and so on. For it is on such differentiated bases, rather than by consideration of overall national aggregates, that most educational decisions and policies – even the most important – have to find both their political support and their final shape.

Two further aspects of our potential catch at first sight may appear to be merely technical, but they have in fact substantive implications. Perhaps the first point I shall make refers rather to the tools we use to catch our Loose-Fish (the nets, lines, harpoons, or what you will) than to the fish themselves.

There has been much discussion among ourselves, and in the social sciences in general, on the question of using quantified data, hypothesis testing and the usual array of statistical estimating techniques to try to make warranted statements about educational phenomena. As suggested earlier, my own view is that there is a role for many different kinds of work, and I am sure that work of a quantitative, statistical kind is here to stay and that our entire array of comparative studies in education will be the better for its presence.

But this is not to deny that serious weaknesses persist in the statistical work that has appeared. For me, perhaps, it is the explanatory models commonly used that pose the most serious and it may be the most intransigent difficulties. These models are correlational of one kind or another – most often multiple regression, or path analysis. In such models the assumption is made that the effects of a complex patterning of variables on some outcome (say, school achievement) can be analyzed as if there could be attributed to each variable a constant strength of association between it and the dependent variable. This is, of course, the regression coefficient. Differences in outcomes in such models are explained fairly simplistically as the summed effects of different values of the independent variables, each multiplied by its own regression coefficient, plus an error term to capture errors in sampling, measurement and model specification. The linear regression model is a highly flexible approach. In particular, should the relationship between the independent and dependent variables be pretty obviously non-linear, there are usually available some quite simple techniques for transforming the data so that linear approximations may be used. Thus, the linear regression approach, in its various forms, has in its favor good explanatory power in multivariate situations, flexibility and generality of use, and hence an excellent standing among the statistical and social science fraternities. Why then do I call for something better?

The problem, as I see it, of applying these regression models to many of our explanatory problems in education (and, particularly when we try to explain variations in achievement, attitudes, career choices, dropout decisions, and the like) is that many of the processes we are trying to map (and certainly all of the pedagogical processes) are neither linear in their naturally occurring form, nor is it very helpful to force them into a framework where they can be handled as if they were linear. For, in reality pedagogical and learning processes are dominated by threshold effects, the presence or absence of catalysts, complex non-linear patterning, limiting factors, and the time-sequencing of events. If this is so, we should not be too surprised that even our most sophisticated multi- and cross-national work to date (I refer to the IEA studies) succeed in explaining relatively small fractions (for example, 30 to 40 percent) of total within-country and across-country variances in achievement. I urge that we accept the challenge to try to do better, by devising and applying more appropriate explanatory models.

Let me conclude this survey of some Loose-Fish I'd like to see us make fast by referring to a cognate statistical-cum-substantive outcome of conventional correlation and regression analyses. In such work, the investigator's attention is naturally focussed primarily upon the search for the regularities, generalizations, the "law-like" statements he can make. And this is quite proper. However, we may tend thereby to overlook those very interesting cases that may lie well off the regression plane, the outliers. Thus, the inner city school that produces excellent results in the face of grave measured disadvantages; the "good homes" that fail in using the conventional socio-economic paths to maintain and advance the class-status of their children; or the region that, against all expectation and statistical prediction, takes on to good effect an unusually heavy financial burden for the schooling of its children – these, and similar "outlier" situations may be the fattest Loose-Fish in our ocean of exploration. I commend them to your attention.

Our Society's Conference, this year as in past years, provides examples in abundance of the Fast-Fish and the Loose-Fish in our field. In some measure, I am sure, our activities over the forthcoming two days will assist us in reconfirming knowledge in areas we have already made reasonably fast; in others I hope it will help us to make what is somewhat loose a little more fast. Thank you for coming to Washington this year. And happy angling!

NOTE

* Harold J. Noah, "Fast-Fish and Loose-Fish in Comparative Education," *Comparative Education Review* 18 (1974): 341-347. Reprinted by permission of the University of Chicago Press.

7

Use and Abuse of Comparative Education*

My favorite anecdote in comparative study is from the field of comparative philology. One day, the story goes, a Spanish-speaking student of Russian language went to her professor and asked him: "Professor, do you have in Russian any equivalent of our Spanish word 'mañana'?" After brief reflection, the professor said to her: "Why, yes. In Russian we have twenty-seven equivalents for 'mañana', but none of them I think conveys the same sense of urgency!"

The more urgent and intractable our educational problems seem to be, the more tempting becomes the notion of a "quick fix." Reports of successes in foreign lands are all that is needed to release a flood of what I call "My Fair Lady prescriptions" – you remember:

> *Why can't the English teach their children how to speak?*
> *Norwegians learn Norwegian, the Greeks are taught their Greek ...*
> *Arabians learn Arabian with the speed of summer lightning,*
> *And the Hebrews learn it backward, which is absolutely frightening ...*

We have all surely noted the fanfare of attention given just at present to the (alleged) merits of the Japanese education system, and the calls for us to learn from Japanese successes and to imitate what we can. A far cry indeed from the years of postwar occupation of Japan, when the shoe was rather precisely on the other foot! There may indeed be some truth to the adage that if you live long enough you will see everything at least twice, the second time the opposite of the first.

Recall, too, the exhibitions of intense interest in the Soviet school system after Sputnik was sent aloft. *What Ivan Knows That Johnny Doesn't* was the apt title that summed up the mood of the times.[1] Later in the 1960s the search for an educational model shifted to Britain and the well-publicized attractions of Open Education in the early school grades. Now it is Japan's turn. Perhaps we should be grateful for small mercies. After all, it was only a relatively small group here in the United States who, during China's Cultural Revolution, urged us to follow that splendid example, by sending our teachers out to the countryside for political re-education, with specific attention to be paid to improvement of their latrine-cleaning skills.

So, there are clearly some problems, if not abuses, to contemplate in the comparative study of education – especially so when the object of the exercise is to find an easy solution abroad for complex problems at home. But it is important not to throw the baby out with the bath water: comparative education does have its valued and legitimate uses, as well.

Although I am not sure that I have anything remarkably new to add, I can only plead that I have given a goodly slice of my academic and intellectual life to thinking and writing on this topic, which will continue, I am sure, to occupy me.

What is comparative education?

There are many definitions. What is common to most of them is the emphasis on the use of data from another educational system, usually a foreign one. Following that emphasis, Max Eckstein and I defined the field as follows in a book we wrote in the late 1960s:

> ... comparative education is potentially more than a congeries of data and perspectives from the social sciences applied to education in different countries. Neither the topic of education nor the cross-national dimension is central to any of the social sciences; nor are social science concerns and the cross-national dimension central to the work of educators. The field of comparative education is best defined as an intersection of the social sciences, education, and cross-national study.[2]

My coauthor and I were engaged in that book in "talking up" the role of the social sciences in comparative education; we thought (perhaps with brash rudeness) that there had been a deal too much historical and philosophical speculation, and that the time had come for some proper attention to what we were pleased to call "the facts," preferably quantified, pressed into the service of social science models of institutional processes and individual behavior. I imagine we must have talked up the benefits of the social science content of comparative education a little too vigorously, for few since then have been prepared to accept our pleas that we were trying only to redress an imbalance, and not to cast out history and philosophy lock, stock, and barrel from comparative study of education.

The Uses of Comparative Education

Properly done, comparative education can deepen understanding of our own education and society; it can be of assistance to policy makers and administrators; and it can form a most valuable part of the education of teachers.[3] Expressed another way, comparative education can help us understand better our own past; locate ourselves more exactly in the present; and discern a little more clearly what our educational future may be. These contributions can be made via work that is primarily descriptive, as well as through work that seeks to be analytic or explanatory; through work that is limited to just one, or a very few, nations, as well as through work that embraces a wider scope; through work that relies on nonquantitative, as well as quantitative, data and methods; and through work that proceeds with explicitly formulated social science paradigms in mind, as well as in a less formalized manner.

Description   Let us look first at the uses of description. Accurate description is a kind of "mapping" of what other countries are doing, or not doing, planning, abandoning, or changing in their educational enterprises. A great deal of this used to go on in departments and ministries of education. Recall the work of the United States Bureau of Education under William Torrey Harris, and of the Board of Education in England. Michael Sadler's series of "Special Reports" on foreign educational developments are a model of this genre. I have always been in special debt to one volume in the series, entitled simply "Education in Russia" and published in 1909 by one of His Majesty's Inspectors of schools, Thomas Darlington. It is a work that reveals quite terrifying powers of observation, assimilation, and reporting.[4]

Help in decision-making   It would be wrong to typify these efforts as "mere description." First of all, there is nothing "mere" about the tremendous amount of effort that has to be exerted simply to acquire systematic, parallel data on educational systems that differ in the particulars of their structure.

Second, accurate, reliable description will often show us that our own problems are not unique, and such knowledge can be most useful. It directs us to search out and try to understand forces and factors at work that transcend the boundaries of our own society. Exercises in mapping the experiences of other countries can feed directly into policy making and decision-taking.   Indeed, as Edmund King has pointed out, comparative studies of education are legitimated and energized precisely to the extent that they originate from the need to make decisions about the conduct of education.[5]

Thus, we worry a great deal about youth unemployment, and we question whether our schools are preparing young people properly for the labor market. This is by no means a uniquely American concern; the British, for example, are struggling with similar problems, as are the French. In such cases, it is not only knowledge of parallel phenomena that is useful but also knowledge of other countries' attempted solutions, and the problems that those solutions are encountering.

These considerations are particularly to be borne in mind at present, as we try to deal with the flood of recent reports on the condition of American education and what we should be doing about it. If we have a tendency to flagellate ourselves for our shortcomings a little too enthusiastically, it may be because we do not understand that other nations are also experiencing severe problems in defining what makes for an education of excellence in the modern world. From Britain to Australia and at points in between, there is currently going on the most vigorous discussion of proposals to change profoundly the content and structure of secondary education. Knowledge of what is being proposed and tried in cognate situations abroad is indispensable for reasoned judgment about what we need to do at home.

Comparative standards   Another important use of descriptive studies lies in the opportunity they provide to estimate the standing of the United States relative to other countries, along dimensions of education that are of interest. This was a major preoccupation in the early years of the nineteenth century; it remains a significant and viable contribution of comparative education. How do our arrangements for the education of the handicapped, the gifted, the very young, and the not so young stack up against those of other countries that we consider our peers? The studies of the International Association for the Evaluation of Educational Achievement (IEA), to which members of Teachers College have made a notably large scholarly and technical contribution, are built on a painstaking mapping of what school children in dozens of countries know in their own and foreign languages, mathematics, science, civics, and the like. Used properly (and, as we shall see, that is not always the case), the resultant inter-country rankings can be powerful pointers toward special problems and needed improvements.

Remedying misperceptions   Even single-nation studies can be immensely useful, especially those dealing with countries that are important to us but where access is difficult. The Soviet Union is a case in point. When I was working on aspects of the financing of Soviet education, the accepted view was that vocational education and higher education were the favored sectors of the Soviet system, and that general secondary education took second place to other sectors that promised a more direct contribution to economic growth. My research led me to a quite opposite conclusion: as far as ruble allocations were concerned, the Soviet authorities had treated general secondary education far more generously than vocational and higher education.[6] Other single-nation studies in comparative education have shown equally unexpected results, and not a few of them have been produced at Teachers College.

Education as touchstone   Only cynics believe that "nations get the governments they deserve," but it may well be that nations get the educational institutions they merit. As the recent report on secondary education from the Carnegie Foundation for the Advancement of Teaching put it: "A report card on public education is a report card on the nation. Schools can rise no higher than the communities that support them."[7] If this is true, then the state of the schools may be an indicator of more than just educational conditions. For example, indifference in the schools to the value of intellectual activity may betoken a more general anti-intellectualism in society; authoritarian classrooms may be reflecting authoritarian political arrangements; and inefficient use of resources devoted to education may simply be an extension of inability to use resources effectively in industry, agriculture, and commerce.[8] If these things are so, and there is a good deal of evidence that they are, comparative education can be a fruitful approach to understanding the values, culture, and achievements of other societies, certainly not in their entirety, but nonetheless a significant portion of what we need to know about our neighbors on this globe.[9]

As I found when I was engaged in a study of educational policies in Austria, the processes of educational policy-making told a good deal about Austrian society in general. I was a member of an international team reviewing Austrian education for the OECD. Two aspects impressed us deeply. One was the emphasis placed on what the Austrians termed "Betreuung," which can be translated as "trust," or "stewardship." Teachers and school administrators, politicians and parents, employers and trade unionists all used the word, meaning by it their sense that the schools bore what I understand lawyers term "a duty of care" for the students. The second was the careful attention to collaborative decision-making, joining government, employers, and trade unions, when figuring out policies for the final years of school and entry into the labor market. Both of these approaches were characteristic of contemporary Austrian attitudes in the wider arena. The concept of stewardship that is normally associated with Aquinas and medieval Catholic thought is alive and well today, and living in Austria.[10]

Naturally, there are also instances where the schools are *not* consonant with important political aspirations or social processes of a given society. Then, an even more intriguing arena is opened for study. Take, say, the Shah's Iran. Like so many of the oil-rich nations, it was a society with two distinct facets, the modern and the traditional. The Shah's schools served the sectors of society that he most wished to develop: business, the army, the towns. But his "modernized" schools flew in the face of the aspirations and world outlook of the more traditionally orientated segment of the nation. Hence, to look at the Shah's schools was to have regard for "official" Iran only.

Meanwhile, traditional Iran lived on, as strong as ever, and nursed its resentments to the point of revolution. Parallel disjunctions were evident in many of the colonial territories before independence, as the schools and universities established by the colonizers produced an elite no longer subservient to imperial interests. Such disjunctions between school and society are keys to understanding the pressures that can build up toward sudden, and often discontinuous, political change.

Origins and influences   Although comparative education characteristically tends to emphasize differences, the basic similarities of formal education across countries are also of interest. With increasing speed, beginning about 1860, the nations of the world have made available the facilities for formal schooling to ever-larger fractions of their populations. The institutional frameworks, the preparation of teachers, the equipment used, the systems of grading and examinations, the issuing of certificates and diplomas – all contribute to the basic commonality of school systems, wherever they are located. Two main factors have been at work to create this standardization: diffusion of educational practices across national boundaries and ever-greater sharing of common objectives for expanding resources for formal education.[11]

Contemporary European practices in education cannot be understood without reference to models developed in the United States. For example, secondary education all over Europe has been powerfully influenced by the American model of the neighborhood, comprehensive high school. Sweden was the leader in the European movement to establish secondary schools that were no longer differentiated according to the social-class origins of their students. The Swedish planners and bureaucrats who effected the reform were well acquainted with the American experience, and took it into account when formulating their plans (even though the American philosophy of decentralized control and predominantly local financing did not appeal to them at all).[12] From Sweden, the comprehensive school movement radiated to influence developments in England, France, the other Scandinavian countries, and recently even Spain and Portugal. In West Germany, some states (particularly those with Social Democratic governments) moved toward the comprehensive pattern – it is, for example, the basic mode of secondary school provision in West Berlin – while the Christian Democratic Länder largely resisted what had become a European trend.[13] In each of these countries, there were local differences and adaptations, but the twin elements of comprehensive secondary education – massive expansion of enrollments and reduction of institutional differentiation – were everywhere in evidence, as they diffused either directly or indirectly from the American example.

Sometimes the diffusion was more forceful, and took on the character of deliberate implantation or imposition. European and American colonial activities have spread a model of schooling that shows every sign of possessing tremendous survivability. For this reason, it is impossible to understand education in, say, contemporary Nigeria, Tunisia, or the Philippines without taking into account the models planted in those places by the British, the French, and the Americans, respectively.

Cross-cultural study of education, then, can identify the potentials and the limits of international borrowing and adaptation. Although nobody has yet tried to do a complete accounting, my own impression is that international borrowing of educational ideas and practices has more failures to record than successes. Transplantation is a difficult art, and those who wish to benefit from the experience of other nations will find in comparative studies a most useful set of cautions, as well as some modest encouragement.

From the particular to the general   I now come to that use of comparative study which I believe to be its most exciting, though perhaps also its most difficult: its potential for establishing the generalizability of what we think we know about education. Of course, results based on research conducted within a single country can be most valuable, and I am aware of the increasing trend among social scientists to emphasize the merits of particularist approaches, and to express a distrust of generalization. This may simply be another swing of the pendulum of fashion in research, or it may have more substantial bases. But comparative education is caught inextricably in what Isaiah Berlin has described as the classic dilemma of those who wish to know about the world, and to act upon it.[14] Do we want to be "hedgehogs," who know one big thing, or do we want to be "foxes," who know many things, none of them presumably very big? Professor Geertz in his recent book, *Local Knowledge,* wants us to settle for lots of little things; one big thing, he believes, is simply not attainable.[15] The debate will not be settled quickly, in comparative education or in any of our other intellectual enterprises. Those enterprises are characteristically partly a matter of science and partly a matter of art. Scientists take the very complex, even the mysterious, and by their work make it ordinary, law-like, explicable. Artists take the ordinary and the humdrum and impart to it wider meaning, even mystery, at times. In this manner, some in comparative study systematically try to move from the particular to the more general; others are concerned with enriching our understanding of a greater number of particulars. While I enjoy the richness of the particular, I am committed to the enterprise of trying to make sense out of (which I take to mean "bring order to") the bewildering variety of educational phenomena we observe. One way that we do this is to take the propositions that arise out of the work done in single countries and test the extent to which they can be said to hold in other situations.

For example, research in the United States has shown that a child's family birth order has some relation (though not a large one) to the child's scholastic achievement. This finding lends support to theoretical models that emphasize the importance for children's school achievement of the time and other resources that parents spend on their children, and the tendency for firstborn children to get more of their parents' (undivided) attention and purchasable resources than do subsequent children. Cross-national studies have shown, however, that the simple relation between birth order and school achievement does not always hold, for example, in Scotland and France. Subsequent research has shown that, rather than birth order, it may be the spacing of births and family size that are of prime significance, and that the effect of birth order on achievement is mediated through family size and the birth rate.[16] In this way, cross-national work has not only pointed toward improved theoretical models but has also, in fact, prevented overgeneralization on the basis of results derived from a single country.

Let me take just one further example. What if we find that rates of return on investments in higher education are falling in the United States? The comparative approach primes us immediately to ask: Where else in the world is this happening? Are there countries that show rising rates of return? Which are they? What are the country characteristics that are related to declining or rising rates of return to education?[17] Is it true that rates of return to education are inversely related to rates of enrollment expansion in the recent past? Such an hypothesis is not unreasonable: as the number of young people graduated increases, we might expect a more abundant supply of labor to drive entry-level wages down, and vice versa. If a relationship of this kind can be observed in a number of countries, we can be somewhat more confident that we are not observing just a chance phenomenon. There is also potential insight to be gained from examining more closely those countries where rates of return are not being driven down, despite a sizable increase in the number of young entrants into the labor market. We can try to answer the question: Under what conditions do rates of return to education hold up?

A comparative approach enlarges the framework within which we can view the results obtained in a single country: by providing counterinstances, it challenges us to refine our theories and test their validity against the reality of different societies; and, by providing parallel results, it can yield important confirmation of results obtained elsewhere.[18]

The Abuse of Comparative Education

After all this sweetness and light, let me now turn to the more problematic side – though I am happy that I can report much less in the way of abuse of comparative education than there seems to be legitimate use.

As I have pointed out, comparative education is an applied field of study, which finds particular justification in the service of evaluation, management, administration, and policy making. Like all applied fields, it is open to potential abuse by those who wish to use its results to support (or oppose) a specific program of change.

Making a case As I also noted when I began, we have special reason to be cautious in the United States when advocates of change rely heavily on reports of a successful program abroad. Diane Ravitch, in her recent book, *The Troubled Crusade,* provides a splendid recounting of the substantial misuse of reports of those English practices in infant education that became known as Open Education. She describes how Joseph Feather-stone's original quite balanced account was soon superseded by exaggerated and distorted reports of what had been going on in a relatively few exemplary schools. American readers were given the impression that teachers in England had found a magic solution to the most fundamental problems of early education: sustaining the children's active interest in inquiry and learning, while building a firm base for future scholastic progress.[19] Without a doubt there were some admirable aspects of some of the things some teachers in England were doing in some classrooms and schools. But of which nation is this not true? The Open Education message became the basis for an over-enthusiastic movement, supported by considerable public funds and extending far beyond the early years of schooling (for which it was developed in England), even into the high school. Of such stuff are present fads and future disasters made. The authentic use of comparative study resides not in wholesale appropriation and propagation of foreign practices but in careful analysis of the conditions under which certain foreign practices deliver desirable results, followed by consideration of ways to adapt those practices to conditions found at home.

A cautious approach to reports of foreign successes is particularly in order for the United States. Education in the United States is characteristically more open to experimentation and new ideas than is the case in most other countries – indeed, too open in the opinion of many observers abroad. In such a climate, the job of the comparative educator often consists in tempering enthusiasm with a dash of realistic reporting. Not so in other, more conservative countries (for example, the Federal Republic of Germany), where resistance to external ideas is much, much greater.

Misinterpreting results Scholars in general are used to seeing their results mis-interpreted by reason of carelessness, ignorance, or intention. And scholars in comparative education are no exception. In the behavioral and social sciences and in historical and philosophical inquiry, responsible scholarship more often than not requires tentativeness in advancing conclusions. Explanatory models are not overly strong, data are often defective, and criteria for confidence in making inferences are subject to dispute. We do the best we can, and, when it comes time to announce our results, they are in effect offered up as hostages to those who can make use of them. Sometimes the use that is made surprises us.

A recent example of misinterpretation of results is probably known to many in this room today, but let me cite it all the same. Barbara Lerner in the Fall 1982 issue of *The Public Interest* sought to answer the question: How are we doing in American schooling, and, in particular, how much have American youngsters achieved in the various school subjects, compared to their counterparts in other countries? Using data from the publications of the International Association for the Evaluation of Educational Achievement (IEA), she concluded, "Relatively little."[20]

As my colleague Richard Wolf pointed out in an incisive critique of the various adjustments Lerner chose to make in the IEA data and the inferences she drew on the basis of those adjusted data, the original findings simply do not support her sweeping conclusion. The achievement picture is much more mixed than she would have us believe: relative to youngsters in other economically advanced countries, American school children performed quite well in some school subjects at some age levels; they did only moderately well in others, and really quite poorly in still other subjects.[21] All of us, no doubt, will agree with Lerner that there is room for substantial improvement in American school achievement levels: we should not be satisfied with the pattern of results that was revealed (especially among blacks and students in the South). But the vital enterprise of raising school achievement levels in the United States is not assisted by misinterpretation of results of cross-national scholarship.

Ethnocentrism   One of the most difficult problems of the comparative method is ethnocentrism. This is the fault of looking at the world primarily from the point of view of the observer's own culture and values. Ethnocentrism has potential for bedeviling comparative education at every stage – from choice of topic to study, through choice of procedures to apply, to judgment concerning the meaning of the results of inquiry.

When we choose to define as a "problem" some phenomenon that is really a problem only from *our* point of view and given *our* set of values, but which is by no means a problem from the point of view of people in other societies, we have fallen into something of an ethnocentric trap.   An oft-cited example of such inappropriate projection of problems has to do with the term "modernization." A great deal of work has been done in comparative education to trace the process and correlates of the so-called modernization process.[22] Special attention has been paid to the contribution that schooling has made to those changes that mark the transformation from a "traditional" to a "modernized" society. Patterns of change that describe well what happened to European and North American societies are assumed to be generalizable to other societies at a later date. Perhaps they are generalizable; perhaps they are not. Although this is a matter for empirical inquiry, the tendency has been to take their generalizability for granted, and to go on from there. This lends a spurious color of definiteness to a process that may go forward very differently from one society to the next.

Projecting our own problems often entails exporting our own concepts, and using them in situations where their fit with reality may not be very good. Thus, despite the efforts of scholars (notably among them, Lawrence Cremin) to broaden our view of education, it remains true that our concept of education is still typically limited to what goes on inside schools. If that broadened view is desirable in the United States, how much more necessary it is for work in societies that have not developed the elaborate systems of formal schooling that we have here.

Elsewhere, I have made this point in the following terms:

> . . .modernization and education in India [is typically] examined on [some such] basis as the number of technical school places opened and filled. This procedure simply reflects the role of formal technical education in Western societies. Yet the most important means of modernization in Indian society may be the increasing availability of automobiles, bicycles, water pumps, and so forth – all the Western-type machines that impose on their operators disciplines of use, maintenance, and repair. Insofar as the comparative educator is interested in examining the relationship between education and development, he would be utterly misled by giving attention just to the formal system of education and neglecting the informal educational effects of introducing Western machinery.[23]

Conclusion

Enough then of abuses, actual and potential. Let me conclude by underlining my belief that, with all its problems, comparative study is a most desirable way of approaching an understanding of education. The challenge is to do it in ways that are valid, persuasive, practically usable, and, above all, enlightening. But, beyond this, I would assert that we need comparative scholarship in general, and comparative education in particular, for a reason that transcends workaday considerations of usefulness.

Our generation, and all those since August 6, 1945, live in a world fundamentally different from that which existed before the bombing of Hiroshima. Before that date, man's inhumanity to man, most violently expressed in war, could be (and was) startling in its destructive effects; but the damage to people, institutions, and things was relatively localized, and recovery in at most a generation or two was the norm. Ours is a different prospect, and, unless we are exceedingly careful, lucky, and, above all, wise, we may be the last generation to inhabit a planet that we would recognize as our Earth.

The special wisdom that we and our heirs must cultivate is the wisdom to get along with our neighbors on this planet, in the company of weapons of quite overwhelming destructive capacity.

However much we may wish that these weapons would simply go away, even the smallest dash of realism must tell us that this will not happen. In a sense that is profoundly Faustian, we have paid for our gifts of intelligence in the coin of permanent fear of global annihilation.

I am sufficiently Aristotelian to believe that knowledge is part of wisdom, though I am a long way from believing that it is the whole of that precious commodity. The knowledge we need more urgently than ever before is knowledge of our own society and of others'. And these two species of knowledge are separable only for purposes of cataloguing them. For the fundamental assertion of comparative study is that we can truly comprehend ourselves only in the context of a secure knowledge of other societies: knowledge that is parochial is partial, in both senses of that word, and therefore potentially dangerous. It is knowledge without completeness, and it is knowledge without appreciation of the rest of the world's experience.

It may be that even our best efforts to negotiate the perils ahead will come to naught, and that humankind will indeed destroy itself in a tantrum of nationalistic and ideological rage. But, by cultivating throughout our society a tradition of rich understanding and knowledge of the other societies with which we share the planet, we shall at least have given the business of species survival our "best shot." Ultimately, I suppose, that is the real test of how well we have used the comparative approach.

NOTES

* Harold J. Noah, "The Use and Abuse of Comparative Education," *Comparative Education Review* 28 (1984), pp. 550-562. This is a slightly edited version of the original paper, delivered as an inaugural lecture for the Gardner Cowles chair, Teachers College, Columbia University, New York, on November 1, 1983.

1. Arther S. Trace, *What Ivan Knows That Johnny Doesn't* (New York: Random House, 1961).
2. Harold J. Noah and Max A. Eckstein, *Toward A Science of Comparative Education* (New York: Macmillan, 1969), p. 121.
3. I do not discuss the uses of comparative education in the education of schoolteachers in this lecture. See Merle L. Borrowman, "Comparative Education in Teacher Education Programs" and three commentary papers by Andreas M. Kazamias, Harold J. Noah, and Cole Brembeck, in *Comparative Education Review* 19 (October 1975) for a presentation of different viewpoints.
4. Board of Education, Special Reports on Educational Subjects, Vol. 23: *Education in Russia* (London: His Majesty's Stationery Office, 1909).
5. Edmund J. King, *Comparative Studies and Educational Decision* (London: Methuen, and Indianapolis: Bobbs-Merrill, 1967).
6. Harold J. Noah, *Financing Soviet Schools* (New York: Teachers College Press, 1966), pp. 109-113.
7. Ernest L. Boyer, for the Carnegie Foundation for the Advancement of Teaching, *High School: A Report on Secondary Education in America* (New York: Harper & Row, 1983), p. 6.
8. A. Harry Passow, Harold J. Noah, Max A. Eckstein, and John R. Mallea, *The National Case Study: An Empirical Comparative Study of Twenty-One Educational Systems* (New York: John Wiley, 1976). See especially Chapter 3.
9. Max A. Eckstein and Harold J. Noah, *Scientific Investigations in Comparative Education* (New York: Macmillan, 1969) presents many examples of the approach under discussion.
10. Organisation for Economic Cooperation and Development, *Reviews of National Policies for Education: Austria – School Policy* (Paris: OECD, 1979).
11. See particularly works published by Francisco O. Ramirez and John W. Meyer, for example, "Comparative Education: The Social Construction of the Modern World System," *Annual Review of Sociology* 6 (1980).
12. Rolland G. Paulston, *Educational Change in Sweden: Planning and Accepting the Comprehensive Reforms* (New York: Teachers College Press, 1968), pp. 30, 100-101, 109, and 124, identifies individuals in Sweden who were influential in spreading the American comprehensive gospel. However, Paulston concludes that the United States experience was too remote for clear Swedish emulation, and that probably the English Progressives had a greater impact on Swedish developments. Of course, English educational reformers who were promoting comprehensive secondary schools between 1930 and 1950 were strongly influenced by American

models. See W.H.G. Armytage, *The American Influence on British Education* (New York: Humanities Press, 1967), pp. 72-76.

13. Max-Planck-Institut für Bildungsforschung, *Bildung in der Bundesrepublik Deutschland: Daten und Analysen* (2 vols.; Stuttgart: Ernst Klett/Rowohlt, 1980) is an indispensable source for contemporary developments in West German education.

14. Isaiah Berlin, *The Hedgehog and the Fox: An Essay on Tolstoy's View of History* (New York: Simon and Schuster, 1953).

15. Clifford Geertz, *Local Knowledge: Further Essays in Interpretive Anthropology* (New York: Basic Books, 1983).

16. R.B. Zajonc, "Family Configuration and Intelligence," *Science* 192 (April 16, 1976): 227-236.

17. George Psacharopoulos, *Rates of Return: An International Comparison* (San Francisco: Jossey-Bass, 1973) examines fifty-three case studies in thirty-two countries, to establish relationships between measured return to education and basic characteristics of the countries.

18. The World Bank has an extensive program of inquiry concerning factors affecting rates of return to education around the world. For a description, see George Psacharopoulos, "Educational Research at the World Bank," *Research News:* 4 (Spring 1983): 5-8.

19. Diane Ravitch, *The Troubled Crusade: American Education, 1945-1980* (New York: Basic Books, 1983): 239-251.

20. Barbara Lerner, "American Education: How Are We Doing?" *The Public Interest* (Fall 1982): 59-82.

21. Richard M. Wolf, "American Education: The Record Is Mixed," *The Public Interest* (Summer 1983): 124-128.

22. See, for example, Don Adams, *Education and Modernization in Asia* (Reading, Mass.: Addison-Wesley, 1970).

23. Noah and Eckstein, *op. cit.,* p. 116.

8

Comparative Education: The State of The Field*

All fields of study appear to be marked by similar phases of growth. In the beginning, contributions to the field tend to be discrete and unsystematic, prompted by the curiosity of the observers and their inherent interest in the subject. There are no rules, just the special insights and motivations of single observers, whose accounts are descriptive and usually lack systematic reporting or an expressed framework of theory.

As work in the field of study increases, reporting becomes more systematic and comprehensive, and the reporters are more self-conscious about the accuracy of their data and more concerned about the ways in which they arrive at conclusions from the data. The curiosity of observers becomes more focused on the possibilities of practical applications of new knowledge, and they are inclined to be critical of their own work and that of their colleagues. Particular types of studies emerge, marked by particular theoretical approaches to the subject, characteristic ways of observing and reporting, and broad agreement on what is or is not relevant. Practitioners in the field become aware of the precedents and of their intellectual ancestors, as well as the kinds of effort their contemporaries are directing at similar targets of study.

Comparative education has demonstrated all these characteristics during its development. The literature includes a wide array of subjects and approaches, symptomatic of the varied motives for studying foreign educational systems. It encompasses narrative description of single nations prompted by interest and curiosity, selective and structured observations motivated by the desire to apply lessons from abroad to the solution of educational problems at home, and encyclopedic codification of the "facts" about many countries. Such work may be impressionistic and even normative, providing a wealth of information and insights about the nations studied. In addition, it often reveals much about the culturally determined predilections of its authors.

Historical reviews of the literature in comparative education show clearly that systematic studies of foreign education increased dramatically as nations began to develop their own public school systems (Brickman, 1960, 1964, 1966; Fraser & Brickman, 1968; Hausman, 1967). Interest in foreign educational practices has been stimulated by nationalism, the growth in international communications, and the aftermath of major wars. For some, the motive was to help develop improved education modeled on foreign practices; for others, foreign study, travel, and teaching were seen as means to ease tensions among nations and foster an international perspective.

Two general questions have especially shaped the investigations of writers in comparative education: Why do educational thinking and practices differ among nations? What are the differences and similarities? The conceptual frame within which answers have been offered becomes evident from a brief review of the literature since the beginning of the 20th century, when Sadler (1900) emphasized the intimate and interactive relation of educational and historical facts.

The education systems of nations differ because of different historical and cultural traditions, but they are similar because there are common elements in human societies. In addition, important events transcending national boundaries have influenced their affairs – the Protestant Revolution, Marxism, the Industrial Revolution, Imperialism (or the achievement of national independence from colonial control), for example. The interplay among such factors has occupied the attention of recent generations of comparative educators.

Comparative education writing has been influenced by several important perspectives. First, the realization that educational phenomena are part of the whole fabric of a nation's culture and history for the most part put an end to works that described and assessed schooling without reference to the larger cultural context of a country. Studies thereafter tended to set educational events against a historical background and to describe the genesis of different types of schools, educational philosophies, and school systems as parts of a series of political and social events. Kandel (1933) and Ulich (1961), especially, focused upon the links among history, national culture, political ideology, and schooling. Much attention was given to "national identity" as the key to understanding a nation's special educational characteristics (King, 1958; Mallinson, 1957). It was conceivable that this approach would end opportunities for comparison because of the tendency to assume that each nation and its education were unique. This danger was averted, however, by the great attention given to common factors and common problems presumed to affect many countries. The major assumption that characterized comparative education work during the first half of the 20th century was that such study could illuminate the past growth and current dynamics of educational change in whole societies (Hans, 1949).

It was not until after World War II, however, that the predominantly historical, philosophical, and theoretical approaches were challenged by more pragmatic considerations. Over a hundred years before, many writers had been prompted to study the schools in foreign countries with a view to improving classroom practices and school system policies in their own lands. From about 1950, this motive prompted a renewal of interest in comparative studies, whether in highly developed nations seeking a way out of the disorder of the postwar period or in the less developed world which was confronting the problems of newly achieved independence. Educational reform and planning for national survival and growth were everywhere of paramount importance.

Economists in particular led the move toward regarding the education system of a nation as its means for investing in human potential, as its way of developing national resources. But the problems were not only economic. The survival of a nation depended as much on its success in dealing with political and social problems as on the most efficient allocation of human resources. For the first time, some nations began to regard reform in education as a possible means of achieving a sense of national unity among disparate sub-populations, a tool for ameliorating gross disparities in status and opportunity among social classes, and a mechanism for improving skills and the quality of life. To study the experience of nations other than one's own seemed pertinent. Comparative study of education and of those social, political, and economic dimensions of society closely bound up with education was encouraged by these developments.

The social sciences thus provided a leavening for the predominantly historical and philosophical approaches of earlier comparative educators. Contemporary work has developed a greater specificity of criteria and a sharper awareness of causal relations. The underlying general questions now tend to be restated more in the following form: What factors in the school system or in the social, political, or other structures of the society explain variability in pupil achievement, administrative structure, school financing, instructional methodology, and other educational phenomena? To the questions of what the similarities and differences in educational practices among nations are and what explains these similarities and differences, a third question was added: What are the outcomes of these similarities and differences?

Comparative educators have for a long time been especially concerned with the availability of data comparable across nations, with controlling the biases of observers and interpreters of data, and with integrating the data, concepts, and analytic techniques of several academic disciplines. The work of international organizations has greatly improved the availability and, to some extent, the comparability of data. Collaborative work involving persons from different nations and disciplines has strengthened the methodological grasp of the problems involved. Further, the use of statistical analysis, model theory, and systems analysis for the purposes of comparative education has been heralded by some practitioners as signifying the emergence of the field as a science.

As a result, a new kind of comparative education research has developed: the empirical cross-national study in which large amounts of data are gathered and analyzed and a variety of social science concepts and techniques are used to test hypotheses about the relations between educational variables and political, economic, and social characteristics (Asher & Shively, 1969; Edding, 1965; Evans, 1968; Farrell, 1970; Lave & Kyle, 1968; Li, 1971). Interest in the methodological problems of cross-national comparison has been sharpened (Bereday, 1964; Foster, 1960; Holmes, 1965), and much attention has been given to the possibilities of using those strategies and tactics that had become commonplace in empirical social science research (Eckstein & Noah, 1969; Noah & Eckstein, 1969). International organizations, such as UNESCO and other specialized agencies of the United Nations, and the Organization for Economic Cooperation and Development (OECD) were able to collect educational and other social data systematically and on a vast scale. These agencies have also made valuable contributions to educational planning and policy efforts, for example, the series of studies on educational finance and planning produced by the International Institute for Educational Planning (a UNESCO agency), and a set of OECD country studies in which national policy and plans have been critically reviewed and analyzed by international teams of educational experts (Organization for Economic Cooperation and Development, 1969-; Unesco, 1964; International Institute for Educational Planning, 1967-1969). Technical assistance programs have encouraged the exchange of skilled professionals among developed and underdeveloped countries, and this has made evident the commonality and immediacy of socio-educational problems in many lands. Thus the burgeoning of data sources, increasing methodological sophistication, the meshing of social science expertise with education, and the presence of urgent problems requiring attention at the national policy level all have combined to give renewed power and variety to comparative studies in education.

An excellent example of this type of work is the massive survey undertaken by the International Association for the Evaluation of Educational Achievement (the IEA project). This project has been devoted to cross-national assessment of student achievement in selected school subjects and attempts to explain variance in such achievement. The first project was a study of mathematics achievement in 12 countries (Foshay, Thorndike, Hotyat, Pidgeon, & Walker, 1962; Husén, 1967). The most recent phases of work covered science, reading comprehension, and literature in 21 countries (Comber & Keeves, 1973; Purves, 1973; Thorndike, 1973), and reports on three more school subjects – civic knowledge and English and French as foreign languages – are in preparation (Farnen, Oppenheim, & Torney, in press; Lewis, 1975; Carroll, 1975). In addition, overall studies of the six-subject surveys are in preparation (Passow, Noah, & Eckstein, 1969; Peaker, 1975; Walker, 1976). Data were not, of course, collected merely on achievement. A vast amount of information in standardized form was obtained on student home background, school practices, teacher characteristics, and the nations' school systems, as well as selected social and economic data. Results were compared at three levels: among students, among schools, and among nations. The main statistical technique used for explaining variance in achievement was multiple regression.

The problems inherent in the new wave of empirical cross-national research are somewhat different from those of the earlier generation of comparativists, but they are not altogether unique. The latter could be faulted on grounds of personal or cultural subjectivity and bias, or because their global perspective was too theoretical, or because their descriptive detail was merely interesting or idiosyncratic and not generalizable. The more empirical studies, even when thoughtfully planned and rigorously executed, are subject to such familiar methodological criticisms as representativeness, the accuracy of data, and the appropriateness of analytical design. Two general concerns, however, are more important. First, the findings should have some relevance to decision making in education (whether at the national policy level or in the school or classroom in particular pedagogical terms), and second, the subtleties of human interaction in the teaching-learning process should not be neglected by undue emphasis upon easily quantifiable and more generally conventional dimensions of education.

In reference to the large-scale survey approach of IEA, the technical problems, while important, are not insuperable. If there is enough time, experience, cooperation among experts, and money, it is possible to reduce weaknesses in sampling, data collection, analysis, and inference to reasonable levels. Relating comparative studies of this kind to policy is a more difficult task, however. At one level is the widespread problem of how to communicate scholarly research findings to practitioners; at another is the selection of problems for investigation and the search for relations among factors that bear upon important professional policy issues. The IEA study does achieve this to some extent. For example, it illuminates the arguments over selective versus comprehensive schooling, documents and refines knowledge about the relation of sex of pupil to achievement in different subjects, and highlights the variable relations between school and home factors in accounting for pupil achievement in different subjects, at different ages, and in different countries. Furthermore, first attempts were made, notably in the literature and civic knowledge studies, to gather and to compare data on noncognitive variables.

The trend of the past decade toward empirical, quantitative, large-scale research has not been without its severe critics (Barber, 1972; Kazamias, 1970). In drawing upon the quantitative techniques of economists, psychologists, sociologists, anthropologists, and political scientists, researchers run the risk of becoming distracted from those topics that are more central to educational studies: curriculum, teaching methodology, and classroom and school organization. Furthermore, it is argued, enthusiasts for empirical methodology may ignore its limitations as an investigative strategy. Critics also tend to stress the inappropriateness of applying models of investigation drawn from the physical sciences to the humane arts, such as education. However, few practitioners are unaware of the differences in orientation inherent in the body of comparative studies:

theoretical and practical, descriptive and analytical, objective and melioristic, philosophical-historical, and empirical. Each orientation has made and continues to make its own particular contribution to the understanding of data and educational problems. But few researchers today will deny the complementary nature of the approaches that characterize the predominantly historical studies of the 1930s and 1940s and the empirical studies of the past decade.

Schooling is a mass enterprise. As such there is value in analyzing its correlates and outcomes, using techniques of mass data collection and analysis. Because education is an international enterprise that is not limited to any particular time and place, it is therefore properly studied cross-culturally. This is not to reject the view of education as a small-scale individual process in which techniques of micro-observation, analysis of small-group behavior, and observations of classroom interaction and culture are desirable. The two approaches should properly be regarded as complementary and, as they are developed, they should contribute to better understanding of the educational process at all levels.

In education and in the social sciences at large, approaches range from attempts to identify the regularities of human behavior in social settings to emphasis upon the special, even unique qualities of the phenomena studied. Comparative education is no exception. At one end of the scale lies a group of works intended to test particular hypotheses systematically: quantified data are statistically analyzed and inferences and predictions are made, with conventional caveats. At the other end are studies of a different nature: colorful, intuitive, eclectic, impressionistic, ranging widely. over history, philosophy, and education, spiced with social comment. Whether a particular piece of work has value is not so much a matter of where it stands on this particular range of alternative approaches as it is of how well the work has been done in its own terms. Comparative education studies include a valuable scholarly tradition in the more humanistically oriented direction, and in recent years the field has been enriched by a growing array of works built upon empirical social science models. Viewed as complementary modes of study, both can contribute substantially to knowledge in comparative education.

REFERENCES

* Max A. Eckstein, "Comparative Education: The State of the Field" *Review of Research in Education 3* (Itasca, Illinois: F.E. Peacock, 1975), 77-84. Reprinted by permission.

Asher, W., & Shively, J.E. The technique of discriminant analysis: A reclassification of Harbison and Myer's seventy-five countries. *Comparative Education Review,* 1969, 13, 180-186.

Barber, B.R. Science, salience and comparative education: Some reflections on social scientific inquiry. *Comparative Education Review,* 1972, 16, 424-436.

Bereday, G.Z.F. *Comparative method in education.* New York: Holt, Rinehart & Winston, 1964.

Brickman, W.W. A historical introduction to comparative education. *Comparative Education Review,* 1960, 3, 6-13.

Brickman, W.W. Works of historical interest in comparative education. *Comparative Education Review,* 1964, 7, 324-326.

Brickman, W.W. Prehistory of comparative education to the end of the eighteenth century. *Comparative Education Review,* 1966, 10, 30-47.

Carroll, J.B. *The teaching of French as a foreign language in eight countries.* International Studies in Evaluation (Vol. 5). New York: Wiley, and Stockholm: Almqvist & Wiksell, 1975.

Comber, L.C. & Keeves, J.P. *Science education in nineteen countries.* International Studies in Evaluation (Vol. 1). New York: Wiley, and Stockholm: Almqvist & Wiksell, 1973.

Eckstein, M.A., & Noah, H.J. (Eds.). *Scientific investigations in comparative education.* New York: Macmillan, 1969.

Edding, F. The use of economics in comparing education systems. *International Review of Education* 1965, 11, 453-465.

Evans, D.R. The use of graphical analysis in educational planning. *Comparative Education Review,* 1968, 12, 139-148.

Farnen, R.F., Oppenheim, A. N., & Torney, J.V. *Civic education in ten countries.* International Studies in Evaluation (Vol. 6), in press.

Farrell, J.P. Some new analytic techniques for comparative educators: A review. *Comparative Education Review,* 1970, 14, 269-278.

Foshay, A.W., Thorndike, R.L., Hotyat F., Pidgeon, D.A., & Walker, D.A. *Educational achievements of thirteen-year-olds in twelve countries.* Hamburg: Unesco Institute for Education, 1962.

Foster, P. Comparative methodology and the study of African education. *Comparative Education Review,* 1960, 4, 110-117.

Fraser, S.E., & Brickman, W.W. *A history of international and comparative education: Nineteenth century documents.* Glenview, Ill.: Scott, Foresman, 1968.

Hans, N. *Comparative education: A study of educational factors and traditions.* London: Routledge & Kegan Paul, 1949.

Hausman, G. A century of comparative education, 1785-1885. *Comparative Education Review,* 1967, 11, 1-21.

Holmes, B. *Problems in education: A comparative approach.* London: Routledge & Kegan Paul, 1965.

Husén, T. (Ed.). *International study of achievement in mathematics – A comparison of twelve countries.* New York: Wiley, and Stockholm: Almqvist & Wiksell, 1967.

International Institute for Educational Planning. *Fundamentals of educational planning.* Paris: Unesco, 1967-1969.

Kandel, I.L. *Comparative education.* Boston: Houghton Mifflin, 1933.

Kazamias, A.M. Woozles and wizzles in the methodology of comparative education. *Comparative Education Review,* 1970, 14, 255-261.

King, E.J. *Other schools and ours.* New York: Holt, Rinehart & Winston, 1958 and 1973.

Lave, R.E., and Kyle, D.W. The application of systems analysis to educational planning. *Comparative Education Review,* 1968, 12, 39-56.

Lewis, E.G. *The teaching of English as a foreign language in ten countries.* International Studies in Evaluation (Vol. 4). New York: Wiley, and Stockholm: Almqvist & Wiksell, 1975.

Li, W.L. A demographic model of student progression. *International Review of Education* 1971, 17, 408-424.

Mallinson, V. *An introduction to the study of comparative education.* London: Macmillan, 1957.

Noah, H.J., & Eckstein, M.A. *Toward a science of comparative education.* New York: Macmillan, 1969.

Organization for Economic Cooperation and Development. *Reviews of national policies for education.* Paris: Author, 1969.

Passow, A.H., Noah, H.J., Eckstein, M.A., and Mallea, J. *The national case study. An empirical comparative study of twenty-one educational systems.* International Studies in Evaluation (Vol. 7). New York: Wiley, and Stockholm: Almqvist & Wiksell, 1976.

Peaker, G.F. *An empirical study of education in twenty-one countries: A technical report.* International Studies in Evaluation (Vol. 8). New York: Wiley, and Stockholm: Almqvist & Wiksell, 1975.

Purves, A.C. *Literature education in ten countries.* International Studies in Evaluation (Vol. 2). New York: Wiley, and Stockholm: Almqvist & Wiksell, 1973.

Sadler, M. How far can we learn anything of practical value from the study of foreign systems of education? *Comparative Education Review,* 1964, 7, 307-314. (Originally published, 1900.)

Thorndike, R.L. *Reading comprehension education in fifteen countries.* International Studies in Evaluation (Vol. 3). New York: Wiley, and Stockholm: Almqvist & Wiksell, 1973.

Ulich, R. *The education of nations. A comparison in historical perspective.* Cambridge: Harvard University Press, 1961.

UNESCO. *Economic and social aspects of educational planning.* Paris: Author, 1964.

Walker, D.A. *The IEA six-subject survey: an empirical study of education in twenty-one countries.* International Studies in Evaluation (Vol. 9), New York: Wiley, and Stockholm: Almqvist & Wiksell, 1976.

9

Dependency Theory in Comparative Education*

*Du musst steigen oder sinken,
Du musst herrschen und gewinnen,
Oder dienen und verlieren,
Leiden oder triumphieren,
Amboss oder Hammer sein.*

Goethe, *Geh! gehorche!*
Kto,kogo?
Russian saying[1]

Introduction

This paper is about an increasingly popular model of world society and national development, and its relationship to work in Comparative Education.[2] We shall call the model 'dependency theory', though whether it is a single theory, a family of theories, or a paradigm, seems to be a matter of some debate.[3] In any event, dependency theory has shaped a substantial body of economic thought in recent years. It seeks to explain the obstacles to the development of poor regions and nations, and has been borrowed by writers on education in general, and by research workers in Comparative Education, in particular.

We propose to outline the main concept of the theory, consider its essential elements, and review some leading contributions to Comparative Education that have proceeded from the standpoint of dependency theory. Finally, we will draw twelve lessons from the discussion, to summarize our assessment of the contribution of the theory to comparative analysis of education.

I. Theory

Dependency theory argues that the world's present state can be most validly seen as the outcome of domination by the 'have' nations over the 'have-nots' and, within nations, by domination of 'have' over 'have-not' classes and interests.[4] This is surely not a new idea. What is perhaps new is acceptance by an increasing number of comparativists that this dichotomy between superordinates and subordinates amounts to a powerful, globally applicable, explanatory model.

The terms that express the key concepts of the theory are: center-periphery, hegemony, and reproduction. They are used to explain the world as it is supposed to exist today (Wallerstein[5] calls it a "world empire"), in terms of the unilateral exercise of power by the center on the periphery, by the hegemonic on the dependent, bolstered through the systematic reproduction in the periphery of the values of the center. Schooling is cast in an especially active role, as reproducing in the young those values, attitudes, and skills best fitted to serve the interest of the dominant groups.[6]

Both past and present are analyzed using the same framework of explanation. The historical record is read as beginning with a missionary zeal, which was soon transformed into explicit, unabashed colonization. The contemporary scene is characterized by the retreat of classical colonialism, and its replacement by a more sophisticated and insidious colonization – that of the mind and the will. Universities and philanthropic foundations, multilateral and national development agencies, book publishers and mass media organizations, even the very artifacts of industrialized society (from automobiles to ballpoint pens to infant feeding formulas) are all viewed as instruments of oppression.[7] The oppressed peoples have merely exchanged physical for mental domination.

This world view claims validity as an explanation of relationships within nation-states, as much as between them. In each country, it is asserted, there is an identifiable center exploiting a periphery, with a dominant class or caste seeking to use schooling to reproduce the set of values and the system of stratification marking its continued hegemony. To that end, some knowledge becomes certified or legitimated as worthy, desirable, and conferring status; other knowledge is neglected, ignored, or even suppressed. Within most nations the goal of thought control has been largely achieved. The people, it is argued, simply do not realize that they are living in a world of ideas and values deliberately created to keep them in subservience. Nor do they understand the vital role played by the schools in producing this "servitude of the mind".[8] Indeed, the very brilliance of the system's success is its capacity to deceive those who serve it into believing they are free, when in fact they have been enslaved.

The harshest criticism is reserved for the curriculum, the body of knowledge ('cultural capital') that is selectively organized and transmitted to students. The periphery, it is said, has been forced or lured into a pernicious copying of the curriculum of the center. Even after release from colonial rule, the disjunction between what is taught and what is needed locally continues. For example, the application of science to agriculture, small scale farming, household management, and hygiene is neglected in favor of concentration on abstract, 'academic' material. The languages of the former colonial masters continue to provide vehicles of instruction, communications, and administration. All this is not simply inappropriate, it is concluded; rather it is at once a consequence of the hegemonic relations between center and periphery, and the means of perpetuating them.[9]

Thus, dependency theory shades over naturally into reproduction theory, which itself arose as a part of the new sociology of knowledge. This holds that the structures and the content of knowledge are most appropriately viewed as forms of property, power, and privilege. There is a natural dynamic leading those societies that have developed the most powerful knowledge yet achieved by mankind, the scientific knowledge of the industrialized states, to impose it on their weaker dependents, thus confirming those dependents in inferiority, establishing their own superiority, and widening the market both for the knowledge itself and for the products of that knowledge. This is the process of reproduction, defined as the extension through time and space of the hegemony of one group over another.

The translation of what began as a theory to explain problems of economic development to the realm of educational affairs has been most vigorous. Neo-Marxist conflict theory, ideological analysis, the study of the dynamics of social institutions, and aspects of psychological conditioning theory, have all joined to form a world view advancing the following propositions: a class-state coerces students in class-ridden educational institutions to support the official ideology; schooling is the apparatus by which the ruling class imposes its (self-serving) values on the working class in order to maintain the status quo; and this is as dramatically displayed within nations (where education is equated with internal colonialism) as among them (where imperialist powers impose a foreign education upon subject nations).[10]   Freire extended the argument somewhat: even the oppressed are shaped into becoming 'oppressors' in their turn, as everyone seeks to become a boss. The prospects for the development of real freedom and individual autonomy are poor.[11]   Bowles and Gintis voiced agreement: schools discipline the young in the interests of serving the existing power structure. This is accomplished via grading, competition, petty rewards and not-so-petty punishments. The educational system dehumanizes by destroying innate originality and creativity.[12]   The emphasis on conflict assumed an even more threatening quality in Bourdieu and Passeron. Knowledge is imposed by the schools, and this imposition is a form of violence visited by the strong (teachers, administrators, and society's leaders) on the weak (the students) in the course of their *formation*, to use the devastatingly descriptive French word for this process.[13]   Educational planning is condemned as a transparent device for extending and intensifying dependency.   Most dependency theorists foresee only an ever-deepening immiseration, as resources continue to be siphoned from the periphery into the center(s). Change is unlikely to occur without violent upheaval; school reform is dismissed as beside the point, a mere diversion from the real business of transforming world-wide power relationships.

We can summarize the various claims and assertions of dependency theory in the form of a half-dozen composite dicta:

1. Dependency theory claims to be a globally applicable, objective approach to understanding how the poorer nations have been deceived and victimized by a unidirectional exercise of power.
2. Dependency theory views educational structures and education content as essential means by which the center exercises thought control over the periphery, reproducing the conditions for its survival and advancement. These means operate not only in obvious ways, but also in ways that are extremely subtle.
3. Dependency theory claims to show that the process of thought control is so powerful that parents and citizens are incapable of recognizing their children's best educational interest, and are helpless to make independent choices in the face of overwhelming ideological hegemony.
4. Dependency theorists tend to deny that we can look to education or educational reform in any important degree for improvement in this state of things: radical (and even violent) rupture of the hegemonic power of the center is required.
5. Dependency theory asserts that the countries on the periphery represent victimized 'good guys'; those at the center are the victimizing 'bad guys'. The latter force so-called modernization on the former, but in fact the fruits of modernization are simply further dependency.
6. Dependency theory claims that the greater a country's degree of dependency, the greater will be a country's difficulties in establishing effective social and educational institutions.

This is an imposing set of claims, and if they are supported we would appear to be in the presence of a formidable general perspective on the development of education and society. We now turn therefore to assess this approach to education, especially as it commands the attention of comparativists.[14] We shall do this on the basis of eight recent research contributions in Comparative Education that have used major concepts from dependency and reproduction theory as a framework for inquiry.

II. Applications

All of the eight articles discussed below use to some extent one or more of the major metaphors of dependency theory: center-periphery, reproduction, hegemony.

Center-Periphery Altbach deals with 'The University as Center and Periphery'[15] in a wide-ranging article. Universities, he points out, may be classified as either "influential" or "dependent", that is, as either creators or distributors of knowledge. Despite their influence within their own territories, universities in the Third World continue to be at a disadvantage in the international knowledge network. They are passive rather than active, serving as agents through which industrialized nations maintain their dominant positions in the world. Altbach views the center-periphery concept as valid within nations, too: the metropolitan nations have their workaday colleges and universities, as well as their world-famous 'flagship' institutions.

Mazrui in 'The African University as a Multi-National Corporation: Problems of Penetration and Dependency'[16] treats the same basic theme as Altbach's: the existence of the metropolitan-based university controlling institutions on the periphery, in this case the typical African university. Mazrui draws a parallel with the activities of multinational corporations which exploit the periphery's resources in the interest of shareholders at the center. He identifies two major functions of the African university: to help meet the colonizers' manpower needs; and to help create markets for the products of Western industry by remaking African values. He indicts African universities on a charge of perpetuating cultural dependency, despite their record of promoting African nationalism and political independence.

While the metaphor, center-periphery, aids us in approaching the variety of educational institutions, nevertheless it can hardly be said to make a unique contribution to our understanding. Essentially, Altbach is describing inequalities among institutions – inequalities of resources (primarily of faculty, but also of physical and financial resources); inequalities of activities (in research, publishing, and positions in the all-important networks of communication); and inequalities of student academic quality. These inequalities may or may not be a result of some socio-economic process related to dependency. That is a hypothesis to be tested. However, what is provided is a series of assertions. The process by which, say, a Chilean university that enjoys only a local reputation is kept in that status by the metropolitan universities of North or South America is not clarified. A more straightforward account, and a more parsimonious one, might simply be based on the concept of choices made under resource constraints leading to inequalities, and would probably do the explanatory job just as well, if not better. As Altbach himself puts it in his final paragraph:

The concept of center and periphery, as applied to the world of universities and particularly to the problems of higher education in the Third World, is a way of thinking about inequalities, institutional and academic hierarchies, and differing roles of academic institutions in a world of complexities. While Third World universities function as peripheries in an international system, they are clearly central to their own societies.(p. 619)

In addition, Altbach notes (p. 612) that, with the help of substantial support, some Third World institutions have achieved excellence. Given that the prime causative differences among universities are between the poor and the wealthy, and the new and the old, and given that it is these differences which determine whether a particular institution is a producer or a distributor of knowledge, we are drawn to conclude that the center-periphery concept merely substitutes new terms for old without adding significant explanatory power.

Mazrui, too, makes use of the center-periphery metaphor primarily as a way of approaching his topic, rather than as an explanatory tool. He concludes his article by identifying three strategies whereby African universities and African nations may become in fact independent, serving their own rather than others' interests. They are: 1. to Africanize admissions requirements, criteria for faculty recruitment, and university organization; 2. to diversify the sources of influence away from an exclusive emphasis on European culture, toward Africanization and 'Asianization' of the curriculum; 3. to counter-penetrate the West, building on the influence that Africa has already had on Western culture (via art, craftsmanship, and music).

The contrast between this advice and the typically pessimistic message of dependency theory is noteworthy. According to most dependency theorists, the outlook for the dependent nations is quite bleak. They are described as being caught inextricably in the toils of a powerful world-wide network of forces, in a system of exploitation, immiseration, and oppression that will not let them go. Mazrui accepts none of this. Indeed, the possibilities of transcending the dependent condition associated with location on the periphery, acknowledged by both authors, undermines the second major metaphor of dependency theory: reproduction. Three contributions illustrate its use in Comparative Education research.

Reproduction Kelly's work is entitled: 'Teachers and the Transmission of State Knowledge: A Case Study of Colonial Vietnam'.[17] The author begins from the standpoint of reproduction:

Although the chapter derives its data from colonial Vietnam, the issues it addresses are relevant to our understanding of the ways in which schooling transmits a set of ideological characteristics favorable to the maintenance of dominant groups and helps reproduce the division of labor in society.(p. 176)

What follows is an exposition of the way in which teachers in colonial Vietnam responded to the role assigned to them. Educational policy in the French colony was a consistent attempt to legitimate certain specified types of knowledge and to use the schools to reproduce the power relationships that would best serve French interests. Here, if anywhere, was the classic colonizer-colonized situation, in which dependency theory and its associated reproduction metaphor might be expected to demonstrate explanatory power to best effect.

But Kelly shows that the story is much more than a simple tale of the colonizers giving the orders, and the colonized obeying. The state issued the most detailed instructions to teachers, training and selecting them carefully to serve French goals, and monitoring their work closely through a far-reaching system of school inspection. Yet Vietnamese teachers contrived to turn the externally imposed school system to their own purposes. They acted independently, transmitted knowledge selectively, and they rejected the French version of moral education and aspects of the official curriculum that were offensive to their nationalist, cultural, and class sensitivities. Even with the most powerful political, juridical, and police powers at their disposal, the French never succeeded in the reproduction goal. Both the teachers who had a westernized training, as well as those who had gone through the 'adapted' Franco-Vietnamese schools, resisted indoctrination. They established professional organizations to nurture their Vietnamese solidarity and rejected attempts to cast them in second-class roles. Kelly concludes with the following cautious verdict:

> The ways in which schools reproduce the division of labor and a set of ideological characteristics favorable to unequal power relations are quite complex. In some instances that reproduction may be less than perfect. (p. 190)

However, the implication of Kelly's work is unequivocal: far from providing a cogent set of explanations for what happened in Vietnamese education under French colonial rule, dependency theory is decisively contradicted by the facts.

If Kelly demonstrates the complexities of an assimilationist educational policy imposed from without on the basis of the Vietnam experience, Barrington shows the problematics of the adaptive approach. His article, 'Cultural Adaptation and Maori Educational Policy: The African Connection' describes the shift in educational policies in the 1930's from assimilationist goals toward an education adapted to the perceived needs of the Maori population in New Zealand.[18] More emphasis was to be placed on the acquisition of agricultural knowledge and skills and on the survival of local culture and handicraft arts. A style of education intended to turn Maoris into cultural Europeans was to be ended. Barrington documents the way in which this change in policy ran parallel to thinking about education for Negroes in the American South and for the indigenous peoples of colonial Africa.

Like Kelly, Barrington proceeds to explain why this officially and rhetorically powerful new doctrine for Maori education failed to take root. Many parents were unalterably opposed to what they viewed as a second-rate education for their children. He quotes from Maori School Records:

> 'A Maori parent is exactly the same as a European', concluded the headmaster of Te Aute, the leading denominational boarding college for Maori boys. 'When I suggest an agricultural course they want their boy to take matriculation'.(p. 9)

Not only in Vietnam, but also in New Zealand, there is little evidence to support the picture of a helpless population manipulated by colonial authorities dedicated to reducing children, through reproduction, to mere objects of dependency. In Vietnam, teachers resisted an imposed foreign curriculum; in New Zealand parents demanded access to one, rejecting the adaptive version. Yet the reproduction metaphor draws no distinction between these two contrasting education programs and between the different indigenous responses. To that extent, too, the metaphor is a weak tool for comparative study.

Bullivant, in his article 'Cultural Reproduction in Fiji: Who Controls Knowledge/

Power?', seeks to clarify some of these complexities by examining the formal and informal process "through which culture is passed on to the developing child" (p. 230).[19] He describes the political and educational relationships between the dominant Fijians and the immigrant Indian population in terms of reproduction. But he concludes that the evidence that Fijian dominance is achieved via use of the educational system and the structure of knowledge is ambiguous. His conclusion is that dominance is exerted more through structures (for example discrimination in favor of Fijians for admission into higher education and in government employment) than through ideological instruments. Moreover, he observes significant concessions made by the Fijians to the cultural claims of the Indian section of the population: "... no one 'cultural arbitrary' is being imposed to the exclusion of the other in a way that might qualify as 'pedagogic action'." (p. 243). What might be interpreted as evidence of dominance is interspersed with many elements of concession, running decidedly counter to the implication of the reproduction approach.

In fact, Bullivant's answer to the question: "Who controls knowledge/power?" is not achieved by reliance on the concept of cultural reproduction. Instead, the complexities of the reproduction process are described and, most important, the transactional nature of the relationships between 'dominators' and 'dominated' is highlighted, as indeed it is by Kelly and Barrington.

Hegemony In using the metaphors of center-periphery and reproduction, the authors cited are all seeking to clarify the nature of hegemony. Bullivant, for example, at the very end of his study falls back on Westernizing agencies as the ultimate source of hegemony in Fiji, and the means by which it is maintained.

> But European influence is strong through the external examination system and the need for all children to learn a common language – English. This plays a major role in determining what kind of knowledge may be taught at the senior academic level, and it can be interpreted as 'pedagogic action' and hegemonic, even though Europeans are a small minority in Fiji.

And again in the following:

> The economy is influenced by a Western ideology of consumption and capitalism together with a heavy reliance on a European-dominated tourist industry .... resulted in structures within Fiji that are .... symbolic of the Western ideology – for example, banks, insurance offices, airlines, car hire firms, and resort hotels.(p. 244)

The author claims that the reality of hegemony is effectively concealed by the pretense at a multiracial curriculum. However, none of this is in any sense proved; it is not even demonstrated. Rather, it is merely asserted, as a way of rescuing the desired conclusion from the evidence produced by the research.

In substantially similar fashion, Altbach concludes his article by sounding the theme of hegemony, after quite properly concluding that the center-periphery metaphor reduces under examination to little more than an expression of inequalities.

> Third World institutions not only confront the reality of the historically and economically based power of the industrialized nations but must also deal with the widespread desire by the industrial nations to maintain their dominant

positions.   This desire, and the specific policies that are used to continue dominance, has been called neocolonialism.(p. 605)

But as with Bullivant, the matter is left to assertion with no attempt at proof.

Three articles that place hegemony at the center of their argument are Berman, 'Educational Colonialism in Africa: The Role of American Foundations, post 1945';[20] Irizarry, 'Overeducation and Unemployment in the Third World: The Paradoxes of Dependent Industrialization';[21] and Sica and Prechel, 'Political-Economic Dependency and Educational Development'.[22]   Berman charges that American foundations, behind a smokescreen of altruism and claims to be rendering only neutral technical assistance, deliberately pursued policies that benefited the givers, not the receivers.   The foundations financed an array of initiatives: the establishment and support of leading universities in strategic areas of Africa; the promotion of social science approaches to problems of development and change; the support of training programs to prepare public administrators; and a variety of programs for teacher training for African students in the United States and for training U.S. specialists in African affairs.   All of this was done, Berman asserts, to enhance prospects in Africa for the capitalist system in general, and for American interests in particular.

> ... There was little humanitarianism in these foundation attempts to develop educational systems in Africa, despite the proclivities of random foundation personnel in this direction.   Education was perceived as the opening wedge ensuring an American presence in those African nations considered of strategic and economic importance...to the governing and business elite of the United States.   The contention that American foundation expenditures in Africa were designed primarily to benefit the recipients cannot be sustained.   Rather, it was through African education that American foundation personnel hoped to exert leverage on the direction of African development, development which would follow lines acceptable to American interests.(p. 225)

> ... The overriding concern of the 'philanthropoids' in Africa has been to train elite cadres capable of running their nations in ways guaranteed to maximize internal growth and political stability, desiderata from the American perspective.(p. 226)

However, Berman's theme of a powerful conspiracy among leading U.S. institutions to assert hegemony over African nations neglects to account for the patent failure of alleged American hegemonic power to even establish (let alone maintain) its ascendancy in Black Africa.   The contemporary African scene is hardly one marked by the rule of American trained "elite cadres ... maximiz(ing) internal growth and political stability", and certainly does not give the impression of an area governing its affairs in the sole interest of U.S. capitalism.   If hegemonic domination was the goal of the U.S. foundations, their failure in Africa has been resounding.

Whereas Berman tends to write in political science terms, Irizarry's orientation is explicitly economic.   He attributes the blame for the severe problems of the underdeveloped countries to their economic colonization by the industrial powers.   He points specifically to the undesirable outcomes of development strategies that seek "accelerated industrialization; that is, the creation and expansion of a modern, industrialized and high-productivity sector of the economy" (p. 338).   Such strategies, according to the author, have failed to eliminate poverty, improve the welfare of the mass of people, provide complete primary education for all, or supply trained manpower adapted to the needs of the economy.

Irizarry points to the paradox of educational systems that produce a surplus of technically trained manpower who cannot find appropriate employment, while at the same time they continue to put most of their emphasis on humanistic and legal curricula. His is one of the clearest examples in the Comparative Education literature of an author asserting the primacy of economic hegemony in the determination of educational structures and outcomes. He asserts that those countries that have developed on the basis of externally injected capital, externally determined models of classical, colonial-type penetration, and accelerated industrialization, have suffered characteristic distortions of their educational systems.

Although Irizarry undoubtedly describes those distortions correctly, he fails to show that their existence is the particular responsibility of hegemonic power, expressed through overseas trade and the international organizations' support of accelerated industrialization. Not a little of what he says about overemphasis of the humanities and the social sciences and exaggeration of the service sector at the expense of industry being paradoxically accompanied by inability of a goodly fraction of the technically trained to find appropriate jobs, can be applied, for example, to the United Kingdom, Greece, Egypt, India, and Denmark – to name just a scattering of countries at different levels of economic development and with widely different previous 'conditions of servitude'.

Like Irizarry, Sica and Prechel examine the role of hegemonic economic power in shaping educational development. Their stated purpose "is to test the empirical utility of the dependency perspective in accounting for one important facet of international inequality, the distribution of education" (p. 387). Specifically they seek to discover whether distributions of education vary systematically with the degree of economic dependency among nations.

The authors assemble data from seventy-two nations representing center, periphery, and 'semiperiphery' countries. 'Distribution of education' was measured by enrollment ratios; 'dependency' was measured by the standard indicators of domestic capital formation, exports, and external public debt (each as percentages of Gross Domestic Product). Either kilowatt hours or GDP per capita was taken as the measure of a country's level of development.

Zero-order correlations reveal that "level of development is very strongly associated with education measures", a finding that is usually taken to support modernization (rather than dependency) theory. The authors then regress the four economic measures on each of the education indicators. Again, they find strong and statistically significant relationships in the expected direction between level of development and the education measures. But contrary to the dependency hypothesis, degree of dependency is usually positively related to educational enrollment ratios, or is not statistically significant. The 'development of underdevelopment' thesis is not sustained. Further analysis produces ambiguous results at best from the point of view of supporting dependency theory and, in some respects, even downright contradiction. Of the nine coefficients that were estimated (three levels of education on three economic dependency variables), only two are statistically significant.

Sica and Prechel try to save something from this apparently complete debacle of the dependency hypothesis, but concede defeat in the end. They suggest that some of their results might be construed as indicating that "as a country develops – as reflected in the increasing percentage of its population advancing from primary to secondary education – it advances into dependency" (p. 392). Yet they concede that other results obtained in their work "indicate(s) – from one view of causality – that education is an important element of development and that its retardation is itself a guarantee of endless dependency" (p. 394). Again, they find some statistical support for the idea that "the road to cultural growth is fiscal autonomy" (p. 397), a notion that is important in the dependency canon. But the figures are disappointingly weak from the point of view of statistical significance. In the end they fall back on the plea that this is not the right way to test dependency theory:

> ... Linear regression models of this sort are probably inappropriate when used to test dependency theory or any other which by its nature is cognizant not only of gross quantitative economic events but also of the finer points of socio-cultural and socio-political idiosyncrasies of each nation. It was, after all, Frank's intimate knowledge of Brazil, Amin's equally strong interest in certain African nations, and so on, which gave rise to the dependency perspective ... Surely an appropriate test of dependency thinking demands a more comprehensive methodological approach.(p. 400)

While the propositions of dependency theory are asserted with a good deal of assurance and conviction, it appears to be difficult, if not impossible, to demonstrate cross-nationally the major implications of the theory in the realm of education. According to proponents of dependency theory, hegemonic power exerted by the center impinges on the countries of the periphery and shapes their social and cultural institutions. These effects should bear at least some rough relationship to the strength of this power, as measured by degree of economic dependency. Yet in Sica and Prechel's inquiry little if any of it can be shown.

III. Evaluation

Two criteria are important when assessing a genre of work for its contribution to education: its capacity to provide persuasive explanations for the phenomena observed or to suggest avenues for further investigation; and its utility for guiding action, that is, its capacity to inform administrators and planners and to help in policy making. Essentially similar criteria apply in assessing the contribution of work done from a dependency viewpoint in Comparative Education. We remind the reader that in no way do we seek to make a critique of the usefulness of dependency theory in economics, or in education broadly defined. Our task has been to focus on the use that has been made of dependency theory specifically in recent research contributions to Comparative Education. The implications of such a critique are not merely academic. They extend to questions of educational policy, planning, and management. Whether explicitly or implicitly, dependency theory notions are woven into national and international education development efforts as well as into evaluations of their outcomes. If the theory is deficient, the bases for action and the criteria for evaluation are rendered suspect.

The eight studies examined are all informative and well executed. However, whether taken singly or together they are far from validating the basic propositions of dependency theory. Although all of the authors begin their expositions with strong avowals of the dependency approach, it is significant that in three instances (Altbach, Kelly, and Sica and Prechel) the conclusions are at variance with some basic propositions of dependency and reproduction theory. In three further instances (Barrington, Bullivant, and Mazrui) the conclusions are such as to make one quite cautious about some of the implications of dependency theory. Only Berman and Irizarry begin and end with full adherence to its validity. If only because of this mixture of outright contradiction and shaded verification, dependency theory cannot be regarded as a particularly powerful or even persuasive addition to theoretical viewpoints in Comparative Education.

Part of our critique relates to assumptions that are made about the conditions under which people live and act. Dependency theory asserts that the poor and the weak are rendered incompetent to judge their own best interests by the process of cultural reproduction. This is achieved by the powerful, who effectively (and often covertly) control access to knowledge and who establish certain values and disestablish others to support their own interests. This viewpoint is well represented in the articles by Bullivant, Berman, and Mazrui. Thus dependency theory asserts that in the colonial era the poor and the weak were effectively subjugated, and that in the post-colonial period a form of thought control is substituted for physical force. Education stands accused as the major instrument of this behavioral manipulation.[23]

What these assertions overlook is the immense complexity of the relations between the center and the periphery. It is an exercise in oversimplification to picture the people of the periphery as mere objects of successful manipulation by the center. While it is obvious that poverty imposes limitations upon people, it is equally obvious that economic power is not without its limits. Some nations on the periphery do indeed appear to be perfectly willing to follow the lead of the center; presumably their leadership has judged that it is in their interest to do so. But others refuse to be client states, in either deed or thought. And there is every condition in between. This disparity in political response is also present in educational affairs. Some nations take their educational cues pretty directly from the center, especially from the nation that formerly exercised suzerainty. Others make every effort to strike out along new paths, rejecting vehemently what they consider to be inappropriate models. Yet other nations adopt quite eclectic approaches, borrowing from a variety of sources, as it suits them, and combining their borrowed practices in novel ways. Nothing in this reality supports any easy assumption that the fact of the center's superior economic power automatically implies cultural hegemony over the periphery.

A second aspect of our critique relates to the assumptions of dependency theory about the nature of power and how it operates (see especially Altbach and Berman). Here, too, dependency theory is liable to the charge that it deals in oversimplifications. Power is not typically a uni-dimensional phenomenon, nor is its action typically unidirectional, as dependency theory implies. Most important, the objectives of the powerful are not always achieved, as Kelly's article demonstrates. Even in circumstances that appear to be extremely advantageous to those giving the orders, there are important transactional elements involved in the relationship between dominated and dominator. Education may indeed be based on a power relationship, as the dependency theorists argue, but it is equally important to realize that the process of education involves more than a mere *exercise* of power. It involves a *transfer* of power, too. To ignore this is to ignore the existence of different stages in the power relationships among nations, cultures, and classes; on the surface, there may seem to be little recognizable difference between the forms of dependence (political, cultural, and economic), but the dynamics, options, and outcomes of any stage may be quite different, and even unexpected. To be powerful does not necessarily mean to be successful in attaining one's goals, or in maintaining that achievement once it has been attained. History is an account of the fall of empires, as much as of their rise; and of the transfer of power, as much as of its exercise. To read it merely as the enslavement of people is simple-minded. Philip Foster emphasized just this caution when he remarked:

> The statement that the school is an agency of conformity is platitudinous ... all educational institutions in any society must, in large measure, perform that function ... (but) viewed in historical perspective the school has been a failure as an agency of conformity and repression.[24]

Concepts of the nature of power naturally influence perceptions of how change occurs. This is the realm of our third major criticism. Dependency theory argues that as long as economic and ideological dependency continues, political independence is merely colonialism under a different name. The role of elites is regarded as essentially unchanged: to serve as the center's local instruments of control over the periphery (the articles by Altbach, Mazrui, and Irizarry are pertinent here). The possibility of improvement in the direction of a greater degree of power vis-à-vis the center is regarded as very small. Apart from Mazrui, who makes a powerful plea to the contrary, this position is maintained in spite of the fact that we have plentiful evidence of successful challenge by the periphery to the power of the center. Here lies the central problem with the dependency approach. Cultural forms (including education) are clearly much stronger than dependency theory assumes. The resilience and vigor of nationalism, local and national languages, and national cultures and historical traditions continue to mock all forecasts about the growth of a global culture.

Dependency theorists have identified international capitalism as the moving force of hegemony, and it is perhaps as a result of this generally anti-capitalist orientation that hegemony has been seen more as a phenomenon of Western influence than Soviet power. However, even in the Soviet realm of influence economic power does not bring automatic hegemony. Despite the immense power of the Soviet Union vis-à-vis Poland, Hungary Romania, and the rest, these countries are far from becoming mere cultural carbon copies of the Soviet Union, let alone dupes of some subtle process of thought control.

Dependency theory and its associated metaphors can make only a limited contribution to Comparative Education, we have argued, because they represent an oversimplification of very complex phenomena. What accounts for this?

One reason is that the theory is borrowed from another field. What may explain features in the realm of economics may not do so elsewhere (and it is worth noting that even in economics, dependency theory is much debated and criticized). As McLean has observed[25], there are dangers in the unthinking transfer of a theory from one field to another. He identifies three major problems: the dangers of "fossilization" (by which he means the failure of the destination field to keep up with improvements to the theory made at the source); basic lack of fit between the source field and the destination; and neglect of key issues in the destination field, as a result of undue concentration of attention and effort on the lines of inquiry suggested by the borrowed paradigm.

Another reason to charge oversimplification arises from the tendency of dependency theorists to ascribe intent to the forces they describe. The reader is given the impression that there is some maleficent force at work on a global scale, generating evil results. Institutions at the center are portrayed as conspiring with their agents at the periphery in some complicated plot to maintain world hegemony. The reader is tacitly invited to identify with the forces of good against the forces of evil. An important objection to this generally rousing tale, is that institutions (schools, universities, foundations, textbook publishers, information and communications enterprises, governmental aid agencies, and so forth), the whole apparatus of putative hegemonic power, cannot have intent and purposefulness ascribed to them. only human beings have purpose, and the habit of confusing purpose with tendency, and of then making moral judgements about tendencies, combines to promote a simplistic view of educational and cultural change.[26]

The third source of what we consider to be excessive simplification lies in a rhetorical trick. Its effect is to protect the theory from criticism. A central proposition of dependency theory is that hegemony is often asserted in ways too subtle for most people to detect: it creeps in, disguised in a rhetoric of benevolence, and subverts its victims. The critic of dependency theory finds that any doubts expressed about this interpretation are turned back against him. His very denials are claimed as further evidence of the demonic power of the forces at work, for do they not show the extent to which he, too, has been successfully thought controlled? The logic is as impudent as it is circular.

The tendency toward simplification also derives from the historical antecedents of dependency theory. Its view of colonialism is old-fashioned. It is based on an outmoded model, that of nineteenth century European imperialism, in which colonies were run by the center purely in its own strategic and economic interest. The imperial powers relied on physical subjugation and bothered themselves hardly at all with education, or thought control, since the subject peoples were regarded as little more than retarded children. Modern dependency theory has updated the classical model by pointing to a mechanism of control developed by the center through education, but the core of the model remains unchanged – a rather simple dichotomy between the exploiters and the exploited, with little if any recognition of the profound changes that have taken place in the world in the relationships between the former imperial powers and the erstwhile colonies. To ignore these changes is anachronistic, and encourages extension of a model derived from a much simpler world into the present, a period characterized by more complex relationships.

A final source of simplification is the lack of caution in using important terms. The basic terms (center-periphery, reproduction, and hegemony) are metaphors, figurative description comprising a particular explanatory paradigm. Useful as they may be for opening a fresh perspective on familiar phenomena the limits of their applicability are not observed. This permits Bourdieu and Passeron to speak of education, in all seriousness apparently, as "violence"[27] and to use the term "reproduction" in their social-educational models, without recognizing that the biological realm from which the term is borrowed makes room not only for faithful copying, but also for mutation from one generation to the next.

For those interested in the use of theory to further research in Comparative Education, the dependency approach is especially disappointing. It offers little help in avoiding many of those worrisome problems common to all social science inquiry: for example, the tendency to find what one is looking for and to stop looking when one has found it. It does not discourage the making of easy assumptions that the association of two phenomena in time and place justifies strong inferences about causation. It does not restrain the researcher from hanging on doggedly to a theoretical perspective well beyond the ability of the evidence to support it. While dependency theory is by no means alone in these problems, the ideological fervor with which it is so often advanced does nothing to limit their frequency.

From this extended critique of the uses of dependency and reproduction theory in Comparative Education research, we draw a dozen lessons:

On people, plots and power

Lesson 1. Although there is not a shred of evidence to show that people in general are unable to recognize the major forces shaping their lives, dependency theory fosters the dubious implication that the majority of humanity are dupes.

Lesson 2. *Pace* dependency theory, neither physical nor 'mental' colonization necessarily succeeds in blinding parents to the best educational interests of their children, as they try to take into account the likely shape of the world in which they will grow up.

Lesson 3. Dependency theory lends itself all too easily to a 'saints and sinners' interpretation of the world. This makes for exciting rhetoric, but yields no great advance in understanding.

Lesson 4. Agencies at the center may indeed operate in the periphery to promote what they view as their own interests, but this is not evidence that they are engaged in a systematic, covert plan of penetration on behalf of some wider interests.

Lesson 5. The relationship between those having power and those receiving orders is by no means a simple one. Dependent people are not necessarily passive, nor are they necessarily disarmed. Power does not flow in one direction alone. Both the colonizer and the colonized influence its workings.

Lesson 6. Given the utter failure to achieve 'first world' objectives in so many parts of the developing world in the past few decades, a complete dependency theory needs to provide a means of satisfactory explanation of that failure, equally with its attempt to document the center's hegemony.

On change and modernization

Lesson 7. Whatever the external obstacles to achieving cultural independence, the developing nations have a goodly share of their own fate in their own hands. The available evidence by no means supports placing all, or nowadays even most, of the blame for cultural dependency on external forces.

Lesson 8. There exist strategies for social improvement, for the regaining of cultural independence, and even for the assertion of countervailing cultural influence. Dependency theory is wrong in holding that there is no way out for the dependent nations short of breaking the relationships between themselves and the industrialized nations.

Lesson 9. Dependency theory attributes too much to economic dependency. Even insightful analyses of economic dependency relationships on the one hand, and educational deficiencies on the other, cannot prove that the latter follow from the former. Dependency concepts do not add distinctly important power to attempts to explain educational deficiencies.

Lesson 10. Contrary to the implications of much of the writing in dependency theory, modernization is a highly desirable goal, not to be denigrated or lightly cast aside out of frustration or resentment.

On methodology

Lesson 11. Dependency theory does not help to control bias in research, nor does it help researchers make good use of counterfactual evidence to improve their theoretical models.

Lesson 12. The center-periphery concept merely substitutes new terms for old without adding significant explanatory power.

Conclusion

Despite the fact that we have found little to admire in its contribution to Comparative Education research, dependency theory represents an approach that currently appeals to scholars in many quarters. What accounts for its attractiveness? What, in a word, have we missed?

In the first instance, it represents a powerful expression of the disappointment and frustration, perhaps even the cynicism, of the latter part of the twentieth century, that has witnessed two global wars, acts of genocide, widespread decolonization without the hoped-for improvement of the lot of ordinary people, and a sense of crisis about the proliferation of weapons of mass destruction. Much store was laid on education. It had been hailed as a sovereign remedy for the ills of the world. Poverty, militarism, hate, political subjugation, and individual abasement would all be conquered by the schools. They have not been, and the disappointment is understandable. If anything, the severity of some of the problems that faced the world in, say, 1950 has increased, not diminished, with time. This was not supposed to happen. The temptation is correspondingly strong to blame the institutions of society for having 'failed'. If among these institutions the schools, on which the highest hopes were rested, have failed the most miserably, they deserve in turn the strongest castigation.

By the same token, dependency theory appeals to intellectuals in the Third World, who are frustrated and impatient with the fact that their nations' problems have not vanished with the coming of independence. Dependency theory fills an ideological gap, and has acquired legitimacy as it has been taken up by social scientists. Intellectuals in the developed world, too, share their colleagues' frustration, and some have added to it a sense of guilt for what they see as capitalism's original and continuing role in the immiseration of the periphery.[28]

The contrast between the vehemence with which the propositions of dependency theory are typically expressed and the weakness of the research results actually achieved, must be regarded as something of a paradox. To continue to hold to dependency theory in the face of such weakness is probably more a matter of faith and values than of social science.

Comparative Education is no stranger to ideology; some scholars have argued that the two are inseparable.[29] Perhaps so; in which case we can assume that as long as the dependency approach answers the ideological needs of researchers, it will remain a popular style of comparative work, despite its formidable logical and empirical weaknesses.

NOTES

* Harold J. Noah and Max A. Eckstein, "Dependency Theory in Comparative Education: Twelve Lessons from the Literature", in Jürgen Schriewer and Brian Holmes, eds., *Theories and Methods in Comparative Education* (Frankfurt am Main: Peter Lang, 1988), pp. 165-192. Reprinted by permission of Peter Lang Publishers.

1. "You must rise or fall, you must rule and win, or serve and lose, suffer or triumph, be the hammer or the anvil." (Goethe, *Go! Obey!*). Kto, kogo: Russian saying, literally: Who, whom? Meaning: Who gives orders, and to whom?

2. An abridged version of this paper was published in *Prospects* 15 (1985), no. 2. under the title "Dependency Theory in Comparative Education: the New Simplicitude".

3. Ingemar Fägerlind & Lawrence J. Saha, *Education and National Development: A Comparative Perspective* (Oxford: Pergamon, 1983), p. 23.
4. A.G. Frank, *Capitalism and Underdevelopment in Latin America* (New York: Monthly Review Press, 1967); Samir Amin, *Unequal Development* (New York: Monthly Review Press, 1974); and Charles K. Wilber (ed.), *The Political Economy of Development and Underdevelopment*, 3rd ed. (New York: Random House, 1984).
5. Immanuel Wallerstein, *The Modern World-System: Capitalist Agriculture and the Origins of the European World-Economy In the Sixteenth Century* (New York: Academic Press, 1974).
6. Samuel Bowles & Herbert Gintis, *Schooling in Capitalist America: Educational Reform and the Contradictions of Economic Life* (New York: Basic Books, 1976).
7. Robert F. Arnove (ed.), *Philanthropy and Cultural Imperialism: The Foundations at Home and Abroad* (Boston: G.K. Hall, 1980); Martin Carnoy, *Education as Cultural Imperialism* (New York: David McKay, 1974); and Philip G. Altbach & Gail P. Kelly (eds.), *Education and Colonialism* (New York: Longman Inc., 1978).
8. The phrase is used by Philip G. Altbach, "Servitude of the Mind? Education, Dependency, and Neocolonialism", in: *Teachers College Record* 79 (December, 1977), pp. 187-204.
9. Michael W. Apple, *Education and Power* (London: Routledge & Kegan Paul, 1982); Michael W. Apple, *Ideology and Curriculum* (London: Routledge & Kegan Paul, 1979); Michael F.D. Young, *Knowledge and Control: New Directions for the Sociology of Education* (London: Collier-Macmillan, 1971); Pierre Bourdieu & Jean-Claude Passeron, *Reproduction in Education, Society and Culture* (London: Sage Publications, 1977).
10. Carnoy, *op. cit.*
11. Paulo Freire, *Pedagogy of the Oppressed* (New York: Herder & Herder, 1972), chapter 1.
12. Bowles & Gintis, *op. cit.*, pp. 11-3, 36-44, *et passim*.
13. Bourdieu & Passeron, *op. cit.*
14. See EDC Occasional Papers, No. 6, "Contributions to the Workshop on Reproduction and Dependency in Education", University of London Institute of Education, Department of Education in Developing Countries, May 1984, especially articles by Brian Holmes, John Lauglo, and Paul Hurst, for a series of valuable pointers and analyses on this theme.
15. Philip G. Altbach, "The University as Center and Periphery", in: *Teachers College Record* 82 (Summer, 1981), pp. 601-622.
16. Ali A. Mazrui, "The African University as a Multinational Corporation: Problems of Penetration and Dependency", in: *Harvard Educational Review* 45 (May 1975), pp. 191-210.
17. Gall P. Kelly, "Teachers and the Transmission of State Knowledge: A Case Study of Colonial Vietnam", in: Philip G. Altbach, Gail P. Kelly & Robert F. Arnove (eds.), *Comparative Education* (New York: Macmillan, 1982), pp. 176-94.
18. John M. Barrington, "Cultural Adaptation and Maori Educational Policy: The African Connection", in: *Comparative Education Review* 20 (February, 1976), pp. 1-10.
19. Brian M. Bullivant, "Cultural Reproduction in Fiji: Who Controls Knowledge/ Power?", in: *Comparative Education Review* 27 (June, 1983), pp. 227-45.
20. Edward H. Berman, "The Foundations' Role in American Foreign Policy: The Case of Africa, post 1945", in Robert F. Arnove (ed.), *op.cit.*

21. Rafael L. Irizarry, "Overeducation and Unemployment in the Third World: The Paradoxes of Dependent Industrialization", in: *Comparative Education Review* 24 (October, 1980), pp. 338-52.

22. Alan Sica & Harland Prechel, "National Political-Economic Dependency in the Global Economy and Educational Development", in: *Comparative Education Review* 25 (October 1981), pp. 384-402.

23. Remi Clignet, "Damned If You Do, Damned If You Don't: The Dilemmas of Colonizer-Colonized Relations", in: *Comparative Education Review* 15 (October 1971), pp. 296-312.

24. Philip J. Foster, "Presidential Address: The Revolt Against the Schools", in: *Comparative Education Review* 15 (October, 1971), p. 271.

25. Martin McLean, "Educational Dependency: a Critique", in: *Compare* 13 (1983), pp. 25-42.

26. Anthony Giddens, *Central Problems in Social Theory: Action, Structure, and Contradiction in Social Analysis* (Berkeley & Los Angeles: University of California Press, 1979), p. 7.

27. Bourdieu & Passeron, *op.cit.*, pp. 11-3.

28. P.T. Bauer, *Equality, the Third World, and Economic Delusion* (Cambridge, Mass.: Harvard University Press, 1981). See, in particular, chapter 4.

29. Erwin H. Epstein, "Presidential Address. Currents Left and Right: Ideology in Comparative Education", in: *Comparative Education Review* 27 (February, 1983), pp. 3-29.

10

The Darling Young*

When W.C. Fields was asked how he liked children, he is alleged to have said, "Broiled!"; but child-hatred as an adult way of life is rarely voiced so bluntly in the so-called advanced countries of the world today. This is not to say that it might not lurk beneath the surface. Bertrand Russell's view is that hostility is natural to the adult view of childhood. For many centuries, according to him, children were seen as limbs of Satan. Then, in the nineteenth century, they came to be regarded as angels of innocence. One could hardly spank those delicate beings who possessed the unique qualities ascribed to them by Rousseau and Wordsworth. So parents invented new devils, no longer theological ones inspired by Satan but scientific ones: Freudian demons of the unconscious; the unbearable pressures of adolescence; the impact of society itself. When parents could no longer wallop the little pests, as Russell put it, they compensated by inventing a new demonology about the young.

Professor Boas' study is devoted to the revolution in thinking whereby children became innocents in the minds of men. It is an elegant *tour de force* of intellectual history based largely on European literary sources. His thesis is that various cults – the Noble Savage, the rural Folk, and later the Irrational – provide different exemplars of a general belief in primitivism. With the passing of the idea of the Noble Savage (coinciding, incidentally, with westward expansion in North America and the decimation of the American Indian) other objects of belief in the primitive were unearthed, all possessing several qualities in common: intuitive wisdom (rather than learning), a keen appreciation of beauty ("Nature I loved, and next to Nature, Art"), and a great sensitivity to moral values. The cult of childhood, the author asserts, is part of a larger history of cultural primitivism which developed synchronously with the advancement of the natural sciences. In his essay, Boas analyzes the changing concepts of childhood during recent centuries and their culmination in radically new views of the child and new assumptions about its nature and characteristics which led to new ways of treating the young.

Origins of Child Adulation

The beginnings of the cult are to be found in sixteenth century skepticism, although its *Urgeschichte* may be traced back to the story of the Christ-child. But Jesus was not really representative of childhood; and, even when the theme of Mother adoring the Child appeared in Renaissance art, it was worship of an exceptional child rather than of children. The origins of what was on occasion to become no less than child adulation lie in a period of European history characterized by rediscovery of forgotten classical texts, vast geographical explorations, new inventions, new sciences, the Protestant Reformation, and the rise of new nations and vernacular literatures. All of these provided the basis for philosophical skepticism and anti-authoritarianism; and, though the author does not delve into it, for the development of scientific methods of inquiry. It was at this point in history, for example, that praise was accorded to animals "who knew good and evil without possessing reason, are virtuous without instruction and have no need of intellect." These attributes were later transferred to children. The theme occurs in Montaigne when he praises animals and primitive man, although his ideas about the training of children remain firm. Boas also shows how seventeenth century theology and belles-lettres gave support to the emerging cult of childhood. He quotes a delightful early example from John Earle's sketch of the child in his *Microcosmographie* (1628) which incorporates several important themes: the Child is like Adam before the Fall; the life of the individual recapitulates the history of the race; growing up is moral degeneration; experience is defacement of original purity; the Child is pure and simple.

Literary Expressions

It was not until Rousseau, however, that such ideas became a full blown theory of the nature of the child and child treatment. Since Boas is interested in the history of the several themes in the cult of childhood – and especially in their literary expression – he does not enter into much discussion of Rousseau's educational philosophy. He is more concerned with relating the portrait presented in Emile to those of other writers and thinkers. Thus he unravels the pertinent strands of the cult of childhood found in Bernardin Saint Pierre's *Paul et Virginie*, that tragic tale of conflict between nature and civilization, or between purity and love on the one hand and official, imposed modesty (properly, sophistication) on the other. It is in Pestalozzi, however, that Boas discerns the very essence of the cults of childhood and cultural primitivism; the belief that those highly lauded traits now being described were actually innate. By the end of the eighteenth century, the child was becoming a new and special being, sui generis.

Boas' gallery of portraits from the nineteenth century shows the further development of a host of important motifs. Wordsworth, of course, points at Heaven which is around us at our infancy, the shades of the prison house closing about us as we grow. Emerson, amongst other themes, offers infant nonconformity as a paradigm for adults. Victor Hugo, exuberant as ever, tells how the innocence of childhood (a naked little girl) has the power to subdue the ferocity of the beast (a lion which is carrying her brother in its mouth). In Swinburne, Boas comments, ecstasy over babies becomes ludicrous. By the end of the nineteenth century the precedent of child heroes and heroines is well established, although the types vary from "such revolting little prigs" as Elsie Dinsmore to the "angelic" David Copperfield and Hans Anderson's saintly child who saw that the Emperor was indeed naked. There are even a few bad boys in Twain and Tarkington.

Law of Recapitulation

Boas is especially interested in the growth of the law of recapitulation, the idea that human development retraces the history of the race. He follows this from its origins through Herder, Comte, Freud and Schopenhauer into its various modern manifestations in the natural and physical sciences as well as social science, notably anthropology.

Just as society becomes aware of the special and meritorious qualities of childhood, so does art come to value the childlike, innocent eye. Boas lightly traces the connections between his main theme and developments in art, Dadaism, Surrealism and on into a variety of contemporary forms. The child draws what he knows is there and what he feels, not only what his eyes show him. By the middle of the twentieth century, artists have claimed the status of children, or perhaps it has been ascribed to them by critics, in so far as they paint "from within", seeking to explore media in highly personal ways. Art, for both artist and child, becomes exploration or therapy rather than aesthetics or communication.

Innocence and Teaching

The key word of the cult of childhood, according to Boas, is *innocence,* and obviously it leads to a new pedagogical system. The major example he quotes is Sylvia Ashton-Warner's book, *Teacher* (1963), a rather surprising choice in several ways. One might have expected the author's interest in the literary sources to have led him rather to her novel, *Spinster,* a far subtler and more persuasive presentation of the same set of ideas, and a far more elegant one. But the choice of Ashton-Warner as an example of the new pedagogical view is arbitrary, to say the least. Educational views based on "the assumption that the child already possesses the wisdom that he needs" have been presented over and over again by a host of writers during the last fifty years, many of them more systematic and thoughtful than she. Boas admits that a detailed study of pedagogical theories since *Emile* is a necessary complement to his study of the cult. Yet he might have given a more appropriate example of the connection between literary themes and pedagogical statements.

Since Boas is concerned with documenting the growing cult of the child, he must perforce omit much. Yet he appears to dismiss all too quickly the anti-child theme which is a part of the history. He does mention that the early statements such as Earle's are in opposition to Calvinist doctrines and the idea of original sin. He also notes that Puritan New England took the "putti" of the Italian Renaissance, angelic little children associated more with profane than sacred love, and transformed them into disembodied faces with wings, for decorations on their tombstones. But the twentieth century emergence of children who were downright evil to which he refers (in Richard Hughes and William Golding), cannot be altogether the new trend that he suggests. It is surely the reemergence of a traditional concept, the Calvinist view of the child in a new guise, compensating, perhaps, as Russell suggests, for the temporary loss of a rationale for treating children in ways that are tough. This anti-child theme, appearing early as part of the doctrine of original sin and later in the idea of children as uncontrolled, passionate, driven by subterranean forces and generally threatening to the adult world – uncivilized in the negative rather than in the Rousseau sense – is the Doppelgänger of the cult of childhood, the Anti-Christ of the Child. The inhabitants of the Island of Flies and the young mutineers sailing under a high wind to Jamaica, did not arrive from nowhere. It would have been interesting to consider where they were hiding during the period from Rousseau to Freud. There are certainly intimations of their immortality in nineteenth century pedagogical writing and practice, to say nothing of the public image (and the private vision). They were at Arnold's Rugby, for example, and were undoubtedly taught their lessons from the McGuffey readers.

Inter-cultural Variations

A few other thoughts occurred to this reviewer as he read the book with growing fascination and admiration. The two rather lovable bad boys in nineteenth century literature which Boas mentions are American; the two evil ones in more recent novels are English. French writers provide the philosophical basis for "the new child", as do some German thinkers, but the child heroes of other European countries to which the author refers just do not compare with the number and variety found in novels in the English language. Is this due simply to his own choice of illustrations of the cult of childhood? Or is there some evidence that the view of the child varies systematically not only over time, as Boas shows, but also between cultures? Study of child-rearing patterns and selected aspects of educational practice and theory have made cultural comparisons possible. There still remains, though, a great opportunity for some of our comparative educators to consider cross-cultural variations in educational phenomena by scrutiny of literary as well as other sources in order to examine culturally different ways of regarding childhood and of implementing these beliefs in education.

The frontispiece to Professor Boas' book is a reproduction of Caroto's painting, *Fanciullo con Pupazzeto* (early 16th century), in black and white, unfortunately, so that the gorgeous red tints are missed. This delightful little girl joyously showing her drawing is modern in both spirit and content, testimony to the long history which Boas, as he admits, merely sketches. Yet his work is replete with scholarly detail and provocative insight. The practice of quoting at length in the original language should not deter any readers; but, as he states, will delight those who wish to see for themselves what the authority quoted actually said. It is a scholarly piece, but not dry, and will give satisfaction and stimulus to all who are interested in children, literature, art, or social and intellectual history. This reviewer, for one, was sorry to reach the final paragraphs where the author merely mentions the many fascinating possibilities for further study, for example, the fullest blooming of the cult of childhood in adult behaviors of various kinds in the United States. He notes that his study needs to be complemented by studies of child-sages, fashions and fads (e.g., collecting dolls, toy soldiers and electric railroads – by adults) and attempts at producing prodigies (Hersey's novel, *The Child Buyer,* takes up this theme), to say nothing of what authors of children's books thought would interest their readers. Many of these topics have indeed been studied and reference to the numerous attempts to handle such data and themes would have provided a useful appendix to this work. They are in fact too many even to mention in this critique, yet none that the reviewer is acquainted with has the erudition, the wit and the scope of Professor Boas' study of the cult of childhood.

One final thought: the word cult carries the suggestion of something cranky and impermanent. What then will be the fate of the adored object, the Child, and the dogmas associated with it? Boas' sketch of the origins and the development combined with the evidences around us today show how the early beliefs and their implications have been amended. Adolescence, for example, seems to have grown out of the cult and replaced the very young child as an object of worship. Boas, without making any real prognosis, takes the optimistic view. If, he says, men have persistently rejected the ultimate vision of the cult of childhood – which he finds expressed in the work of Norman O. Brown – and have always insisted on growing up, "we can only conclude that there is after all something congenial in maturity." Yet, as one considers contemporary fashions and other adult behaviors, art and literary forms, leisure-time activities, and domestic or foreign political affairs, the basic motifs of the cult of childhood appear appallingly persistent: the Irrational; the Naif; the Egocentric; the Simple; the Intuitive.

Maturity may be congenial, as George Boas puts it. One sometimes wonders if it is congenital.

NOTE

* M.A. Eckstein, "The Darling Young: an Essay Review" of *The Cult of Childhood.* George Boas, London: The Warburg Institute, University of London, 1966, 106 pp., in *The Record/Teachers College Columbia University* 69 (October 1967): 91-95. Reprinted by permission of Teachers College Record.

11

The Comparative Mind: Metaphor in Comparative Education*

The thesis of this paper is based on three arguments: first, that comparative educators make extensive use of metaphors in their thinking and writing, and that while this has great strengths it also contains some real problems in the process of advancing knowledge; second, that comparing is inherent in human thinking as a developmental process; and third, that comparing through the use of metaphors is a fundamental and characteristic way by which researchers in all areas of knowledge seek to extend our understanding of the world around us, The metaphors we use presuppose or imply theories; the theories (or models) which purport to explain or account for phenomena contain specific metaphors, whether implicit or explicit. One of the more important themes of the paper is that the unexamined metaphor, like the unexamined life, may have limited value.

Metaphors in Comparative Education

There are three major ways in which we all approach the substance of our field: as teachers, as students and researchers, and as users of the knowledge accumulated to make, implement, and evaluate policy.[1] Most of what follows relates to the second approach, study and research, though it has implications of course for the other two. Furthermore, we should acknowledge that the ideology, values, and techniques of comparative education are not unique to our field but are common to philosophy and the social sciences. They are as helpful and as problematic for us as for our colleagues in other scholarly fields. Like them, we seek to establish transnational laws about social phenomena, specifically, generalizations about education that are valid for different societies. Like them, too, we ponder whether this is at all possible, either because each society or culture is unique or because social science is an inappropriate or inadequate means to establish generalizations comparable to those of the physical or natural sciences. And like them, we often do ourselves a disservice, either by attending too closely to one nation or type of nation or by not being critical, self-conscious, and creative enough about the images, metaphors, and paradigms that we employ in our comparisons. On the one hand, we may be too parochial or one-sided, and on the other, too many-sided in the attempt to make sense of the great unknowns that we study.

The first task, then, is to examine some of the basic metaphors current in the field, for it is through them that we communicate with one another.[2] Since metaphors are at the very least implicit comparisons, it is only to be expected that they will abound in our literature.

A quick dip into recent issues of the *Comparative Education Review* will net a rich catch of metaphors: Brown's reference to "Hard Core" ideology in Chinese educational policy, and Harrison and Glaubman's examination of "Open Education" (October 1982); Psacharopoulos's metaphor for higher education as "the top step of the learning ladder" and his use of the phrase "prescription for economic development" (June 1982); Masemann's use, in her review of various sociological and anthropological approaches to educational research, of familiar terms in reference to functionalist views, for example, "structures," "life process", etc. (she is to be complimented for being self-conscious and analytical about metaphors) (February 1982); Thomas La Belle's mention of "the national character" of nonformal education, Merritt and Leonardi's use of the terms "immobility and accommodation" when discussing responses to various secondary school reform efforts in Italy, Clignet's reference to the "Natural History of Educational Interactions," and Sica and Prechel's dwelling on "dependency" as a metaphor for educational relationships (October 1981); Eisemon's use of the idea of "center and periphery" in writing about science in universities, and Young's evocative and colorfully phrased description of the African university as "at once child of decolonization and intended parent of national development" (June 1981). This assortment of metaphors is random. At some other time we might join in the intriguing game of collecting them and pinning them down, like butterflies, in some order. But what follow are a few generic examples of metaphor, chosen to illustrate how they are used and the kinds of ideas they comprise.

The first example is quite simple and obvious but a pervasive and important use of metaphors to identify nations and cultures. Perhaps the best-known examples may be taken from Edmund King's *Other Schools and Ours*,[3] in which certain chapter titles serve primarily as powerful instructional devices:[4] "France – the Central Light of Reason," "The U.S.A. – a Nation on Wheels."

When proceeding from the individual case to the variety of cases under study, that is, the many nations of the world, we tend to group them into categories. We refer, for example, to developed and underdeveloped nations, selective and nonselective secondary school systems, centralized and decentralized administrations. Some nations are loosely called Third World countries in contrast to those of the First and Second Worlds, often without adequate identification of their common features. Such groupings of what, on the face of it, appear to be similar items are often no more than a preliminary sorting of the cards. We may not yet have seriously considered, let alone answered, the question, Similar with respect to what? We have not yet, in many instances, identified our rules of correspondence, and when we begin a closer examination we often find that the exceptions to the rule are more numerous than the items that conform. As we ponder the anomalies, the exceptions to the rule, and the possibilities of a new paradigm, the similarity of relations among the items is likely to change. Yet we stubbornly persist in retaining familiar categories, even when they force very dissimilar items into the same set and do not serve to explain what we seek to understand. And the reason for this persistence is quite simple: we are bound by the metaphors we create.

Both kinds of examples cited so far use metaphors to describe. They do not necessarily explain anything, even though they purport to do so. But the following examples do explicitly intend to explain: they propose connections and interactions, they suggest causes, and they even intimate the future.

The founding fathers of our field, working from a progress-oriented model, referred to the "warp and woof" of the social fabric into which schooling was woven; they noted the "forces" of society that shaped educational ideas and practices and the intellectual "currents" that moved not only school events but also the various configurations of political realities. Their paradigm included a number of significant assumptions: not only the sense that our subjects of study, nations or school systems, can be sorted into certain groups (e.g., developed and less developed, industrialized and unindustrialized), but that movement from one to the other is likely if not inevitable and represents some form of progress (by definition, in the conventional English usage, a Good Thing). In this same spirit of progress we have accepted the familiar analogy, influential in history and anthropology in particular, between changes in human societies and the development of the human individual: some societies are like human infants – simple and primitive; others are mature, complex, and sophisticated – like human adults. The metaphor of the growing human contains certain expectations and values, draws our attention to some, similarities and differences rather than others, focuses on some research questions rather than others. The implicit value judgments are obvious.

A second general model, the so-called radical paradigm, as Kazamias and Messialas term it,[5] has enjoyed increasing attention over the past decade or so, though it, like the notion of progress, is rooted in nineteenth century political thought. It has at its center the ideas of power and conflict and generates a number of evocative metaphors: reproduction, dependency, imperialism. Education thus becomes a means of exerting power, and elites use schooling as a mechanism for maintaining their hegemony over those with little or none. Unlike the first model, which is progress oriented and ecological and which conceives of education as the trigger or the yeast for general social growth and improvement, the second sees education as the tool or the conduit through which elite groups maintain their advantage over lesser groups.

To say that school developments are milestones on the road that leads inevitably to national improvement or are triggers for social progress does help to give us a perspective on a confusing and complex set of information. Such statements may even be true, but they are certainly inadequately founded either in theory or in fact and at best represent only possible parts of the picture. To say that the schools are instruments to maintain political power supplies a different and similarly limited perspective on complex events and phenomena. This view of the schools is familiar and simple, though not for that reason necessarily simpleminded, and also usefully illuminates otherwise hidden or disregarded aspects of our subject. To cite yet another metaphor, it is all well and good to liken the education system to a factory, whether in Lloyd Warner's sense of a social sorting machine[6] or in the more complex sense of a processor of human potential for the labor market (i.e., the production-function model), but this model, like the others, takes us only so far. Most of the metaphors we use to understand and to communicate with one another shed some new light on the subject. At the same time, they all leave too many questions unanswered and more unasked.

Ernest Nagel's comments on explanation in the social sciences appear especially appropriate here. He observes that a number of very different concepts (or variables) that cut across cultural differences have been used as the bases for transnational generalizations. But, he continues: "The social laws that have been perhaps most frequently proposed in terms of such concepts state orders of supposedly inevitable social changes, and maintain that societies or institutions succeeded one another in some fixed sequence of developmental stages. None of these attempts or proposals has been successful. . . ."[7] He goes on to suggest that what may be needed are more abstract conceptualizations, that is, metaphors more removed from the familiar notions used in the daily business of social life.

At the very least, our metaphors in comparative education help us to describe, and there is of course a limit to the extent that they explain. A powerful metaphor, however, both describes and explains and then goes even further:[8] it articulates new ideas, invites further exploration of similarities and differences, and generates new analogies which include features not yet fully understood and previously undiscovered. Our metaphors in comparative education are really quite simple, drawn from nature and from everyday life. They serve the purpose of bridging some of the known and the unknown. They cast the unknown into a shape that helps us grasp some of its elements. But so often they are used without consideration of what they really say or imply or of how far they can take us in exploring the territory. They must therefore be scrutinized critically lest they limit our thinking. And they must be challenged by new conceptualizations that have the potential of answering more questions and provoking yet new ones.

Comparison and the Development of Human Thought Processes

Needless to say, comparative education is not the only place where comparison goes on. Figurative thinking and comparing are, I believe, inherent in human thinking and in fact mark a fundamental step in the cognitive development of the young. This is indicated in developmental theory in general and particularly well illustrated in Piaget's formulation of stages of development. The general idea is that there is a set sequence, that under normal circumstances each stage follows the preceding one, and that each stage is a precondition for the next.

In describing intellectual development, Piaget identifies five characteristic stages: (1) sensorimotor thinking (the earliest, pre-speech); (2) emergence and development of symbolic thought (approximately 1½-5 years); (3) articulated or intuitional representation (approximately 4-8 years); (4) concrete operations (9-12 years); and (5) formal operations. A word or two about stages 2 and 3 (i.e., those stages that coincide with the development of speech and are therefore the foundation of adult conceptualization) will suffice to make the initial point.

Stage 2 is associated with a dramatic increase in language use and indicates a fundamental development in mode of thinking that shapes an individual's life-long intellectual activity. Language begins to be used as a representation of action instead of being merely an accompaniment to it, as in the earlier infant stage. No longer just a part of the action, language evokes action.[9] This development marks a large spurt forward toward using language as a conceptual symbol system.

To narrow our focus momentarily, two key concepts that Piaget uses to describe thought processes at this stage recall theory and practice in comparative education as illuminated by Bereday some years ago: "juxtaposition" and "syncretism."[10] In Piaget, these terms refer to alternative modes of thinking by which children think, explain, and communicate at this crucial phase of intellectual development. To juxtapose simply means putting items together without relating them to one another, although some explanation (some nascent idea of cause and effect) is at least suggested or implied in the ways in which the parts or the details are placed next to one another. Syncretism, by contrast, is thinking about the whole without relating it to the parts (a sort of primitive Gestalt conceptualization).

All this mental activity is what Piaget calls "pre-conceptual thought," and it is clear that the subsequent stages of development rest upon this second stage and are shaped by it. But it may even be argued that juxtaposition and syncretism represent comparison in its simplest and least developed form.

Piaget describes stage 3 as the threshold of operational thinking. Just as the preceding stage was marked by a rapid increase in speech, so this one is marked by increasing social involvement and sharing, as well as further language development. So far as thought processes of this stage are concerned, juxtaposition and syncretism begin to decline, and the details and the totality begin to be seen as a related whole.

This outline of Piaget's stages of mental development is sufficient for our purposes. At all stages, and with many examples drawn from his own careful observation of children, Piaget illustrates the growth of intellectual ability by drawing attention to how the young relate things: one thing to another, details to the whole, self to others, single items to classes of items (i.e., single facts to variables). Under normal circumstances, by the time adolescence is reached a "complete" system of thinking is available to the individual. It is a system independent of the context, an autonomous instrument that can be applied to all kinds of data. Propositional thinking and hypothesis-deductive reasoning are among the by-products. And all the way through, relating and comparing have been central.

The purpose of this brief disquisition on Piaget is to argue (if this is indeed at all necessary) that comparison is inherent in human thinking and that the development of this one faculty is in fact entwined in the development of all the human thinking processes. Cultivation of the one faculty is thus a particular form of advancing the total capacity to think, the capacity to draw meaning from things and experiences and to generate new ideas from them.

Metaphors and the Progress of Knowledge

The third leg of the argument addresses the question of how we think generally in advancing knowledge at a more sophisticated level: as students and as researchers seeking to expand our grasp of the world around us. We are here concerned with the ubiquitous use of metaphor as a tool for achieving knowledge, explaining parts of the unknown, and expanding understanding.

A familiar example of the role of metaphor in scientific discovery was dramatically presented in the television series and the book by Jonathan Miller entitled *The Body in Question*. It was not until the sixteenth century that William Harvey conceived of the way in which the heart functioned, as a pump for the circulatory system. This notion, with some elaborations, remains valid to this day. Harvey himself acquired no startling new evidence (the empirical evidence provided by Vesalius was certainly adequate, and what Galen knew in the first century, though incomplete, was not irrelevant). Why then, asks Miller, did it take so long – at least sixteen centuries – for understanding of the heart to develop to this point? Because satisfactory metaphors for thinking about what was seen were lacking: "In primitive societies, where technical images are few and far between and very simple at that, most explanatory metaphors are drawn from nature.... But the development of technology created a new stock of metaphors – not simply extra metaphors, but ones altogether different in their logical character,"[11] Only after pumps and pumplike engines had become widely used in mining and civil engineering, and only when fountains and fire-fighting equipment had become familiar sights in the growing cities of preindustrial Europe, was it possible for the pump to be thought of and accepted as a satisfactory metaphor for the working of the human heart.

Another example from human anatomy is even more familiar. More has been discovered about the workings of the brain in the past two decades than in several preceding centuries. Consider some of the terms widely used by cognitive psychologists and educators to describe various brain functions: thinking is "information processing"; learning to read, to comprehend, and to communicate consists of encoding and decoding symbols; consciousness is "a feedback mechanism"; memory is a matter of "data storage and retrieval." The most illuminating contemporary metaphor for the brain is the computer. It is irresistible because it helps to fill in pieces of a model that purports to explain an unknown territory for whose description we lacked a language. In this way, it provides us with a theory of human functioning that explains large parts of what was previously a mystery to us.

In his analyses of the logic of scientific explanation, Ernest Nagel provides a host of examples from mathematics and physics to demonstrate how general analogies and particular metaphors serve to bridge the gap between familiar facts and new experiences and to articulate new theories.[12] In a similar vein, Thomas Kuhn, discussing the role of what he calls paradigms, cites examples from the physical sciences of new models or conceptualizations (he frequently uses the term "puzzle-solutions") facilitating giant steps forward from the known into the unknown regions of scientific knowledge.[13]

It is not in the physical and natural sciences alone that metaphor plays an important role in discovery. In the social sciences generally, and in history specifically, much of our knowledge is shaped by powerful metaphors. We use such terms as "the forces of history"; we refer to the youth, maturity, and decline of peoples or cultures, to the ebb and flow of social movements, to the rise and fall of nations. As Isaiah Berlin points out, this metaphorical language conveys the idea of an inexorable, fixed time order.[14] Such metaphors may be misleading, but they are pointers to categories which are helpful, if only to a limited degree. (It is worth noting that the metaphors that Berlin cites are all, to use Miller's phrase, "drawn from nature," simple and primitive.)

It is tempting to continue listing more of the metaphors we have lived by in expanding our grasp of the universe. But we must now pay some attention to examining the nature of the metaphor in our thinking, its function in helping us discover new knowledge, and some of the problems as well as advantages entailed in using it.

Common speech is full of expressions that were originally used figuratively but have now lost their original meaning and are used literally: the leg of a table, for example, or the head of a hammer. And it is probably impossible to compose more than a few sentences without having recourse to an explicit metaphor, since figurative speech is a common tendency in human communication. This tendency may not, for most people, be deliberate or conscious, though in the hands of a poet, scientist, or teacher the metaphor is likely to be thoughtfully and self-consciously used, but as Nagel observes, "the widespread use of metaphors . . . testifies to a pervasive human talent for finding resemblances between new experiences and familiar facts. . . ." "Analogies help to assimilate the new to the old, and prevent novel explanatory premises from being radically unfamiliar." And ". . . the desire to explain new domains of fact in terms of something already familiar" has controlled important developments in the history of scientific knowledge in all areas and disciplines.[15]

We must, however, draw attention to a number of caveats associated with how metaphors work. A metaphor or a model may be used to express a theoretical formulation, but it is not itself a theory. Correspondence must be demonstrated between the set of phenomena requiring explanation and the model itself, and, as Nagel argues, in attempts at scientific explanation there are certain rules of correspondence. A model may be an intellectual trap as well as a valuable tool if some inessential part is mistaken for a key feature of the theory it represents. The researcher will become distracted by spurious problems in his attempt to make the model fit the facts (or vice versa) and thus be led into unproductive efforts, all because of this basic error of confusing the model with the theory itself or, to put it in other words, of mistaking the vehicle for the journey.

As already indicated, figurative expressions are so fundamental to human thinking and communication processes that the use of a metaphor may not always be a deliberate or conscious act. If we do not pay attention to the limits of the resemblances between the reality and the metaphor or the familiar and the new (or between any of the sets of items we are comparing), we risk serious error. We may take a concept from a domain where its use is legitimate and use it in another where it is not. As Nagel points out, "... words like 'force,' 'law,' and 'cause' are occasionally still used with decided anthropomorphic overtones that are echoes of their origins." Nevertheless, a sense of even vague similarities between the old and new may be a starting point for an advance in knowledge, and "when reflection becomes critically self-conscious ... [these vague similarities] may come to be developed into carefully formulated analogies and hypotheses that can serve as fruitful instruments of systematic research."[16] In another context, that of explanation in political science, Isaiah Berlin also acknowledges that metaphors may distort as well as explain. But in the end, he is not seriously concerned: "the fact that many metaphors have proved fatal, or at least misleading, [does not] tend to show that all metaphors can or should be eliminated...."[17]

The history of the development of human knowledge provides many examples of metaphors that failed to explain phenomena satisfactorily, leading researchers into unproductive directions and unsolvable puzzles. While it is in the nature of such conceptual models to serve the purposes of explanation for a period (perhaps a very long one), eventually they fail in the face of new and unanswered puzzles. Then the old metaphor, well established in the minds of experts in a field of study, serves as an obstruction to further solutions. This pattern of development is exactly what Kuhn argues in his disquisition on the role of paradigms in scientific revolutions. Explanatory models, he argues, have similar functions: "Among other things they supply the group with preferred or permissible analogies and metaphors. By doing so they help to determine what will be accepted as an explanation and as a puzzle-solution; conversely, they assist in the determination of the roster of unsolved puzzles, and in the evaluation of the importance of each."[18] But the "group," that is, a given scientific community, may be forced to confront what Kuhn terms an "anomaly" or a "violation of expectation." In the face of such a puzzle, a new paradigm is proposed, one that replaces the previous one that was inadequate to explain the unexpected phenomena. A paradigm is an entire set of beliefs, values, and techniques associated with a particular field of study, and it includes a set of concrete puzzle-solutions in the form of models or examples. A scientific revolution occurs when a general and widely held paradigm is replaced by another that is fundamentally different. The new paradigm marks a large advance in knowledge because it provides new models and metaphors for understanding. By the same token, the old metaphors are shown to have been incorrect, at least in part, or misleading and limiting in their explanatory power.

These observations on the role of metaphors in knowledge cannot be concluded without some reference to language and aesthetics. In the *Poetics,* Aristotle praises the metaphor: "The greatest thing by far is to have command of metaphor." But the argument made here goes beyond the traditional view of metaphor. It is not merely a decorative rhetorical device, as Aristotle views it, but a characteristic form of human communication that is used, whether well or not, in teaching and in study. Metaphor is inherent in human thinking, and its main function is to help us bridge the known and the unknown, as children, as adults, and as researchers. The very nature of thinking, as I. A. Richards observes, is metaphoric and proceeds by comparison: "What is comparison? It may be several different things: it may be just a putting together of two things to let them work together; it may be a study of them both to see how they are like and how unlike one another; or it may be a process of calling attention to their likenesses or a method of drawing attention to certain aspects of the one through the co-presence of the other."[19]

Conclusion

To summarize my argument, metaphor is comparison. It is inherent in human thinking and communication, and it is central to furthering the progress of science, not just the physical and natural sciences, but all sectors of human knowledge. There are some real problems involved in using metaphors, for they may impede progress in discovery, but they serve as valuable tools when used consciously and with deliberation, even though they may, in the first instance, emerge in that flash of intuition and insight that characterizes great scientists and great poets. The metaphors that prevail in comparative education, as in the social sciences generally, need to be critically examined and new ones invented, since those we rely on are rather simple, overworked, derivative, and limiting. We need periodically to reexamine first principles and earlier practices. The very metaphors we use to represent our own field of study need scrutiny. For example, we might again consider the concept of comparative education as natural history, perhaps regenerating interest in comparative educational taxonomy; or we might conceive of our work as a geography of education and direct our creative energies toward developing original and visionary maps of the world educational scene with new and provocative projections. Metaphors, if they are to be illuminating and useful, must be scrutinized critically and new ones periodically considered.

What then, in conclusion, is the comparative mind? In the first place, like all other human mental activity it is inclined toward figurative thinking, using metaphors, models, and paradigms to explain the unknown in terms of the known. But the comparative mind is also like the minds of others engaged in the deliberate search to extend knowledge. It is curious, especially drawn to puzzles concerning human behavior. It is creative and flexible, being capable of moving back and forth between the particular item and the whole pattern, between the facts and the variable, between data and theories, between contemplative study and other kinds of activity. In sum, the comparative mind is a particular case of the general human cognitive condition and an even more particular case of the inquiring mind, whether scientist, philosopher, or artist. And its most special attribute is that it is drawn to the fascinating game of solving complex puzzles and playing with ideas and facts through comparison – and the use of metaphors.

NOTES

* Max A. Eckstein, "The Comparative Mind: Metaphor in Comparative Education," *Comparative Education Review* 27 (1983): 311-323. Reprinted by permission of the University of Chicago Press.
1. Edmund J. King, "Students, Teachers and Researchers in Comparative Education," *Comparative Education Review* 2 (June 1958): 33-36; and Robert L. Koehl, "The Comparative Study of Education: Prescription and Practice," *Comparative Education Review* 21 (June/October 1977): 177-94.

2. It may be helpful at this point to distinguish between metaphors and several other terms frequently used in this essay. "Metaphor" (deriving from a Greek root meaning "to transfer") is the figure of speech in which a name or a descriptive term is transferred to an object different from, but analogous to, the one to which it is properly applicable. A "paradigm" (also from a Greek root, connoting "to show side by side," i.e., to juxtapose) is a pattern or exemplar. A "theory" is, of course, a scheme or system of ideas held to explain or account for a set of facts or phenomena, or a statement of what are held to be general laws, principles, or causes. And "model" refers to a representation of a theory in some kind of structural form; here the phenomena are related to one another in terms of the set of ideas composing the theory. Any theory, model, or paradigm is likely to comprise a major metaphor (or set of metaphors); alternatively, any metaphor suggests or assumes a theory, model, or paradigm.

3. Edmund J. King, *Other Schools and Ours*, 5th ed. (New York: Holt, Rinehart & Winston, 1979).

4. Richard Boyd, "Metaphor and Theory Change: What Is 'Metaphor' a Metaphor For?' in *Metaphor and Thought*, ed. Andrew Ortony (Cambridge: Cambridge University Press, 1979). Boyd distinguishes between pedagogical metaphors (used for instructional purposes) and metaphors that function to cover gaps in knowledge.

5. Andreas Kazamias and Byron G. Messialas, "Comparative Education," in *Encyclopedia of Educational Research*, 5th ed.(New York: Macmillan, 1982), pp. 309-17. See also, e.g., Robert L. Koehl, "Cultural Imperialism as Education: An Indictment, *Comparative Education Review* 19 (June 1975): 276-85; Martin Carnoy, "Education as Cultural Imperialism: A Reply," *Comparative Education Review* 19 (June 1975): 286-89; Philip G. Altbach and Gail P. Kelly, *Education and Colonialism* (New York: Longmans, 1978); J. Karabel and A.H. Halsey, eds., *Power and Ideology in Education* (New York: Oxford University Press, 1977).

6. W. Lloyd Warner et al., *Who Shall Be Educated?* (New York: Harper, 1944).

7. Ernest Nagel, *The Structure of Science: Problems* in *the Logic of Scientific Explanation (*New York: Harcourt Brace, 1961), p. 465..

8. Zenon W. Pylyshyn, "Metaphorical Imprecision and the 'Top-Down' Research Strategy," in Ortony, ed., pp. 420-36.

9. Jean Piaget, *Play, Dreams, and Imitation* (London: Routledge & Kegan Paul, 1967); P.G. Richmond, *An Introduction to Piaget* (New York: Basic, 1970); Ellen Winner et al., "First Metaphors," *New Directions for Child Development* 3 (1979): 29-41.

10. George Z. F. Bereday, *Comparative Method in Education* (New York: Holt, Rinehart & Winston, 1964).

11. Jonathan Miller, *The Body in Question* (New York: Random House, 1978), p. 181.

12. See Nagel.

13. Thomas S. Kuhn, *The Structure of Scientific Revolutions* (Chicago: University of Chicago Press, 1970).

14. Isaiah Berlin, *Concepts and Categories* (New York: Viking, 1979); see esp. his chapters on "Logical Translation" and "The Concept of Scientific Inquiry."

15. Nagel, pp. 108, 46, 95-96.

16. Ibid., p. 108.

17. Berlin, pp. 158-59.

18. Kuhn, p. 184.

19. I.A. Richards*, The Philosophy of Rhetoric* (London: Oxford University Press, 1938), p. 94; see esp. his chapter on "Metaphor." For further illumination of the function of metaphor as a cognitive instrument (in linguistics and philosophy), see also

Boyd (n. 4 above); Max Black, "More about Metaphor," in Ortony, ed. (n. 4 above), pp. 19-43; Hugh G. Petrie, "Metaphor and Learning," in Ortony, ed.; George Lakoff and Mark Johnson, *Metaphors We Live By* (Chicago: University of Chicago Press, 1980).

Part II: SCHOOLS IN CONTEXT

12

The Elitist and The Popular Ideal: Prefects and Monitors in English and American Secondary Schools*

A basic function of educational systems is to purvey social ideals of authority and responsibility. Within its schools, society at large sanctions a regime which is not only a particular form of social order but also a potent teaching device. The youngster at school is exposed to a series of lessons which may complement, reinforce or contradict other teachings of his environment. In any event, they make widely approved assertions about the nature of leadership, about good or bad behavior and the consequences of each. Each day, the attitudes, actions and responses to one another of teachers, principals and pupils help to create a disciplinary climate through which pupils learn, among other things, their present and future places in a social order. At school, a youngster learns whether authority is for or against him, whether it is constant or unpredictable, fair or unfair, kind, cruel or venal. When the rules for diagramming sentences have long been forgotten, the impression of a disciplinary regime imposed by the school may well have the power to influence an adult's attitudes and behavior.

As one visits secondary schools in different countries, one is impressed by the many variations in pupil-teacher relationships and in classroom atmosphere. There are of course similarities too, yet as one moves from country to country, or from region to region, one cannot but note differences in the behavior that is licensed or forbidden and in specific techniques of control which may be used. The mid-Western American high school, the traditional German gymnasium, the English grammar school, – each of these is the setting for a different social order and social atmosphere, with different underlying assumptions about discipline and authority and different techniques for purveying them. In particular, the part played by students themselves in maintaining a given disciplinary climate is worthy of note.

An excellent example of how this function may be carried out is provided by the Prefectorial System found in English secondary schools. This paper analyzes aspects of that system, and seeks parallels in the American high school. The process of comparison between two countries linked by common cultural and political traditions reveals different ways of thinking about authority and contrasting styles of social control and social education.

The Prefectorial System in England

With the increase in the number of schools in England during the nineteenth century, the new institutions understandably used as models schools of long standing and established tradition.[1]   The new grammar schools offered an education to a new, growing and powerful segment of the population: the manufacturing middle classes. Yet earlier goals and methods persisted in subsequent developments. The prefectorial system and the house system are two examples of the great influence of traditional (and today still private) education upon the public system of schools.

Today, the prefectorial system operates in many English schools in various ways. Even at the primary level, the practice of having class or school monitors prepares the way for its operation at the secondary level. While the tradition of "fagging"[2] has been abandoned in all but a few private boarding institutions, prefects are commonly appointed in many kinds of secondary schools.   Though their functions today vary extensively, their significance in the authority systems of many schools remains considerable.[3]

Most commonly, prefects are appointed by the Headmaster from among the senior pupils of the school (Sixth Formers), generally on the recommendation of their teachers. There might be about twelve in a school of five hundred pupils. Apart from seniority *per se,* criteria for selection include academic ability, non-scholastic activities, and personal attributes such as good character and leadership qualities. The student's mere presence in the Sixth Form would imply a measure of academic superiority or at least persistence, as well as some eminence among the school population. The school games captains, society chairmen, the editor of the school magazine, all these are also likely to culminate their school careers as prefects.

Prefectorial duties generally include the policing of school premises and activities in various ways, thus relieving teachers of certain everyday minor supervisory chores. Prefects' powers include the awarding of minor punishments such as extra assignments, detention after school hours and recommendation for more serious punishment. At one time, physical punishment by prefects was sanctioned, but this is no longer so, at least officially, in public (i.e., state) schools. Prefects may have formal meetings to discuss their problems and activities, but the schools generally permit little real delegation of power or independent responsibility.   The prefects are often a headmaster's private police force, exerting a predominantly repressive and punitive discipline, and exacting obedience to an external and imposed authority.

The former Headmaster of a well-known English grammar school, while acknowledging the Public School and aristocratic origins of the prefect system, emphasizes its positive aspects:

> ... prefects are drawn from all senior forms, and they are a compact body set apart from the form system. Ideally, they are respected by staff and by boys, and by both are expected to maintain a high standard of behaviour and a high standard of justice. Their duties in Grammar Schools are generally confined to maintaining an orderly movement of boys about the school, suppressing inconvenient exuberance, and taking an important part in the organization and administration of regular or special school functions.[4]

He argues that the privileges and powers of promotion to prefectship are limited so that ostentation and abuse of power are rare. Unlike prefects in the Public Schools, they may not use corporal punishment, nor use younger boys as "fags":

It is perhaps because of these two limitations on their power that the authority of the Grammar School prefect is less aggressive, less leader-conscious, than that of his Public School counterpart, and there can be no doubt which of the two systems of authority is the better adapted to the social conditions of the world today.[5]

There is no doubt that such delegation of authority and responsibility by teachers to pupils can provide many opportunities for the prefects to assist the young and learn to use authority. Younger pupils, too, are obliged to experience the rule of their seniors before they move on to exercise power themselves. In the intramural hierarchical system, the influence of prefects falls equally upon all younger pupils, thus eliminating discrimination between those of different abilities and social backgrounds. Finally, the prefectorial system has proved to be an efficacious device for ensuring that leaders in the student community use their energies on behalf of the staff rather than for potentially rebellious students.[6]

On all sides, there is general recognition that the prefectorial system is an important part of the educational experience which has to do with the development of character and responsibility. A student will learn from the experiences undergone within the power system of the school, and the common ground of both supporters and critics of a prefectorial system is a concern for the appropriateness of what is learned in this area. If the lesson is inappropriate, or simply wrong, much damage can be done:

> Orthodox schoolmasters regard the last two years of school as the most valuable, because it is then, as a prefect, that the young man learns the art of managing and ruling those below him. In fact it is just these years that are most harmful... At the crucial age when he is becoming an adult, he learns that traditional might is right and that autocratic power is absolute, and this in a democratic world which is trying hard to struggle out of these infantile conceptions.[7]

Davies[8] also emphasizes the traditional authoritarianism of the system and proposes that more than a merely repressive power be given to the selected few. Preparation and training for leadership is required,[9] power must be more diffused, and the school population as a whole must have a greater involvement in the running of its affairs, he argues.

The influence of the prefectorial system on those who are now adult may be discerned in the attention devoted to it in autobiographical writings as well as in strictly professional sources. For many, the officially sanctioned power system among students proved to be cruel, discriminatory and immoral, to say the least.[10] For others, it is castigated as an educational device wrongly used.[11] Like the army non-commissioned officer, the prefect has been privileged by promotion from the ranks. He is thus rewarded by exemption from certain restrictions and punishments, and given the power to inflict upon transgressors some of the consequences of their actions. The rewards of limited status, limited power, and freedom from irksome limitations upon personal liberty are important aspects of becoming a prefect.[12] Criticism is therefore directed both against the abuse of power which the system permits and the whole authority ethic which it represents.

Certain schools have contrived to introduce changes in the selection, preparation and functions of prefects so that negative aspects of the system could be eliminated. In certain cases, teachers, senior students and the current group of prefects all nominate future school prefects.[13]   In preparation for this, form prefects are elected yearly in lower classes of the school.   Secondary schools have encouraged varying degrees of involvement by pupils in decision-making.   In most cases, however, the head teacher retains at least a final veto on appointments.

In contrast to the attempts of certain schools to improve or to adapt the prefectorial function to changed circumstances, the following extract from a discussion on the secondary modern school is pertinent:

> We have no prefects to enforce them [school rules]: prefects would not, in any case, make sense in a community in which all have an equal and interested stake in the life of the school and its efficient and smooth running.[14]

Behind the criticisms and reforms of the prefectorial system lies of course the debate on satisfactory definitions of authority and government in the school.   In effect, criticisms of the traditional system within school are criticisms of the traditional social system outside the school.   The prefectorial system of the Public Schools, copied by the grammar schools which are now an important part of the public system of education, is criticized to the degree that it has not been adapted to its new environment.   It is also criticized according to the degree that it has not moved away from a centralized and elitist authoritarian system, reminiscent of a society where opportunity for advancement and for participation in decision-making was very much limited.[15]

The U.S. High School

American schools, like their English counterparts, seek to maintain a certain social order, and to teach their students lessons about leadership, authority and responsibility. There are some students in the American high school who enjoy a more active and more influential role in the school's authority system than others.   They may carry out tasks similar to those of English prefects.   But, particularly to the English observer, there appears to be no such thing as a Prefectorial System.

In one sense, the honor students found in certain high schools might be compared with the prefects of an English school.   They form a scholastic elite and usually occupy prominent places in extra-curricular activities and school affairs.   The leading athletes of the high school, the sports stars, may be another group which in some respects is comparable with the English school's elite.   They may be socially eminent, influential models for younger pupils, heroes for the school community (and often for the adult community as well).   But though they may possess an informal influence, they are not endowed with official power by the school to maintain a given regime.

A closer approximation to the English prefect is perhaps provided by the American service squad member, monitor or school aide.   This is one of a group of high school students who has varied responsibilities connected with maintaining order on school premises.   He may, for example, supervise traffic in corridors and in the cafeteria to ensure orderly and safe movement; he may be a monitor who, in addition to maintaining order and quiet, runs errands for teachers, escorts visitors within the building and fulfils similar "service" functions in the school.   The basis of selection for such responsibilities varies considerably, though a combination of nomination and approval by teachers and willingness by pupils generally determines membership of this group.   Academic criteria, in the form of minimum scholastic standards, are often included.   A badge, pin or other form of insignia is often given to such pupils as a mark of office.

The wide variety of names used for the high school student with the special functions which have been described is indicative of the lack of uniformity of practices and ideas in this matter. It may also be symptomatic of a lack of any clear consensus about what the general authority ethic is and how it should be implemented. One thing is clear, however, and it is that students in American high schools do assist in maintaining order and that some of them do have a supervisory role over their fellows. Their activities are best characterized by the term "service" which is often officially used to describe their tasks. However, though there may be privileges of certain kinds attached to these responsibilities (status, insignia), it is rare that there are any powers to punish or reward. Monitors can rarely do more than report an offender to a teacher. In certain instances they may be able to assign punishments, though this is rare and likely to be the result of unusual local conditions.[16]

The Student Council is generally an officially sponsored agency in the American high school, where students may make decisions and see that they are carried out.[17] Standards of behavior, dress and other matters may be discussed and defined at student council meetings and rules established for the whole school. Council members and officers of the student organization are elected by their peers for certain terms and have some powers to initiate action and to enforce or at least influence standards. The way in which this process is carried on is important in setting the "disciplinary tone" of the school. Though it may be referred to as student government, it rarely merits this description, since it is usually characterized by "limited" experiences in democratic procedures (nominations, elections, committee work etc.) and by the coordination of certain student extra-curricular activities.

The type of student participation in the orderly running of the school which tends to be quite widely encouraged is a form of supervised selfdirection. Rules of conduct in the parking lot, corridors, lunch room and study halls, for example, may be reached by student and possibly faculty discussion, and selected students are responsible in some way for the maintaining of order, not as policemen but as leaders of the school community.[18] Student leaders may be appointed or elected; their power to influence the behavior of others may be the force of their own personalities, or their informal powers of various kinds, but it is rarely any explicitly stated punitive or rewarding authority.

This type of social order, which varies from school to school but does represent a definable norm, is not without its critics. There are those who see it as encouraging license because rules are not imposed and enforced by properly designated authority (i.e., teachers). There are others who see it only as a feeble attempt to avoid outright authoritarianism, leading to a rather insidious manipulation of people (young and old). The regime remains directive, they argue, though it has the appearance of non-authoritarianism and permissiveness, and the trappings of student selfdetermination.[19]

The American high school pupil's involvement in the disciplinary regime of the school thus appears to be varied and diffused. Opportunity for supervision of pupils is given, there are selected elites, responsibilities of different kinds are given to pupils, and sometimes official and unofficial status and influence overlap.[20] Pupils may have many opportunities for leadership within the school community, but authority is generally quite widely dispersed, and rarely provided with punitive powers.[21] There is little evidence that the school or teaching staff characteristically selects a group of students to carry out extensive disciplinary mandates in any official or systematic way.

Conclusion

While the Prefectorial System is a well-established and common phenomenon in English secondary schools, it has no precise equivalent in the public high schools of the United States. In view of the contrasting patterns of historical and social circumstance, this is hardly surprising. Different social conditions and ideals demand different school procedures.

This is not to say, however, that many of the functions carried out by English prefects are not pursued by American students. Authority, power and status are distributed among secondary school pupils in both countries. But the systematic sponsoring and consistent reinforcement which the official school regime gives to one selected group in English schools has no real parallel in the United States. In America, power and status are widely dispersed among formal and informal elite groups, partly supported by the school administration, rarely singled out for general privilege and power. The contrast is between two systems of pupil participation in school affairs, and between two ways of thinking about the social order. In both countries there is a leadership group in society which the school system in some measure selects, trains and elects. In England the process is as striking as its product. It is, after all, with England that the term *Establishment* is associated. But in the United States the schools treat this function differently and the Establishment, or its equivalent, is an animal of a different color. In this example, as in others, school and society provide reflections of one another, though not necessarily in identical images.

In the case of England, the authority system of the school in its most pristine form is authoritarian and elitist. Prefects are sharply differentiated in status from their fellow pupils, and their symbols and powers are formalized into a fairly clearly defined and widely recognized institution – albeit one that is severely criticized and strongly pressured to change. Several assumptions about authority are evident: that it emanates from above, that one must serve well in order to rule, that its concomitant is public service. The cloak of authority must be worn with certainty and conviction, though modestly. Acceptance, by leaders of their privileges and obligations, and by followers of their leaders, is an important feature of thinking about authority in England. The example of such institutions as the police and the civil service confirm this outlook in England,[22] contributing to the picture of those in authority as a select group of unswerving, inflexible, obedient and dutiful beings. The regime of the schools is quite consistent with such widespread social attitudes and assumptions.[23]

In the United States however, pupil participation in the school's authority system has a rather different character. Authority does not appear to emanate exclusively or even mainly from above. It is achieved in a "free market" of influence, striving and prestige drawn from a variety of sources – individual attributes, and peer group as well as official school judgements. But such achievement does not so clearly nor officially set one pupil off from another; it is not recognized as such by all concerned. Distinctions are unclear, semi-official and eternally in the making. As a result, authority is in a very real sense "popular": its major justification is social necessity, and it is governed by exposure to the limelight, to rules of procedure, expediency and consensus. Great emphasis is placed upon individual participation in democratic processes. Thus the appeal to "the public," at least ostensibly, for confirmation in power, and the importance of popularity, adaptability and responsiveness to the pressures and needs of a given time and place. The theme is a familiar one, with echoes from Franklin, the Constitution and Tocqueville: authority is associated with power which is a corrupting influence upon those who achieve it. Its source is the consenting public who must therefore constantly act as supervisors of those in or near positions of power. In the United States, institutions such as the Civil Service and the police force suffer by their association with government and authority, earning poor status, distrust and constant surveillance from the public. The schools provide, on a modest scale, a breeding ground and an exemplar for general social thinking on the subject of power and authority in the United States.

While this paper has been mainly concerned with differences between the two countries described, the fundamental common features which make comparison possible must not be forgotten. In both situations, the educational system seeks to prepare the young for the adult social order, to induce them to accept models of thought and behavior which their mentors provide. At school, all are groomed for adult society, while some are selected and trained for particular functions and powers. The young are instructed at the same time as social order is maintained in the school. In addition to this basic similarity of function, there may be similarities in the characteristics of those selected for authority roles and in the demands placed upon them. There are also common values exemplified by the two systems. However, this paper has sought to consider differences in the basic model of each system, in the respective means used to achieve selected ends and in the general assumptions about authority which each case reveals. One may be more brutal than the other, or more insidious, more or less efficient, enlightened or consistent with prevailing social values. But evaluation of the systems, whether on grounds of morality or efficiency or ultimate implications for society is a separate subject for study.

There is one obvious qualification to the generalizations made. In both countries each school is marked by the special stamp of its own community, principal or student body. In both countries too there is a wide range of outlooks and practices, as well as much questioning of traditional or conventional practices by schoolmen and social critics. Yet with all the variations, there remains a characteristic mode, a style, a key-note. In the United States, it is the familiar suspicion of any overt and institutionalized authority or privileged group combined with a traditional reliance upon checks and balances. In England, it is the Prefectorial System.

NOTES

* M.A. Eckstein, "The Elitist and the Popular Ideal: Prefects and Monitors in English and American Secondary Schools," *International Review of Education*, Vol. XII, No. 2, 1966, pp. 184-193. Reprinted by permission of Kluwer Academic Publishers.

1. At William of Wykeham's school (established 1387) eighteen seniors were to maintain discipline and report misdeeds; praeposters were appointed at Eton in the sixteenth century for supervisory and disciplinary duties. The precedent of appointing prefects was established well before Dr. Arnold raised his Sixth Form at Rugby to what has been described as the "status of Apostles". Harold Nicolson, *Good Behaviour*. Boston: Beacon Press 1960, p. 264.

2. "Fagging" – system whereby junior pupils performed menial tasks for seniors.

3. Paul Nash, "Training an Elite: The Prefect-Fagging System in the English Public School", *History of Education Quarterly*, Vol. I, No.1, March, 1961, pp. 14-21.

4. H.A. Ree, *The Essential Grammar School*. London: George G. Harrap and Co., Ltd., 1956, p. 38.

5. *Ibid.*

6. E.B. Castle, "The English Public Schools: Character and Responsibility", *Yearbook of Education*, 1958, Yonkers-on-Hudson: World Book Co., pp. 206-14.

7. T.C. Worsley, *End of the Old School Tie.* London: Secker and Warburg, 1941.

8. H. Davies, *The Boys' Grammar School Today and Tomorrow.* London: Methuen and Co., Ltd., 1954 (2nd ed.).

9. See, for example, Roy Harris, "A Study in the Assessment and Guidance of Prefects in a Comprehensive School", *Educational Research* IV, June 1962, pp. 238-40, which argues that prefects, and other pupils, would benefit from a guidance course, comprising some elementary psychology.

10. See, for example, George Orwell, "Such, Such Were the joys..." (1950), *A Collection of Essays.* Garden City, N.Y.: Doubleday Anchor Books, 1954, pp. 9-55; and Brian Inglis (ed.), *John Bull's Schooldays.* London: Hutchinson and Co., Ltd., 1961.

11. "As a political institution, as a device for training guardians for the British Empire... the Public Schools deserve respect. They seem a good deal more ingenious, if only slightly less painful, than the Chinese communes". J.D. Pringle, "The British Commune: Thoughts on the 'Public School'", *Encounter* 16.2, Feb. 1962, pp. 24-28. The discussion is concerned with such features as boarding children away from home, developing character through a Spartan regime and team games, and administering discipline via prefects. Except for the first, these measures have greatly influenced secondary education in general.

12. Tangible rewards, in the form of privileges, do however exist, though their value may be merely symbolic: "Only the Sixth Form may use the front steps. The marble steps are only for the use of prefects and sub-prefects... The use of umbrellas is confined to the Sixth Form" (from the Rules and Regulations of a well-known London school). Prefects often have insignia of rank such as a gown or badge, freedom from certain school rules – e.g., dress regulations – and a private commonroom.

13. Samuel Everett, *Growing Up in English Secondary Schools: Significance for American Practice.* Pittsburgh: University of Pittsburgh Press, 1959, p. 187.

14. A.W. Rowe, *The Education of the Average Child.* London: George G. Harrap and Co., Ltd., 1959, p. 51.

15. Rupert Wilkinson, *The Prefects.* London: Oxford University Press, 1963

16. The system of a New York school in which a squad of 600 pupils supervise corridors, classroom, lunch hall, entrances and exits, and has the power to give detentions, refer pupils to teachers, and to report pupils to parents, is a rare one. The total pupil population is 6,000, the building is large and many-storied, and traffic problems and safety hazards are very great. Conversations with teachers responsible for the service squad confirm that such an extensive delegation of power and responsibility to a body of "non-coms" is rare, and a function of the special problems of size and location of the school.

17. Over 90 per cent of U.S. high schools have a student council, though great variations exist in functioning, degree of importance, range of activities. For fuller discussion, see Robert W. Frederick, *The Third Curriculum: Student Activities in American Education.* New York: Appleton-Century-Crofts, Inc. 1959; and Gerald M. Van Pool, "The Student Council", *Bulletin of the NASSP,* 48, 294, Oct. 1964, pp. 42-53.

18. See, for example, Donald W. Empey, "Student Self-Direction, Flexible Scheduling and Team Teaching", *Bulletin of the NASSP,* 47, 280, Feb. 1963, pp. 118-24.

19. Edgar Z. Friedenberg, *The Vanishing Adolescent.* Boston: Beacon Press, 1959; Paul

Goodman, *Growing Up Absurd.* New York: Random House, 1960.

20. Recent studies strongly suggest that the informal processes, elites and authorities are of greater significance and influence than those officially recognized by the school. See, for example, C. Wayne Gordon, *The Social System of the High School.* Glencoe, III: Free Press, 1957; James S. Coleman, *Social Climates in High Schools,* Cooperative Research Monographs. Washington D.C.: U.S. Department of Health, Education and Welfare, 1961.

21. One institution which may exert a powerful controlling influence upon student behavior is the high school fraternity. The power which senior members can exert upon their inferiors in the organization might be compared with that of prefects upon junior members of their schools. However, fraternities are not part of the officially sponsored high school regime, they are illegal in many states, and membership may be grounds for immediate expulsion from school.

22. G. Gorer, *Exploring English Character.* N.Y.: Criterion Books, 1955.

23. There is no intention of asserting that English social thinking on these matters is inflexible. Indeed, there is little doubt that the pattern described is a rapidly changing one.

13

Ultimate Deterrents: Punishment and Control in English and American Schools*

There may still be those who think of the English secondary school as described in *Tom Brown's Schooldays,* where punishment was summarily dispensed in violent ways. The cane-wielding Ichabod Crane of the *Legend of Sleepy Hollow* tends to be regarded, however, as an eccentric remnant of former days, no longer characteristic of American schooling. Yet in both countries, corporal punishment remains one of the penalties of various seriousness visited upon pupils who break school rules.

An examination of disciplinary policy in English and American schools provides indices of general thinking on educational matters in these two countries, bound by common antecedents and close contemporary ties, yet differing in basic elements of their social assumptions and practices. The ingenuity of teachers on both sides of the Atlantic in devising punishments for their more recalcitrant pupils is by no means limited to beating them or excluding them from school. However, these are two common results of grave infractions. As serious deterrents, they are more likely to be given careful attention in law or local school regulations, and less likely to be used capriciously. When examined in context as part of a disciplinary policy and as measures to implement a particular regime in school, they suggest definitions of authority and responsibility, of tradition and change, indicative of the respective national patterns of schooling of which they are part.

Administrative and Legal Sanctions for School Punishments in the United Kingdom and the United States

The decentralized nature of both English and American school systems creates obstacles to defining national policy in any educational matter. The necessary information must be sought in local or regional regulations, in the statements of representative individuals or groups and in the actual conventional practices within the schools. However, both countries define and distribute authority and responsibility in ways revealed through their respective administrative patterns as well as pronouncements.

In England, the forms of punishment to be used in schools, or for that matter in the home, are not laid down by Parliament or the Ministry of Education. However, teachers in England are considered *in loco parentis.* They thus assume some of the rights and duties of parents and are obliged to take reasonable steps to carry out their professional duties. The principle has been laid down in legal precedent and also endorsed by

Parliament.[1] Considerable discretion is thus left to teachers, whose practices are determined by convention and general usage rather than by formal policy statements of any kind.

On the other hand, most local education authorities do have some regulations dealing with corporal punishment,[2] and the Ministry of Education has one requirement, namely, that all cases of corporal punishment be recorded in a special book.[3] Local regulations vary, being broadly concerned with preventing abuses and regulating the use of this disciplinary device. However, the teacher, in general, operates within a large, permissive framework with rather few limitations set by the various levels of the administrative hierarchy.

In the United States, as in England, the teacher is empowered to punish pupils if necessary and appropriate in the circumstances as a normal part of his responsibilities, and is also considered as being *in loco parentis* in this matter. The courts have frequently upheld the right to administer corporal punishment, to suspend or expel pupils, or to give other kinds of punishments, after carefully examining both the letter and the spirit of the specific act. However, even parental powers are not unlimited in this matter, and it has been suggested that in actual fact, "school personnel cannot go so far under the law as can parents."[4]

As to the regulations provided by various levels of the administrative hierarchy, the Federal Government has no direct control or authority in education, so that the responsibility for setting educational policy and ensuring development towards it devolves upon State Boards of Education. In most cases much of this responsibility is in turn delegated to local Boards of Education. It is generally at the local level that rules of student behavior and the consequences of infractions are defined, and the regulations which govern teachers' practices in punishment are made. The only limitation upon local practices is that they be consistent with State policy and the broader provisions of the Constitution.[5]

The school and the teacher in the United States therefore operate within a setting in which the immediate community is likely to provide a more or less detailed policy on punishments within the general framework of State and common law on the subject. In England, on the other hand, fewer detailed specifications appear to exist, the immediate community is little involved, and the precedents are provided by common law, common expectations and traditional usage.

English School Policy

The idea of corporal punishment, or of using "the cane," is a familiar one to the English. Teachers, pupils and parents alike generally associate the cane with the headmaster's study or the schoolroom as a natural consequence of certain infractions of rules. However, there has been increasing debate and controversy on its efficacy or desirability in recent decades, even at the national, Parliamentary level. For the first time, information has been systematically gathered on school punishments on a national basis.[6]

Teachers and principals in England may normally administer corporal punishment if they see fit, subject to local regulations and the sole Ministerial requirement mentioned above. The rules laid down by local authorities mostly cover the powers of head teachers and their assistants, types of instruments of correction, conditions under which these may be used, and safeguards such as penalties for disregard of the regulations.[7]

A significant feature which emerges from the consideration of the English regulations is a concern for "authorization," i.e., professional competence of the teacher. His qualifications and his professional role provide sanction enough for him to use corporal punishment (or other punishments if necessary). The comment of the moderately conservative London *Times Educational Supple*ment sums up a fairly typical attitude. In discussion of a proposed children's charter at the United Nations Commission on Human Rights, a motion by the Soviet delegate which would have denied the teacher the right to spank was defeated. The paper's comment was as follows:

> The teacher has rights, too, and these must include the right to spank. He (or she) may never elect to avail himself of it. But it is a right he should have. Possessing the right, let him grapple in solitude on a wet Sunday with the rights and wrongs of corporal punishment. The decision should be left in his hands.[8]

While no local education committee completely prohibits the use of the cane, partial prohibitions do exist in most areas. The predominant concerns are to avoid cruelty and excess, to ban male teachers from punishing girls in coeducational schools and to forbid unauthorized teachers from inflicting corporal punishment. However, though the majority of such committees seem to be satisfied with existing regulations,[9] it depends on individual head teachers and staff whether caning is used at all, and if so, how much.

Gradual, voluntary abandonment of use of the cane appears to be the major tendency in recent years.[10] Local education authorities have made efforts to steer schools away from corporal punishment by reports of successful changes in policy and suggestions about more desirable regimes.[11] However, there is resistance to any diminution of the school's punitive powers and in some quarters a call for even greater firmness may be heard.[12]

In the matter of expulsion or suspension, English policy is again defined, for the most part, by local authority and the school itself. It is the legal responsibility of Local Educational Authorities to provide an education suitable to their age, ability and aptitude for all children of school age. Suspension from school is "normally within the jurisdiction of the head and is usually the limit of his power, but there are some schools where the head is authorized to expel."[13] In the case of expulsion, procedures laid down by the school and local authorities include the right of appeal to the Minister of Education.[14]

An exchange of letters in the *Times Educational Supplement* raises certain major issues involved.[15] A fourteen-year old girl was expelled from a grammar school for "uncooperative and troublesome behaviour." The action was defended on various grounds, including the interests of other pupils and the school at large. It was argued that expulsion is a last resort used only with the agreement of the school staff in view of the likely effect upon the whole school community. The action was, however, criticized since it raised the difficulty for the child of obtaining entrance to another grammar school. The head teacher concerned had suggested that the pupil attend the local secondary modern school, but this would in all likelihood rule out the possibility of the pupil taking the General Certificate of Education and preparing for University entrance. Editorial discussion of the case emphasized the "necessity of retaining the power to expel, in extreme circumstances, for the sake of preserving a school environment which good parents desire for their children and should receive from the national system."[16]

However, expulsion implies a rough hierarchy of schools in a universal, compulsory educational system. It may be regarded in effect as a form of demotion within the system. The editor therefore suggested, in the interest of fairness, that non-grammar schools also be included within the hierarchical system, and that, for example, an educational authority with several secondary schools in its area could assign one as a final resting place until fifteen years of age for the pupil who was "unamenable to the discipline of the others."

Discussion of this case illustrates the paradox inevitably involved when the principle of universal attendance is accepted, while the final deterrent of expulsion is retained. In England, the tripartite organization of secondary education permits this measure to be used as a device for demotion from the grammar school, the more selective and higher status secondary institution. However, the anomaly persists in other types of schools.

In summary, it is generally accepted in England that the schools may have to punish pupils on occasions, that local regulations and common law are enough to prevent abuse but that schools and teachers are generally the proper authorities to decide upon rules and the consequences of infraction. Decisions about usage and about change in practice are to be left in the hands of head teachers and staff though change in disciplinary policy may be of considerable public interest and concern. Nevertheless, there is considerable resistance to encroachments upon the teacher's powers and right to self-determination. The general English approach is that if change is to come, it should not be through the diminution of either the school's authority or the professional autonomy of teachers.[17]

American School Policy

Corporal punishment does not appear at first glance to be an important or common part of American school discipline. As one English observer writes of schools in the Middle West:

> Formal classroom discipline, in the traditional sense, is not a common feature
> in the contemporary American school scene, and punishment, other than bad
> marks or expressed disapprobation, is almost unknown.[18]

As a measure of the disuse of physical punishment in some communities, a problem was raised in Stamford, Connecticut, in 1959 when the Board of Education decided to endorse corporal punishment in extreme cases. No one appeared to know what instruments of correction should be used or where to obtain them.[19]

Teachers in the United States are normally permitted to chastise pupils physically if circumstances warrant and if the intention and the act are neither malicious nor unreasonable.[20] However, the variety of State pronouncements on corporal punishments gives some indication of the regulations to which teachers are subject. These range from a complete ban in one case (New Jersey) to specific authorization for teachers to use reasonable force (in five States). However, most States do not explicitly refer to the teacher's statutory authority.[21]

Local regulations are no less varied than those of the States, but are rather more specific and detailed in defining policy, the reasons for it, and approved practices and procedures. Of eleven major cities, five expressly forbid corporal punishment in their public schools.[22] In the six major cities which do sanction it, regulations demonstrate great concern for the mental is well as the physical health of pupils. They not only emphasize the legal and moral rights of schools to punish according to specific procedures, but also include safeguards of various kinds against the abuse of such rights.[23]

While most principals in the United States have the right to administer corporal punishment, only 45.5 per cent of classroom teachers have such power.[24] As in England, however, urban educational authorities circumscribe and regulate the schools in this matter more than do rural areas.[25]

Though it is apparent that the policy on corporal punishment varies considerably in the United States, it is also evident that there are changes in opinion and pressures towards changes of current policy. In New York, for example, where discretion as to the use of corporal punishment is left to local boards of education, a bill which would have prevented local authorities from outlawing physical punishment was passed by the State Legislature in three successive years, only to be vetoed each time by the Governor.[26] The Superintendent of Schools in Washington, D.C., where corporal punishment was banned, recently called for the restoration of such powers to the schools.[27] General concern over discipline problems in the schools has in recent years resulted in much support for the idea of a generally "tougher" regime in the schools[28] and the call for restitution of the power to use corporal punishment where it has been banned. Characteristically, the pressure emanates from a variety of sources, both professional and lay, and is exerted in the press and in state and local governmental bodies.

In the case of suspension or expulsion, policy is similarly defined for the most part at the local school board level. While state statutes often set forth conditions for expulsion, in most cases pupils may be expelled by official action of the local school board.[29] Since expulsion immediately raises questions as to the pupil's statutory right to attend school it must be ensured not only that the decision to expel is not made maliciously, but that it is the only remaining measure which can be taken to ensure the general well-being of the school. In disputed cases, therefore, the courts, if appealed to, will weigh the respective rights and powers of the school system and of the parent and pupil, assuming the pupil's obligation to submit to the reasonable rules and actions of the school system.[30]

The courts have often been required to rule on a school board's powers to expel pupils. They have in the past upheld expulsion of pupils who refused to salute the flag or to submit a certificate of vaccination. They have generally supported bans on membership in secret societies and antifraternity rules of various kinds.[31]

Local policy on suspension from high school is frequently specified in detail to pupils. General offenses, such as disorderliness and insubordination, as well as specific anti-social or criminal acts (stealing or carrying dangerous weapons, narcotics or alcohol) may be listed in handbooks distributed to students.[32] Improper dress is a common cause for suspension from school.[33]

In rare instances, expulsion may be invoked as a punishment for poor school work, as distinct from other forms of misconduct. The adoption of such a policy by a school board in California was considered unique by one professional journal.[34] Expulsion, in California and elsewhere in the United States, is more commonly associated with disobedience, defiance, habitual profanity, immorality or any other moral or physical habits or disabilities as might be inimical to the welfare of other pupils.

In summary, American school policy on discipline varies widely and is subject to change. The serious measures which have been studied here are used as last resorts, generally for serious misbehavior rather than for school work. Such criteria as moderation, reasonableness and positive intent are invoked in cases of disputed acts of punishment, but local regulations, state and common law are the sources of authority to punish. Specific regulations, generally greater in number and detail in urban than in rural areas, both sanction and delimit the powers of schools and teachers.

Just as the authority to control pupils is located in the pattern of local regulations and conventions, so too do changes in policy take place in local and regional school governments, depending upon public discussion and resolution of the issues. It may well be that in the absence of commonly accepted sanctions and policies on a broad national basis, the tendency is encouraged to define the details of a discipline policy with increasing specificity lest any person question a particular act.[35] The actual powers of teachers and school in any particular location depend upon the interplay between a variety of forces in the community, in which teachers are included but not necessarily prominent.[36]

Comparative Discussion and Conclusions

Though school discipline may have changed since *Tom Brown's Schooldays* and *The Legend of Sleepy Hollow,* sanctions for the use of quite severe punishments, such as physical chastisement and expulsion, are strong in both England and the United States today. However, this review of regulations, laws, conventions and opinions suggests important and even basic differences between the two countries.

In England, sanctions for punishment are provided by the professional status of teachers, the traditional independence of the school as an institution, and their authority in decisions about the proper ways of educating the young. In the control and punishment of pupils, English schools and their staff are a stern and independent force.

The contrast with the United States is quite evident. American teachers and schools do have the right and the responsibility to set standards of behavior, to define and inflict punishments where appropriate. However, this authority is not located primarily in the independent and stern institution of the school. It is rather dispersed among the political and other lay authorities of the immediate and surrounding communities. The teacher's status is subject, not superior or independent, not "professional" in the English manner. Punishment must be not only justified but also defended. Comparatively speaking, great attention is given in the United States to defining a particular policy and to setting up specific limitations and safeguards to disarm the public. This effort serves to circumscribe the school's freedom of action.

The underlying assumption in England is that the institution has the right and the responsibility to maintain a disciplinary regime, that professional competence is generally a reliable enough guard against abuses, and that changes come best from within the institution. The American assumption, however, is that the public through its formal and informal agencies of government must act as a perpetual watchdog over its institutions, inspecting and initiating changes wherever necessary. The result is that, whereas in England traditional sanctions support an authoritarian disciplinary regime in schools, relatively independent of other powers, in the United States the various forces encourage the school to be an institution with limited authority, ever-reminded of its dependence and responsibility to serve the community around it, and rather hesitant to insist upon the use of overt punitive measures to maintain a specific type of disciplinary regime.

A number of variables account for specific differences in policy and practice within each country as well as between them. The example of corporal punishment shows that in both countries there is a difference between rural and urban areas, punitive power being more circumscribed in the towns. In both countries too, there are variations from a more to a less punitive approach, though in the United States these are at the discretion of local school government, while in England they are at the discretion of individual schools. Furthermore, the range of statutory provisions is generally greater in the United States.

Finally in both countries there are conflicting pressures for change and for maintaining or reasserting the *status quo*. Here again, however, the direction of major forces, the sources from which they emanate and the ways in which they operate differ between England and the United States. In the United States, the currently dominant call is for more and stricter discipline. It is heard in many public circles, in the press, in government, and also in the school hierarchy. In England, however, whereas a similar range of differing voices may be heard, the direction of change is predominantly towards lessening the degree of punitiveness, the autonomy and authoritarianism of the schools. In addition, the channels through which pressures for change are exerted are professional and internal (the "suggestions" of the Ministry, the influence of local authorities, professional training), though public debate and influence are important forces.[37]

The use of expulsion as a disciplinary device in both countries is recognized as an admission of failure to cope with the malefactor and reflects a concern for the general good of the school community. Since this measure contradicts the principle of universal education, the concern for the constitutional rights of the individual must be weighed against the problems raised by his presence in school. However, the situation in England is a special one in that expulsion from a (selective) grammar school does not necessitate exclusion from public education, but rather demotion within the secondary education system. The disciplinary device in such a situation has overtones for the academic standing of students and is a potentially powerful instrument in this area. The same feature is not generally apparent in American schools, where policy on punishment is limited to conduct generally and where the comprehensive high school is the usual form of secondary education.[38]

In reviewing the current situation in both countries together, there appear to be several significant aspects involved. Where a trend towards urbanization is occurring, the concomitant educational developments, such as growth in the size of schools and of the educational enterprise, bureaucratization and specialization, lead to a greater specification and codification of disciplinary policy. Rules are considered and recorded, and cases of infraction are noted. In a sense, then, disciplinary procedures become more circumscribed and somewhat more inflexible. Secondly, and apparently at the same time, the growth of knowledge, research and "enlightenment," encourages efforts to install a less overtly punitive approach by the school, and a diminution of the independent authority of teachers. Finally, the need to cope with a wider range of pupil ability, interest and aspiration as a result of encouraging longer school attendance, leads to growing concern not only by teachers but also by the public, about youthful indiscipline as a social phenomenon and a social threat, with consequences such as demands for greater strictness as well as greater flexibility. Thus the changing environmental circumstances and the educational adaptations to them produce a variety of conflicting pressures to change the school's ideas and practices in discipline. These pressures are characteristic of the prevailing scene in England and the United States.[39]

Study of these aspects of disciplinary policy in schools of England and the United States demonstrates differences between many of their respective educational and social assumptions. The role and responsibilities of schools differ between the two countries;

so too, do the relationships of teachers and schools to other forces around them, administrative and social. Specific disciplinary purposes and practices differ from one country to the other. Whereas in the United States, local rules and regulations add to the evidences of a characteristic and ebullient pluralism, the case of England reveals a greater uniformity and a more affirmative and independent posture on the part of those entrusted with the task of educating the young.

It may be tempting to conclude that the major lesson to be drawn from this comparative essay has to do mainly with the differences in practice, approach and style between the two countries studied. The fact remains, however, that within each country there are wide variations and contradictory tendencies, that these overlap between the two countries, and that any emphasis upon differences must be severely qualified. The contemporary trends and debates demonstrate responsiveness to changing ideas and conditions in both instances, thus underlining comnonalities as well as differences. Certainly, the responses and adaptations to changing circumstances take place in a specific cultural context and are greatly determined by it. Yet, in the long run, it may be the similarities of contemporary conditions and concepts which will prevail over the respective precedents, patterns and outlooks of such closely related countries as England and the United States.[40]

NOTES

* M.A. Eckstein, "Ultimate Deterrents: Punishment and Control in English and American Schools," *Comparative Education Review* 10.3 (October, 1966), pp. 433-439. Reprinted by permission of the University of Chicago Press.

1. G. Barrell, *Teachers and the Law* (London: Methuen, 1958), p. *155 et seq.; Childrens and Young Persons Act,* 1933, S.1 (7).
2. National Foundation for Education Research in England and Wales, *A Survey of Rewards and Punishments in Schools* (London: Newnes Educational Publishing Co., 1952), Chapter 4.
3. Ministry of Education, *Administrative Memorandum No. 301,* Oct. 11, 1948. The status and responsibilities of the national authority in education have increased rapidly in the last twenty-five years. However, it does not provide, maintain or control schools directly, nor does it employ teachers. The Ministry does not specify curricula, methods of teaching or specific policy on educational matters. It is responsible, however, for developing a national policy which it pursues by inspecting and assessing schools, setting minimum standards, providing a clearing house of information and expert advice not through directives but by means of suggestions, e.g., *Primary Education: Suggestions for the Consideration of Teachers and Others Concerned with the Work of Primary Schools* (London: Her Majesty's Stationery Office, 1959).
4. E. Edmund Reutter, Jr., *Schools and the Law* (New York: Oceana Publications, 1960), p. 67.
5. Two important trends are evident in the U.S. with reference to responsibility and power at different administrative levels: a. the growth of the Federal Government's involvement in education; b. the consolidation of school districts. This suggests a general unifying and uniforming trend with an accompanying decrease in the degrees of independence and variety at the local level. See, Hollis P. Allen, *The Federal Government and Education* (New York: McGraw Hill, 1950); Dawson Hales, *Federal Control of Public Education: A Critical Appraisal* (New York:

Bureau of Publications, Teachers College, Columbia University, 1954), Chapter IV.

6. Discussion in the House of Commons led to a national research project on the general subject of punishments and rewards in schools and the particular matter of corporal punishment. See Hansard, *Extracts from the Official Report of the Proceedings of the House of Commons,* 24 April, 1947.

7. Ninety-nine of the 136 local education authorities canvassed in the study which resulted from Parliamentary discussion were found to have such regulations. National Foundation for Educational Research in England and Wales, *op. cit.,* pp. 72-3.

8. *Times Educational Supplement,* April 17, 1959, p. 637.

9. National Foundation for Educational Research in England and Wales, *op. cit.,* pp. 69-70.

10. *Ibid.,* Chapter V.

11. London County Council, *Punishment in the Schools* (London, 1952); Education Department, West Riding County Council, Be*haviour and Delinquency in Secondary Schools* (Wakefield, Yorks., 1961).

12. See, for example, the motion demanding restoration to teachers of "unfettered disciplinary control" at the annual Conservative Party Conference, 1961; also, *Times Educational Supplement,* Oct. 3, 1958, p. 1454, and Oct. 13, 1961, p. 478.

13. G.R. Barrell, *op. cit.,* p. 103.

14. "It is incidental to the authority of a headmaster to expel from the school over which he presides any scholar or student whose conduct is such that he could not any longer be permitted to remain without damage to the school. This is, however, not to be exercised arbitrarily. It may be questioned and, although no doubt a large discretion must be allowed, it must not be exercised wantonly or capriciously." Lord Chief Justice Cockburn in *Fitzgerald v. Northcote* (1865), 4F and F656. Quoted by Barrell, *op. cit.,* p. 164.

15. *Times Educational Supplement,* Aug. 3, 1962, p. 140; Aug. 10, 1962, p. 161.

16. *Times Educational Supplement,* Aug. 17, 1962, p. 179.

17. This is consistent with the traditional English approach towards educational change where legislation has generally been permissive rather than mandatory and where the growth of central authority has been balanced by attempts to retain self-determination at the local level.

18. John N. Wales, *Schools of Democracy* (East Lansing, Mich.: Michigan State University Press, 1962), p. 20. Corporal punishment, he found, was not a common practice in Michigan schools, though it is found occasionally, particularly in private or parochial schools.

19. *Times Educational Supplement,* December 11, 1959, p. 723.

20. Laws on cruelty to children and legal sanctions for moderate, reasonable punishment by parents or teachers are the usual legal yardsticks for such acts. N.E.A. Research Division, "The Legal Status of the Public School Pupil," *Research Bulletin 26* (Washington, D.C.: The Association), February 1948.

21. Three States do refer explicitly to the teacher's powers *in loco parentis.* In most cases, however, the decision on policy and on how far it should be defined in regulations devolves upon local boards of education. N.E.A. Research Division, *Research Memo 1959-11* (Washington, D.C.: The Association, 1959).

22. Washington, D.C., Chicago, Baltimore, Philadelphia and New York. See, *Rules for the Public Schools of the District of Columbia,* July, 1953, p. 35; *Rules-Board of Education of the City of Chicago,* May 9, 1956, Sec. 6-22; *Rules of the Board of School Commissioners,* Baltimore, Md., Sept. 22, 1955, Article V, Section 6b.

New York City couples the ban with an embargo on "punishment of any kind tending to cause excessive fear or physical or mental distress." New York, N.Y., *By-Laws of the Board of Education,* April, 1958, Section 90:15, p. 77. Philadelphia recognizes that while State Law may permit corporal punishment, local policy forbids it since it "tends to vitiate the fine human relationship between teacher and class" and "it involves unjustifiable risks on the part of the teacher." Board of Education, Philadelphia, Pa., *Administrative Bulletin No. 22,* December 1957, p. 52.

23. In several cities, for example, corporal punishment may specifically only be used as the last resort; in others, parents must be informed before such action, or there must be witnesses, or a written report. Some rules specify the instrument of correction, or the target. See, for example: *Administrators' Handbook,* Dade County, Fla., July 1, 1957, pp. 3202-05; *Rules and Regulations,* Board of Education, Minneapolis, Minn., 1953, p. 29; *Regulations of the Department of Instruction,* St. Louis Public Schools, 1951, p. 76; *Rules and Regulations,* Board of Education, Houston, Texas, Section 4a: 15.

24. Teachers' power to administer corporal punishment: Principals 74.3%; elementary school teachers 44.7%; junior high school teachers 30.3%; senior high school teachers 22.1%. National Education Association, R*esearch Bulletin 34.2,* April 1956, pp. 63, 87.

25. Teachers permitted: Urban 31.6%, Rural 66.1%; Principals permitted: Urban 68.5%, Rural 83.0%. National Education Association, *ibid.,* pp. 63-4.

26. The so-called Corso Bill was supported by a number of teachers' groups such as the New York High School Teachers' Association and the Bronx Teachers' Association and opposed by New York administrators and other teachers' groups. See, *World Telegram and Sun,* March 18, 1959, April 9, 1959, *New York Herald Tribune,,* "The Corporal Punishment Debate," February 15, 1959.

27. The local Board of Education refused to give such authorization. However, the House of Representatives District of Columbia Committee supported a bill to repeal the law; this was passed by the House (277-53) and sent to the Senate for approval. See, *Christian Science Monitor,* February 21, 1963; *New York Times,* May 14, 1963.

28. "We have found ample evidence showing a direct connection between the namby-pamby attitude of the educational hierarchy and the collapse of discipline in our schools," was the conclusion of a Brooklyn grand jury investigating crime in the public schools. They recommended that teachers be authorized to use "reasonable force" in disciplining troublemakers. Judge Samuel Leibowitz, in accepting their report and approving their stand, said: "We who deal with the problem of crime in our schools know through bitter experience that unless we return our teachers to a position of authority held in former years, we may as well throw up our hands." *World Telegram and Sun,* January 22, 1959. Reflecting a similar call for increased power for teachers, the American Federation of Teachers passed a resolution favoring the use of physical force in maintaining classroom discipline: *World Telegram and Sun,* August 21, 1959.

29. E. Edmund Reutter, *op. cit.,* p. 68.

30. N.E.A. Research Division, "The Legal Status of the Public School Pupil," *Research Bulletin 26:3-38,* February, 1948, pp. 26-30.

31. N.E.A. Research Division, *op. cit.;* M.K. Remmlein, *The Law of Local Public School Administration (New York: McGraw Hill, 1953), Chapter 7; Robert Hamilton and Paul R. Mort, The Law and Public Education 2nd ed. (Brooklyn:*

Foundation Press, 1950), pp. 513-20.

32. Glenn F. Nolan, "Handbook for Discipline*," Bulletin of NASSP,* 43, 249 (October 1959), pp. 15-16,

33. E.g., *New York Times,* December 1, 1961; November 14, 1962.

34. "Student Behavior Policy," *The Clearing House,* 33, 6 (February 1959), pp. 348-52.

35. See, for example, the opinions expressed in Glenn F. Nolan, *op. cit.* The author strongly approves of the San Bernadino discipline handbook which is a useful guide, he says, and has a "soothing effect on irate parents. It quiets recalcitrant students. It has a steadying effect on the administrator." In other words, the printed codification of policy gives the school a needed tool for disarming conflicting authorities.

36. Thus, the national constitutional principle of "balance of power," which the United States attempts to achieve by dispersion of authority between legislative, executive and judicial branches, is paralleled in educational matters by the attempt to ensure that no interested party has independent authority in disciplinary policy.

37. Gradual erosion of the relative independence from public pressures of English schools and teachers may well be encouraged by features which appear to accompany growth of school populations, urbanization, increase in school purposes and functions: formalization of rules, increase in disciplinary incidents, growth of bureaucratic machinery.

38. Of course, in those rare cases in the United States where selective high schools exist, a similar significance is apparent. In a sense, special schools for incorrigible discipline problems do provide a comparable device, for example, in the 600 Schools of New York City. Transfer to such a school, though it may be given a psychological rationale, is a result of a serious and continuous disciplinary problem, and is conceived of as a demotion within the public education system. See recommendations of New York Teachers' Guild in 1956 with regard to enlarging such provisions: American Federation of Teachers (AFL-CIO), *Discipline: What For and How?* (Chicago: American Federation of Teachers, 1957), pp. 26-27.

39. Two recent items confirm the general findings of this essay: the reports and comments upon yet another statement on "punishment in Schools," this time by the Educational Institute of Scotland, in *Times Educational Supplement,* October 15, 1965; and the article by Richard M. Grummere Jr., "Discipline in the Dark: on Beating School Children," *The Nation,* December 6, 1965.

40. This article is based on one section of the author's Ph.D. dissertation, "A Comparative Study of Discipline in English and American Secondary Schools; Rewards and Punishments As Socializing Agents," New York, 1964. Teachers College, Columbia University.

14

Metropolitanism and Education*

This study grows out of two closely associated concerns. First, the growth of large cities and the problems that vex them are important to the interested parent or citizen, as well as to educational policy makers and planners. Second, the increasing typicality and commonality of the urban environment and the pervasiveness of the influence of large population centers in and beyond their own countries, makes this theme a natural subject for the use of comparative analytical methods. The first is a more pragmatic consideration, while the second may be more academic and theoretical. They are complementary, however, in that policy and practice both draw on and test theory.

The metropolis is a special form of the urban environment, an exceptionally large population concentration within a given country, whose influence is great nationally and extends beyond its national boundaries. In commerce, communications, and politics its importance is clearly recognized. As a center which attracts talent in varied field., its significance is evident. It is characterized by social and economic heterogeneity, high levels of population mobility, and a disproportionate concentration of skilled manpower and economic activities of particular types. Of particular importance to the social, political, and economic influence which the metropolis radiates is the fact that it is here that the centers of communication and distribution of ideas are located.

However, as an educational force, the role of the metropolis has been neglected. It trains and produces people of all ages, through many kinds of formal and informal agencies. The importance of this process lies in the fact that there are special, even unique circumstances that characterize the metropolis, a pattern of social, economic, and political conditions which signify a special quality of existence. Inevitably, this must be bound up with education and with schooling. The twin rationales for this study are: first that the educational implications of metropolitan conditions deserve further study; and second that these educational implications transcend national boundaries.

The Metropolitan Phenomenon

Like schooling, the experience of living in a metropolitan setting is relatively new so far as most of the population of the world is concerned. True, schools and cities have existed for thousands of years. But in the twentieth century the two experiences, of formal education and of urban living, have become common to the majority of people in the developed world.

Industrialization and the growth of technology are marked by the growth of cities, the increase in formal schooling for all, and more specialized, advanced education for many.   Through his growing technological knowledge, Man has been able both to ignore and to meddle with his natural environment.   His artifact, the city, was a function of new inventions: social, political and economic.   The metropolis is its latest manifestation, rapidly becoming the human settlement of the twentieth century.   As their conditions of existence, needs and beliefs converge, the inhabitants of Amsterdam, London, Paris, New York, and other urban agglomerations come to form a global community transcending their national boundaries.   No citizen in modern society can escape the influence of the metropolitan economy, communicational system or culture, even though he may not reside in the metropolis.

Whether physically or socially, the metropolitan environment is identifiable: an intricate transportation network, high concentration of residential, industrial, and cultural facilities.   Flux is the theme of the metropolis: people are in constant movement, from home to work, in and out of buildings, vehicles, shops and places of entertainment.   Streets are filled with people and objects in rapid motion, window displays and billboards are renewed constantly, and the physical environment is always undergoing change, demolition, rebuilding and refurbishing.   People, too, are in transit, not only in the strictly physical sense.   They change residence, employment, they sample new tastes and styles.   Metropolitan areas generate their own peculiar forms of human interaction and their own political and economic systems.

Within the metropolis divergences between the various subgroups are striking: inner city and suburban residents, the urban poor and the propertied, salaried middle class are separated spatially and politically as well as by economic status.   As the contrasts sharpen, polarization becomes a danger to the organic life of the metropolis and a refutation of its promise of a better life for the many.

The contrast between rich and poor, favored and disadvantaged, has long been characteristic of the city.   In the modern metropolis, however, its sharpened form represents not merely a simple numerical increase but a difference in scale so great as to be qualitatively different.   For it is accompanied by a host of other civic problems deriving directly from the rapid rate and size of growth of the metropolis.   The mere presence of so many people overloads facilities for public transportation, housing, health, recreation and schooling, creating grave problems of pollution and congestion, to such an extent that the modern metropolis has been described as ungovernable.

As former patterns of behavior and life change radically, the accretion of such large human settlements presents social and educational problems of the first magnitude. Understanding of the new environment does not keep pace with the growth of either the metropolises, or their attendant problems.   The field of metropolitan studies is in its infancy.   In particular, how the phenomena of metropolitanism are related to the form and function of education remains especially obscure.

Much of the specifically educational writing about the metropolis is pragmatic.   It emanates from concern with a current issue, such as racial integration, curriculum improvement, and administration and control of schools.   It is concerned with coping with pressing emergencies.   Prescriptions and normative descriptions prevail while an analytical, comprehensive view of the metropolis and metropolitan education is largely lacking.

Education in the Metropolis

If, as Plutarch said, the City is the teacher of man, then the modern metropolis can be regarded as the total learning environment. The child who grows up in the metropolis is educated in ways and content that are unique in human history and, certainly, not by virtue of his formal school experience alone. The metropolitan phenomenon constitutes a set of unprecedented conditions, generating a process of socialization that distinguishes metropolitan Man from all others.

There is a danger, of course, in asserting that metropolitan education is simply a function of growing up in the large city. Like the philosopher who states that all of life is education, we may be using a definition so comprehensive that it is useless. Similarly, there is danger in emphasizing the novel aspects of metropolitanism, for the historically-based recurrent aspects of the human condition may thereby be obscured. Nonetheless, the impact of this setting upon the people, young and old, who inhabit it, is so strong and so evident, that we feel justified in speaking of a "total metropolitan educational environment."

This environment contains, first, institutions entrusted with the formal task of daily instruction, primarily schools, colleges, and universities. To these is added a variety of school-system sponsored activities, both formal and informal. Next there are the activities of myriad non-school agencies: churches, philanthropic societies, youth organizations and interest groups concerned with conveying messages and skills of many kinds to the young and adult populations.

The cultural facilities of the metropolis, libraries, museums, theaters, concert halls, also fulfill educational functions. And there are other locales, too, which enrich the metropolitan educational environment; the park, the playground, the apartment house or street block, the corner candy store, all are educational settings, as is the very physical environment which strikes the senses and shapes the sensibilities of the city-dweller. And finally, there are the media through which information and ideas are disseminated: words, visual and oral, and pictures, in books and periodicals, on radio and television, in cinemas and posters – all are part of the total educational environment of the metropolis.

One important theme of recent research has been, what type of institution and operation is most appropriate to the metropolitan situation? The modus operandi of our schooling, it has been argued, is a function of a former social system (rural, stable, characterized by little geographical or social mobility, for example); it still operates as if former conditions persisted. Thus, it is argued, contemporary problems arise from the persistence of the traditional model in a technological, mobile metropolis.

How to remedy the disjunction between schooling and the metropolitan environment is an urgent matter. In New York City, for example, innumerable proposals and experiments have addressed themselves to the problems of the big city school system. They have been directed at administrative reorganization in order to change the basis of policy and decision making and the day-to-day direction of the schools, new ways of selecting and preparing teachers and ancillary personnel, and a reappraisal of traditional instructional methods and curriculum practices. All of these are the schools' responses to characteristic conditions of New York: urban congestion, the flight to the suburbs that produces inner city blight, ghettoization, civil disorder, rising costs, wide-spread poverty and limited economic opportunity within the inner city aggravated by racial hostility. All testify to the growing inability of the city's agencies to cope with the maintenance, let alone the improvement, of basic services such as welfare (including education), communications and police. The story is the same wherever there is comparable growth: metropolitanization produces pressures to which the educational system is forced to respond. If then the metropolitan setting and style of life are increasingly characteristic, if the quality of education is at once a factor of this trend and affected by it, then education must be seen as part of the web of interrelationships linking the social, political and economic factors in the metropolis.

Not only have other metropolitan centers in the United States been faced with similar pressures and issues, but so too have metropolitan centers in other parts of the world. London, notably, has reorganized its administrative structure and is grappling with problems raised by characteristic features of the metropolitan setting: population density, growth in the size of the school system, and racial and socio-economic heterogeneity, polarized into homogeneous neighborhoods. Clearly the experience of big cities in general and their school systems may provide guidance for any particular city to help clarify its problems, suggest alternatives and project possible outcomes of specific measures. Thus, the comparative dimension offers great potential. Strangely enough, any systematic comparisons which would make such help available do not yet appear to exist. Planners, whether in education or in other area, who draw attention to foreign examples may provoke interest, but are hard put to persuade their clients that a foreign example has any relevance to their own situation. Yet the big cities of the world do in fact provide a species of laboratory for the researcher. Systematic comparison should reveal the common dimensions and problems of metropolitanization, the alternative responses to these developments, and also some evidences as to their outcomes.

The Present Study: Scope and Rationale

Comparative education has for a long time been characterized by descriptive, mainly historical accounts and normative studies of education and other national institutions. They have provided disappointingly little help either for the researcher in understanding the dynamics of the system he wishes to explain, or for the educational policy maker who wishes to improve on what exists. One reason for this, we submit, is that the units for comparison have usually been entire nation states, thus obscuring important differences within countries.

In an attempt to use some sub-national units, this study considers selected elements of the educational systems of four large cities: Amsterdam, London, Paris, and New York. London and Paris are the capital cities of their nations: Amsterdam and New York are not. But all four are old-established centers of commerce, communications and political power, and each contains its country's largest concentration of population. All are, of course, examples of Western civilization and any conclusions we reach on the basis of our investigation will be correspondingly limited.

Ideally, our working definition of metropolis would be a large population concentration, comprising both city proper and its suburban extensions. Though we are interested in the functional whole, a cultural rather than a geographical area, in fact we are limited by existing definitions, largely administrative, for these are the categories in which the data for this study have been collected. London has revised its traditional and outdated administrative boundaries, and has moved to a regional framework; Paris is moving in this direction; New York and Amsterdam have so far not done so. Consequently, we have been forced to make do with what exists: the Inner London Educational Authority and Greater London; the Académie de Paris and the Department of the Seine; Amsterdam; and New York City.

We have elected to study two facets of metropolitan school systems located in four metropolises: the characteristics of teachers and the patterns of perceived success of the respective school systems. We hypothesize that in both respects, the four cities not only differ from the norms of their respective national settings, but they differ in the same direction from nation to nation. We predict that both metropolitan teachers and what we have termed the perceived success of their school systems are marked by features peculiar to the metropolitan setting: its heterogeneity, mobility, concentration of expertise, and so on. In Chapters 3 and 4, these expectations, their rationales, data and analyses are presented and discussed.

The purpose of this study is, however, not limited merely to identifying similarities and differences within and across countries. We try to extend it to explanations of what we find, by considering why certain differences between metropolitan and national norms are less marked in some countries than in others, and why, the differences are sometimes in unexpected directions, or inconsistent.

NOTE

* Excerpt from Max A. Eckstein and Harold J. Noah, *Metropolitanism and Education: Teachers and Schools in Amsterdam, London, Paris and New York.* New York, N.Y.: The Institute of Philosophy and Politics of Education, Teachers College, Columbia University, 1973: 1-3 [Occasional Paper No.1].

15

Teachers and School Success in Amsterdam, London, Paris, and New York*

This investigation is a first step toward comparative, systematic study of education in metropolitan areas. Four large cities (Amsterdam, London, Paris, and New York City) were selected and data were assembled on the characteristics of teachers and on the perceived success of school systems, in both the metropolises themselves and in their respective nations.

The Characteristics of Teachers

One of the basic propositions tested in this study is that there is a metropolitan type that transcends the particular nation in which large cities develop. With respect to teachers, this translates into the generalization that teachers in a large city in a given country resemble teachers in large cities in other countries more than they resemble non-metropolitan teachers in their own land. Specifically, we hypothesize that teachers in large cities are very much alike and that they differ from their respective national norms in similar ways.

The teacher variables considered here fall into three groups: basic vital characteristics (such as age and sex); educational characteristics (such as levels of formal education, professional training); and professional characteristics (such as job mobility and membership in professional organizations).

It is predicted that, compared to their national counterparts outside the big city, metropolitan teachers are younger, more mobile, and more likely to be male. Furthermore, it is believed that they will be found to be better educated, though not necessarily in the formal/professional sense, and more likely to move out of teaching into some other career after a period of time. In this sense, therefore, they might be described as less professionally committed. However, being younger, more mobile, probably having a higher proportion of males than the national teacher cadre, they might well be more open to change not only in their personal careers but also in their teaching lives (with respect to changing posts and to being involved in educational innovations).

The rationale for this expected profile of the large-city teacher is fairly clear. It is drawn from the larger picture of life in the metropolis, one of relatively high rates of geographical and economic mobility, especially among those beginning their professional careers, and of higher pay levels and more opportunities for advancement in the nation at large.

Table 15.1 presents data on the characteristics of teachers for the four cities and the four nations on a series of selected indicators.

Table 15.2 presents a series of indexes, based on these data, which permit comparison among cities. Indexes were obtained in the following manner. For each indicator, the national figure was equated with 100. The corresponding figure for the metropolis was then expressed as an index with the national average used as the base, i.e., metropolitan values were expressed as percentages of national values on each indicator. Inspection of the metropolitan indexes then makes possible some statements about the direction and extent of deviations by metropolitan teachers from their respective national norms and comparison of the indexes across nations.

The results of the analyses in Table 15.2 make possible the following generalizations. Teacher cadres of metropolises differ from their respective national norms in the following ways: they include a larger proportion of younger teachers and a smaller proportion of older teachers; they contain a higher percentage of women; they tend to be better qualified academically and, while containing a larger proportion of teachers with superior credentials, have a smaller proportion without full qualifications; they contain a larger proportion of teachers with limited experience, this being consistent with the data on age; they are less prone to belong to professional organizations; they are likely to devote less time to preparing for classes (though this is not true of time spent marking classwork); they are less likely to read professional journals regularly (though more likely to have attended a professional conference during the past year); and they include a larger proportion of part-time teachers.

We have not been able to assemble evidence that would enable us to test the propositions that, compared with their colleagues elsewhere, teachers in the metropolises exhibit a higher rate of mobility out of teaching to other occupations; that they are more innovative in their teaching; or, that they are more varied in their social origins.

The generalizations that we can make do not, of course, apply in every single case, nor, where the data tend to point in the same direction, are the differences always of the same extent. On age, Paris is an exception to the generalization made above, with a lower proportion of young teachers than the national norm (but still with a slightly lower proportion of older teachers, too). This fact is easily explained by reference to the professional reward and promotion system in France and by the general preeminence of Paris secondary schools in the French educational system. The teacher cadres of Amsterdam and New York stand out as especially youthful. The data on teaching experience are, as might be expected, consistent with those on age.

We had hypothesized that the metropolitan teacher cadres are more masculine than the national norms. We find, on the contrary, that with the exception of New York, they are not. Instead they are more feminized, with the extent differing very markedly from country to country.

One explanation for the fact that females form a smaller proportion of teachers in New York City than in the United States as a whole might be that women have more employment opportunities other than in teaching in New York than elsewhere. However, since this is probably true for the other major cities in this study, that explanation is not sufficient. A more sturdy explanation might refer to the relatively high salaries, the high proportion of administrative positions (relative to classroom positions), and the extensive opportunities for additional part-time employment, that might make a career in teaching in New York more attractive for males than is usual in the United States. In any event, it should be noted that the United States has the most feminized teacher corps of the four nations and that the present trend is toward an increase in the proportion of male teachers.

In general, the data on teacher experience and qualifications do support the expectation that metropolitan teachers are a somewhat more variegated group than their national counterparts. Amsterdam stands out as having the greatest contrast between metropolitan and national standards and Paris stands out with the least. While the latter is clearly explicable by the nation-wide standardization and direction of education, the reason for Amsterdam's striking departure from national norms is not so apparent. The answer may well lie in the greater opportunities for secondary and higher education offered by Amsterdam compared with the rest of the country.

The data on teacher mobility show mixed results, with London and New York having a slightly larger proportion of teachers with relatively less staying power than the national averages, and Paris and Amsterdam both having a smaller group of teachers with five years or less experience in their current schools than is average for the nation. If it can be assumed that younger teachers tend to be more mobile, these data on turnover are consistent with the data on age and experience for London, Paris, and New York.

On the variable "professionalism," metropolitan teachers tend to be below national norms according to the indicators used here. While these data are not cross-nationally complete or reliable, there is a widespread impression that metropolitan teachers are more likely to hold additional part-time employment, though whether this is moonlighting in teaching or in other occupations is not established.

Does the lower level of professionalism of metropolitan teachers occur in spite of, or because of, their relatively higher levels of qualifications? Is it that metropolitan teachers simply do not need to read so many professional journals, belong to professional organizations, and devote so much time to preparation as do their less qualified colleagues in the provinces? Or, is it that their environment places more pressure on their time and provides greater opportunities for other activities, including extra employment or preparation for different careers? These questions, unanswerable without further data and analyses, relate to the interplay between metropolitan environmental conditions and the particular characteristics of its teacher cadres. However, another set of questions points to the possible relationship between these characteristics of teachers and the extent to which metropolitan school systems are successful according to the several criteria conventionally used. It is to that dimension that we now turn.

The Perceived Success of School Systems

Success is a highly debatable term in education. And, much of the argument about school issues derives from differences in unexpressed definition of the word "success," which may very well obscure fundamental differences in values. In this study, we attempt no refinements at the philosophical level and no more justification at the operational level than to say that the indicators of success used have been chosen to cover several dimensions of the term, and are conventionally put forward by school systems and discussed by teachers and parents as important and relevant criteria. It is for these reasons that we use the qualification "perceived," to emphasize the relative nature of the word "success" and to avoid any hint of absoluteness in the operational definitions referred to in this study.

All school systems are concerned with the achievements of their pupils and measure these from time to time by means of examinations or tests in particular subjects of the curriculum at various levels. In addition to the regional and national assessments within countries, we have been able also to obtain achievement scores in science and native language from the I.E.A. Project.[1]

While the achievement of pupils is one important measure, a series of additional indicators is conventionally used as a criterion of institutional or system success. This includes such items as average class size (or teacher/pupil ratio); the system's ability to retain pupils beyond the age of compulsory schooling and to usher them on to more than minimal qualifications (retentivity); and the degree to which the system has developed special facilities for those pupils who are not within the normal range of competencies (facilities for special education).

These by no means exhaust the possibilities for data collection on measures of success. In particular, we would have liked to assemble evidence of the extent of satisfaction or dissatisfaction with the school system expressed by teachers, pupils, parents, and other public voices. The kind and extent of criticism leveled at school operations, attempts to disrupt schooling by strikes and demonstrations, and even the amount of vandalism against school property are all likely to be indicative. However, the difficulties in obtaining documented evidence of a comparable nature for both metropolis and nation are especially acute here. Impressions, of course, abound, and are cited here and there in this study. But in the absence of hard, comparable data, we have been forced to limit severely the indicators of perceived success used in the analysis.

It is hypothesized that the achievement of metropolitan pupils differs from national norms by being, on the average, higher, more diversified (having a larger spread) and, in particular, by having a larger proportion of high achievers; that metropolitan school systems show more pupils per teacher, more facilities for special groups, and greater retentivity. Finally, we can consider as a mark of dissatisfaction with the public schools the extent to which parents seek alternative arrangements for their children in private and parochial schools, and hypothesize that in the metropolis parents will be more likely to choose non-public school alternatives.

The rationale for these expectations is drawn from our general profile of big city populations and structures. Metropolitan pupils, we assume, are more heterogeneous than those in the rest of the nation, as are the teachers, whether by socioeconomic origin, ethnic, or religious affiliation, or other dimensions of life style. They will represent a more diversified set of behaviors, attitudes, and aspirations which might be expected to reveal themselves in more diversified levels of achievement in school. But, because of the concentration of wealth and high-level schools, we would also expect to find in the metropolises a relatively larger concentration of high achievers. Not only will pupils and teachers represent a more diversified group, but so also will parents, whose educational aspirations for their children will be more varied than those of the nation as a whole.

Population size and higher density are expected to yield two results: more pupils per teacher (or more overcrowded classrooms) and more developed facilities for special educational provisions. Finally, school systems in large cities might be expected to have greater powers of retaining students beyond compulsory schooling for several reasons. The array of opportunities is larger; horizons and aspirations of students broader and higher; occupational vistas are more numerous and more likely to require higher educational qualifications than in locations outside the metropolis.

Tables 15.3a through 15.3d present the quantified data on selected indicators for each city and nation, while Table 15.4 presents indexes based on the data which permit comparison of the direction and extent of divergence of each city from its national norms.

The results of the analyses in Table 15.4 permit the following generalizations: school achievement of students in the four metropolises tends to be higher than the national average on some measures and lower on others; school retentivity is usually higher in the metropolis; the big-city school system is more highly developed in the sense of providing more special facilities for special groups outside the normal range of primary/secondary schooling; and these school systems have more pupils per teacher and more overcrowded classrooms. We hasten to add, however, that although these generalizations are permitted by the comparative analyses, the data are not always complete or consistent. The picture is mixed, with enough variability to require careful scrutiny of each indicator and each city.

For Paris and Amsterdam, all the indicators of achievement show means higher than the national, except for science in Paris. For London and New York, the achievement norms are mixed: the IEA results also show that pupils in the metropolises do rather better than those in the nation at large, New York being marginally better and London markedly so. But in the basic skill areas, especially reading, both cities fall below the national norms. In achievement at the higher level leading to continued full-time education beyond the secondary level, Paris and Amsterdam are above the national norms, New York is below, and London the same or slightly below. However, other evidence from England suggests that the comparison of metropolitan and national means probably obscures very different distributions of patterns of success in achievement, with a pattern approximating a normal distribution nationally and a tendency toward a bimodal distribution, with high proportions of both high and low levels of achievement in London. This phenomenon, we suspect, is not limited to London alone, it may well be a general metropolitan phenomenon and would explain some of the inconsistencies among indicators of success, especially for achievement and retentivity.

Rates of staying on at school beyond compulsory schooling are, on the whole, consistent with rates of continuing on to higher education, except in the case of London. In Paris and Amsterdam, as in the case of achievement, retentivity is above the national norms, while in New York retentivity is below. However, in London, retentivity is higher while rates of continuing to university or other full-time education after schooling are lower.

In each country, the metropolis tends to have developed a more elaborate system to accommodate those pupils outside the normal range of the primary/secondary schools. The ratio of pre-school and special education pupils to primary pupils is higher in the metropolis compared with the respective national norms, sometimes extremely so (one exception: Amsterdam, pre-schooling). As to the last dimension of system development, the finding that classes in the city are larger should be considered more as a function of the factor of population density, than of deliberate choice. Rural classes and the number of pupils per teachers, we assume, are smaller simply because pupils and schools are more dispersed

Attention must now be given to the relative size of the private sectors of schooling in nation and city. In London and New York, metropolitan parents are considerably more likely to select an alternative to the public school system for their children than is the norm nationally, while in Paris the reverse is true. We cannot include Amsterdam in this comparison because the familiar distinctions between Church and State schooling simply do not obtain. Even for England, France, and the United States, policies and practices in this matter differ in each case. The distinctions, furthermore, may be denominational, or on the basis of social class, or a combination of both. However, if in these last three instances, schooling is considered simply as the alternative to the public school system and as an option used by parents according to their degree of satisfaction/dissatisfaction with the public schools, then we could assert that, on this measure, schools in Paris are more successful and those in New York and London less successful than their respective national norms in satisfying the preferences of parents.

Finally, in reviewing all the indicators of perceived success discussed here, and notwithstanding the mixed results, it is possible to discriminate among the four cities. Relative to their respective national norms, New York rates low on most measures, London high on some but low on others, Paris and, on the whole, Amsterdam, too, rate high. If we rank the four cities in descending order of perceived success of the school system relative to their national norms, then, the final order appears to be: 1. Paris; 2. Amsterdam; 3. London; and 4. New York.

Relating Teacher Characteristics and School Success

We do appear to have generated considerable evidence to support one central and two subsidiary propositions. The first is that there are certain definable and measurable characteristics of teachers and schools in metropolitan areas that differentiate them systematically from their respective national norms. The secondary propositions are that the metropolitan/national differences run mostly in the same direction in the four countries examined and differences in degree of contrast (and sometimes in direction) can usually be ascribed without difficulty to certain identifiable characteristics of the national educational system.

Specifically, we have found that in the four countries examined, the teacher cadre of the metropolis differs from that of the nation as a whole by containing a larger proportion of younger teachers and a smaller proportion of older teachers; by having higher educational and training qualifications on the average and also a smaller proportion without full qualifications; and by being less professionally committed. In these respects our findings support our initially stated hypotheses. However, in one important respect our initial hypothesis is not confirmed: metropolitan teachers are not more likely to be male than teachers elsewhere in the nation. Only in New York city is this so. Moreover this result is found in spite of the fact that the school systems of the metropolises tend to contain a larger proportion of secondary school teachers (who tend to be male) and a smaller proportion of primary school teachers (who tend to be female). We find it difficult at this point to suggest why this is so.

With respect to the perceived success of the metropolitan school system, relative to that of the nation as a whole, once again our initial hypotheses are largely supported by our findings, though we would wish to emphasize that we are far removed indeed from providing firm confirmation. There is some weak evidence that school achievement levels in the metropolis are higher than elsewhere (except in New York) and that the distribution of metropolitan achievement scores perhaps tends to be bimodal to a greater extent than in non-metropolitan areas. Certainly, the special facilities of metropolitan areas are greater and the retentivity of their schools higher; but their teacher/pupil ratios are less favorable and parents in metropolises are more likely than other parents to select a non-public school alternative for their children.

Let us now attempt to associate the relative characteristics of metropolitan teachers with the relative perceived success of metropolitan school systems. Table 15.5 ranges the four metropolises from left to right in descending order of relative perceived school success, based upon summary of the comparative indexes given in Table 15.4. That is, the Paris school system *relative to France* is first, because it is perceived to be more successful than any of the other three; New York's school system *relative to the U.S.* is perceived as being less successful than any of the other three, and is listed last. Amsterdam ranks in second place, London is third.

In the body of the table the metropolises are ranked on 17 aspects of teacher characteristics (based on comparative indexes in Table 15.2). A high rank indicates a high value for the metropolis in question *relative to its national norm*, and not necessarily a high value in absolute terms (though this is not, of course, excluded). Thus, in the first line, the ranks indicate that New York has the highest proportion of young teachers *relative to the U.S.* norm, and Paris the smallest *relative to the French* norm.

Looking down the column for Paris, it is noteworthy that Paris, the city with the highest relative success ranking, has not only the smallest relative proportion of young teachers and the highest of older teachers, but also the lowest proportion lacking full qualifications, the highest with high qualifications, readership of journals about teaching and attendance at educational conferences. At the same time, Paris has the highest relative proportion with a degree and the lowest with over four years of full-time post-secondary education.

The composite picture that is thus conveyed is of a teaching force that, relative to France as a whole, is older, more female, more qualified by education and training, more stable and more professionally committed than are London's teachers relative to England and Wales, Amsterdam's relative to the Netherlands, and New York's relative to the U.S. Especially in the case of New York, there is an impression of a relatively very young, male, highly unionized, professionally uncommitted and mobile teaching cadre, with education and training qualifications not much different from those of teachers in the U.S. as a whole.

Amsterdam also has a large number of extreme ranks, but no clear pattern of variables emerges. London, too, demonstrates no clear pattern, with few extreme ranks. None of the immediately preceding analysis is meant to imply that the relative superiority of Paris teachers' characteristics is *causally* related to the perceived success of the Paris school system. This can be by no means demonstrated with the evidence we supply. Instead, though, we would suggest an *associative* relationship: a teaching cadre in Paris that looks relatively "old-fashioned" is associated with a school system that is perceived to be relatively highly successful.

That this is so is probably due to antecedent factors common to both sets of observed phenomena: such factors as rates of demographic and social change, the pace of educational reform, system size, adequacy of financing metropolitan enterprises in general and education in particular, and the prestige attached to metropolitan institutions.

What is peculiar to the metropolis and what distinguishes this type of human organization from others is its educational function. It is in this role that the metropolis appears to be unique. It is at once the progenitor, importer and exporter of culture, a powerful agency of education in its national and international contexts. People, ideas, and skills are attracted to the large city. In the metropolitan setting, their ideologies and technologies are generated, institutionalized and disseminated. The metropolis is itself the means for routing people and knowledge, defining and sorting them for the nation and for the world. The goods handled by this distribution system are ideas, skills and values; the operation is, therefore, centrally an educational one.

Ideally, then, we would want to shed some direct light not only on the schools and other institutions of formal education, but also upon the educational roles and function of the entire metropolitan environment – its streets, stores, jobs, museums, art galleries, presses and broadcasting studios. In this exploratory study, we have been unable to do this, and we have instead concentrated on a number of selected aspects of the formal school system. Obviously there, too, we have only scratched the surface of the range of topics awaiting attention. However, our particular purpose has been achieved: to test the propositions that cross-cultural study of like sub-national units can be done, and that it is, at least potentially, interesting and illuminating.

Table 15.1
Characteristics of Teachers: Intra- and International Comparisons

	AMST.	NETH.	LOND.	E&W.	PARIS	FRANCE	N.Y.	USA.
Age								
% under 30 yrs*	45.0		42.0			36.8	65.0	33.9
% under 27 yrs*	33.0	18.8	42.0	32.7	14.0	18.8	43.1	34.4
% over 48 yrs*	11.0	26.2	12.0	18.5	22.0	24.5	12.0	17.5
Sex								
% females	60.8	38.8	63.0	57.0	54.8	50.3	59.2	67.3
Qualifications								
% lacking full qualification for post	11.0		18.3	12.3	22.3	26.0	4.7	4.9
% possessing high academic qualifications	57.6		28.6	22.2	77.7	74.0	4.7	30.3
% specialists with no university degree	22.0	86.5	25.0	51.2	14.0	7.3	0.0	0.0
% with over 4 yrs. post-sec. Full-time education	89.0	35.7	13.0	9.0	56.0	54.5	94.0	83.5
Experience								
% with 3 yrs. or less						24.2	39.0	21.0
% with 5 yrs. or less	56.0	21.7	42.0	36.3	29.0	32.3	59.0	38.0
Turnover								
% of teaching force leaving p.a.	25.0		13.3	10.6			14.3	19.5
% less than 5 yrs. in current school	22.0	54.3	72.0	64.5	41.0	54.1	76.0	59.9

Professionalism

% working for supplementary income	25.0		29.0	23.0				20.0
% who are members of largest union			97.0	80.0			25.0	59.9
% who are members of gen. Teaching assoc.	56.0	74.6	73.0	81.6	67.0	74.6	76.0	77.3
% who are members of subj. matter teaching assoc.	56.0	27.5	12.0	28.6	43.0	54.5	56.0	48.1
% spending less than 3 hrs./wk:								
preparing lessons	22.0	27.1	33.0	24.9	4.0	1.9	26.0	7.0
marking	0.0	13.6	30.	21.3	4.0	3.8	15.0	14.0
% who regularly read journals:								
about teaching	33.0	49.3	28.0	44.6	29.0	27.8	35.0	50.7
about subject	78.0	57.5	48.0	49.4	61.0	63.7	56.0	58.4
% attendance at ed. conf. in past year	56.0	53.6	56.0	50.5	70.0	42.5	44.0	61.4
% of teachers teaching full-time	44.0	83.5	67.0	92.3	81.0	89.3	93.0	91.7
% of teachers not teaching full-time			14.6	5.5				

*Data for these indicators were usually derived from different sources. This explains the apparent contradiction in, for example, the N.Y./U.S.A. data (where there appear to be more teachers under 27 than under 30 years).

Sources:

Amsterdam and the Netherlands
Bureau van Statistiek der Gemeente Amsterdam, *Statistiek van het Onderwijs te Amsterdam (1968/'69, Deel I).* Amsterdam 1970.
Jahrbock 1970. Amsterdam. Bureau van Statistiek, 1970.
Planning and Development in the Netherlands, Vol. III, No. 1/2.1969.
Council of Europe, *School Systems: a Guide.* Strasbourg, 1965.
Central Bureau voor de Statistiek, *Statistiek van het VWO, HAVO en MAVO 1968/69.* 's-Gravenhage, 1970.
Materials supplied by personnel of City School System, Amsterdam.

London and England/Wales
Greater London Council, *1968: Annual Abstract of Greater London Statistics.* London, 1969.
Department of Education and Science, *Statistics of Education.* Vol.1: Schools (1968); Vol.4: Teachers (1968); Vol.1: Schools (1969). London, 1969, 1970.
Materials provided by Dr. A. Little, Director, Research and Statistics Group and additional personnel of I.L.E.A.

Paris and France
Ministère de l'Education Nationale, *Statistiques des Enseignements (1968-69).* Nos. 3.1; 3.2; 3.3. Paris, 1969.
Ministère de l'Education Nationale, *Tableaux Statistiques 1969-70.* Paris, 1970.

(Mimeo. doc. no. 3870)
Ministère de l'Education Nationale, *Etudes et Documents No.19.* Paris, 1971.

New York and the United States
National Education Association, Research Division, *The American Public-School Teacher,* 1965-66. Washington, D.C., 1967
New York State Division of the Budget, *Statistical Yearbook 1970.* Albany, 1970.
University of the State of New York, State Education Department, *Annual Educational Summary 1968-69.* Albany, 1969.
New York City Public Schools, *Facts and Figures 1969-1970.* New York, 1970.
Materials supplied by Division of Teacher Education, City University of New York and Central Board of Education, New York City.

Table 15.2
Characteristics of Teachers: Comparative Indexes

INDEXES	AMST.	LONDON	PARIS	N.Y.
(rate for nation is always 100)				
Age				
under 30	-	130	-	127
under 27	176	128	74	189
over 48	42	65	90	69
Sex				
female	157	111	109	88
Qualifications				
lacking full qualifications	-	149	86	96
possessing qualifications	-	129	105	115
with no univ. degree	25	49	192	-
with over 4 yrs. full time post-secondary education	249	144	103	113
Experience				
with 3 yrs or less	-	-	-	186
with 5 yrs or less	258	116	90	155
Turnover				
leaving teaching p.a.	-	125	-	73
with 5 yrs. or less in current school	41	112	76	127
Professionalism				
working for supplementary income	-	126	-	-
membership of largest inion	-	121	-	42
membership of general teaching association	75	89	90	98
membership of subject matter association	204	42	79	116
less than 3 hrs. per week for preparation	81	133	211	371
less than 3 hrs. per week for grading	-	141	105	107
regular reading of journals about teaching	67	63	104	69
regular reading of journals about subject	136	97	96	96
attendance at educational conference in past year	104	111	165	72
teachers teaching full-time	53	73	91	101
teachers not teaching full-time	-	265	-	-

Table 15.3a
Patterns of School Success: Intra-National Comparisons

		Amst.	Neth.
Achievement			
% of elem. student who fail (1968)	Public	5.0	-
	Denom.	4.9	-
Science achievement means*		26.0	17.8
Reading comprehension means*		34.3	25.2
Reyentivity			
% of 15 yr. olds in school 1968/69		84.1	77 ⎤
% of 16 yr. olds in school 1968/69		64.1	58 ⎬ 1969
% of 15 yr. olds in school 1968/69		45.5	39.4 ⎦
System Development			
Average class size, elementary	Public	31.4	-
	Denom.	29.3	-
	Total	30.4	-
		1:23.8	1:29
Teacher/pupil ratio			
Ratio of primary pupils (Index 100)			
to pre-school		28.9	34
to special ed.		6.3	4.9

Sources:

*IEA data
Bureau van Statistiek der Gemeente Amsterdam, *Jaarboek 1970.* Amsterdam, 1970. Pp. 264-5, 272.
Bureau van Statistiek der Gemeente Amsterdam, *Statistische Mededelingen No. 170: Statistiek van het Onderwijs te Amsterdam 1968/69.* Amsterdam, 1970. Pp. 28, 30.
Gemeente Amsterdam, *Statistische Mededelingen van de Afdeling Onderwijs No. 74: Openbaar Onderwijs Staat der Schoolbevolking.* Amsterdam, 1970.
Central Bureau of Statistics, *Statistical Yearbook of the Netherlands 1971.* The Hague, 1971. P. 82.
Council of Europe, *School Systems: A Guide: The Netherlands.* Strasbourg, 1965. Pp. 28-29.

Table 15.3b
Patterns of School Success: Intra-National Comparisons

		Lond	E & W.
Achievement			
% of pupils who are good readers (1967)		10	16.7
% of pupils who are poor readers (1967)		17	8.6
% of school leavers bound for university	B	6	6
	G	2	3
for Col. of Ed.	B	1	1
	G	4	5
for other full-time ed.	B	4	8
	G	5	11
Science achievement means*		26.8	21.3
Reading comprehension means*		32.4	25.3
Literature achievement means*		22.5	16.1
Retentivity			
% of leavers leaving at 14 yrs. (all			
maintained schools 1997/97)	B	33	46
	G	32	47
Pupils aged 16 as % of those aged 13			
3 yrs. previously		36.3	30.2
Pupils aged 17 as % of those aged 13			
4 yrs. previously		17.5	16.1
System Development			
% of all pupils in private schooling		6.4	4.7
Av. Teacher/pupil ratio – primary		26.2	27.8
– secondary		15.9	15.9
Ratio of primary pupils (Index 100)			
to pre-school (2-4 yrs.)		7.4	5.0
to special ed.		4.4	1.5

Sources:

*IEA data
Department of Education and Science, *Statistics of Education 1969: Vol. 1, Schools.* London, 1970 Pp. 2, 8, 23, 27, 100-101, 142.
Department of Education and Science, *Statistics of Education 1968: Vol. 4, Teachers.* London, 1970.
Central Statistical Office, *Social Trends. No.* 1, 1970. London, 1970. Pp. 126, 128-131.
Greater London Council, *1968: Annual Abstract of Greater London Statistics.* Vol. 3, London, 1969. Pp. 132-133, 136, 139-143.
Data supplied by officials of I.L.E.A.
Inner London Education Authority Statistics Group. *School Leavers.* London (n.d., mimeo.). Pp. 3-6, 9-26.
Inner London Education Authority, *Literacy Survey: Summary of Interim Results of the Study of Pupils' Reading Standards.* London (n.d., mimeo.).
Department of Education and Science, *Reports on Education.* Dec. 1970, No. 67.

Table 15.3c
Patterns of School Success: Intra-National Comparisons

		Paris	France
Achievement			
% receiving graduating diplomas at end of 2nd cycle long (1969)	Académie	20.7	17.8
	Ville	91.2	85.9
% of candidates passing baccalaureat (1967-68)	Académie	90.6	
Mean scores in 3rd class			
verbal aptitude	Ville	34.06	30.75
Numerical apt.		18.49	18.21
Spatial		27.77	24.92
Science achievement means*		17.0	18.3
Retentivity			
% scolarization in 1st cycle (public and private)	Académie	75.3	72.4
% scolarization in 2nd cycle (public and private)	Académie	44.5	34.6
System Development			
% of all pupils in private ed. in all 1st cycle		15.4	20.0
Average class size (primary)		29.0	26.3
% overcrowded classes (35 pupils or more, primary)		10.0	6.4
Ratio of primary pupils			
(Index 100) to pre-school	Ville	52.8	38.8
to special ed.	Ville	8.6	3.6

Sources:

*IEA data
Ministère de l'Education Nationale, Service Central des Statistiques et Sondages, *Indicateurs Relatifs aux Disparités Regionales 1968/9 en Matière d'enseignement du Second Degré.* Paris, 1971 (Doc. No. 3932).
Ministère de l'Education Nationale, *Statistiques des Enseignements 1968-69.* Paris, 1970. Vols, 2, No. 1; 4, 1; 6, 2.
Materials supplied by Mlle, Bacher, Institut National d'Etudes du Travail et d'Orientation Professionelle, and by officials of the central statistical services.

Table 15.3d
Patterns of School Success: Intra-National Comparisons

	N.Y.	*U.S.*
Pupil Achievement		
Performance on standardized achievement test, expressed as grade equivalents:		
4th grade reading	4.6	4.7
study skills	4.2	4.7
math skills	4.3	4.7
8th grade reading	7.8	8.5
study skills	7.9	8.5
math skills	7.3	8.5
Science achievement means*	22.8	21.5
Reading comprehension means*	27.8	27.3
Literature means*	17.7	16.5
Retentivity		
H.S. graduates as % of 9th graders 4 yrs Previously	65	71.6
System Success		
% of all pupils in private schools	27.9	13.8
Teacher/pupil ration (elem.)	23.4 or 28.0	24.8
Ratio of elem. pupils (Index 100)		
to pre-school pupils	19.6	9.2
to special education pupils	17.4	7.3

Sources:

*IEA Data.
New York State Division of the Budget, *New York State Statistical Yearbook 1970.* Albany, N.Y., 1970. Pp. 201-204, 212.
United States Bureau of the Census, *Statistical Abstract of the United States.* Washington, D.C., 1970.Pp.105,113,115,122,125.
New York Dept. of City Planning, *Plan for 1969: A Proposal Vol. 1: Critical Issues.* New York City, 1969.Pp.99,104.
New York City Public Schools, *Facts and Figures 1969-70.* New York, 1970. Pp. 58, 59, 61, 66, 75
New York State Dept. of Education, *Annual Education Summary, 1968-69.* Albany, N.Y. 1969, P.11.
Material provided by officials of New York Central Board of Education.
City School District of the City of New York, *Summary of City-wide Reading Test Results for 1969-70.* New York, 1970 (mimeo.). Pp. 2, 3, 13.
Board of Education of the City of New York, *Analysis of City-Funded per Capita Costs and Staff Ratiosfor 1969-70.* New York, (n.d., mimeo.). Pp. 1, 2.
Board of Education of the City of New York, *Community District Profiles for 1969-70 School Year by Newly Aligned Community School Districts.* New York, (mimeo.). Pp. 1, 2.

Table 15.4
Patterns of School Success: Comparative Indexes

	AMSTERDAM	LONDON	PARIS	NEW YORK
ACHIEVEMENT		Good readers 60	Graduating,	*4th Grade*
		Poor readers 198	2nd cycle 116	Reading 98
				Study skills 89
		Destination of	Baccalaureat 106	Math skills 91
		Leavers:	105	
				8th Grade
		Univ. B 100	*3rd class*	Reading 92
		G 67	verbal apt. 111	Study skills 93
		Col of Ed B 100	num. Apt. 102	Math skills 86
		G 80	spatial 111	
		Other		
		FT Ed B 50		
		G 46		
IEA Science	146	126	93	106
Reading Comp.	136	128	-	102
Literature	-	140	-	107
RETENTIVITY	15 yrs. in	Leavers B 72	1st Cycle 104	H.S. Grades
	school 109	at 15 G 68	2nd Cycle 129	91
	16 yrs. 111	Stayers		
		at 16 120		
	17 yrs. 115	at 17 109		
SYSTEM	T/P Ratio 82	T/P Ratios:	Av. Class	T/P Ratio 94
DEVELOPMENT		prim. 94	size 110	or 112
		sec. 100	% over-	
			crowded 151	
Pre-school/primary	85	148	(Ville de	213
			Paris) 136	
			(Académie) 117	
Special ed./prim.	129	293	(Ville de	238
			Paris) 238	
			(Académie) 125	
Rel. of private	–	136	77	202
to public schooling				

Table 15.5
Rankings of Metropolises: Characteristics of Teachers Relative to Their National Norms

| | *Rankings on Relative School Success* | | | |
	1st *PARIS*	*2nd* *AMSTERDAM*	*3rd* *LONDON*	*4th* *N.Y.*
I. AGE. Relative prop. of young teachers	4	2	3	1
of older teachers	1	4	3	2
II. SEX. Proportion female	3	1	2	4
III. QUALIFICATIONS.				
Proportion lacking full qualifications	3	-	1	2
Proportion without degree	1	3	2	-
Proportion with higher qualifications	1	-	3	2
Proportion with over 4 years of full- time post-secondary education	4	1	2	3
IV. EXPERIENCE.				
Proportion with 5 years or less of- teaching experience	4	1	3	2
V. PROFESSIONALISM.				
Membership of general teaching association	2	4	3	1
Membership of subject matter association	3	1	4	2
Less than 3 hrs. per week for preparation	2	4	3	1
Less than 3 hrs. per week for grading	-	3	1	2
Regular reading of journals about teaching	1	2	2	2
Regular reading of journals about subject	2	1	2	2
Attendance at educ. conference in past yr	1	3	2	4
Teachers teaching full-time	2	4	3	1
VI. TURNOVER.				
Proportion with 5 years or less in current school	3	4	2	1

NOTES

* Max A. Eckstein and Harold J. Noah, Metropolitanism and Education: a Comparative Study of Teachers and School Success in Amsterdam, London, Paris and New York, *Comparative Education Review* 18 (October 1974): 359-373. This article summarizes an investigation conducted by the authors under the auspices of the Institute of Philosophy and Politics of Education, Teachers College, Columbia University and funded by the Ford Foundation and the Institute.

1. The International Association for the Assessment of Educational Achievement has recently completed a comparative study of student performance in science and native language (known as the IEA Project). Samples of students at several age/grade levels were tested in twenty-one countries (though not all of the countries participated in all tests). In addition to performance data, the study gathered information on student background and on teacher and school characteristics.

16

Toward a Strategy of Urban-Educational Study*

Educational responses to the process of urbanization appear in many forms: literacy and health campaigns in South American *favelas*, decentralization of school administration in New York City, new curricula and instructional methods especially tailored for racial or socioeconomic minority groups in London and Liverpool. The pressures are varied and complex, including population mobility and congestion on an unprecedented scale, changes in the modes of living and aspirations of hosts of people, upheaval in their physical, economic, social and political environments. And the concomitants of these developments are crises in city school systems. Educational thinkers and practitioners all over the world are seeking to meet these new contingencies and to plan and implement educational systems for burgeoning urban populations.

The Metropolitan Context

Despite the extensive studies which have been made on the subject, the concept of urbanization remains a complex and confusing one. It overlaps considerably with the processes of industrialization and modernization and is, in fact, sometimes used as a synonym for them. On occasion, an index of urbanization may be used as a proxy for one or the other concept.

The basic and most simple indicators of urbanism are demographic: population density, a settlement in a given location of more than a certain number of people. Even here, a problem arises which, though it may not be so serious for a national study, is fundamental for cross-national research. Little consensus has existed on the degree of density or the size of the population cluster which makes an urban centre. Census-takers in one nation may define an urban centre as a population of over 250 people (Denmark), in another as a grouping of over 40,000 (Korea). The work of the American team, International Urban Research, has gone far in developing a standard for international comparisons and in collecting the data for such study on the basis of Standard Metropolitan Areas (S.M.A.), a term and a concept employed in the U.S. Census.[1] This is defined as follows: a population of at least 50,000 people, living in a territory comprising a central city (or cities) and adjacent areas with an economic relationship to the centre, and predominantly (over 65 per cent of the labour force) engaged in non-agricultural employment.

The definition includes more than merely the numbers of people in an urban unit. It comprises also compactness of territory (the city-centre and its periphery) and an economic indicator, and thus supplies a functional definition of practical value for identification, measurement, and comparison. Much useful work has been done to show the extent to which a given nation is urbanized, the sizes and rates of growth of urban centres within and among nations, all in a relatively clear quantified form.

In incorporating the territorial and economic indicators, the definition of International Urban Research moves beyond a simple nose-counting concept. It is, nonetheless, a limited definition. The urban unit is not merely a relatively large and dense settlement of people working in non-rural occupations; it also characteristically comprises a population which is extremely diverse economically, socially, ideologically, and very often also racially and religiously. Social heterogeneity is a significant feature of the urban setting; '....the heterogeneity of a city's people gives rise to complex patterns... The total impression is a confusion of types, or different colours, different creeds, the young, the old, the rich, the poor'.[2]

It is this characteristic, heterogeneity, and the mutual dependence and interaction of the several populations comprising an urban centre, which are most germane to the educator. They point to the existence of an urban culture and to the peculiarity and the educational importance of the experience of living in it. An urban location is not merely a given large number of inhabitants, grouped in and around a city centre and spilling over from its traditional physical or administrative boundaries. An urban centre, and by extension an urbanized society, is characterized by a special life-style and a set of relationships in which a large number of identifiable and differentiated social groups are involved. The economy is organized around a complex division of labour and the labour force incorporates a wide differentiation of economic roles and skills. People are joined together into a community more by physical proximity, spatial interaction and mutual dependence, than by sameness of tasks, commonality of past experience, or family relationships. While the administrative boundaries may or may not coincide with the settlement pattern, the urban population is in many respects a separate unit of municipal government. It is further characterized not only by high density of population (and therefore of housing and employment facilities), but also by its wealth of recreational, educational, and general social service facilities (such as health and government). Finally, complex transportation systems and extensive use of communications media, whose headquarters are situated in the urban centre, bind the inhabitants together in a network of mass communications.[3]

The urban location is traditionally regarded as the place where opportunity lies. Migrants from the country and from abroad have in the past accounted for much of the rapid growth of cities. But economic opportunities or cultural riches are not the only attractions. Any person can find others like him in the city. Elsewhere he may be a lone individual; in the city, he can at least be a member of a minority group, and find some security either by joining it or by losing himself in anonymity. The inhabitants of the cities of the world form a kaleidoscope of sub-cultural minorities, that is, groups who are in one way or another not in the national mainstream. The city may have been so powerful a magnet for them that they make up a numerical majority of its population. Yet the lure of opportunity and the frustration of unsatisfied ambitions are a source of serious tension.

The 'new urbanization', taking place with extraordinary rapidity in the less-developed nations possesses its own outstanding features.[4] Here, the most striking characteristics are underemployment, or redundant labour, poverty on an immense scale, division of the population into the very rich and the mass of poor, with a relatively small and separate middle group of government employees, merchants, and teachers. But the rate of growth of cities in underdeveloped countries is a most dramatic fact. A high proportion of the inhabitants of such cities are not urban in the sense described above, but are rather recent rural transplants. When studying onrushing urbanism in those lands which have not undergone the process of industrialization experienced by most of Europe during the nineteenth century, it is essential to note its special characteristics. It is also important consider how far (if at all) the processes and particular relationships of phenomena are similar in the 'new' and older situations.

To the extent that a nation's population lives an urban way of life, to that extent is the nation urbanized. But the size of an urban centre or the proportion of a nation's population living in densely populated areas are inadequate indicators of the general phenomenon. Numbers alone are not enough to describe it; style, quality and conditions of life, social and economic population 'mix' are dimensions of a definition which will permit discrimination among the different types of urban condition.

Several types of urban existence may be identified among the historical and contemporary instances, and the process of 'urbanization' is not the same everywhere. A developmental theory seeks to explain this: the several major urban types represent different stages of development of population centres and the process of urbanization has different features according to the overall level of development of the nation. Thus, the preindustrial city grows into the urban centre, then to the modern metropolis, then into megalopolis, for example, with major variations according to the historical period in which the process began, or to certain local features (*vide* such terms as the European city, the mediaeval city, the cathedral or university city). Architects, city planners and historians as well as social scientists have contributed generously to the creation of such a theory, though its ethnocentric nature and apparent determinism continue to be a source of considerable concern and debate among specialists.

One striking feature distinguishes the urban mode of life in less developed nations from that of the more developed. The traditional distinction between rural and urban applies less and less to the latter situations. In the United States, to take the prime example of advanced development, geography and administrative boundaries no longer adequately differentiate urban life style from the modes of existence in adjacent rural areas. For one reason, as mobility, technology, and mass communications have advanced in efficiency and complexity, many aspects of rural existence lose their traditional uniqueness. Relatively few people in the United States live in a completely non-urban cultural setting. But a second factor is even more compelling, the growth of metropolitan areas to such an extent that they cover large regions and incorporate several cities, towns, and urban areas. New York is the centre of the largest urban agglomeration in the world, spilling over into adjacent counties and states, extending beyond suburbia into 'exurbia' some thirty miles and more from Times Square. Yet even this may be an inadequate unit for some considerations. The geographer, Jean Gottmann, speaks of Megalopolis, 'an almost continuous stretch of urban and suburban areas from southern New Hampshire to northern Virginia,' extending along 450 miles of the Atlantic coastline. Other 'World Cities'[5] have not yet reached the scale of New York, and may never do so. Yet they demonstrate metropolitan expansion far beyond the traditional and familiar urban dimensions and present a scene and problems quite different from, say, Bombay or Rio de Janeiro, though they may point the way to future developments around the world. Especially in considering the problems and the needs for education, as well as those of transportation, government, health and the economy, the whole metropolitan area must be regarded as the unit for investigation.

Schooling in the Metropolitan Setting

When school problems in the city become the topic of public concern, they are rarely *sui generis*, but rather arise from more general conditions: population growth, change in the age composition of communities, economic progress, manpower and finance problems, and so on. Changes in the composition of populations, in social and political ideology, in economic organization, create school problems. The size and density of the urban community, its heterogeneity, its interdependence, the interactions of its human components, and above all, its mobility and changeability – in fact, those features discussed above – are the sources of educational problems and debates in large cities.

From both the local and the global perspectives, three major categories of problems confront the educational observer. First, there are the political and economic issues: who shall run the schools for urban populations? Who shall make which types of decisions? How shall administrative power be distributed between local, regional and national levels of authority? And how is the effort to be planned, financed, and implemented? The second and third groups of problems are more directly pedagogical. One has to do with personnel (students, teachers, and administrators) and calls for responses to the changing populations in the schools of densely settled areas. The pupil populations of urban schools pose new problems, not only because of numbers, but also because of their backgrounds, aspirations, and competencies. As a concomitant and as a consequence, ought there not be new criteria, new job descriptions and therefore new training programmes for those seeking employment in the schools? And finally, closely associated with the previous set of questions, what of the curriculum, the pedagogical methods and tools, and the patterns of internal school organizations? Are these changing as a response to new conditions? Are changes desirable? What is the relation of such innovations to educational outcomes?

One example of a major current issue in two big cities confirms both the widespread nature of some phenomena and the peculiarity of the local cases. The physical growth of metropolitan centres all over the world, but especially in the more developed countries, has created economic and administrative problems for city school systems everywhere. The decentralization controversy in New York, and the administrative reorganization which London underwent in 1965, are examples of responses to the same kind of pressure. The New York situation is different, of course, in that its current educational problems are as much a function of the United States' historical problem of segregation of Negroes as of the sheer size of the city. The city has been 'ghettoized' into communities which are either black or white, either poor or reasonably well-off, either inner-city or urban. Yet, the situation in London has similar features. Growing residential congestion at the centre has, as a result of considerable planning, been controlled, but the flight to the suburbs is evident. The influx of migrants from Asia and the Caribbean has created sizeable culturally, racially, and economically homogeneous enclaves different from the mainstream of the society. The phrase, 'town of villages' takes on a new meaning in today's London, where, as in New York, one moves from one cultural world to another as one moves around the city. In some senses, London's educational problems are unique, for they are part of the national effort to raise standards, adapt and modernize, and to implement a set of social and political principles through reform of school organization and practices. Yet in this, too, there are similarities with the basic considerations in the United States and elsewhere. The precedents and recent developments may differ, but the general process and contingencies are widespread.

When this discussion is extended to other aspects of schooling, the comparability of the two cases becomes sharper. Even though there is a strong precedent in the United States for public participation in educational decision-making and a strong tradition of parental exclusion from this activity in England, neither of the two cities conforms strictly to these principles. Through its appointed Board of Education and its extensive and highly centralized supervisory and administrative machinery, New York has effectively excluded parents and local citizen groups from the type of influence they have enjoyed in other communities in the States. In London, as in New York, the power of a local community to influence school decisions at large or in a district varies, but the relatively high degree of school autonomy and progressiveness of the Educational Committee and its administration have resulted in responsiveness to public demand. As a consequence, despite the differences in national practices and local provisions, London and New York recognize that parents, as well as local and regional administration, must somehow participate in educational decisions in their own cities.

The trend toward homogeneity of local communities within the urban setting creates very special problems for educational thinkers and practitioners. The most serious current issue in the United States and, with local variations, in other parts of the world, is the existence of gross differences in educational facilities, motivation and achievement according to urban sub-culture and residential community within the metropolis. The moral problem is not new; where there is national commitment to a set of democratic principles, such self-perpetuating social injustice cannot be tolerated. The economic and political aspects are generally realized too: when a given group of people does not fully utilize a society's educational facilities, manpower is wasted and 'social dynamite' is stored up. But the persistence and even the growth of such divisions diminishes the potential made available by urban organization and life. It also threatens the very existence of the city as a social, economic, and political unit and as the nerve centre of the nation.

As a result of 'ghettoization', the student clientele of an urban school may be categorized according to a single label: low income, or any of the recent euphemisms (deprived, underprivileged), immigrant (meaning black, Puerto Rican, Asian, culturally different and racially distinct), middle class. The labels are either socioeconomic, racial or religious, and serve as simple indicators of the special nature of the community. It is not yet clearly understood whether it is the empty pocket or the skin colour which accounts for the special nature of a given community and, by extension, of the children in a particular school. What is more generally conceded, however, is that the school institution is often unsuccessful in making the majority of some groups of youngsters productive or even minimally educated and responsible citizens, able to compete on the educational ladder or as adults in the economic society. Where an urban centre has succeeded in providing some measure of schooling for the whole range of its population, an appreciable minority has not been able to profit. In some extreme cases, a complete breakdown has resulted; in others, schools remain open but have abandoned any pretence of operating as educational institutions. Teachers and pupils engage in no productive communication, curriculum is abandoned, the formal school organization has no function except, possibly, to enforce attendance. In addition, the separate components of the school situation – parents, administrators, teachers, pupils – work against, instead of with, one another. As a particular situation deteriorates, the whole educational enterprise is effectively blocked by the actual withdrawal of one or another of these groups (student dropouts, teacher strikes, withholding of funds or other facilities, for example), or by its passivity.

Little agreement exists on the best means of solving the problems of metropolitan schools. Judging from the nature of both the arguments and the proposals, there appears to be little agreement on what the problems are. *Exposés* of the horrific conditions in city slum schools are common in the United States. Radical and romantic nostrums are almost as frequent, reminders of the noble muckraking and progressive spirit of the turn of the century. More money and more devotion are the main deficiencies, as many of these writers see it; but a new curriculum, new teaching means and objectives and a new kind of concern for human relationships are some of the more specific targets. Wide agreement does exist on the need for making curriculum more relevant to students, and not only the poor and the urban; and for considering ways of making teaching more effective through the use of new tools (books and educational hardware) and new patterns of organization (grouping practices, student participation in school government).[6] In addition, attention is being given to the question of using adult manpower more effectively, not only by use of teaching machines and other devices, but also by employment of 'para-professionals.' These may be housewives who assist the classroom teacher in several ways, depending upon their competence and desires, possibly marking homework, more usually distributing and collecting materials, keeping records, more rarely assisting in individual or small-group instruction. The significance of this development is not purely as a school facility. It recognizes the growing trend toward part-time employment of mothers; it also provides sorely-needed job opportunities in a convenient location for poverty areas; and it draws into the schools, as active participants, adults who may otherwise have remained passive outsiders.

If attention tends to be devoted to the school problems of cities in the more advanced countries of the world rather than to the exploding urban communities of South America, Africa, and Asia, it may be due to the ethnocentrism of writers, to which fault this author is no exception. But it is also due to the dearth of systematic and reliable data on the large cities of the undeveloped world and the rapidity with which information becomes obsolete. The economic, social and political problems of 'new' countries are replicated in the educational aspects of their cities. The overriding considerations are to retain what progress has been made so far in developing educational facilities and to extend at least some minima to the majority of the inhabitants. All the more reason why attention should be given to describing the dimensions of schooling and its urban settings (social, economic, political), to investigating their relationships and identifying the special problems of the school and its context in non-Western, underdeveloped nations. Where resources are scarce and priorities are numerous, planning is paramount and an information base for such planning needs to be created.

Need for Research

It is clear that the problems of metropolitan schools are too important and broad in scope to be left to the educators alone. But they are also beyond any other single group, be they politicians, economists, sociologists, teachers, or parents. Research on the subject, as well as planning for the future, is the responsibility of and the opportunity for the several social and behavioural science disciplines, collaborating to share concepts, data, and techniques.

While there is wide agreement that something needs to be done, that more money and facilities are required for schools to serve the urban poor more successfully, and while there is no lack of proposals to solve the problems of big-city schools, little consensus exists beyond this point. Solutions in a given location tend to be piecemeal, *ad hoc* responses to immediate pressures, resting upon no more solid a basis than faith, limited research, and a strong sense of what appears to be politically expedient at that moment. Yet the big cities of the world provide a species of laboratory for the researcher. Comparison could reveal not only the range of educational alternatives offered to deal with the several dimensions and problems of urbanization, but conceivably some evidence as to their outcomes. The experience of large cities, studied systematically and comparatively, may help to clarify the relationships between aspects of schooling and the urban environment in which they occur and even project the possible outcomes of specific measures for the guidance of a particular group of city educational planners.

But much work has to be done before useful investigation can be achieved. There is, first of all, an extraordinary lack of basic information on the subject. Second, there is a noticeable absence of empirical investigation and verifiable results. And third, there is a dearth of useful validated theory on the subject.

Urban sociologists and political scientists have written extensively on urban and metropolitan areas, producing many individual case studies, considerable information on urban composition and organization, and a theory on urban growth and development. Yet the information has been of little value for the educator, or at least it has not yet been utilized. The demographic and spatial dimensions of urban development have been quite fully explored, but little is known with much degree of certainty about those aspects of urban life most relevant to the educator.

In order to achieve an information base for comparative study and understanding, a host of new maps are needed of the cities of the world, maps which depart from the familiar topographical style and offer more than figures of population density and land utilization. They must, in addition, reveal the location of groups of children according to such educationally relevant criteria as parental occupation and educational level, for example, and sub-cultural groupings other than socioeconomic. Such maps should also present data on residential patterns over time. The most up-to-date educational details, such as school efforts at innovation, and pupil achievement, are needed to complete the map. With such information, planners may be able to chart the educational needs and obstacles of the future.

But this is only the beginning. Planners also need to know if given administrative devices do in fact have predictable outcomes, whether dispersal of the decision-making process, for example, does in fact lead to amelioration of educational problems in any identifiable respects. They need to know whether there is any relationship between educational expenditure in general and improvement, between certain kinds of expenditure and specific kinds of change. A lengthy list of questions is awaiting investigation, concerning teachers, their selection, preparation and use in the system, and about curriculum and methods. The answers will be insufficient if based merely upon single innovations under specific and limited conditions. But on the basis of systematic, comparative, controlled investigations, some generally valid conclusions may be drawn about schooling and its social context.

One special area is the politics and economics of metropolitan school systems. The political, institutional concomitants of educational innovation may be studied at several levels, from case studies of schools attempting new programmes and policies which cause social and political community repercussions,[7] to the comparative study of power and decision-making in big-city schools.[8] The economic dimensions, too, pose several types of unanswered questions: for example, the relation of a city's overall educational level to that of the nation, and the significance of comparative disparities; the relation of school production of trained manpower at various levels of skill to the metropolitan and to the national economies; the efficiency of the school system as an economic organization according to the resources available. Here too, then, lies the opportunity to engage in studies which delve beneath description, beyond mere amassing of information.

In short, basic information on the environmental conditions of metropolitan areas and on their educational characteristics are sadly lacking, not only for those nations just beginning to bring schooling to the mass of their populations, but even for the highly developed countries of the world. Furthermore, descriptive and evaluative information on specific educational problems in big cities and efforts to solve them needs to be more widely disseminated. But far more important, such information must be gathered and arranged in such a way as to permit investigation into the connections between educational and other phenomena. Only on such a basis, will it be possible to lay bare the educational correlates of metropolitan environments.

Conclusion

Metropolitanism is the life-style of this century. It is already so characteristic of technologically advanced countries that the residents of Paris, London, New York and other urban agglomerations form a trans-national community of the like-minded, with converging beliefs, lives, needs and conditions of existence. Growth of urban centres in the undeveloped world is part of the same general phenomenon, radically altering past forms of behaving and living. The divergencies within the metropolis are sharp, between the various sub-groups such as inner-city and suburban residents, between the urban poor and the propertied, salaried middle class. They are a danger to the organic life of the metropolis and a refutation of its promise for a better life. Yet the separation between schooling and its metropolitan setting appears sharper still: schools 'short-change' the children of affluent suburbanites and of ghetto-dwellers alike, though in different forms, as they serve their immediate communities with greater or less efficiency. They often also seek deliberately to remain above and apart from many aspects of their environment. In physical form as well as function, schools and especially colleges and universities in the city are reminiscent of mediaeval fortresses, turning their backs on the heterogeneous vibrant, complex metropolis. Interdependence being the main feature of this modern form of living, the interaction between education and its big-city settings is the priority for research on a comparative basis.

In this essay, the author has attempted to be descriptive rather than prescriptive, and theoretical rather than practical. Not that the intention was to be *im*practical; the purpose has been to set metropolitan-educational problems in some tentative theoretical framework. Only with such a framework is it possible to proceed to investigate some of the specific relationships that link the schools and their educational problems to their settings. And only through systematic testing of general propositions (parts of theories) against the evidence of the real world is there any hope of using insight and understanding to explain.[9] For reality tends to be obscured by the data and the immediacy of problems, and only systematic, comparative, empirical investigation can expose the principles which explain them.

The study of education and of efforts to ameliorate the lot of deprived city dwellers and protected suburbanites is a highly subjective enterprise, prone to ideological bias, political expediency and economic exigencies. By striving for objectivity and clarification which systematic investigation promises, a useful, indeed, a practical contribution is possible.

NOTES

* Max A. Eckstein, "Toward a Strategy of Urban-Educational Study," in Joseph A. Lauwerys and David Scanlon, eds., *World Year Book of Education 1970* (London: Evans, 1970): 19-29. Reprinted by permission of Evans Brothers, Ltd.

1. International Urban Research, *The World's Metropolitan Areas* (Berkeley, California: University of California Press, 1959).
2. Emrys Jones, *Towns and Cities* (New York: Oxford University Press, 1966), p. 133.
3. Scott A. Greer, *The Emerging City: Myth and Reality* (New York: Free Press, 1962), Chapter 2.
4. Scott Greer, Dennis L. McElrath, David W. Minar and Peter Orleans, *The New Urbanization* (New York: St. Martin's Press, 1968).
5. For example, London, Paris, Tokyo, Moscow, Randstad (the ring-city of Holland), and the Rhine-Ruhr region of Bonn, Cologne, Düsseldorf and their environs. See Peter Hall, The World Cities (New York: McGraw-Hill Book Company, 1966).
6. Much less attention has been directed at the suburban aspects of metropolitan education (see, for example, Alice M. Miel, *The Shortchanged Children of Suburbia* (New York: American Jewish Committee, Institute of Human Relations Press, 1967), or at the role of the urban wealthy in the schooling (public and private) of the metropolis.
7. Leila Berg, *Risinghill: Death of a Comprehensive School* (Harmondsworth, Middlesex: Penguin Books. 1968).
8. Marilyn Gittel and T. Edward Hollander, *Six Urban School Districts: A Comparative Study of Institutional Response* (New York: Frederick A. Praeger, 1968).
9. For exposition and examples of this view with special reference to the field of comparative education, see: Harold J. Noah and Max A. Eckstein, *Toward a Science of Comparative Education* (The Macmillan Co., 1969), and Max A. Eckstein and Harold J. Noah (eds.), *Scientific Investigations in Comparative Education* (The Macmillan Co., 1969).

17

International Study of Business/Industry Involvement with Education*

Introduction

This study investigates the involvement of business and industry with the education and training of young people aged 14-18 (middle and upper secondary level) in three industrialized countries: Britain, the Federal Republic of Germany, and France. The principal aim is to compare and contrast these countries' experience, practices, and policies, in order to expand knowledge of these developments among members of the business and educational communities in the United States. As a preface to the discussion of the project's purpose, we describe the scope of the project in terms of: the three countries, related U.S. projects, changing involvement of business and industry, employers' concerns about schools, employers' involvement in education/training, and the specific goals of the study.

The Three Countries   We have selected these nations for study because they combine similarities and variations. They are sufficiently similar to one another and to the United States to support valid comparisons, while they simultaneously vary importantly in the areas to be studied. The features that they share with each other and with the United States are: a representative political system which encourages initiatives from nongovernmental interest groups; a mixed free-market economy in which private ownership predominates, but where public policy plays an influential ground-setting role; a highly developed, technologically advanced economic system; a public education system that provides universal tuition-free access to schooling through at least age 18; and widespread, strongly supported opportunity for continuing and higher education beyond that age.

However, along with these commonalities, these nations represent a considerable range of practices intended to meet broadly similar aims of preparing young people for employment and citizenship. France has a highly centralized system of educational administration, management, and finance; German education is organized on a decentralized basis at the national level, but is highly centralized within each *Land*; the English system is decentralized to the local level, but with the central government retaining considerable general authority. The nations have had different economic experiences in the last few years, England having had the most economic difficulty, Germany the least. And, as we will point out later in greater detail, the countries have had quite different approaches to preparing young people for the transition from school to work.   Quite substantial differences may be seen in the degree and pattern of business/industry involvement with the schools.

Changing Involvement of Business/Industry   Before the mid-1800's in the now industrialized nations, the preparation of young people for their working lives took place mostly in the workplace. But this is no longer true. Over a period of some 100 years, secondary and post-secondary schooling has assumed ever greater responsibility for preparing young people for working life. However, this vast expansion of public education in most industrialized nations appears now to have reached something of a plateau. In the United States, the private sector is expressing increasing concern at how the schools prepare (or fail to prepare) young people for employment, and schools are opening themselves to many new ways to fulfill this task.   In particular, active partnerships are developing in different forms across the country (Timpane, 1982; Peirce and Sagan, 1983; Mann, 1984).

The study is concerned with the two broad categories of business/industry involvement in education and training: what employers and their associations say about the schools; and how they actually participate in education and training.

Employers' Concerns About Schools   Employers' complaints about the deficiencies of formal schooling are longstanding and widespread. They charge that the schools are ineffective in teaching a basic set of skills and attitudes. Specifically, they charge that the schools teach an inadequate curriculum, that they leave students ignorant of the real merits of business/industry (and even promote hostility to business/industry enterprise), that the credentialling system used in education is confused, confusing, and unhelpful in the hiring process, and that the schools are run inefficiently.

Hoping to improve matters, employers and their organizations in all three countries are making a similar set of proposals for change. They want the schools to pay much more attention to the practical applications of knowledge, to tone down their preoccupation with preparation for entry into higher education, and to be more responsive to employers' priorities for entry-level workers.   In pursuit of these objectives, employers urge that specific job training be done under their supervision, and not by the schools. They ask that the quality of teachers be improved; in particular, they advocate much greater exposure of teachers and students to business and industry, so that young people do not learn false notions about the world of work. They ask that the schools adopt business/industry's concern for the efficient and productive use of scarce resources.

Employers' Involvement in Education/Training   Though the criticisms and proposals for change tend to be quite similar across countries, the nature and extent of employer involvement in education/training vary greatly. This is partly the result of precedents, and partly the result of current conditions and institutional arrangements.

In Germany, for example, starting before World War I, great emphasis has been placed on the systematic education, training, and credentialling of young people for entry into work. A system has been developed (the so-called 'dual system') in which educational authorities, employers, and trade unions cooperate to provide opportunities for young people to enter apprenticeships while continuing their general education on a release-time basis. This has flourished in spite of the fact that employers cannot count on public funds to defray their job-related training efforts.

In France, a quite different model has been adopted. Notions of education/industry partnerships are quite new, and young people receive most of their job-related training in vocationally-oriented secondary level institutions financed by the government. Nevertheless, as in Germany, it is accepted as a national responsibility that young people be provided with the opportunity to acquire a vocational, entry-level qualification.

The British, in contrast, have been reluctant until most recently to assert a national youth training policy, whether executed solely in the schools, or shared between schools and employers. Credentialling for job entry has been largely left to the uncoordinated initiatives of employers and their organizations, while the schools have been charged with the responsibility for academic credentialling. However, the contemporary British scene is marked by a notable change in government attitude, accompanied by many central government initiatives to encourage development of a mixture of the French model of school-based job preparation and the German model of partnership between the schools and employers.

Principal Questions to be Answered What is the nature and extent of current business criticism of the secondary and post-secondary educational system?

What are the specific changes in educational organization and curriculum being proposed by business?

To what extent and in what specific ways is business currently cooperating with educational institutions in the education and training of young people?

What factors influence the extension of business-education partnerships?

What is the potential of, and what are the limits to, business/industry collaboration with education?

Criticisms and Recommendations

Two major aspects of business/industry involvement in education and training are: the criticisms employers and their associations voice concerning the schools, and the recommendations they make for improving education and training.

Employers have been complaining about deficiencies of formal schooling ever since the establishment of national systems of education. Their criticisms of the schools continue unabated, and are directed at both the schools' curricula and at their organization and management practices. . . .

Business/industry involvement with education goes far beyond voicing complaints, and extends to making both general and specific recommendations for change. In spite of significant differences among the three countries in educational goals, structures, and processes, there is remarkable similarity of view expressed by employers and their organizations in Britain, France, and Germany, regarding what needs to be done in the realm of secondary education.

Business people wish to see the distance between the world of work and the world of the schools sharply diminished, and to that end they propose changes in school curriculum, in teacher training and in-service education, and in the management and structure of the school system. . . .

Although the recommendations made in the three countries are remarkably similar, both in premises and in specifics, the posture taken by business/industry toward its "educational responsibilities" varies.

In France, business organizations tend to defer more to the education authorities and the teaching profession than in the other two countries, although their claims to a voice in educational policy are growing. In Germany, where business/industry involvement in training policies is long-standing, there is no hesitation on the part of business organizations in making recommendations for far-reaching change. In Britain, business organizations, taking a relatively new stand, assert the necessity for business to get involved in setting policies for education, and even business/industry's positive right to do so. They point out that not only does the world of work have a *special* claim to be heard, but that education and business are mutually dependent, have common interests and many common purposes, and must therefore cooperate as partners. (Association of British Chambers of Commerce 1984)

Participation

Business/industry has become involved with the education of young people beyond simply offering criticisms and making recommendations for change. Since roughly 1975 their active participation has been stimulated by a number of increasingly important factors. The downturn in economic growth and a sharpening of economic competition among nations, combined with increasing numbers of young people in the age-groups leaving school, resulted in rapidly rising youth unemployment rates. These reached quite unprecedented levels in France, for example, where the percentage of unemployed males aged 15-19 increased from about five to over twenty per cent in the period from 1974-82, and in the UK, from a similar level to nearly thirty per cent.(OECD 1984:2, 26) In Germany, however, the rise was much smaller, from close to two and a half percent to about seven per cent. These figures were interpreted as demonstrating the extent to which the existing structures and content of secondary schooling had become outdated, despite the prolongation of schooling for many. Moreover, technical progress had apparently eliminated many low-skilled entry level jobs formerly available to school leavers, creating a problem which had every prospect of worsening in the future. Thus there was a widespread feeling that even when economic growth rates improved, and the size of the entry level age groups fell, a severe problem of adequate education and training of the young labor force would remain.

The result has been a new focus in all three countries on the requirements of so-called "transition education", in which business/industry would play a larger role than ever before, not only in its more usual training function but especially in an increasing contribution to general education. This has called for changes in the legislative and regulatory frameworks for education and training, for changes in financial arrangements, for novel institutional functions and provisions, and for greater acceptance of business/industry as a full partner in a total national education and training enterprise.

The following three sections ... are devoted to the context and the experience of each of the three countries, as business/industry participates in activities aimed at a more directly work-relevant education. These endeavors take a variety of forms, among which are: providing an increasing number of teachers and students with opportunities to observe life in the work place and to gain practical experience; joining with the schools in twinning and partnership arrangements to improve communication and cooperative work ties between the world of learning and the world of earning; providing schools with material and human resources, and opportunities to collaborate directly with business/industry; and sponsoring many kinds of activities, local and national, designed to encourage the development of work-related skills, an appreciation of the importance of efficiency in production, and a more positive attitude toward business/industry....

1. *Britain*

Two main characteristics distinguish business/industry involvement in the education and training of young people in Britain: active encouragement of local firms' participation by the national voluntary organizations of employers; and local collaboration of individual firms with schools and LEAs.

Legislation and initiatives of government agencies have been important in setting out the guidelines for these activities, revising the organizational frameworks necessary, and providing financial incentives for companies to increase job training opportunities.

In the course of developments over the past decade, the traditional separation of academic general education from vocational training has narrowed. Business/industry has contributed to new thinking and practice in general education, has expanded its training activities, and has participated in revisions of examinations and proposals to introduce new credentials, and new forms of assessment.

Business/industry involvement over all aspects of education and training is of recent date, and has been growing rapidly. The series of new initiatives and the blurring of the distinctions between academic and vocational education has led to anxiety over what **is** regarded as vocationalization of the school curriculum, and rising tension between the Manpower Services Commission and the Department of Education and Science. As a memorandum submitted to a House of Commons committee by Imperial Chemical Industries noted: ".... the national organizational relationships between MSC and DES undoubtedly have within them the potential to generate unsatisfactory local competition which can only in the end act to the disadvantage of the young people themselves." (Great Britain. House of Commons 1983, 218) ....

2. *France*

France has had a strongly developed system of vocational training in the regular school system, alongside a relatively limited system of apprenticeship training. On the initiative of the Ministry of Education, employers' groups were involved in establishing the curricular outlines and content of this vocational preparation, but they were excluded from participation in school-based training as well as from involvement in academic education in the schools.

This exclusionary policy has been greatly modified in recent years, with a good deal of central government encouragement for business/industry to offer teachers and students information, counselling, work experience, tools, materials, and opportunities for collaboration on specific production projects.

Other changes proposed to encourage business/industry participation in education and training have focused on simplifying the financial arrangements for reimbursing firms providing such facilities, and on adapting the content and organization of training programs to the needs of small and medium-sized firms.

It is commonly assumed that French administrative style calls for central control of every detail of local operations, in the interest of insuring uniformity and equality across the entire country. However true this may be of school organization (and there are some doubts that it is indeed the case), it is decidedly not true with respect to involving employers with the school system and with training. Instead of detailed direction from the center, the central authorities and the national organizations have chosen recently to promulgate general frameworks of law and encouragement, leaving the regional and local organizations to determine the extent and the form of their activities in detail. As a consequence, there are substantial differences in employers' involvement to be observed, both among the various geographical regions of France and from one economic sector to another ....

3. *Germany*

The long-standing and highly regulated participation of business/industry in training is an outstanding feature of the German system. It is characterized by clear definition of roles and responsibilities by the national government, specification of training content and standards by federal agencies (with business/industry participation), provision by employers, and supervision, evaluation, and enforcement of regulations by regional and local employer-and-worker boards. The system reaches the majority of youth and enjoys high status. It exemplifies the adaptation of a traditional apprenticeship system to the requirements of a contemporary economy.

However, this intensive involvement of business/industry in work-related training is not matched with respect to school-based education and training, though a few isolated examples of firms' involvement can be identified. In any event, the contrast between the elaborate organization of the dual system and the reliance upon individual and local initiatives with respect to the secondary schools is marked.

Comparative Discussion

Business/industry involvement with the schools is a two-way street. It requires schools to reach out to employers and the workplace, and employers to involve themselves with the school system. As a result, joint programs, partnerships, and twinning arrangements have been established, requiring formal and informal provisions at local, regional, and national levels to take care of legal, financial and administrative details.

While collaboration between business/industry and the schools is widely supported rhetorically, it has not proved to be easy to install and maintain in practice. By tradition, business/industry has been excluded from direct participation in general education in the secondary schools, and the schools continue to maintain a certain degree of defensiveness against what they view as "outside interference" in their work. At the same time, business/industry continues to feel that it has a special expertise and interest in vocational training, and should be its main provider.

This exclusion of business/industry from general education has been modified somewhat in recent years, as schools have recognized that they need to improve collaboration with the world of work. It is increasingly conceded that educators need to become better informed about employers' wishes; that, as education becomes more costly, it can profit from the material and political support the business sector can provide; and that the schools need access to the workplace in order to bring a greater degree of realism and sense of immediacy to their curricula. Also, as the general education component in vocational education curricula has grown, the distinction between general and vocational education has become less well defined. Finally, as secondary schooling has become less exclusively a preparation for university entrance, its significance for the economic welfare of the nation has been enhanced, and business/industry's role as a "social partner" in the definition of secondary schooling has become more legitimized.

1. Three models

The three countries present three different models of providing transition from school to work, with consequent differences in the way business/industry participates in education. In the first model, broadly represented by France, most of the preparation of young people for work takes place within the school system, under the control of the Ministry of Education. In the second, represented by Germany, the responsibility is divided between the school system and employers in a "dual system", in which most of the training is provided by employers in the workplace. Britain exemplifies a mixed model, with neither schools nor employers having a monopoly over any part of transition provisions. (Furth January 1985, 7-11) In Germany, the roles and responsibilities of business/industry have been specified in great detail within a well-established and on the whole well-regarded system; in France, they are in the process of being established; in Britain, however, adaptation and *ad hoc* local arrangements are the rule, though recent years have seen important legislation and the development of new government and business/industry agencies to advance and direct changes.

The three countries differ, too, in the extent to which young people of school age participate in general and vocational education (CEDEFOP 1983, 3), and in the extent of school attendance as compared with apprenticeships. (OECD 1984: 1, 44)

The following figures are for the 16-17 year old age group in 1981.

	School	Apprenticeship	Ratio	% of youth involved
U.K.	30	9	3/1	39
France	60	11	6/1	71
Germany	39	52	4/5	91

These percentages make clear the extent to which entry workers in France are more "schooled" than is the norm either in Germany, or in Britain (Lutz 1981, 76-77), and they document the extent of German business/industry responsibility for preparing young people for entry into work. Only in Britain does the majority of school leavers still enter the employment market without any formal transition, whether in school or in firms, and without any form of credential, despite increasing retention by the schools and the growth of the Youth Training Scheme.

Transition education   Recent years have witnessed a progressive blurring of what were formerly quite sharp distinctions in France and Britain between the institutions constituting the school system, and those of the world of work. A new set of arrangements for the transition of young people from school to work is emerging in all three countries, though at different rates. Because these new transition institutions and programs are attracting an increasing number of young people, they constitute a severe challenge to the traditional arrangements for both schooling and apprenticeship. The pressures for change not only engender new forms of practice but also create tensions and adaptations of traditional modes of operation in several areas: governmental roles, legislative and regulatory action, financing, and the distribution of power and authority between national and local centers.

Each nation is dealing with these tensions and pressures for change in its own way, depending on its institutions and precedents, and current economic and demographic conditions. But in all three nations, the new conditions of transition have brought with them additional pressures for business/industry to become involved, and an increased willingness on the part of business/industry to do so.

Tensions and pressures   In Britain, as the jurisdictional boundaries between the educational authorities' schools and the employers' training arrangements have blurred, uncertainties about the eventual limits of change have grown. This is evidenced in fears that current plans of the politically and financially well-supported Manpower Services Commission to extend the Youth Training Scheme from a one- to two-year program of employment, education, and training will undercut the Department of Education and Science, which is also trying to make school curricula more relevant to employment and more attractive to young people. The British worry especially about what they see as an undue vocationalization of the school curriculum. In France, too, the government is concerned that new transition programs might empty the LEPs and, as it is committed to maintaining a variety of educational and training arrangements (traditional *lycées*, LEPs, apprenticeships, and apprenticeship centers), it has tried to move forward on a broad front, first providing financial and political support to the LEPs, then to apprenticeship arrangements, then to the traditional *lycées*, all the while encouraging extension of business/industry involvement in schooling.

Germany's long-standing practice of having employers participate in the transition of youngsters from school to work, via the offer and operation of formal apprenticeships, has meant that Germany has not had so far to go as the other two countries in expanding the involvement of employers. Consequently, Germany has not experienced the wrenching adjustments that the introduction of new transition arrangements has brought about in England, and even to some extent in France.

Indeed, in Germany, if there has been change in the demarcation of responsibilities for transition education, it has been in a direction opposite from that of Britain and France. The tendency in Germany, especially under Social Democratic governments, had been to strengthen the school-based modes of training while faulting the traditional apprenticeship arrangements on at least three grounds. Specifically, the dual system has been charged with being overly and narrowly craft-based, and for that reason unresponsive to the needs of modern technologically-advanced industry; crudely exploitative of the cheap labor of young apprentices, in the interest of higher profits; and inherently incapable of meeting the quantitative demand for training places. However, attacks on the dual system along these lines have not gone unanswered (Lutz 1981, 85), and the return to power of a Christian Democratic government at the Federal level has encouraged business/industry organizations to become more active than ever in support of a continued, and even expanded, role for employers in both defining the content of education and in providing young people with opportunities for transition to work.

In France there has been a fairly clear and highly developed school-based system for equipping young people with academic and vocational knowledge; and in Germany the dual system also has been very clearly defined across all the *Länder*. Because of the absence of a uniform, central direction of their system of schooling and transition, the British may well have experienced unusual tension and difficulty in the process of adjusting the connections among schooling, training, and work. The British had left school matters largely in the hands of local authorities, and training matters in the hands of professional and industrial organizations. The result has been a hodgepodge of *ad hoc* arrangements, satisfactory-to-excellent in some areas (for example, advanced skill training of a relatively few young people), but only fair-to-poor for the majority entering lower skilled employment.

As concerns the impact of changes in transition education on administrative arrangements for providing education and training to young persons, Germany had a relatively easy task, given its long tradition of business/industry involvement. Britain, on the other hand, has had to create new mechanisms for incorporating business/ industry organizations in educational planning and practice. In a somewhat startling paradox, the poor economic record of Britain in the past decade has led a Conservative government, inclined toward a laissez-faire rhetoric on most social and economic matters, to adopt an interventionist tone in educational policy, with the goal of providing radically altered transition arrangements for young people into work. Alongside an official policy of encouraging collaboration between firms and education authorities at the local level, the central government's Manpower Services Commission has become the chosen instrument for defining and executing education and training policy. The justification for this accretion of responsibility on a national scale has been largely in terms of the MSC's (alleged) keener appreciation of the skill requirements of the British economy as a whole, and of business/industry in particular.

While the British have been moving quite rapidly away from their traditional mode of decentralization, in France more responsibility for both the organization and funding of programs of transition education has been recently assigned to the localities, perhaps as a reaction to the traditional practice of initiative and control from the center (Jallade 1985,178-9).

2. *Financial and Economic Aspects*

Financing It is not possible to provide estimates of the money value of the resources provided by business/industry to the schools. The firms do not generally keep separate accounts of outlays, and in many cases the assistance is given in kind, rather than in cash. Business/industry involvement with the schools is entirely voluntary, and government incentives to become involved are diverse and indirect. Moreover, as far as training programs are concerned, there are substantial differences among the countries in modes of financing, and in the ultimate burden of costs.

In Germany, employers and apprentices bear the entire cost of within-firm training and education; the costs of release time vocational school are borne by the *Länder*. Attempts were made in the 1970's to introduce a payroll training tax-plus-subsidy program, in order to impose some penalty on firms that avoid their training "obligations" and to reward those who do offer training. But these attempts failed on constitutional grounds. German employers presumably recoup part of their training costs from the relatively inexpensive labor of apprentices. It has been estimated that 40 per cent of total training costs are covered from the sale of apprentices' output (*Nettokosten der betrieblichen Berufsbildung*, cited in National Economic Development Council 1984, 17)

The British have adopted an opposite mode of financing, offering employers sizeable public subsidies for in-firm job placement and training. As one observer has put it: "...the New Training Initiative of 1981 has effectively buried the long-standing principle that the financing of industrial training is the responsibility of employers." (Ryan 1984, 31) Youth wage-rates in Britain tend to be set quite high (about 60 percent of adult workers' rates), and the differential has been shrinking, so that employers' reluctance to offer jobs and training without substantial subsidy is understandable.

As already noted, the French rely on the payroll training tax-plus-subsidy device (something that the British had previously adopted as part of Industrial Training Board programs). This lessens the direct impact of training costs on general tax funds. However, the payroll training tax presumably erodes the French company tax base to some degree, curtailing the flow of general tax revenues to Paris; and the French government spends heavily for the support of pre-service training of secondary school youth in publicly-funded *collèges* and *lycées*. Given these considerations, not only the British, but also the French systems of financing training can be regarded as relying heavily on public funding, compared with the German approach.

The state of the economy   Apart from adjustments in the traditional machinery of government and the financial arrangements governing firms' training efforts, economic conditions are likely to be a crucial factor shaping the nature and extent of business/industry participation in education and training. All three countries have experienced economic recession – France and Britain quite severely, and Germany noticeably, but more moderately.

The effect of economic downturn on business/industry efforts in education and training is likely to be somewhat ambiguous. Faced with a relatively abundant labor supply, firms will tend to curtail training, because they do not need to offer training opportunities as an additional recruitment incentive. They also have an incentive to call for more vocational training in the schools, in order to shift training costs to the public purse. But, working in the opposite direction, a slacker labor market implies less labor mobility. This means that firms do not have to fear quite as much the loss of newly-trained labor to competitors, thus giving them some incentive to maintain their training efforts.

In contrast to these ambiguities, government policies in all three countries have been strongly directed at promoting more business/industry involvement in education and training. This seems to have been prompted by two considerations. First, governments in Britain and France have now accepted the responsibility (long recognized in Germany) for providing a systematic, national approach to preparing young people for entry into work. Second, each nation views itself as being in severe economic competition with other industrialized and trading nations, and believes that success in that competition will depend importantly on the skills and adaptability of the labor force. Both considerations have argued strongly in favor of an enhanced role for business/industry in education and training. Thus, Britain, with the poorest economic record of the three, has witnessed the most change in government activity aimed at increasing such involvement; Germany, with the best economic and employment record (and also the most business/industry involvement already) has seen the least. France lies somewhere between these two extremes.

3. Conditions for Effective Partnerships

Special note should be taken of pilot programs mounted by the European Community in its member nations (including the three countries which are the focus of this study). The programs have been used to identify the conditions necessary for successful cooperation between business/industry and the schools. The first phase of these programs, the "Transition of Young People from Education to Working Life," began in 1976, prompted by a widespread concern about rising youth unemployment. The second, projected as a three-year phase, began in 1983 and is similarly focussed on changing education to facilitate entry into working life. Ministers of Education of the ten member nations of the European Council called for action to assist the States to develop their policies for young people aged 14-18.

The current program consists of thirty pilot projects to try out novel approaches to the youth transition problems faced by the member nations. (European Community Action Programme 1984) Whereas the projects in the first phase were designed to encourage change within the schools, the second phase is more concerned with the relationship between schools and other local agencies: industry, businesses, and public and private youth services. The aim is to help these agencies become aware of the part they can and must play in the transition of young people to adult and working life, and to improve their ability to collaborate successfully with the schools. The majority of pilot projects . . . are concerned with arranging work experience opportunities for students as part of compulsory education, and developing better guidance and counselling.

The key concept of these efforts is "partnership," and the European Community report on developing a new curriculum in transition programs for the 14-18 year age group stresses a number of key factors for success, covering the context, content, and methods of instruction. The report goes on to argue that consideration must be given to the physical setting in which programs are offered, which should conform to both the nature of the instruction and the characteristics of the students. The social context is also important, that is, the relationships among staff and learners, respectively. The implications for success in developing a work experience program are thus considerable, covering changing the attitudes and skills of staff, new methods of assessment, possible new formal regulations, and changes in the ways of providing resources. (European Community Action Programme 1984, 9-17) Some specific examples illustrate the difficulties that can arise:

> . . . when staff are recruited from industry and commerce it is essential that they fully understand that successful production is *not* the major aim. The aim is the development of the young people, and this involves an acceptance, on their part, of student participation. The staff have to realize that, within the limits of acceptable risk, wrong decisions are themselves a learning situation. *Ibid.*, 48)

The following caveat is also instructive with reference to the content of instruction:

> A tendency exists to presume that because the working situation...is 'real', young people will automatically acquire all the knowledge they need of the adult world. This is not true. (*Ibid.*, 49)

Assessment of work experience programs in the Schools Council Industry Project in Britain has identified other conditions likely to influence successful collaborations between business/industry and the schools. Such programs are more likely to be successful if they are not run from 'the center' by LEAS, but are instead decentralized to school departments. (Jamieson and Lightfoot 1982, 144) Guidelines for projects and assessments after the fact all emphasize the need for proper planning and management; equal and full involvement of all the parties concerned, after lengthy orientation and opportunity for learning about the priorities of each participant and the conditions under which they operate; clear identification of respective responsibilities and accountability for performance and outcomes. Working relationships in the schools (between teachers, the head, and the LEA) are different from those in a firm (between, for example, a manager, his managing director, and the shareholders). (Dept. of Education 1981, 14) Failure to appreciate these differences leads to problems in implementing even an agreed-upon program. The new partners, whether teachers, or workers and supervisors from business/industry, require preparation to perform in the new milieu.

4. Findings of the Comparative Study

The major findings of the comparative study may be summarized as follows:

– Employers in all three nations make similar criticisms of the schools. These include: lack of connection of school curricula with the world of work, the schools' preoccupation with academic study and credentials, inadequacy of basic skill training, and the consequent unpreparedness of school leavers for work.

– Their recommendations for change, aimed at repairing these deficiencies, are also very similar. They want a more "practical" curriculum, greater knowledge and appreciation of the world of work on the part of both teachers and students, and more efficient management of the schools.

– Business/industry participation is organized in substantially different ways in each of the three countries, though specific types of activities tend to be repeated.

– The three nations represent three different models of transition education and training: school-based (France), firm-based (Germany), and a mixed model (England).

– There is considerable variation in the extent to which business/industry is involved in secondary transition education, from extensive (in Germany) to relatively low (France).

– In Germany, there has been little change over the last few years in either the extent or the structure of business/industry involvement in education and training. This is in sharp contrast to both France and Britain (the latter, particularly), where the trend of government policies has witnessed remarkable shifts. These shifts have, in turn, produced substantial tension between the traditional authorities governing education and the newly created ones.

– In Germany, employers bear a large proportion of the costs of training, recouping much of this by utilizing the relatively cheap labor of apprentices; in Britain, the wage costs of trainees are rather high for employers, and government tries to reduce these by offering employment and training subsidies. In France, too, the combination of a secondary school-based vocational and technical training and a payroll training tax implies that a large fraction of total education and training costs are covered either directly or indirectly by public funds.

– There is no evidence from these three cases that any particular mode of financing (by State, employer, or trainee) or administration (local or central) is to be preferred as a way of involving business/industry, though presumably the greater the reliance on public funding, the greater the risk that changes in government budget priorities will adversely affect business/industry involvement in the future.

– Business/industry continues to have an important if not dominant role in vocational training. In spite of the sizeable increase in business/industry interest in secondary education, the base from which it began was extremely small, and its involvement, therefore, remains limited and sporadic, especially as regards the general education system.

– If business/industry involvement in general education is to be successful, and even expand, careful attention has to be given to establishing the conditions and appropriate institutional arrangements for collaboration between business/industry and the schools. Some progress toward this in France and Britain is noted; in Germany the dual system has for long provided these conditions for vocational and technical training, though relatively little has been done to expand collaboration with respect to general education.

In Britain, business/industry involvement with education is shaped primarily by the national voluntary organizations of business and by local initiatives, nowadays with substantial governmental encouragement The result has been an assortment of *ad hoc* arrangements, rather than a system, though there is a good deal of agreement that it is precisely a system that is needed. In France, government encouragement (and rhetoric) for business/industry to get involved is also quite strong, but the major locus of change remains the schools, with relatively little willingness to accord business/industry more than a supplementary specialized role in preparing young people for work. In Germany, there is little substantial change to be seen in the traditional ways of involving business/industry with the education and training of youth. By and large, Germany is satisfied that it has come a long way in involving business/industry in the preparation of young people for work (certainly much further than all of the European countries, other than perhaps Austria and Switzerland). Certainly, Germany has already encompassed much that both the British and the French are seeking to establish. Under the circumstances, it is not surprising that these two countries look to Germany as something of a model of transition to work.

A common set of challenges has produced a common set of ultimate goals, and a common realization of the need for development of substantial frameworks of support for collaborative arrangements between business/industry and the schools. But at present, we see a noticeably different pattern of responses in each country, as they seek to transform their quite different current arrangements for upper secondary and transition education.

Implications for the United States

The current condition of American secondary education has been the target of much critical comment from almost every quarter of society, in particular from government, the educational community itself, parent groups, churches, and employers, and we can readily recognize elements of the European scene that have close parallels in the United States. As a result of conditions similar to those in Europe, employers in the U.S. have not merely stepped up the volume and frequency of their criticisms and recommendations concerning the schools, but they have sought to build effective partnership roles with them. In doing this they have given notice that they no longer regard their proper relationship toward the schools as being that of passive consumers of whatever kinds of young people the schools see fit to graduate (or, worse still, allow to drop out). As in Europe, American employers have increasingly expressed the view that schools have a critical role in determining business/industry profitability and even viability. Without putting it in so many words, American employers and their representative organizations are acting on the premise that school policies and practices are too important to be left to the educational authorities alone ....

Lessons for the United States

Clearly, on both sides, of the Atlantic, the level of business/industry involvement with the secondary schools is higher than it has ever been. This is not just a matter of promoting vocational education, which has been the traditional arena of business/ industry involvement; rather, it has extended to the general secondary schools on a fairly broad front. The reason is not hard to find.

A common set of pressures has brought business/industry, government, and education more closely together.   On both sides of the Atlantic there is heightened concern for economic growth and international trade competitiveness.   This forms, perhaps, the central issue for business/industry, and it has been the primary stimulus to employers to form partnerships with the schools. At the same time, the costs of public education are rising, and corporate taxpayers are as prone as individual taxpayers to want to see value for money, secured by introducing in the schools the allegedly superior practices of business.   Third, schools and school-based credentials are increasingly viewed as virtually mandatory gateways to employment. Coupled with the phenomenon of high and persistent youth unemployment, this has produced a universal acceptance of the notion that educational programs cannot be left simply to school personnel and teachers alone. Finally, while education has never been far from politics, the attempts made in the last two to three decades to reach and to deal equitably with all social groups by expanding access to schooling have strengthened the political nature of educational policy-making, attracting increased attention from business/industry and its representative organizations, along with that of other interest groups.

However, the institutional context and the history of school/business/ government relations differ substantially from one nation to another, to create a unique setting in each place. Unlike Britain, France, and Germany, the U.S. is typified by the existence of an exceptionally large, complex, and decentralized system, with a relatively slight federally-mandated framework to coordinate it; a school policy-making process that is highly responsive to local community pressures and interest groups; a pervasive suspicion of the idea of planning in the public sector, and a powerful anti-trust, anti-monopoly tradition that makes it difficult to develop a legislative framework for collaborative efforts in the economic sectors. The result is a scarcity of mechanisms to facilitate joint planning and cooperation of schools, business/industry, and government.

Given all of this, what are the lessons of comparative study for the U.S.?

It is a cliche that successful borrowing of foreign practice is exceptionally difficult to arrange, and can even be quite dangerous, giving rise to more and worse problems than those the borrowed practice sought to remedy. Although Britain, France, and Germany have all established frameworks to support partnerships between the world of work and the world of the schools, they have done so in different ways. Knowledge of the options actually chosen is useful, but none of them should be taken as prescriptive for the U.S. There is no 'miracle bean' for overcoming the substantial barriers standing between business/industry and education. If the European experience shows anything, it is that supporting institutions must be aligned to the political traditions of each particular country. But, even so, can we make practical use of the evidence from abroad? We believe that there are two important, related lessons to be learned from the European experience.

Barriers to change   The first lesson is that, although both educators and business/ industry representatives may agree that collaboration can produce sizeable benefits all round, barriers to change should be considered as both expectable and strong. Distrust, inertia, and fear of external influences are present on both sides, so that even a joint interest in bringing about change in schooling does not easily prevail over the attitude commonly held by business people that educators are ignorant of "the real world," wasteful in their deployment of resources, and at times downright subversive of the business ethic. Nor will a strong interest among educators in attracting increased support for the schools by itself overcome the view that, in their quest for profits, business people are unconcerned with the personal growth and development of individual youngsters, and that they are prone to act in ways destructive of the finer things of life. While there may be enough truth in both views to sustain them as social myths, their persistence is a major obstacle to collaborative participation. In Europe, school people's suspicions of business/industry intentions are probably much stronger than they are in the U.S., and this may be one of the reasons why governments there have felt more strongly the need to establish formal frameworks in which partnerships might go forward.

The Need for Frameworks Both in Europe and the United States, there are long-standing tensions between the different levels of government, federal, state, and local, and between government at any level and the private sector. The U.S. differs from France and Britain (and even from Germany) not just because it has a federal system, with its concomitant decentralization of power, but because of the powerful, entrenched principle of checks and balances. Collaboration among the political actors has been limited for this reason, and this has been a major cause of fragmented and short-lived programs and policies.

A second lesson we can draw is that the European nations have benefitted from the establishment of legislative or quasi-legislative frameworks in which business/industry involvement with school systems can be organized and assisted, information disseminated, and effective practices institutionalized.

In all three countries it has been recognized that, without such frameworks, initiatives tend to weaken and fade away. Establishing such frameworks enables good practice in one locality to be more easily disseminated on a wider stage. The long-standing system in Germany, the rather more recent developments in France, and the quite new structures in England all point to the desirability of such frameworks. While voluntarism, a characteristic U.S. style, is effective in promoting experimentation and innovation, it is unlikely to be sufficient for long-term sustained development, dissemination, and institutionalization. The current administration's "New Federalism," which has called for state and local governments, corporations, parents, and youth to share responsibility in tackling the education and employment problems of young people, has given rhetorical encouragement to increased involvement and collaboration by these groups. But it remains to be seen whether these activities will endure to bear important fruit. To date, efforts in the United States consist almost entirely of one-to-one partnerships between businesses and schools, sometimes sponsored and guided by a local or regional organization (for example, the New York City Partnership and the Boston Compact), but as often as not outside even such relatively loosely organized frameworks. Indeed, the necessity to consider building more permanent structures of collaboration is emphasized by Mann, at the conclusion of his survey of collaborative efforts in twenty-three U.S. cities, cited above:

> Virtually everything that is now being done is project-based, i.e., episodic, special purpose, tacked on and usually at the periphery of the school's core technology of teaching and learning. That is a short leash for the schools and a fragile base for long term partnership. If public/private partnerships continue to be dominated by small projects supported by small grants, they will have done some good. But they will also fall short of the sort of assistance and improvement which the movement promises. All city systems need to think about how to lever the interest so far shown from the business community into the sort of enduring situational alliance that can support big city schools and the children they serve.

The anti-planning and anti-trust traditions of the U.S. combined with the localism of schools systems hinder the development of more permanent frameworks that could sustain long-term collaborative arrangements between school systems and business/ industry. However, we need not surrender to the argument that it takes France's unitary system of government or even Britain's more limited but still important central government powers to establish legislative and organizational frameworks of this kind. The lesson from Germany is that a federal political structure may present extra difficulties, but that it is not an insuperable obstacle. Despite a federal system in which the *Länder* guard their autonomy in education as jealously as do the states here, and despite business/industry's equally strong resistance to government "interference", Germany has found it possible to establish and systematically improve frameworks within which Federal and regional governments can work with employers and trade unions to further business/industry partnerships with the school system.

In order to achieve such a framework in the U.S., Federal government encouragement will certainly be necessary, but the primary action will presumably need to be at the State level. The practical policy question for the U.S. is to figure out how State governments can work together with national forums (for example, the Council of Chief State Education Officers, the U.S. Chamber of Commerce, the Committee for Economic Development, the National Association of Manufacturers, and the major trade unions), and with local and regional forums, to promote business/industry partnerships with the schools.

We should take heart from the fact that in Europe even sovereign nations, not just federal states, have been able to arrange ways of collaboration across national boundaries. For example, the Organisation for Economic Cooperation and Development in Paris has done research on the process and results of transition from school to work, and the Council of Europe's IFAPLAN in Brussels has arranged for joint action to encourage, publicize, and assess pilot projects in several very different and independent nations. This suggests at the very least that a similar effort might be undertaken within the boundaries of the U.S. with reasonable prospects of success.

Conclusion

The United States has already had some success with partnerships between business and government: North Carolina's Research Triangle Park is a prime contemporary example; in the past the building of the railroad network and the enlistment of private industry in the war effort have been others. At present, according to H. Brandt Ayers ("The 'Long Arm' Meets the 'Invisible Hand,'" *New York Times*, February 2, 1987), the conditions for creating "a new ethic of public-and-private partnership" are again in the making.   The problems now before the nation – school deficiencies, youth unemployment, and poverty – are so serious that no single agency or level of government can deal with them, and just as the problems of transition from school to work were not created by the schools, or government, or business alone, so they cannot be solved by any single interested party. The rapid recent growth of business/industry partnership arrangements with schools in the United States indicates growing recognition of this.

At the very least, we might pay attention to the British example of the establishment of the Manpower Services Commission, the French government's vigorous encouragement of local employers' collaboration with the secondary schools, and the German success with the dual system of apprenticeship-plus-continued-schooling. We should review the legislative actions taken in each country and the means used to mobilize and distribute resources of money, time, and effort. And we should seek to create a set of support frameworks for public-private partnerships, responsive to regional differences. Attention paid to the menu of successful European initiatives would surely yield important dividends for U.S. business/industry – and for the schools.

NOTE

* Harold J. Noah and Max A. Eckstein, *International Study of Business/Industry Involvement with Education.* New York: Institute of Philosophy and Politics of Education, Teachers College Columbia University, 1987 [Occasional Paper Number 4]: pp. 1-3, 5-14, 15-19, 23-25, 29-30, 32, 33-40. For a summary of this project report, see: "Business and Industry Involvement with Education in Britain, France, and Germany" in Jon Lauglo and Kevin Lillis (eds.), *Vocationalizing Education: an International Perspective.* Oxford: Pergamon Press, 1988, pp. 45-68.

REFERENCES

Association of British Chambers of Commerce (1984). "Business and the School Curriculum." London: Association of British Chambers of Commerce.

Ayers, H. Brandt, "The 'Long Arm' Meets the 'Invisible Hand,'" *New York Times*, February 2, 1987

CEDEFOP (1983). *Youth unemployment and vocational training.* Luxembourg: Office for Official Publications of the European Communities.

Confederation of British Industry (1981). "Memorandum", in Great Britain. House of Commons. Education, Science and Arts Committee (session 1981-82). *The Secondary School Curriculum and Examinations: with special reference to the 14 to 16 old age group* Vol.II.

European Community Action Programme (July 1984). *Education for Transition: the Curriculum Challenge.* Brussels: IFAPLAN (Working Document 23WD84EN).

European Community Action Programme (1984). *Thirty pilot projects.* Brussels: IFAPLAN.

Furth, Dorotea (January 1985). "Beyond Compulsory Schooling: Problems of the 16-19 year olds." *The OECD Observer.* 132.

Great Britain. House of Commons (1983). Education, Science and Arts Committee (session 1982-83). *Education and Training, 14-19 year olds. Minutes of Evidence together with Appendices.* London: Her Majesty's Stationery Office.

Jallade, Jean-Pierre (1985). "The Transition from School to Work Revisited." *European Journal of Education.* 20: 2-3.

Jamieson, Ian and Martin Lightfoot (1982). *Schools and Industry.* London: Methuen.

Lutz, Burkart (1981). "Education and Employment: Contrasting Evidence from France and the Federal Republic of Germany." *European Journal of Education.* 16: 1.

Mann, Dale (1984). "All That Glitters: Public School/Private Sector Interaction in Twenty-Three U.S. Cities". New York, NY: Teachers College, Columbia University. Mimeo.

National Economic Development Council (1984). *Competence and Competition:*

Training and Education in the Federal Republic of Germany, the United States, and Japan. London: National Economic Development Office.

OECD (1984:1). *Meeting of the Education Committee at Ministerial Level. Item 6b. Policies for Post-Compulsory Education and Training.* Paris: Organisation for Economic Co-operation and Development.

OECD (1984:2). *Youth Unemployment in France: Recent Strategies.* Paris: Organisation for Economic Co-operation and Development.

Peirce, Neil R. and Deborah Sagan (1983). "Business Increasingly Sees Quality Education as Vital to Its Interests". *National Journal*, October 15, 1983, pp.2109-2113.

Ryan, Paul (April 1984). "The New Training Initiative after Two Years." *Lloyds Bank Review.* 152.

Timpane, Michael (1982). "Corporations and Public Education in the Cities". New York, NY: Teachers College, Columbia University. Mimeo.

Part III: ACHIEVEMENT, ASSESSMENT, AND EVALUATING LEARNING

18

Comparative School Achievement*

Achievement has been a central topic of interest to comparative educators since Marc-Antoine de Jullien first proposed his comprehensive schema for studying foreign educational systems in 1817 (Fraser, 1964). Throughout the nineteenth century, as school systems were developing in the more industrialized nations of the world, observers traveled abroad to study those practices and policies that might explain differences in the achievements of students and the contributions of a nation's schools to the well-being of their respective societies. American and other educators described and commented upon schooling in other countries and on their presumed outcomes, limited severely by the data available and the lack of research sophistication of their times.

A century later, in the aftermath of two world wars and of the dissolution of great European-based empires, new nations as well as old again concerned themselves with the potential of their school systems to serve their interests: economic growth, political stability, social development, and educational advancement. Comparative study was stimulated by the twin desires to learn from foreign examples and to seek yardsticks against which to measure performance. With the growth in communications through national and international organizations, the accumulation of educational and social data, and the rapid advances in research concepts and techniques, the possibilities of cross-national study of educational achievement were considerably enhanced.

Substantial progress may be observed from the early statistical studies and impressionistic observations of the later nineteenth century to the more systematic empirical studies of the mid-twentieth. Studies of curricula, examinations, textbooks, teacher training, and instructional practices compared across several countries, began to appear with increasing frequency, as did efforts to assess pupil attainment in such areas as arithmetic and reading (Eckstein, 1977). Nevertheless, despite its centrality as a topic for comparative investigation, achievement was relatively neglected in contrast to other aspects of education. The reasons are clear: cross-national assessment of student school performance is fraught with problems of equivalence and comparability, complicated by differences in national objectives and practices, and confounded by verbal and conceptual ambiguities. Small wonder then that comparativists leaned heavily upon such system variables as retention rates and promotion figures from one level to the next. Enrollment or attendance figures are generally available, rates can be calculated from official statistics, and thus seemingly reliable and objective measures may be used. That such figures are themselves not altogether unambiguous is acknowledged, but for international comparison, they appear to be far less troublesome than curriculum content, student performance, and instructional methods.

The IEA Project

The first concerted effort to compare achievement levels according to internationally accepted measures is represented by the massive research project of the International Association for the Evaluation of Educational Achievement: the IEA Project. It began in the late 1950's when researchers from a dozen countries convened under UNESCO auspices to consider the feasibility of conducting such research. The report on the pilot study (Foshay et al., 1962) concerned itself with many of the administrative and methodological problems involved in international collaboration on this scale, while the mathematics study (Husén, 1967) presented the results of the first completed survey of student achievement in twelve countries.

Subsequent phases of the project encompassed six additional school subjects: science (Comber & Keeves, 1973), literature (Purves, 1973), reading comprehension (Thorndike, 1973), English and French as foreign languages (Lewis & Massad, 1975; Carroll, 1975); and civic education (Farnen, Oppenheim, & Torney, 1975). Twenty-one nations participated, though not all were involved in each subject. In addition to the achievement data of samples of students at several school grade-levels, information was gathered on the students' home and school backgrounds through questionnaires administered to principals, teachers, and the students themselves in each country. The IEA Project was an ambitious attempt along the lines of the Coleman study in the United States and the Plowden report in Britain to perform simultaneous national replications. And the central purpose of all this activity was to answer the question "What factors best explain differences in student achievement?" (Postlethwaite, 1974; Härnqvist, 1975).

That differences in achievement existed was clearly evident. In each subject at each age and grade, achievement was compared at several levels: among students within nations, among schools within nations, and among nations. In mathematics, for example, Japanese students scored higher than those in all other nations at the same age/grade levels. Although the differences were not great, younger students (primary level) from Sweden and Italy performed better in the reading comprehension tests, while lower secondary students from New Zealand and Italy did well. In the same subject, average national scores of older students differed considerably, closely associated with the extent to which nations retained students of the appropriate age-group through the final year of secondary schooling. In English as a foreign language, Swedish students performed better than those of the other nine nations participating. And in science, secondary school students from New Zealand and Germany led those of other nations involved in the study.

It was inevitable that some educators would respond to the fact that students from their own nation performed higher or lower than students from other countries in a subject. However, the researchers properly insisted that national averages could in no way be regarded as the results of an international competition, for obvious reasons. Their quest was for the associated factors that might explain the differences observed.

The six volumes on achievement in the several subjects cited above contain a host of data and interpretations relating to their own areas, but three additional IEA publications review the project as a whole: a technical report on the methodology (Peaker, 1975), a summary discussion of the findings as a whole (Walker, 1976), and a review of the findings in relation to differences of school-system structure and organization and socio-economic characteristics of the twenty-one nations involved (Passow et al., 1976). Looked at in its entirety, the project confirmed and extended much that was known or suspected about the factors affecting student achievement: home background, comprising essentially the educational and social status of parents, by far the most influential force; school characteristics of various kinds; and features of the national educational system. But the relative significance of individual factors and of groups of variables was found to vary considerably among different countries, age levels, and subjects of study, provoking new questions about why achievement levels vary.

A number of more specific points may be selected from the total project to illustrate its capacity to illuminate and to provoke new questions. Although home background factors tended generally to be more important than school-related characteristics, this fact varied greatly by subject, by grade level, and by nation. In science and foreign languages, for example, school factors were generally of greater significance than they were in reading comprehension and civic knowledge. Although, as expected, nations differed in curriculum content and curriculum emphases in particular subjects, they also differed in their orientations toward the subject matter itself and the very nature of learning. The mathematics study had revealed, for instance, that students of the United States were more inclined to guess than those from Belgium; the literature survey showed that students' attitudes toward literature and their approaches to interpreting and evaluating it also differed according to nation or culture. Certain achievement differences (science, foreign languages) were linked with sex. The study as a whole confirmed the gap that separates the less developed countries of the world (Chile, India, Iran, and Thailand participated in several phases of the study) from the rest, in school resources and student performance as much as in economic development. Finally, among the several more obviously policy-related aspects of the study, it was evident that national achievement norms tended to be lower in those nations that maintained nonselective school systems and relatively open access to upper secondary education.

Although the IEA Project is a landmark in quantitative comparative research – rigorous in design, catholic in perspective, comprehensive in scope (Inkeles, 1977) – its very strengths may also account for some of its limitations. The decision to perform a cross-sectional study and use linear multiple regression as the primary analytic tool imposed certain limitations from the beginning. Inevitably, explanations for the phenomena observed could only be based upon correlations among variables, a far cry from causal associations (Bridge, Judd, & Moock, 1979). The variables themselves comprised groups of separate but presumably associated indicators for samples of specified student populations, expressed in average values. And the cross-sectional approach made it impossible to investigate the developmental aspects of education, except by tentative inference. Just as causation cannot be assumed from correlation, the cumulative effects of schooling cannot be adequately considered merely by comparing the achievements of three (or more) different age levels at one time. Average values may obscure suggestive or significant relationships, and the difficulties of actual or proxy variables remain intractable. However, these deficiencies are generic to this particular research mode and common to all similar social science research. The IEA Project, despite its limitations, goes a long way to realizing many of the objectives of comparative study of education as outlined by Jullien over a century and a half ago.

That such issues have been taken to heart is indicated by certain new approaches in IEA work currently under way: revised replication of the mathematics study, which will incorporate a longitudinal dimension; smaller-scale observational studies of classroom interactions, which will attempt to remedy the neglect of subtler, qualitative aspects of teaching-learning processes; and a movement from largely uniform international measures to tests that contain both an international core and sections tailored to the concerns and the curricula of individual participating nations.

Comparative Research Findings

The possibilities of the IEA six-subject study have not yet been fully exploited. The data bank with its mass of educational and related information is available for new and revised analyses by the scholars of the world. Since the publication of the original IEA volumes, a slow but steady stream of studies has used these data for various purposes, often in conjunction with the results of additional research, both in a single nation and in several countries.

Home and school influences   The IEA results confirmed what had already been concluded from similar national-survey research studies and a host of more limited ones: on the whole, home background matters more than school-related variables in accounting for differences in student school performance. With one exception, specific school characteristics did not clearly or consistently relate to variance in student cognitive achievement.

Some have used this broad generalization to argue that in the absence of political or economic reforms that would radically alter the nature of home and society, changes in educational policy and practice can have little effect. Yet the evidence suggests otherwise. Although most school factors examined in the IEA Project bore no direct, consistent relation to achievement, the indicators of "opportunity to learn," that is, time devoted to teaching and studying a particular portion of knowledge in a subject, were important cross-nationally. Furthermore, school factors in general were substantially more influential in certain subject areas rather than in others – in science and foreign languages, for instance, rather than in reading comprehension in the native language and in civic education. The relative influence of school compared with home factors tended to increase with the age of the student. And, finally, the amount of influence ascribed to school factors varied from nation to nation. The conclusion can only be that differences in school policies and practices do matter, but that much remains to be explained: when, where, how, and why?

Several writers have raised the question, "Why do the IEA studies and similar large-scale surveys, such as the Coleman report, shed no more light on the influence of home and school factors on student achievement?" One answer proposed (Marjoribanks, 1973) is that the two environments are rather broad concepts, crudely measured and aggregated , and therefore unlikely to account reliably for more than small proportions of variance. The author reanalyzed a number of small-scale studies from England, the United States, Canada, and Australia, focusing upon the "learning sub-environment," those psychosocial factors that appear most likely to affect a student's cognitive performance at school. These include such factors as the intellectuality and "achievement press" of parents and their ambitions, aspirations, and attitudes toward school achievement. Marjoribanks found these to be highly predictive of children's school achievement in their different national settings.

The argument is taken a step further in the analysis of data from one less developed nation (Uganda) compared with certain evidence from the IEA Project (Heyneman, 1976). Although home background appears more influential in the developed countries, the effects of schooling on cognitive achievement appear relatively greater in the case of less developed nations. One inference to be drawn from such work is that there may be a threshold effect at work: at certain levels of social and educational development, school factors are highly influential; at more advanced levels, home background becomes more significant. Furthermore, this effect may be true not only between nations but also between segments or strata of society within a given nation.

On this issue of relative influence, it can be concluded that, in all likelihood, home backgrounds differ from each other far more than schools do, at least for the measures used in large-survey research. Secondly, the very nature of the research design may obscure rather than highlight the associations among factors: the need to use large numbers of indicators; the decision to aggregate a number of measures for a particular variable. The very comprehensiveness of studies that seek to test many elements of a complex explanatory model at one time is also a deficiency. Fine distinctions, qualitative dimensions, and exceptional relationships – all potentially highly significant – may be lost in the manipulation of average values. It is left to researchers without the resources and scope of the IEA teams to reanalyze portions of data already collected and, in complementary and exploratory smaller-scale studies, to investigate portions of the conceptual model. In this way, they can direct attention to specific variables in both the home and school environments of students and their relation to one another under specific conditions.

Teachers and instruction   The data base and the research model of the IEA Project enhanced the possibilities of systematic comparative study of teacher characteristics and instructional methods. For example, the first global study of reading and writing (Gray, 1956), a UNESCO sponsored project, laid the foundations for comparisons of educational conditions and standards of literacy in the world. Nearly two decades later, a collection of essays and studies (Downing, 1973) delved further into the subject, although still limited by the lack of a unified set of concepts and information. Examples of individual efforts in various subject areas may also be found in Halsall's thoughtful attempt to study attainment differences in French in Holland, Belgium, and England (Halsall, 1963); in Trace's comparison of curriculum and textbook content in the United States and the U.S.S.R. (Trace, 1961); and in Wiersma's study of academic achievement of prospective teachers (Wiersma, 1969). Yet even the evidence from IEA studies provided no clear answers. On the whole, teacher and instructional variables bore no general, consistent relationship with variance in student achievement that was statistically significant.

It was left to subsequent analyses of IEA data and to reviews of additional information to cast light on the subject. One study concluded (Avalos, 1980) that neither higher academic qualification nor longer preservice preparation of teachers were in themselves important in explaining differences in student achievement, although they might be in conjunction with other variables. The same author also found that differences in instructional method were not influential, although she found discovery methods more effective than expository teaching at higher levels of intellectual achievement. This study, of data relating to less developed nations, is in part substantiated by two additional works (Husén, 1978; Simmons & Alexander, 1980). Although neither found clear and consistent, significant relationships among teacher training, several other school-related variables, and achievement, Husén's analyses firmly rejected the null hypothesis that the sixteen teacher-related variables studied were unrelated to achievement. Four characteristics were rather more important than others: qualifications, experience, amount of education, and knowledge. In addition, two demographic characteristics were important under specified conditions: teacher's sex and teacher's age (older teachers may be more successful with older, that is, upper secondary students). Finally, positive teacher expectations, so far as they could be identified, tended to produce positive results.

Simmons and Alexander (1980) found that teacher certification and academic qualifications were not so important at primary and lower secondary as at upper secondary levels and in certain subject areas (notably science). However, in their search for evidence to influence educational policy decisions in less developed nations, they found teacher experience did have a positive effect on academic achievement in the lower grades (although it was not so important at upper secondary levels). In general, they concluded that gross expenditures on teacher salaries and school facilities were not significant, but that teacher motivation (as indicated by time spent on preparation and by membership on curriculum-reform committees) was a positive factor in student achievement. Finally, Simmons and Alexander found that the amount of homework done, the physical conditions at home, and the amount of reading done were all important predictors of student achievement. The conclusions are that increasing the quality or quantity of most of the traditional inputs to schooling, such as teacher training or expenditures per student, is not likely to increase student achievement. However, affective skills taught by the schools may be more important than cognitive skills, especially for post-school benefits (higher earnings and satisfactions in work).

Finally, still with reference to practice in less developed nations, Heyneman (1978) reviewed the published evidence on the relationship between availability of textbooks and academic achievement. Studies covering twelve nations were reviewed, including the IEA Project, Heyneman's own investigations in Uganda, and a number of other works. The availability of books is a consistently good predictor of academic achievement, Heyneman concluded, although the reasons why the associations are stronger in some cases and weaker in others are not at all clear. He recommends that investment in reading materials is likely to improve cognitive achievement in less developed nations.

All of the studies reviewed in this section exemplify the potentialities and the limitations of quantitative analysis made possible by IEA and similar investigations. They raise questions about the conventional wisdom on which educators base their actions; they are suggestive about possible and conceivably unanticipated association among variables; and they indicate most clearly that smaller-scale, rigorous studies of particular sets of phenomena are necessary to complement the broader surveys.

Sex and achievement   Much remains to be discovered about the relationship between sex and school achievement. Although the issue of separation of the sexes in school is quiescent in many countries, it remains controversial in various places because of social and religious values and customs. However, comparative study reveals that even where schools have been integrated, achievement often depends on the sex of the student. The sex of the teacher is probably also an important factor.

The IEA studies extended the general awareness that, on the average, sexes perform differently in given school subjects; what was known to be true in certain instances, was found to be true internationally. Boys do better than girls in civic education, mathematics, and science, with the exception that, in some countries, girls excel in biology. On the other hand, although the differences are sometimes slight, girls tend to do better in foreign languages, reading comprehension, and literature. Such findings add to what is known about sex differences in education globally: literacy skills as estimated by United Nations statistics, enrollment and attendance figures, curricular and vocational choices, and achievement in specified school subjects (Finn, Dulberg, &

Reis, 1979).

It can be no coincidence that male teachers appear to be more successful with their students' science achievement too, while their female colleagues are better able to enhance their students' foreign-language performance (Husén, 1978). As one comprehensive review of the topic makes evident (Finn, Reis, & Dulberg, 1980), patterns of performance are inextricably bound up with behavior models suggested in schools by teachers and textbooks, by curriculum exposure, by academic supports, and by vocational expectations and opportunity – all of which are deeply rooted in society's ideas and practices.

Yet the evidence is not all in, and the psychological and sociological dynamics remain unclear. Why, for instance, does it appear that male teachers influence male students positively in the middle grades, but negatively at upper secondary levels (they also influence female achievement negatively at the upper secondary level) (Simmons & Alexander, 1980)? In a four-nation study of reading achievement (Johnson, 1973-1974), boys scored higher than girls in Nigeria and England, while the reverse was true of samples of primary pupils from Canada and the United States. And a selection of IEA data (Passow et al., 1976) suggests that in those more developed nations of the world, where primary-school teaching is perceived as a career for females, primary-school achievement in basic skills (mathematics, reading comprehension) tends to be lower; where primary-school teaching is seen as a career for either sex, such achievement is higher. Comparative study demonstrates that school-achievement differences between the sexes are not easily or quickly reduced, even as social practices develop, economic conditions change, and school practices vary.

National School Policies   The continuing debates over how particular school policies affect performance are unlikely to be stilled easily, for they are often rooted in fundamental differences of philosophy, political ideology, and social values. It should make a difference whether compulsory schooling begins earlier or later, how long it lasts, whether classes are smaller or larger, at what age students are moved from primary to secondary levels of schooling, and what mechanisms, if any, are used at important transfer points. The controversies over the effect of classroom grouping policies or the merits of selective versus comprehensive schooling cannot be assessed with respect to student achievement alone, for they are also involved with political and social effects.

These and many similar issues have been studied both in one-nation case studies and in cross-national investigations. In the IEA Project especially, in addition to the several volumes devoted to the separate subjects of study, the National Case Study volume (Passow et al., 1976) discussed associations between such issues and student achievement. However, since the nations were not selected as a sample for particular research purposes (participation was on a voluntary basis) and the ranges they represented on such variables were limited (and unrepresentative), no clear associations were found between such factors as national average class size, forms of compulsory schooling, and achievement. However, a number of suggestive points emerged, indicating that further analyses and added data would be fruitful.

The question of the effect of selective versus comprehensive secondary schooling may demonstrate how comparative study may dispel some confusion. The IEA Project produced national achievement norms for each participating nation in different subjects for students at different levels. On the whole, achievement norms were demonstrably lower in those countries that retained larger proportions of their youth in the education system by means of nonselective transition from primary to secondary levels and by providing various forms of comprehensive secondary schooling. It is to be expected, therefore, that such countries would have a wider range of student ability in the samples tested at middle and upper secondary school levels, and that national averages would consequently be depressed in comparison with those countries restricting advancement through the school system. However, as IEA analyses demonstrate, if comparisons are made among the top 5 to 9 percent of achievers in each country, the differences among countries are sharply reduced. The best students tend to achieve at very similar levels in different countries, regardless of whether the school system is more selective or more comprehensive.

The issue of how increased access to more schooling may affect outcomes is but one of the current concerns in the United States as in other nations of the world. So too are the issues of how to provide for cultural, linguistic, and other "exceptional groups" whose achievement levels are demonstrably below national norms and whose participation in the mainstream of national life is limited. Bilingual education programs and compensatory school schemes of various kinds have developed in many countries of the world in order to meet similar kinds of problems: transient foreign workers in Sweden and West Germany, the Francophone communities of Canada, Asian refugees in the Netherlands, Indian and Jamaican immigrants in Britain, the poor in rural or urban areas everywhere. Such efforts to use the school system to achieve particular social as well as educational objectives are increasingly being described and analyzed in the comparative literature.

However, as these examples of policy questions indicate, student attainment in basic skills such as reading the native language or in standard school subjects is but one way of defining the outcomes of different school policies. School achievement may also be considered as the capacity of the school system to produce what the educators, citizens, and the leadership of a nation deem important. To evaluate the performance of an education system calls for some understanding of the goals, costs, demands, and needs of the nation for which it provides. Although societies may agree on certain broad social and personal objectives of education, the many varieties of practice, organization, and criteria for evaluation among the schools of the world indicate that, in fact, the ends, the means, and the processes connecting them may vary considerably. Thus, Coombs and Lüschen (1976) propose four criteria by which to assess system performance comparatively: effectiveness, efficiency, responsiveness, and fidelity. They acknowledge the existence of many output measures, some more usable than others, but note the problems involved that may explain why so little has yet been achieved in comparing the achievements of school systems relative to their particular respective priorities and objectives. They conclude with a number of hypotheses suggestive of policy-oriented research.

Valuable as the comparative research has been, its potential for informing specific policy has been severely limited. One cause for this fact may be that the researchers have not adequately translated their findings into forms that educational practitioners and policy makers can grasp. In this respect, comparativists may be at one with other researchers in education and the social sciences generally. A second cause, quite evident in the IEA Project, lies in the research strategy that resulted in conclusions about the relative importance of one factor compared with another over entire nations. Eckstein (1977) summarizes the argument:

> Teachers, curriculum makers, and educational policy makers, however, usually wish to know something more specific. They are more interested in those variables over which they have some control than in those less amenable to

their decisions. They need to know the effect upon achievement of varying a particular item under rather specific circumstances. They are less interested in influencing achievement on an average, national basis than in, say, rural as compared with urban settings, boys vis-à-vis girls, students in poor neighborhoods as distinct from wealthier communities. What provides the largest increments to achievement for low achievers? For average or high achievers? The answers to these and similar questions require analyses that partition the national samples (singly and across groups of nations) so as to investigate relationships among variables for specified groups of students, e.g., rural/urban, poor/wealthy, high achievers/low achievers. The potential of the I.E.A. studies to inform policy making in education was neglected because insufficient attention was given to policy questions and because authors did not take care to express their findings in appropriately concrete form. (pp. 354-355)

Conclusions

The scope of this article has been restricted in two important senses. First, the word "comparative" has been taken to mean cross-national, although this is by no means the only possible usage. Much educational research is "comparative" in the intra-national sense and faces similar possibilities and obstacles. Second, the term "school achievement" has been taken to mean student cognitive performance, rather than other contributions of a school system to individual or social benefit. As a result of these limitations, a substantial body of literature on both the politics and the economics of education has been excluded (e.g., Blaug, 1978; Merritt & Coombs, 1977; Messialas, 1977). It should also be noted that the discussion is based on two significant assumptions. The explanatory model for school achievement presupposes that there are explicit causes of differences in student performance and that they may be discovered in the patterns of relationships among a number of environments: the home, the school, and the larger contexts of the whole culture or society. And, it is held that comparative school research, whether of achievement or of other aspects of schooling, contributes substantially to our understanding of the complex processes of education and thereby to informing policy.

By moving outside the boundaries of a single nation, comparative study enables the researcher to include variables that may not be available at home. For instance, some practices, such as beginning age and duration of compulsory schooling, are generally uniform within a nation, so that the effect of varying this policy cannot be studied without comparison. Similarly, it may be possible to increase the range of variability of a given factor by using cross-national data when a given nation exhibits only limited variations. In fact, certain important policy differences and outcomes can only be investigated through cross-national comparison. As Wolf (1977) effectively demonstrates in his discussion of student performance in the United States in the IEA Project, reference to the larger number and wider range of variables represented in other countries can be most illuminating.

A second value of comparative study is its capacity to extend generalizations, to expand the scope and validity of a given finding. The conclusion of a one-nation study in education may hold true for a particular school system, but of necessity omits consideration of important national variables. Comparative study broadens the applicability of the conclusion, or, if not, poses new questions about the educational processes under investigation.

This is in fact the third value of comparative studies in achievement: their heuristic potential. They increase the number and variety of phenomena for study; challenge the conventional wisdom in education; and, most important of all, as Bloom (1976) suggests, enhance the theoretical models posited to explain achievement.

All questions concerning school achievement do not require cross-national treatment, although comparison at a lesser level is likely to be necessary. Nor can the conceptual and operational difficulties of cross-national research be avoided. But the history of comparative education over the past century provides ample evidence of progress in defining important educational questions, developing means for studying them, and revealing, with increasing degrees of specificity, the possibilities and limits of such investigations (Noah & Eckstein, 1969). The variety of educational practices and their outcomes in the many nations of the world may be regarded as a series of natural experiments created by different political, social, and economic circumstances. Comparative study investigates their meanings and seeks to relate them to persistent problems in understanding education.

NOTES

* Max A. Eckstein, "Comparative School Achievement." Reprinted with permission of Macmillan Library Reference USA, a Division of Simon & Schuster Inc., from *Encyclopedia of Education Research*, 5th Edn. Vol 1: 323-329. Copyright 1982 by the American Educational Research Association.

Avalos, B. Teacher effectiveness: Research in the Third World – Highlights of a review. *Comparative Education*, 1980, *16*, 4554.

Blaug, M. *Economics of Education: A Selected Annotated Bibliography* (3rd ed.). New York: Pergamon Press, 1978.

Bloom, B. Human *Characteristics and School Learning*. New York: McGraw-Hill, 1976.

Bridge, R.G.; Judd, M.; & Moock, P. *The Determinants of Educational Outcomes. The Impact of Families, Peers, Teachers and Schools*. Cambridge, Mass.: Ballinger, 1979.

Carroll, J.B. *The Teaching of French as a Foreign Language in Eight Countries*. Vol. 5 of *International Studies in Evaluation*. New York: Wiley; Stockholm: Almqvist & Wiksell, 1975.

Comber, L.C., & Keeves, J.P. *Science Education in Nineteen Countries*. *Vol.* 1 of *International Studies in Evaluation*. New York: Wiley; Stockholm: Almqvist & Wiksell, 1973.

Coombs, F.S., & Lüschen, G. System performance and policy-making in West European education: Effectiveness, efficiency, responsiveness and fidelity. *International Review of Education*, 1976, *22*, 133-153.

Downing, J. *Comparative Reading: Cross-national Studies of Behavior and Processes in Reading and Writing*. New York; Macmillan, 1973.

Eckstein, M.A. Comparative study of educational achievement. *Comparative Education Review*, 1977, *21*, 345-357.

Farnen, R.F.; Oppenheim, A.N.; & Torney, J.V. *Civic Education in Ten Countries*. Vol. 6 of *International Studies in Evaluation*. New York: Wiley; Stockholm: Almqvist & Wiksell, 1975.

Finn, J.D.; Dulberg, L.; & Reis J. Sex differences in educational attainment: A cross-national perspective. *Harvard Educational Review,* 1979, *49,* 477-503.

Finn, J.D.; Reis, J.; & Dulberg, L. Sex differences in educational attainment: The process. *Comparative Education R*eview, 1980, *24,* S33-S52..

Foshay, A.W.; Thorndike, R.L.; Hotyat, F.; Pidegon, D.A.; & Walker, D.A. *Educational Achievements of Thirteen-year-olds in Twelve Countries.* Hamburg: UNESCO Institute for Education, 1962.

Fraser, S. *Jullien's Plan for Comparative Education, 1816-1817.* New York: Columbia University, Teachers College, 1964.

Gray, W.S. *The Teaching of Reading and Writing.* Paris: UNESCO, 1956.

Halsall, E.A comparative study of attainments in French. *International Review of Education,* 1963, *9,* 41-59.

Härnqvist, K. The international study of educational achievement. In F.N. Kerlinger (Ed.), *Review of Research in Education* (Vol. 3.). Itasca, Ill.: F.E. Peacock, 1975.

Heyneman, S.P. Influences on academic achievement: A comparison of results from Uganda and more industrialized countries. *Sociology of Education,* 1976, *49,* 200-211.

Heyneman, S.P. *Textbooks and Achievement: What We Know* (World Bank Staff Working Paper No. 298). Washington, D.C.: World Bank, 1978. (ERIC Document Reproduction Service No. ED 179 044)

Husén, T. *International Study of Achievement in Mathematics: A Comparison of Twelve Countries* (2 vols.). New York: Wiley, 1967.

Husén, T. *Teacher Training and Student Achievement in Less-developed Countries* (World Bank Staff Working Paper No. 310). Washington, D.C.: World Bank, 1978.

Inkeles, A. The international evaluation of educational achievement. *Proceedings of the National Academy of Education,* 1977, *4,* 139-200.

Johnson, D.D. Sex differences in reading scores across cultures. *Reading Research Quarterly,* 1973-1974, *9,* 67-86.

Lewis, E.G., & Massad, C. *The Teaching of English as a Foreign Language in Ten Countries.* Vol. 4 of *International Studies in Evaluation.* New York: Wiley; Stockholm: Almqvist & Wiksell, 1973.

Marjoribanks, K. Psychosocial environments of learning: An international perspective. *Comparative Education, 1973, 9,* 28-33.

Merritt, R.L., & Coombs, F. S. Politics and educational reform. *Comparative Education Review,* 1977, *21,* 247-273.

Massialas, B.G. Education and political development. *Comparative Education Review,* 1977, *21,* 274-295.

Noah, H.J., & Eckstein, M.A. *Toward a Science of Comparative Education.* New York: Macmillan, 1969.

Passow, A.H.; Noah, H.J.; Eckstein, M.A.; & Mallea, J. *The National Case Study: An Empirical Comparative Study of Twenty-one Educational Systems.* Vol. 7 of *International Studies in Evaluation.* New York: Wiley; Stockholm: Almqvist & Wiksell, 1976.

Peaker, G.F. *An Empirical Study of Education in Twenty-one Countries: A Technical Report.* Vol. 8 of *International Studies in Evaluation.* New York: Wiley; Stockholm: Almqvist & Wiksell, 1975.

Postlethwaite, N. Introduction, and Target populations, sampling, instrument construction, and analysis procedures. *Comparative Education Review,* 1974, *18,* 157-179.

Psacharopoulos, G. *Returns to Education: An International Comparison.* San

Francisco: Jossey-Bass, 1973.

Purves, A.C. *Literature Education* in *Ten Countries.* Vol. 2 of *International Studies in Evaluation.* New York: Wiley; Stockholm: Almqvist & Wiksell, 1973.

Simmons, J., & Alexander, L. Factors which promote school achievement in developing countries: A review of the research. In J. Simmons (Ed.), *The Education Dilemma: Policy Issues for Developing Countries in the* 1980s. Elmsford, N.Y.: Pergamon Press, 1980.

Thorndike, R.L. *Reading Comprehension Education in Fifteen Countries.* Vol. 3 of *International Studies in Evaluation.* New York: Wiley; Stockholm: Almqvist & Wiksell, 1973.

Trace, A.S. *What Ivan Knows that Johnny Doesn't.* New York: Random House, 1961.

Walker, D.A. *The IEA Six-subject Survey.* Vol. 9 of *International Studies in Evaluation.* New York: Wiley; Stockholm: Almqvist & Wiksell, 1976.

Wiersma, W. A cross-national comparison of the academic achievement of prospective secondary school teachers. *Comparative Education Review,* 1969, *13*, 209-212.

Wolf, R.M. *Achievement in America: National Report of the United States for the International Achievement Project.* New York: Columbia University, Teachers College, 1977.

19

National Case Study Report*

[From Chapter 1: Context and Content of the National Case Study Report]

The IEA Six Subject Study and Comparative Studies in Education

IEA achievement studies constitute the largest multinational and international study of the cognitive outcomes of schooling ever attempted. The present series of IEA publications, of which this volume represents but one small part, surveys and analyzes school achievement and its correlates in 21 countries and in six school subjects. IEA work thus constitutes a massive contribution not only to the literature of pedagogy, in general, but also to international and comparative studies in education.

Comparative studies in education have been developed out of a variety of motives. Simply the need to know what is happening in the educational systems of other lands was the earliest, and remains one of the strongest, supports. This has been reinforced by the intense interest of policy makers in foreign examples, in the hope that there might exist abroad some useful lessons to improve domestic practice. Thirdly, comparative studies of education held the promise of enriching both theoretical and empirical understanding of the processes taking place within schools, and the interconnections between schools and society. In response, comparative education has developed in a number of characteristic ways. First, there has been heavy concentration on the collection of data: what is going on abroad? and how best might the data be organized to demonstrate the similarities and differences among countries? Second, there has been great emphasis on the cross-national study of "problems" in education and between school and society, in the hope that policy makers wrestling with intractable problems of, say, Church-State relations, Teacher Training Curriculum, School Budgets, and so forth, might have their decisions informed by an understanding of the variety of conditions and attempted solutions abroad. Third, comparative education has proceeded in the direction of testing hypotheses about school processes and their relation to societal phenomena against the evidence drawn from several countries. On occasion, such research hypotheses have been derived from single-nation (case) studies; alternatively, the propositions tested have emerged only "after the fact," following extensive, sometimes even global, efforts at data collection and analysis.

IEA studies represent progress along all these dimensions. A vast amount of descriptive data has been amassed to describe what is in fact going on, but this was done with some well-defined aims in mind. Attention was focused upon the task of measuring levels of school achievement cross-nationally, and the related problem of investigating variations in levels of school achievement, particularly in those countries and among those students in all countries where achievement levels were unusually low. Moreover, from its very inception, IEA work was intended to provide the opportunity of testing the validity of a number of clearly enunciated hypotheses, using data from many countries. Thus, the format of IEA work is a series of replicated studies, for which special instruments were devised, appropriate to all the cases (countries) studied, to collect data on school achievement and on as many variables as were thought to be useful for explaining achievement.

The National Case Study and the IEA Six Subject Study

IEA studies are all concerned with identifying and explaining sources of differences in school achievement. The six subject studies approach this problem from the perspective of students and schools within each country. They are less concerned with the general characteristics of the nations – their societies and school systems – than with analysis of differences in the characteristics of the students tested, the schools they attend and the teachers. On occasion, the subject studies refer to national factors, such as economic level, school system structure, selectivity and the like, but these factors do not play a central role in the subject study analyses.

The National Case Study (NCS), on the other hand, puts the structure of the nations' school systems and the leading dimensions of their social-cultural-economic systems at the very center of the analysis. Thus, we may characterize the approach of the subject studies as "micro," while the NCS uses a "macro" approach, employing the country rather than the student or school, as the unit of analysis.

In this way, the two sets of studies constitute complementary, strategies for answering the basic questions: What factors are associated with what differences in school achievement, and to what extent?

Countries differ in important respects with regard to their culture, socio-economic systems, and their educational systems. It is reasonable to suppose that at least some of these features will affect the way schools operate, the way teachers teach, and the way students learn. In other words, there **is** some basis for supposing that some factors of a society and an educational system can be used to predict and/or explain particular features of a country's pattern of educational achievement.

More than this, there has now passed into the realm of "conventional wisdom" a host of preconceptions about the relationship between societal and educational structure on the one hand and educational achievement on the other. For example, comprehensive schools are said to "lower standards;" centralized educational administration is believed to raise educational achievement across a country; student achievement is supposed to suffer when the social status of teachers is low, and to gain from a high innovative capacity of the school system. Such is the conventional wisdom: the job of the National Case Study inquiry was to try to find out if it is indeed supported by the facts.

[From Chapter 4: Conclusion]

Review and Summary of the Findings

....The National Case Study data do extend knowledge about the socio-cultural, economic, and pedagogical context of the participating IEA countries but not sufficiently to provide firm generalizations about organizing and implementing an educational system. What we are left with insofar as the policy-planner is concerned, are a number of hints and possible implications which need to be examined on both a within-country and a cross-national basis. The correlations of the indicators with achievement, it must be repeated, deal with achievement in Science and Reading Comprehension. An educational system has broader goals than achievement in these subjects, goals of both a cognitive and affective nature, goals dealing with individuals and the society. These were not considered in the NCS analyses, and the policy-maker must perforce consider these other goals, and make decisions on a wider basis than that of measure school achievement alone.

There are four distinct kinds of implications to be drawn from the NCS data. Some findings suggest that the policy-makers might take "positive action" if increased achievement in Science and Reading Comprehension is desired. Some findings suggest that certain aspects of the so-called "conventional wisdom" are not borne out cross-nationally, and policy-makers would do well seriously to query such wisdom. Some findings suggest that policy makers should seek to make *qualitative* rather than quantitative changes and recognize that "more" alone may have little bearing on the question of "better" or "worse." And, finally, some findings suggest that even though there is a strong relationship between achievement and specific variables, other values should lead policy makers to look to different means of affecting achievement. For instance, a strong inverse relationship between achievement and economic development would not imply that nations reduce efforts to raise the GNP but rather they should study ways of improving the quality of school life, using an increasing level of affluence.

Implications for Further Research From its inception, the National Case Study gave promise of fewer implications for educational policy, than did the six subject studies. These focus much more than does the NCS on within-school variables, which are more susceptible to manipulation by school administrators and policy makers. The NCS deals typically with broad system characteristics of countries that are both more difficult to change and which reveal change only after quite long passages of time. The above discussion on policy implications has emphasized that the best that the NCS exercise could be expected to show is a number of rather gross associations, factors to be considered when attempting to reach conclusions about decisions on school policy. Commonly held assumptions might be questioned and previously neglected factors might receive more attention. Proof of definite associations and assertions of causal connections, leading directly to choice among policy options are not to be expected.

In the IEA study of Mathematics achievement, an effort was made to describe the several national educational and social contexts that should be taken into account, when considering the implications of the results. The NCS attempted to build on this example, and to go beyond it by looking at a wider range of country system characteristics; by including factors that are not easy to quantify and scale, as well as those that are; and by seeking time-series as well as cross-sectional data. It will have been evident that in all these respects a great deal of improvement is possible. Future research should try to cover far more comprehensively than was possible in the NCS such matters as differences by country in home environments, the political context of schooling, the connection between jobs and educational credentials, and the style of student-teacher "transactions" inside and outside the classroom – to name only a few.

Collection of time-series data on many variables proved to be very difficult, exceeding the statistical resources of most countries. Yet a good model of the factors influencing school achievement must be cast in terms of past inputs and processes. Insofar as social and educational systems change very slowly it is possible to use cross-sectional data as proxies for conditions in the past, and the NCS (and the other IEA studies) have relied upon the validity of this assumption. However, it should be recognized that it *is* an assumption, and research should continue to expand efforts to collect and use longitudinal data in explanatory models of cross-section achievement differences.

In international research in education, as in other social studies, cultural bias can be a serious pitfall. The multi-country collaborative nature of the IEA enterprise went far to eliminate such bias, and the instruments developed to measure student achievement appear to be, so far as is possible, neutral, or, if not neutral, at least not systematically biased with respect to national systems of education. Yet the very selection of school achievement as the criterion variable may be culturally biased, for it is a concept generated within and commanding particular attention in developed, Western-type societies. Even though achievement may include non-cognitive dimensions, such as associated skills and attitudes, even though it may be a value thoroughly acceptable to the educators of forward looking, but as yet less-developed countries, the IEA studies, and the National Case Study in particular, assume that school achievement is considered to be equally desirable (vis-à-vis other school and social objectives) among all people and in all countries. However, it may be that some people, countries or cultures simply value other outcomes of schooling (or of the use of young people's time and other national resources) more than they do achievement. And, while achievement appears to be a Western-generated criterion, it may not be an equally prized objective of schooling even among developed countries.

Although the subject committees gave varying amounts of attention to non-cognitive achievement in their respective areas (civic attitudes, literary tastes, science attitudes, for example, were particularly important and potentially illuminating), the NCS did not exploit the possibilities generated by these results. Future research should expand the analysis to investigate relationships between countries' system characteristics and such non-cognitive outcomes of schooling. Moreover, it is important to estimate the extent to which countries differ in the priority they accord to school achievement, compared to other outcomes of schooling.

For the most part, the statistical models employed in the subject studies explained only quite small fractions of the total observed variance in scores, between students and between schools. The reader will have noted also that the analyses employed in the NCS discovered few close fits between social, cultural, political and educational system characteristics and country achievement differences. There are a number of possible reasons for these, on the whole disappointing, results, reasons that apply as much to the explanatory models used in the subject studies as to the NCS approach.

First, measures on both the input and output sides may contain large amounts of error. Error in the measurement of variables severely limits the explanatory power of statistical models, and in this respect the NCS probably suffered more than did the subject studies. Thus, the plight of the NCS Committee might be compared with that of a marksman condemned to shoot at a poorly defined target with rifle and bullets deficient in a number of unknown respects. Future work should give higher priority to improving the quality of measures, particularly on the input (independent variable) side of the equations.

Secondly, low explanatory power can arise from misspecification of the model. There are various aspects of this problem. There may have been omission of important variables. However, in view of the large number of variables used in both the subject studies and in the NCS, this is unlikely to have happened. A more damaging misspecification may have been the implicit assumption in the NCS study that, in general, the several explanatory variables can be used as if they are associated with achievement in a straightforward, additive and essentially non-interactive manner. If this assumption is incorrect, if in fact differences in the patterning of inputs are important for explaining differences in achievement, then the low values of correlation coefficients reported are not unexpected. Future NCS-type work, then, should try to assemble patterns of countries' system characteristics, and relate these to differences in school outcomes. If this is to be done, however, it will require a larger number of nations than was available from the Six Subject Survey, as well as the use of more sophisticated statistical techniques.

The third aspect of possible misspecification resides in the possibility that the significance (for outcomes) of a particular factor may not be its quantity, or even its role in some overall pattern, but its timing. Two countries' systems may supply equal amounts of several resources, but in one country the timing of these inputs may suit children's growth and achievement more than in the other. An analogy from agriculture is perhaps apposite. Two farmers may labor an equal number of hours on very similar fields and with similar equipment, seeds, fertilizer, and so on. If one farmer times his operations consistently better than the other, the size of their harvests can be expected to differ sharply. The NCS did not probe such questions in the context of school achievement, and future research might well try to do so.

The most interesting, and perhaps the most useful, approach to cross-national research proceeds not in terms of existing country-wide units, but on the basis of subnational units. This means that it may be more interesting (for comparative work) to inquire about the correlates of achievement *within, say, metropolitan areas across several countries,* or *among the children of the poor,* or *among girls, each group taken together across nations,* than it is to regard individual countries as the logical, or only, units of analysis. This is not to deny, of course, that policy makers and researchers within each country will place first priority upon knowing the contributions made by such factors as metropolitan location, parental poverty, or sex to achievement in their own country. But that is by no means the end of the story, and comparisons across countries are inevitable. Here, the technique to be used is not simply a comparison of system-wide derived regression coefficients (although that can be valuable, especially if care has been taken to standardize definitions, measurement and scaling of variables across countries), but rather a cross-country pooling of data, partitioned by such factors as location, parental characteristics, teacher characteristics, levels of school finance, and so forth. This would enable the researchers to answer the question: How far, across all country units, *among girls,* are certain characteristics of homes, students and schools associated with achievement; how, if at all, do these associations differ among boys? Cognate questions could be asked about the production of achievement in metropolitan areas compared with rural areas, in poorly financed schools compared with well financed ones, and so on.

The NCS Committee did attempt a pilot investigation along these lines, but problems connected with the way schools were sampled defeated the attempt. It remains as a most fruitful line for crossnational research.

A final point concerning the value of partitioning samples for regression analysis bears on the utility of the results to policy makers. Because, in general, IEA regression analyses have taken the entire country sample as the universe to be explained, policy makers may find the results much less useful than they might wish. The results of linear multiple regression analyses done on aggregated country samples conceal a great deal of the information that they need. The reason for this becomes clear if one reflects on the nature of the information that a partial regression coefficient conveys. It tells the reader the *average* value of the strength of the association between the dependent variable and a particular independent variable, all other independent variables being held constant at *their* average values. Such an explanatory approach is able to clarify the connections between achievement and other factors, and to assign relative weights to the importance of one factor compared with others, *on average, over the entire country*. Policy makers, however, usually require something more detailed than such average indications. They need to know the effect upon achievement of varying a particular item under rather specific circumstances. Policy considerations are directed not at influencing achievement levels in "average," country-wide settings, but typically they deal with the problems of achievement in, say, rural vis-à-vis urban settings; of girls vis-à-vis boys; and of students in poor neighborhoods as distinct from wealthier neighborhoods. What is the incremental achievement value of increasing expenditures for schools in, say, poor neighborhoods? In wealthier neighborhoods? What provides the largest increments to achievement for low achievers? For average achievers? For high achievers? Thus, the policy makers' questions require analyses that do not hold the values of the other independent variables constant at their average country level, but which partition the total sample, in such a way that the associations between a dependent variable (say, achievement) and a particular independent variable (say, current expenditure per student) can be investigated separately for specified groups – e.g., poor children and rich children; urban center children and rural children; poor urban center children and rich urban center children.

In a sense, then, the NCS study can be regarded as an inevitably weak substitute for within-country regression analyses done on partitioned samples. Comparing, say, India, Iran and Thailand with the United States, England and Germany does underline the contrast between the way home, school and student variables are associated with achievement among poorer people, as compared with more affluent people. But there are severe problems in relying upon aggregate cross-national analysis to fulfill this role: the number of dimensions for partitioning countries soon exhausts their number, so that cell sizes become very small, or even zero; the results are always subject to challenge on the ground that national idiosyncrasies are at the root of all observed results; it is obviously not expedient to have to deal with all the difficulties involved in cross-national measurement and scaling of variables, if within-country research can answer some of the important policy questions as well, or better; and, finally, it is often more difficult to see how results obtained from cross-national research can be applied to the problems of a given country.

The role of an NCS-type study in the future, then, becomes one of trying to use national system characteristics to assess and explain problems and paradoxes that remain after as much variance as possible has been explained using partitioned national samples and partitioned pooled data.

This report has, it is hoped, reconfirmed the potential of crossnational studies of schooling, based upon broad cultural, societal and educational measures. However, the caveats attached to findings are numerous, and the study is, perhaps, best regarded as an interim report. The goal of a coherent, reliable, persuasive explanatory model of school achievement differences is still far distant; and many problems of measurement, scaling, and comparability of variables remain intractable. The present state of the art in empirical comparative educational analysis leaves much to be desired. For we are all as yet in the position of one of W.S. Gilbert's comic opera criminals, endlessly expiating his misconduct, serving as a cautionary example to others:

> *And there he plays extravagant matches*
> *In fitless finger stalls,*
> * On a cloth untrue*
> * With a twisted cue*
> *And elliptical billiard balls.*

* Excerpts from A. Harry Passow, Harold J. Noah, Max A. Eckstein, John R. Mallea, *The National Case Study: An Empirical Comparative Study of Twenty-One Educational Systems*. New York: John Wiley and Sons, and Stockholm: Almquist and Wiksell, 1976. International Studies in Evaluation VII: 12-14, 299-295. Reprinted by permission of John Wiley and Sons.

20

International Study of School Achievement*

Policy makers in education say they want to make schools "more effective." What knowledge will help them achieve that goal? They need answers to such questions as: How do children's minds work so that they learn, can perform, and continue to learn? (Psychology) How do teachers teach successfully? (Pedagogy) How do home environments facilitate or hinder children's learning and teachers' teaching? (Sociology, anthropology) How do societal factors, school system patterns and internal school arrangements interact with the previous questions? (History, economics, political science, administrative science, systems analysis, etc.)

If we knew all these things, the ways they are patterned and how they interact, we would be in a position to make firmer assertions about pedagogical matters and the probable outcomes of particular educational decisions. Policy makers informed by this knowledge could then perhaps concentrate on their proper function, which is to make moral decisions. (Philosophy)

The research work conducted by the IEA (the International Association for the Evaluation of Educational Achievement) over the past fifteen years represents a massive attempt to answer a few of these questions. Twenty-one countries participated in what was, without doubt, the largest international effort ever made to collect and analyze primary data on schooling and its correlates.

Nine volumes (eleven, if we count the two volumes in 1967 on the mathematics study, or twelve, if we go back to 1962 and the pilot study report); 200 million pieces of information; $5,000,000 of international costs and perhaps half as much again of local, individual country costs; hundreds of thousands of manhours of labor; two international conferences (one just held in November 1973 at Harvard University) all are devoted to trying to find out what principal factors, if any, make a difference to the school achievement and attitudes of young people from different class backgrounds, in different types of schools, in different countries.

Three recent volumes detail the study of education and school achievement in science, literature, and reading comprehension. Six further volumes will appear in the next year or so. Three will deal with teaching, learning and achievement in English and French as foreign languages, and in civic knowledge; a fourth will contain the socio-educational profiles of the several countries; a fifth will be a technical report; and the last will attempt a summary of the entire project.

The conclusions so far are not very startling. No great cornerstone of our understanding about the factors influencing school achievement is either erected or overthrown. The home background of children, as measured by father's education and occupation, mother's education, and number of books in the home, stands out as an internationally strong variable in "explaining" variations in school achievement. Few of the directly school-related variables, such as sex of teacher, teachers' experience or training, size of school, quantity of homework, and type of curriculum come through as important in all the nations tested, though here and there, one or another school based variable shows up with a statistically significant coefficient in the regressions. The one consistently important school-related variable is "opportunity to learn": that is, when the curriculum has provided for students to learn a given area of knowledge, when teachers have actually taught it, and when the internationally devised tests included it among the questions asked, students did better. Again, not an earthshaking conclusion.

It could *not* be established that differences among school related arrangements bear any direct, simple, universal relationship to differences of school achievement especially when home and general environmental factors are held constant. Note that this *does not mean* that "school makes no difference." To conclude that, IEA would have had to compare test scores of children without any schooling with the scores of children who had had some standard amount. That was not done. What the IEA results do point to is the probability that within countries (and probably even across countries) homes differ from each other vastly more than do schools. Consequently, although most children get a lot out of school, the big variations in achievement observed around that basic level are attributable more to home than to school differences.

The IEA investigation provided three levels of analysis: between-children, between-schools, and between-nations. Hence, a good beginning has been made to answering such difficult questions as: Do the ways in which different countries sort children into different types of schools matter at all? If so, in what particular respects?. Thus, the sorting of children by social class of the home appears dramatically in the results of between-schools analysis in Scotland and England, in contrast with Sweden, where individual school populations are much more heterogeneous. Adding school related factors (after the home factors have been put in) to the equations for Scotland and England does not add much explanatory power to the model; adding them in Sweden made a great deal of difference. Hence, IEA work begins to allow us to specify the school and home contexts in which some factors are important for achievement, and others less so. The IEA results show, too, the degree to which the term "less developed" must be applied to school systems, and not just to economic systems. Four less developed countries (Chile, India, Iran, and Thailand) participated. The gap between mean school achievement levels in the developed and less developed world is very wide. Thus, at the Population I level (10-year olds), the grand mean score for science in the developed countries was twice that for the less developed; in reading comprehension, similarly. These comparative measures of the combined effect of home, school, and environmental factors on school achievement are the first ones of their kind. They underline the enormous tasks facing the poorer nations of the world in raising the level of knowledge and basic educational skills of their young people. It is precisely because of their relatively high levels of school competence that the richer nations of the world can begin to think in terms of some "de-schooling." For the poorer nations, who have hardly reached first base in the organization and operation of their school systems, the notion of "de-schooling" is a cruel joke.

Among other significant questions treated in the present corpus of IEA work are: the differences in achievement that are linked to sex, from subject area to subject area (especially in science), and from country to country; the extent to which comprehensive secondary schooling lowers mean national scores, but leaves virtually unaffected the scores of the top achievers in each country; the relatively high importance of certain school and home factors that are composited under the label, "learning conditions," for explaining achievement in science, and in French and English as foreign languages; and their relatively low importance for reading comprehension and civic knowledge; and the first attempts to measure cross-national differences in students' attitudes to literature and their modes of evaluating the merits of a piece of writing. This list, however, barely scratches the surface of the rich store of data and inferences to be found in IEA publications.

Where does the study of the factors affecting school achievement go from here? Most obviously, subsequent work, designed to replicate the individual subject studies after an interval of five or ten years, can use that opportunity to improve the validity, reliability, and scaling of important variables. In addition, close inspection of the data already collected in each country will identify schools that lie far off the regression plane, so-called "outlier" schools, that appear to produce extraordinarily high (or low) scores in association with extraordinarily unfavorable (or favorable) circumstances. Such schools should become the subjects of detailed on-site studies, to isolate the proximate causes of their "non-predicted" behavior.

Aggregative social science models that rely on data amassed from many thousands of individuals in a score of countries are naturally likely to contain large amounts of error. After every reasonable effort is made to fill in gaps, to check responses, to control coding, keypunching, and data storage, mistakes and gaps are still inevitable. But this first and most obvious difficulty with this kind of work is, in the end, not the most serious. Given time, money, patience, and a few more tries at what is a brand new area in education and social science studies, such problems will be controlled.

More intractable is the problem of adequately modeling the processes at work in the homes, schools, and classrooms of the world. The model used in the present IEA studies is an avowedly simplistic one, designed to facilitate the use of linear multiple regression as the primary analytic tool. Together with linear scaling of variables, this assumes that, for each variable entering the regression, at no matter what quantitative level, its contribution to achievement outcomes will be a constant proportion of that level. Thus, we assume that for a given population there will be a single value of the regression coefficient that can be applied equally to, say, a low level of "home background" factors and to a high level. This is the average value of the association between home background and school achievement. Whether that average value reflects anything of practical importance in the real world depends on close scrutiny and testing of the underlying data. . . . .

Some critics may wish to deny totally the validity of the IEA approach. They will point to the essentially small scale nature of the educational process – teachers and students interacting in a given classroom at a moment of time. They will reject an analytic technique that ignores all these individual interactions and studies instead the circumstances around the teacher-student-home interaction. It appears to us that an either/or choice is not necessary. Rather, our stance should be to encourage diverse, and essentially complementary, modes of analysis. Because education is a small scale, individually based process, techniques of micro-observation, analysis of small group behavior, and observation of classroom interaction and culture are vital. But we know, too, that schooling is a mass enterprise and, as such, there is value in analysing its correlates and outcomes using techniques of mass data collection and analysis. Both techniques have their place and their role. As we develop each of them we should approach a better understanding of schools in their micro- and macro- aspects.

NOTES

* Harold J. Noah and Max A. Eckstein, "International Study of School Achievement," in *Notes on Education* 4 (1974): 6-9.

IEA Publications

Arthur W. Foshay et al., *Educational Achievements of Thirteen-year-olds in Twelve Countries* (Hamburg: UNESCO Institute for Education, 1962); Torsten Husen (ed.) *International Study of Achievement in Mathematics: A Comparison of Twelve Countries,* 2 vols. (New York: John Wiley and Sons, 1967); L.C. Comber. and John P. Keeves, *Science Education in Nineteen Countries* (New York; John Wiley and Sons, 1973); Alan C. Purves, *Literature Education in Ten Countries* (New York: John Wiley and Sons, 1973); Robert L. Thorndike, *Reading Comprehension Education in Fifteen Countries* (New York: John Wiley and Sons, 1973). In press: E. Glyn Lewis, *English as a Foreign Language in Ten Countries,* John B. Carroll, *French as a Foreign Language in Seven Countries,* R.F. Farnen, A.N. Oppenheim, and Judith V. Torney, *Civic Education in Ten Countries,* A. Harry Passow, Harold J. Noah, and Max A. Eckstein, *The National Case Study: An Empirical Comparative Study of Twenty-One Educational Systems,* G.F. Peaker, *An Empirical Study of Education in Twenty-One Countries: A Technical Report,* D.A. Walker, *The IEA Six-Subject Survey.*

21

Reflections on the IEA*

In a world of rampant nationalism, it is a wonder that the IEA exists at all. Schooling is only too often the very embodiment of nationalism, and nations are fiercely protective of the school systems they have built. To open them to international scrutiny requires a degree of willing cooperation, mutual trust, and genial forbearance that is, to say the very least, rare among nations. Thus, quite apart from the quality of IEA published results (which I happen to think is generally high) and their utility (which I think is great), the IEA shines forth as a good deed in a naughty world.

Empire or Commonwealth?

Purves had, at one time, thought of titling his article "The IEA Empire" (personal communication from Postlethwaite). Better to call it "The IEA Commonwealth." From its beginnings to the present, the IEA has lacked all the attributes of empire. The association has never had, nor is there now, an emperor or empress (though the IEA has profited singularly from the steadfast, forceful, and nurturing leadership of Torsten Husén and T. Neville Postlethwaite). It has no fixed boundaries, no stable territories. Nations, and even parts of nations, join voluntarily, participate in this or that aspect of the IEA's work as they please and as they can raise the resources, and may freely secede. An empire requires imperial subjects; the IEA has none. An empire requires tribute, flowing from the periphery to the center; in the IEA, tribute is neither paid nor collected. Moreover, over time, the IEA has become progressively more decentralized. The international coordination of testing, data analysis, and even reporting is no longer located in a single headquarters (Hamburg and then Stockholm) for all projects; instead, each project finds an international home in one or another of the countries participating in the project. No empire was ever quite like this!

As Purves shows so clearly, one of the IEA's most important achievements has been to provide a framework within which research personnel can learn to improve their skills in analyzing the operation of their school systems.[1] Out of active international instruction and interchange of ideas, a vigorous fraternity of scholars and administrators has emerged, energizing and extending the reach of comparative education. Perhaps the IEA is best viewed not even as a commonwealth but rather as a latter-day incarnation of Robert Boyle's seventeenth-century "invisible college," operating on a global scale. For that reason, it is wholly fitting that over the years the *Comparative Education Review* has devoted so many pages to reports and comments on IEA work and now devotes a second entire issue to some of the association's current work. Its inquiries continue to represent the most sustained, imposing, and ultimately, I dare say, most heuristic work in comparative education that we have yet seen. As Philip Altbach has recently written, "Whatever criticisms one may have of aspects of the IEA research, it is perhaps the most widely cited and influential research done on an educational topic from a cross-national perspective."[2]

Let me declare my interest. For a period of 9 years, 1967-76, I was a student enrolled in this "invisible college," working for a brief period in Stockholm but mostly in New York City, on materials that eventually appeared as the *National Case Study* volume in the Six-Subject Survey series.[3] Since then I have enjoyed alumnus status, having been discharged more or less honorably from the college. I owe a colossal debt to all those with whom I worked in and around the IEA for a postdoctoral education in comparative education provided during those 9 years. The reader should bear in mind, then, when reading what follows that I am definitely parti pris.

Country Mean Scores

From first to last, IEA spokespersons have consistently deprecated the alacrity with which commentators seize on the figures of mean national achievement scores, and they deny that the scores, taken without the benefit of a great deal of other knowledge, have much meaning. The tests were not devised primarily in order to make total score comparisons between countries possible and certainly not as yardsticks for an 'international contest.' "The mere fact that algebra and geometry items were included in the tests for the 13-year level in spite of the fact that these topics were not dealt with in some countries should discourage national comparisons."[4] Husén emphasizes the same point: "The media and the general public focused on the national means, in spite of the cautions issued by IEA researchers who tried to play down the tendency to perceive the exercise as an 'Olympic Game' or 'horse race.'"[5]

I take the contrary view. I continue to believe that, on the whole, it has been a strategic error for the IEA to take this cautionary stance to the national mean figures. First, it gives the impression that IEA researchers do not really believe that the means are valid and reliable; that they do not in fact reflect (relative to other nations) what schoolchildren in a given nation know of science, or mathematics, and so forth; and that the means might be significantly different if testing were to be repeated. This is an unfortunate impression to convey because the IEA has devoted an extraordinary and by all accounts successful effort to insure that the tests reflect the curriculum, that the samples of students to be tested are good probability samples, and that the scoring procedures are systematic and accurate. Moreover, *pace* Husén's observation cited above, even where it is true that those taking the test have not had the opportunity to learn some of the material in the test, that in itself is an important datum. A country that chooses to teach algebra to its 13-year-olds presumably gains an "advantage," which should be properly reflected in the country's total score.

Second, the protestations contra international comparisons of national mean scores do not ring true. They engender the kind of skepticism a parent might feel when his 13-year-old son is observed deeply immersed in the pages of *Playboy* magazine and who, when asked what he is doing, replies that he is studying the advertisements for audio equipment. The national mean scores may not be *the* most interesting aspect of IEA published results, but they are very high on the scale of legitimate as distinct from prurient interest – and rightly so.

Third, national mean scores (given that they are valid and reliable statistics) have told us some very important things. They have told us that, for comparable populations in school among the industrialized nations, the range of the means is by no means large, nor is it consistent across school subjects and age-groups. Rather than deny that the country mean scores had importance, the more pertinent message would have been that schools on average do about as well by their pupils in one (developed) country as in another. This has been evident from the very beginning of IEA-type work, when the Pilot Study of School Achievement was conducted (June 1959-June 1961) under the auspices of the UNESCO Institute for Education in Hamburg. At the time, Thorndike had this to say:

> It is clear that the variation between national means is small in relation to the variability of scores within any one country. [Between-country variability as a percentage of within-country variability ranged from a high of 16.2 percent (mathematics) to a low of 5.2 percent (science).] National differences represent a minor rather than a major component of these results. And the probability is that they are over-estimated rather than underestimated, because the countries that did relatively well on the tests were in several instances those that were known to have tested an up-graded sample of their populations. We suspect that with truly representative national samples, the differences would have been reduced. Of course, the participants in the survey were all countries with a basically European culture, and with well-developed educational systems. A greater heterogeneity in national cultures and educational levels would probably increase the national differences, perhaps substantially.[6]

The first wholly-IEA study (the 12-nation mathematics study) produced results with similar implications: the country with the lowest mathematics score for 13-year-olds (Sweden) had a score only about one-quarter of a standard deviation from the grand mean; Japan, with the highest score, was about three-quarters of a standard deviation above the grand mean. The range from top to bottom was just over 1 standard deviation, or 15.5 points on a 70-point test. Six of the 10 countries clustered tightly around the grand mean (with a range of about 0.4 standard deviations, or 5.8 points).[7]

Are these "big" differences? Husén thought so: "Differences between countries in average score are quite marked."[8] I suppose that what is big and what is small is a matter of perspective and context. But surely it would be imprudent to dismiss the hypothesis that, on the evidence of test scores of 13-year-old children in mathematics, Finland, the Netherlands, Australia, England, Scotland, and France are all nations "from the same population" and that the United States and Sweden are hardly much different. Whatever the variations in their educational and social systems, taken together they are not associated with much difference in national mean mathematics scores for this age-group.

For older students, the range of national mean scores opened up (1.6 standard deviations for the preuniversity grades taking mathematics; 1.5 for the parallel groups not taking mathematics). But, after adjusting for the differences in retentivity of 17-19-year-old students across the nations, Gilbert Peaker could observe that the data "strongly suggest that the amount of mathematical talent is very much the same in all these countries, though the policies used to develop it differ."[9] Alex Inkeles, commenting on the results of the Six-Subject Survey, is as definite. "I read these results as telling us that, given broadly comparable material to work with, the school systems of the more developed countries are, in general, turning out students of broadly comparable competence in the subject tested."[10]

Rosier now provides us with preliminary cross-national results for science achievement, specifically, data on *p*-scores (percentage correct responses) on six items given to 14-year-old students in 14 countries/systems.[11] Two of the countries are "developing" (Singapore and Thailand); the rest are "developed." Let us assume that the scores are representative of results on the entire test (a large assumption, but these data are all that we have at the time of writing). The overall mean is 57 (i.e., 57 percent of responses to all six questions in all 14 countries were correct). The cross-national range is 19.1 (Japan high, 69.2; Italy low, 50.1). However, three countries (Israel, the Netherlands, and Norway) fall within +3 points of the mean of 57; and seven countries (Australia, English-speaking Canada, England, Finland, Poland, Thailand, and the United States) fall within − 5 points. This is a noteworthy degree of clustering. It might be interesting to compare it with the clustering of national averages of 14-year-old children's heights or weights.

Of special interest is the position of Thailand, whose mean *p*-score of 54.3 is above England's 52.3, English-speaking Canada's 53.7, and Poland's 53.7. Here is a "developing" nation that may have raised the science education of its junior citizens to an impressive level – a veritable *défi thai*.[12] In terms of GNP per capita, the World Bank ranks Thailand as fifty-fifth from the bottom of 126 countries listed. Compare Thailand's per capita income of $820 (in 1983 U.S. dollars) with the United Kingdom's $9,200 and Canada's $12,310.[13] Recall that one of the most solid crossnational findings of earlier IEA studies has been that mean achievement scores of the less developed countries (LDCs) are substantially and consistently lower than those of the more developed countries (MDCs). As between these two "worlds," it is as if we are indeed dealing with two different populations, each clustered quite closely about its respective grand mean. This is what Walker had to say in his summary volume on the Six-Subject Survey: "It was also apparent at an early stage that the material [for science achievement] from the developing countries (Chile, India, Iran, Thailand) would, in many of the analyses, require to be treated separately from that of the developed countries.... The most striking fact to emerge from the table is the large difference between the two groups of scores in Reading Comprehension, i.e., those of the three developing countries and those of the remainder."[14]

Should Thailand's preliminary results hold up when we have the complete figures, the implications are quite important: the "necessary" connection between a low level of income per capita and low level of school achievement will have been shown to be not necessary at all. Perhaps after reading Anderson's report of the Classroom Environment Study, we should not be surprised at this possibility. The conclusion he labels generalization 3, "the nature of classroom teaching is quite similar in all countries," is a powerful pointer to the results IEA has published.[15]

Perhaps, though, the dispersions of achievement scores about the national means (the standard deviations) might tell a different story. A good deal of the IEA evidence is that they do not. Nations are really quite similar in the degree of dispersion of scores generated in association with schooling. This is hardly the place to present a detailed, comprehensive analysis, so let me simply cite results from the Six-Subject Survey and the 1967 mathematics study. In science achievement, population I (10-yearolds) and population 2 (14-year-olds) each exhibited remarkably similar cross-national standard deviations. For population 1, the grand mean of the country standard deviations was 7.9 *(N* = 12), and the range went only from 7.1 (French-speaking Belgium) to 9.3 (U.S.A.); for population 2, the grand mean was 11.8 *(N* = 14), and the range went from 8.8 (French-speaking Belgium again) to 14.8 (Japan). Nor was the cross-national "dispersion of dispersions" much greater for population 4 (the preuniversity grade): grand mean was 9.9 *(N* = 14), low standard deviation was 7.9 (French-speaking Belgium, yet again), and high was 12.1 (Scotland).[16]

Postlethwaite reported standard deviations of mathematics scores for population 1b (the grade in which most students are 13 years old). Again, with the exception of only one country, England, there is notably tight clustering of the standard deviations for the 12 nations about the international grand mean.[17]

Within very broad limits, the industrialized nations taken as a whole do much the same things in their classrooms and secure broadly comparable results. The big differences are within-nation and even within-school.

Focusing on Within-Nation Differences

If the cross-national differences in school achievement are not large, does this mean that IEA work is fundamentally irrelevant to comparative education? There would have been a time in the development of the field when this would have been the received opinion. Comparative education was viewed as primarily, if not exclusively, concerned with describing, explaining, and perhaps profiting from knowledge of the differences among countries. This is certainly not the case today. We have come to recognize that a valid cross-national comparative study will often proceed by demonstrating the ways in which different combinations of factors are associated with broadly similar outcomes. This, more than the underlining of achievement differences, has been the largest knowledge-enhancing contribution of IEA achievement studies. At the end of a detailed critical review of the nine volumes reporting the Six-Subject Survey, Ellis Page made the point this way: "But if the IEA had done nothing more, it contributed a great deal in showing how standard were some of the patterns of explanation, when seen internationally. This is a high accomplishment, especially given the difficulty of interpretation of some of the questions asked about the schools, curriculum, etc., in an international context."[18]

Evaluation of the Evaluations

People have taken notice of IEA work. A bibliography published in 1979 lists about 300 items from all corners of the world.[19] There have been many new publications since then. It is well beyond the capacity of any one reader to know, let alone assimilate. Technical reports, reports of analyses, policy reports, school-subject reports, country reports, international reports, reports on IEA organizational matters, doctoral dissertations, journal articles and reviews, secondary analyses, parallel studies – the list goes on and on. Let me select just three pieces of scholarship from this enormous literature.

All three are evaluations of IEA work that have appeared in the U.S.: Inkeles's review of the nine volumes associated with the Six-Subject Survey; Page's review monograph, "The Methodology of International Evaluation of Educational Achievement"; and Theisen, Achola, and Boakari's article, "The Underachievement of Cross-national Studies of Achievement," which won the CIES award for the best article appearing in volume 27 of the *Comparative Education Review*.[20] Although all three pieces contain some generous huzzahs for IEA work, their overall tone is highly critical. I would like to pool those criticisms in as brief a compass as I can, comment on their appositeness, and suggest that they do not contain much that was not known to IEA researchers.

Inkeles faults IEA work for being "underanalyzed" in four main respects: inconsistencies in design, models of analysis, and reporting across the subject areas; failure to express the results in accessible form, so that comparisons across countries might be facilitated; failure to analyze the relation between school achievement and separate social groups (social class, race, religious, or ethnic groups); and failure to evaluate the influence of national context as a determinant of student performance. He expresses regret that the IEA chose to assign a low priority to analysis of the gain in scores between grades. He suggests that it is very important to identify children's capabilities at the point of entry to school, especially when trying to explain why children in the developing nations get low scores on the tests. In addition, Inkeles questions the wisdom of choosing populations on the basis of age, when the same age may mean quite different accumulated years of school attendance (grade level) in different countries.

Page faults the IEA for not spelling out the objectives of its work clearly enough (not as well "as in a typical doctoral dissertation"), although he does derive seven objectives from a foreword by Husén to the science study.[21] He criticizes what he judges to be an overwhelmingly "environmentalist" tone in IEA work and neglect of possibly important genetic factors to explain differences in school achievement. Specifically, he would have liked the IEA to test sibling pairs in order to control for genetic and home-background factors ("the IEA missed a great opportunity").[22] Together with Inkeles, Page deplores what he sees as IEA's "fragmented view of the school curriculum."[23] Instead of seeing it as a whole, the IEA has chosen to study the curriculum subject by subject, even failing to test broadly the same set of students across all school subjects. He retains the gravest doubts about the cross-national validity of the tests, given the problems raised by translation, nor does he give the IEA high marks either for following Bloom's taxonomy of objectives or for assigning test items to just four of these categories.[24] Again, with Inkeles, he faults the IEA reporting for inconsistencies (especially the failure to maintain consistent definitions across the studies of each of the major explanatory "blocks" formed for regression analysis), confusing presentations, and gaps (no indexes, no lists of tables, on occasion no full presentation of the test items, and no systematic presentation of means and standard deviations of all variables, independent and dependent).[25] Finally, and also echoing Inkeles, Page expresses disappointment at what he sees as excessive tentativeness and ambiguity in the announced conclusions as to what makes a difference for school achievement both within and across countries – "an uncertain trumpet" is his wonderfully chosen metaphor.[26]

Inkeles and Page accept and even embrace the basic IEA approach via cross-national regression models, "merely" asking that it be done better. Not so Theisen, Achola, and Boakari. They argue that explanatory models formulated in terms of national units will be "difficult to standardize in terms of both variable inclusion and measurement." The principal need is to measure variables at the local idiosyncratic, rather than at the national aggregate level. Otherwise, studies will most likely yield results that will be misleading when used at the local level, which is the "level [at which] educational policies, if they are to be effective, must be designed and implemented."[27] The major problem, they suggest, is with the sampling strategies, which

have been designed to reflect aggregate levels of achievement; individual students, not school systems or districts, have been the unit of analysis. Under most sampling schemes, one or two schools from a defined geographical or administrative boundary are selected in the first stage of a multistage sampling process. Subsequently, a handful of individual students are chosen randomly from these schools for inclusion in the final sample. As a result of the low number of students drawn from each school and because of randomly distributed variations in ability among the sampled elements, achievement data may only marginally reflect the importance of school and community characteristics on learning.... Furthermore, the statistics resulting from samples may be highly unstable as a result of the small number as of cases taken from each school.[28]

This is a truly formidable massed array of criticisms, and it by no means exhausts either the total presented in these three commentaries or, of course, the additional criticisms that have appeared elsewhere. But they will certainly do for now. What can one say in response?

Virtually all of the points summarized above have been made and published by IEA researchers and report writers themselves. This is not to justify decisions made or not made in the course of IEA work but merely to underline the extent to which individual scholars worked with resources that were meager relative to the immensity of the tasks they had assumed, under deadlines that approached all too quickly, and ever mindful that international work forces compromises between the ideal and the possible. Such compromises inevitably end up closer to the possible than to the ideal. . . . . The closing pages of one IEA report, the National Case Study, summarize the critical comments of particippationts in the work.[29]

Many of the Inkeles, Page, and Theisen et al. recommendations – especially those that ask for a more uniform approach to model building, variable identification, construct building, and statistical procedures – require a much greater degree of central control than has proved possible in an international, voluntary organization, which attracts researchers with very different levels of expertise and sophistication. To the extent that the IEA is adopting an even more decentralized organization of its international work (partly because it is so difficult to raise funds for international coordination, and partly in order to reduce the weight of "advanced" countries in decisions), uniform approaches may become even more difficult to achieve. Nevertheless, criticisms voiced particularly by Inkeles and Page about the inconsistencies, relatively arcane and hence confusing statistical measures, and sheer gaps in reporting data and results are probably only too valid. On the evidence of the papers collected in this issue of the *Comparative Education Review,* they are being taken to heart, and a determined effort is being made to remedy the problems.

One point in conclusion is of particular importance for scholars in comparative education. There is a tendency to limit consideration of IEA work, its merits as well as its shortcomings, to just that work contained in the international studies of achievement in school subjects. This neglects the fact that there is as much, if not more, IEA literature written from the perspective either of a single nation or of a single topic other than school achievement. These works present further, often extremely detailed, analysis of data collected within a country or about a particular aspect of education. Naming only the merest few, I refer to Wolf's *Achievement in America* and Pidgeon's *Achievement in Mathematics* to illustrate the first category; and Postlethwaite's *School Organization and Student Achievement,* Noonan's *School Resources, Social Class, and Student Achievement,* Bergling's *The Development of Hypothetico-Deductive Thinking in Children*, and Purves and Levine's *Educational Policy and International Assessment* to illustrate the second.[30]

It was said of Sir Christopher Wren, the great architect-rebuilder of London in the seventeenth century, Si monumentuum requiris, circumspice ["If you want to see his monument, look about you!"]. Similarly, if you want to see (the living) monument to the IEA, just take a look at the 1979 bibliography of works from, using, and about the IEA noted above. It reveals a formidable, if oft-times messy, piece of research architecture.

NOTES

* Harold J. Noah, "Reflections," *Comparative Education Review* 31 (1987), pp. 137-149. Reprinted by permission of the University of Chicago Press.

1. Alan C. Purves, "IEA: An Agenda for the Future," *International Review of Education* (in press).
2. Philip G. Altbach, "The *Review* at Thirty," *Comparative Education Review* 30 (1986), pp. 1-11, at 8.
3. A. Harry Passow, Harold J. Noah, Max A. Eckstein, and John R. Mallea, *The National Case Study: An Empirical Comparative Study of Twenty-One Educational Systems* (New York: Wiley, 1976).
4. Torsten Husén, ed., *International Study of Achievement in Mathematics: A Comparison of Twelve Countries* (New York: Wiley, 1967) 2: 26.
5. Torsten Husén "Policy Impact of IEA Research" (in this issue).
6. Arthur W. Foshay et al., *Educational Achievements of Thirteen-Year-Olds in Twelve Countries* (Hamburg: UNESCO Institute for Education, 1962), p. 16.
7. Husén, ed., pp. 26-27.
8. Husén, ed., p. 26.
9. G.F. Peaker, "International Study of Achievement in Mathematics," *Trends in Education* 9 (1968): 42-48, at 45.
10. Alex Inkeles, "National Differences in Scholastic Performance," *Comparative Education Review* 23 (1979): 391.
11. Malcolm J. Rosier, "The Second International Science Study" (in this issue), table 2.
12. There was a foretaste of Thailand's potential given in the results of the Six-Subject Survey: Thailand's 14-year-olds did about as well on the test of reading English as a foreign language as Italy's, and better than Finland's. See Glynn Lewis and Carolyn E. Massad, *The Teaching of English as a Foreign Language in Ten Countries* (New York: Wiley, 1975), p. 102.
13. *World Development Report 1985* (New York: Oxford University Press, 1985), pp. 174-75.
14. David A. Walker, *The IEA Six-Subject Survey: An Empirical Study of Education in Twenty-one Countries* (New York: Wiley, 1976), p. 81, 113.
15. Lorin W. Anderson, "The Classroom Environment Study: Teaching for Learning" (in this issue).
16. L.C. Comber and John P. Keeves, *Science Education in Nineteen Countries* (New York: Wiley, 1973), p. 159.
17. T. Neville Postlethwaite, *School Organisation and Student Achievement: A Study Based on Achievement in Mathematics in Twelve Countries* (New York: Wiley, 1967), p. 96.
18. Ellis B. Page, "The Methodology of International Evaluation of Educational

Achievement," *Proceedings of the National Academy of Education* 5 (1978): 19-48, at 45.

19. T. Neville Postlethwaite and Arieh Lewy, *Annotated Bibliography of IEA Publications (1962-1978)* (Stockholm: IEA, University of Stockholm, 1979). The title is somewhat misleading because many of the items listed had no IEA imprimatur.

20. Inkeles, Alex, Ellis B. Page, Gary L. Theisen, Paul P.W. Achola, and Francis Musa Boakari, "The Underachievement of Cross-national Studies of Achievement," *Comparative Education Review* 27 (1981), pp. 46-68.

21. Comber and Keeves, pp. 10-11.

22. Page, p. 31.

23. Ibid., p. 32.

24. B.S. Bloom et al., *Taxonomy of Educational Objectives,* Handbook 1, *Cognitive Domain* (New York: McKay, 1956)

25. Page, pp. 43-45.

26. Ibid., p. 36.

27. Theisen et al., p. 47.

28. Ibid., p. 46

29. Passow et al., pp. 291-95

30. Richard M. Wolf, *Achievement in America: National Report of the United States for the International Educational Achievement Project* (New York: Teachers College Press, 1977); Douglas Pidgeon, *Achievement in Mathematics: A National Study in Secondary Schools* (Slough: National Foundation for Educational Research in England and Wales, 1967); Postlethwaite's *School Organization and Student Achievement* (n. 17 above); Richard D. Noonan, *School Resources, Social Class, and Student Achievement* (New York: Wiley, 1976); Kurt Bergling, *The Development of Hypothetico-Deductive Thinking in Children* (New York: Wiley, 1974); Alan C. Purves and Daniel U. Levine, *Educational Policy and International Assessment: Implications of the IEA Surveys of Achievement* (Berkeley: McCutchan, 1975).

22

The Two Faces of Examinations*

Introduction

All over the world, major aspects of the school system are being reassessed in response to changing social, political, and economic demands. One common and important response by educational systems has been the prodigious expansion of secondary school enrollments, and consequently there is a greater diversity of abilities and aspirations in the student body. In turn, this has been accompanied by demands for more options, and by growing utilitarian and instrumental concern for the applicability and economic relevance of the curriculum and credentials. A particular consequence is that governments as well as politicians, parents and employers have afforded increased importance to vocational considerations. To meet the new demands, the organization and structure of school systems, the content of instruction, and the selection and preparation of teachers, have all come under review. National policies are formulated to work directly on school practices, through regulation, as well as indirectly, via financial incentives and sanctions, teacher training, and exhortations, studies and recommendations issued by prominent individuals or commissions.

One of the potentially most powerful mechanisms for achieving change in education is the external examination system, especially examinations taken toward the close of secondary schooling. In recent years educational policy makers have recognized what was known by the Imperial Chinese court over a thousand years ago and by those who laid the foundations of state-funded elementary and secondary education in nineteenth and early twentieth-century Britain: that a national external examination system can be a powerful instrument for moving schooling in a desired direction. As a consequence, many agencies, including governments, look to examinations to influence how teachers go about the business of teaching, how students attend to learning, how universities select their students, and how employers choose new workers.

This paper selects eight countries for study: China, England and Wales, the Federal Republic of Germany, France, Japan, the Soviet Union, Sweden, and the United States. First, we identify the targets of changes in the examinations taken toward the end of secondary school. We then examine instances of governments using changes in the examinations to initiate or accelerate wider educational change, as well as instances where examination systems have acted as barriers to change. The paper closes with some observations on the nature of examinations and of the ways in which their dual roles have played out in the eight countries.

211

Examination systems appear to be exceptionally resilient, able to adapt well to pressures for change. Indeed, while the extent and specifics of change in examinations vary markedly from country to country, the social and educational importance of the credentials gained through them seem hardly to have diminished. The substantial changes introduced in recent years in the *baccalauréat* and the *Abitur* attest to the adaptability of these traditional examinations, while they continue to retain their status as essential mechanisms for directing students to, and within, institutions of higher education, and for regulating the scholastic activity of teachers and schools. In Japan, the examinations at the end of primary and junior high school, and especially the examinations taken at the end of senior high school, provide the common (some would say, the major) motive force driving the entire schooling enterprise. In the People's Republic of China, the university entrance examinations are a critical device for allocating the severely limited resources for higher education. In England and Wales, while particular examinations have come and gone during the past 40 years, the underlying social and educational significance of the examinations has been conserved. Indeed, the fact that the British government has been eager to break decisively with traditional constraints and has emerged as the leading actor in the nationalization of external examinations and tests is compelling evidence of the status school examinations continue to enjoy. Even in the Soviet Union, where the examinations for the school completion certificate have relatively little importance, the separate entrance examinations to institutions of higher education carry great weight.

Nevertheless, the experience of two countries may be cited in contrary evidence: the United States and Sweden. As we shall see, in the United States the market for tests may be vast and extensively patronized, but there is a widespread (and even growing) suspicion of external examinations. Sweden has gone further, by actually discarding the uniform national examinations that used to be taken at the end of secondary school, though it has been replaced by a nationwide system of regular assessment.

While the United States and Sweden may be cited as being especially critical of end-of-secondary-school examinations, examinations everywhere draw a mixture of praise and criticism, on both educational and wider social policy grounds, and for a variety of alleged merits and defects. They have earned praise because, it is claimed, they provide objective, fair, public criteria for selection; they supply valuable educational data; and they establish and maintain a de facto canon of knowledge to be learned and norms of achievement, stimulating student learning and teacher effort. Furthermore, where educational deficiencies are identified, it is asserted that examinations can be used to assist in the remedy. In this way, examinations are seen as potentially useful levers of change.

On the other hand, in the last decade or two, the claim made by examining bodies that their examinations are fair measures of academic ability and the further educability of persons, irrespective of gender, ethnic and cultural origin, and location has been sharply disputed. Instead, examinations have been roundly accused of being inherently, if not deliberately, biased. They are charged with overloading students with work, raising anxieties in students and their families, depersonalizing schooling, discouraging creativity, and supporting credentialism and "the diploma disease." The examinations are said to hinder school- and teacher-initiated innovations, restrict teachers' professional autonomy, and act as barriers to correction of all these alleged defects. In fact, some consider examinations to be inherently hostile to educational reform and therefore to be necessarily instruments of the status quo.

We do not here propose to examine all of these familiar arguments for and against examinations. Instead we focus on what we see as the inherently two-faced nature of external examination systems: that is, while many instances can be cited of examination systems that are or have been used to initiate and reinforce educational change, there are equally instances of their serving as obstacles to change. Moreover, examination arrangements that at one time were promoted as levers of change in education may in the ordinary course of time turn into quite effective barriers to further change. The present paper identifies these dual aspects of secondary school leaving examinations, citing data from the experience of the eight countries listed.

The Targets of Examination Policies

National examination policies and practices may be directed at securing changes within schools, within other sectors of education and the broader society, or at supporting changes in the political or ideological sphere. Obviously, internal school arrangements and procedures will usually constitute the prime target of changes in examinations, especially such features as the curriculum (not only the official, intended course of studies that describes what teachers are supposed to teach, but also the curriculum that teachers actually teach, as well as the curriculum that students in fact master). Thus changes in examinations are often deliberately designed to affect instructional content and instructional effort (perhaps also instructional methods), and especially to affect the intensity of effort exerted by students.

In addition, demands for accountability impel governments and educational authorities to seek out and implement ways of acquiring "hard data" about the "products" or "outcomes" of schooling, by assessing students and thereby evaluating the quality of the schooling provided at social expense. Changes in examination systems are designed not only to improve data gathering, but also to establish appropriate differential criteria for increasingly diverse school populations, as well as to signal changes of acceptable standards of achievement for the school population as a whole.

Opening secondary education to the nonacademically talented and to children of "nontraditional" families has created pressure to elevate the status of explicitly nonacademic, as well as vocational, education. This combines with the pressure to produce needed skills for the labor force and even with ideological preferences for a polytechnical education. The extent to which the result is to modify the older, rather job-specific craft/vocationally oriented preparation, or to introduce a genuinely polytechnical element into the general academic program, or both, naturally will vary from country to country. In any event, changes in the structure and content of examinations and in the credentials they validate, may be introduced specifically to raise the status of nonacademic curricula.

But changes in examination practices can also influence processes beyond the secondary school system. For example, the allocative function of examinations requires little emphasis. Although the allocative function is especially evident where opportunities are strictly limited, even in rich and generous societies the most desirable postsecondary opportunities, whether of work or study, are by definition in short supply. Changes in examination subjects, syllabi, regulations, standards or credentials are all ways to alter who gets rewarded with which jobs and study opportunities. Nor need all these changes be made in unison. For example, the standards for successful performance may be altered without the form or content of the examination undergoing any change whatsoever. Or a credential that in the past had provided unrestricted access to the university may lose some part of its "open sesame" character. Sometimes a quota system is introduced for entrance to certain areas of study (the *numerus clausus),* or a second-tier examination is instituted, usually by individual institutions or employers facing an excess of "qualified" candidates.

Finally, changes in examinations may be directed at what are essentially political/ideological issues: nation-building in a post-independence society, or the promotion of social justice and the achievement of greater equity among social groups. In excolonial countries, the pre-independence secondary school leaving examination was normally imported from the colonial power. After independence, the slogans "Bring the examination home" and "Indigenize the curriculum" have conveyed an attractive political message. Indeed, until such changes are made, the new nation is unlikely to feel truly independent of its former colonial master. Similarly, social justice may demand that examination standards and content be changed, in order to accommodate the special circumstances of specific social groups: workers who faced limited educational opportunity at the time they were in school, women, the rural population, ethnic minorities, and the handicapped. It is often judged that their interests will be advanced by providing multiple types and levels of examinations and credentials.

Instead of "selecting-out," the stance that characterizes traditional hiring and postsecondary/university admission practices, examinations may be restructured to serve the purpose of "selecting-in." The emphasis on passing or failing is reduced, tempered by a view of examination results as simply one element in a broad array of counselling and guidance measures. To facilitate this new use of examination results, the concept of student portfolios and student profiles may gain support, especially where it is recognized that, while reliance on a single pass/fail set of examination results may suit an allocative process restricted to a small and fairly homogeneous student population preparing for a limited set of study and work experiences, it will no longer serve for use with a vastly enlarged population of young people.

To summarize, then, across the eight countries of our study, changes in examinations have been used as levers to promote change in three broad areas of education and society. In order of greater to lesser frequency of occurrence in the eight countries, these targets of examination change are: (1) to move the school curriculum in a specific direction, for example, to make it either more rigorous, or less rigorous, or to help make it either more uniform, or less so, across the entire country, or to change its character by encouraging the incorporation of more vocational or "practical" elements; (2) to help shift effective control of education either toward, or away from, the center; and (3) to help achieve specifically political goals, for example, repudiation of a previous government's general political line, or achievement of more social equality.

Examination Change and the Curriculum

Standards In England and Wales, as in the United States, through most of the 1960s, criticism of the schools was characterized by charges that schools were too oppressive, too demanding, and too inclined to evaluate and label students. Examinations and tests were seen as symbols of the problems of education, certainly not as potentially part of the solution. In both countries a reversal of the tenor of criticism appeared in the late 1960s. In England the new direction was signalled by the publication of a series of so-called Black Papers, beginning in 1969, culminating in Rhodes Boyson's *Crisis in Education* (Boyson, 1975). The critics charged school and university curricula with being unstructured and watered down. Domination of school policy by education professionals had substituted faddish, "easy" subject matter in place of knowledge that had proved its worth over time. As a result, it was alleged, Britain was sinking into mediocrity, unable to produce the quantity and quality of graduates required by a first-rate nation. It was absurd, the Black Paper critics asserted, to try to organize the educational system on the basis that there should be no clear winners and losers. The message of an effective education system should be that there *are* winners and losers, with examinations allocating the prizes.

A degree of support from more official quarters was not long in coming. In 1976 a parliamentary committee concluded that too many options were available far too early in secondary education, and recommended consideration of a core curriculum, to be determined under the leadership of the Department of Education and Science (DES) and Her Majesty's Inspectors. In the same year, concern for acquiring data to use in judging the efficiency (or inefficiency, as the government suspected) of education's use of public resources led to the establishment of the Assessment of Performance Unit. In 1977, the DES itself expressed the need to prune drastically an overgrown curriculum, to concentrate on essentials rather than continually to expand options, to reduce the wide range of differences between schools, and to introduce a core curriculum within a national framework.

Although these calls for change were initiated under a Labour government, the policy direction survived the shift to Conservative government. In fact, a direct line leads from these preliminaries to the passage of the Education Act of July 1988, as educational reform took on new life in 1987.

The Act provides for many quite revolutionary changes in education. Among them are: the establishment of a national core curriculum (to cover at least 40 percent of total school time) and a national system of continuous assessment of students' achievement (at 7, 10, 14, and 16 years of age). Together with a new examination for "all" (the GCSE), these innovations are intended to change principals' and teachers' behavior in ways that will support the core curriculum, and elevate standards of achievement.

In the United States, the rhetoric of criticism, and some part of the reality of action, have proceeded along quite similar lines. As in England, until the late 1960s most criticism of the schools came from the "progressive" viewpoint, though there were those like Arthur Bestor and Admiral Hyman Rickover who called for a return to basics, and tougher standards. As evidence of low average achievement levels accumulated from National Assessment of Educational Progress (NAEP) reports, IEA studies, and statistics of declining SAT and similar test scores, a host of voices called for a tougher curriculum, fewer options, and a return to emphasizing basic, agreed-upon knowledge.

Although the education scene in the United States may appear at first sight to be hopelessly chaotic and uncoordinated (and compared to many more tightly organized national systems of education it *is),* there have been a number of occasions when a consensus on next practical steps of change arises, when most of the actors start talking the same language, and when many begin acting on broadly similar lines. This certainly happened when the "reform" movement in the United States concurred on more and tougher testing and examinations of students (and teachers) to support the business of learning.

Publication of *A Nation At Risk (*1983) signaled the opening of this phase, which continues to show unexpected signs of strength even six years later. By 1989, most states were requiring regular assessments of students' academic achievement, and were increasingly mandating explicitly defined minimum course requirements and levels of achievement for the award of a high school graduation diploma. The National Assessment of Educational Progress has received an infusion of Federal government funds, and a strengthened mandate to report its findings in ways that can inform the educational policies of the several states.

However, what marks off the United States from most other countries is the refusal to implement a national core curriculum, or to bring the Federal government in any way into the business of constructing a national high school leaving examination. These things, as in the Federal Republic of Germany, remain wholly state prerogatives. To date, though, very few states have seized upon the idea of state-organized high school leaving examinations as a lever to implement curriculum change. New York with its long established Regents examinations and California with its Achievement Tests are the outstanding exceptions. Instead, the task is left to the Educational Testing Service and the College Entrance Examination Board, essentially private bodies, whose influence on the curricula of the high schools is nevertheless vast, through ETS's Scholastic Aptitude Test and the College Board's Achievement and Advanced Placement tests.

Three years of nationwide consultation and consensus building led by the College Board resulted in the publication of *Academic Preparation for College: What Students Need to Know and to Be Able to Do* (CEEB, 1983), the so-called Green Book. This was followed by a set of suggestions on how to achieve the competencies and knowledge specified in each of the six basic school subjects. The intent of the Board was "to suggest curricular change (and then to modify the tests to reflect such changes as did occur) and not to force curricular change by first changing the tests" (Valentine, 1987: 164). While the Board is currently giving priority to reforming its testing instruments, it specifically abjures use of college admission tests as a means of changing the secondary school curriculum.

By contrast, in France and the FRG, the secondary school curriculum has been regarded as too demanding and restricted, excessively focused on academic material, and too theoretical to be of use to secondary school graduates. As a result, in both of these nations, a previously unitary (single criterion) general academic and rather difficult examination has been eased. Differentiation to suit various student circumstances, aspirations and inclinations has been introduced, together with much more optionality. Certain subjects were altered to suit students following different programs, and answers graded differently according to student specialization. Thus, multiple standards replaced a more single standard in the end-of-school examinations in both countries, as a means of implementing the several goals of reform: to improve access to post-compulsory schooling, to diversify the curriculum, and to increase optionality for students.

In the Federal Republic of Germany, where provincial autonomy in education remains a jealously guarded prerogative, changes in the *Abitur,* central to the processes of national educational reform, have been slow to arrive, but in the end have been very substantial. The effort to modernize the secondary schools and at the same time to achieve some measure of comparability of curriculum and standards of achievement across the Länder soon produced broad agreement in principle among the Ministers of Education on the nature and aims of the examination and on reciprocal recognition of the credential (1950-51). However, only after reform plans had been instituted by the Länder and in the early and middle 1970s were minimum national requirements for the *Abitur* agreed upon (1979). Earlier Federal law (January 1976) provided certain guidelines to regularize admission to higher education, including a reduction in the number of university specializations subject to the *numerus clausus,* and reaffirmation of the *Abitur* as the major requirement for university admission (though now with differential weighting of subjects according to the relation of those subjects to success in a specified university program). The 1979 agreement endorsed the more relaxed pattern of optional basic and main courses which had now been established, with higher standards of performance required for any subject offered in the former group and less demanding standards for the "main" subjects. The numbers of students taking and passing the *Abitur* increased both absolutely and relatively. The number of applicants to higher education rose from 79,000 in 1960, to 225,000 in 1981, and to 245,000 in 1988; about 7 percent of 19-20-year-olds were in higher education in 1960, compared with 11 percent in 1970, and 21 percent at present. As a result, a mounting chorus of criticism about declining standards has been heard from the schools, the universities, and sections of the public. The reforms had begun to have their effect, and the results were found by some to be deplorable!

A "reform of the reforms" arrived in late 1987. The Conference of Ministers of Education of the eleven Länder revised minimum standards for the *Abitur,* and called for higher standards. From 1989 on, student options have been limited. Candidates must take continuous courses up to the examinations in at least two of three required subjects: German, a foreign language, mathematics; one of these subjects must be taken in the exam; and the importance of history and natural science is enhanced. Moreover, through changes in the weighting system for different subjects, the value of marks for basic courses is to be increased and those for main subjects reduced. By changing the formulae by which marks for achievement in the various subjects add up to an overall grade for the total *Abitur,* the ministers intend to reverse some slippage in curriculum and standards. But differences of standards among the Länder have made it necessary to develop a weighting system for university admission, doubts persist about comparability, as well as on such fundamental questions as the validity of results from oral examinations, which are still widely used, and about the predictive power of *Abitur* scores for success in higher education.

The conflict over standards and the effect the *Abitur* has on them is by no means over. Concern persists about the pressure on students of successive school tests leading up to the final State examinations, and over their heavy workload, and there is discussion of a proposal to reduce the duration of the *gymnasium* from 9 to 8 years to bring the age of graduation in line with other nations in the European community (pilot projects are already under way) and to deal with international equivalence of credentials. But if that proposal is accepted, the *Abitur* may then be taken a year earlier, again provoking concerns about decline in academic standards.

In France, too, reform of secondary schooling has been tightly bound to reform of the terminal credential, the *baccalauréat.* Increasing access and diversifying the curriculum were major objectives pursued as early as the 1950s. The *baccalauréat* came increasingly to be seen as a narrow, humanities and mathematics-oriented, academic selection device for higher education.[1] However, a series of changes instituted since that time have made it an extraordinarily differentiated and complex system. The four major specializations which existed in 1950, have been increased to 38 (1988), and now cover a range of general academic and technical/professional specializations. Changes in the *baccalauréat* have brought about radical and significant changes in the French education system. One consequence has been that the number of students sitting for the examination has increased astronomically, and so have the rates of success. *Baccalauréat* awards have grown from 30,000 in 1950, to 60,000 in 1960, to 200,000 in 1970, and to over 300,000 in 1988.

In addition, a system of weighting compulsory subjects according to specialization is intended to maintain broad curriculum standards while at the same time being responsive to the need for multiple standards. The examination in mathematics, for example, is longer and more demanding for candidates specializing in mathematics and science, and the results more heavily weighted in the final result, than for candidates in the humanities. By the same token, the examinations in, for example, philosophy and French, while of the same duration for all candidates, are more heavily weighted for those in the humanities.

Given the variety of student options and the degree of local autonomy, concern about problems of equivalency, i.e., comparability of standards, is considerable. The diploma is national, providing the legal right to enter any university in France (nowadays for the first two years only), but the examinations are regionally implemented. Each *académie* chooses questions from a national list of topics and grades student performance according to national guidelines. It is a "hard" examination, but less hard in some places and subjects than others. Thus the number of candidates and their rates of success vary substantially between regions and *séries* (type of *baccalauréat)*.

Successive governments have announced the target of 80 percent of the age-group at *baccalauréat* level by the year 2000. Moreover, the report of a recent commission recommends an increase in the options available to candidates, a *bac à la carte* to contain a number of common required subjects, and an even greater variety of optional ones, possibly to be taken in two stages.

In France, therefore, what was once an examination system which guarded the schools against the pressures of change has served as an effective means for implementing changes in the education system. The current Minister of Education, M. Jospin, has announced his intention of reducing the length of the school day, and the frequency of grade repetition, possibly compensating for this by a longer school year. He wishes to increase the number of technical and vocational *baccalauréats,* and to reduce the heavy emphasis upon mathematics in order to improve educational opportunity, despite persistent criticisms of falling standards.

In considerable contrast to the FRG and France, Sweden today relies on a nationally provided, but locally administered, system of regular assessment of the individual student's achievement. Sweden has abandoned the *studentexamen,* once equivalent to the *Abitur* and the *baccalauréat.* As part of its larger plan to reform secondary schooling, the Swedish government began to introduce exceptions to the traditional practice of university selection by examination results alone in the early 1950s, and had adopted a totally new system by 1972, consonant with its policies of universal comprehensive schooling and open access to postsecondary education. Since that time, no school leaving examination has been required, only certification that a given program of study was satisfactorily completed (27 lines are defined for the alternative programs of study at upper secondary level). However, locally administered, school-based assessment according to national guidelines is mandatory in the final years of secondary school.

Non-Academic Curricula   Four nations, Germany, Sweden, France, and England and Wales, have recognized the potential of changing the structure and content of examinations to increase the attractiveness of vocationally oriented secondary schooling. Germany has done the most, and did it earliest. Alongside the academic *Abitur*, Germany established a host of federally recognized specialized vocational examinations and qualifications in developing the dual system of employer-sponsored apprenticeships and continuation schooling provided by public education authorities. The academic examination, the *Abitur,* was protected from pressures to vocationalize it, and has retained its superior status, but careful cooperation among the formal associations of employers, Federal and Land education authorities, and trade unions in devising syllabi, setting and administering examinations, and awarding qualifications, has meant that the nonacademic qualifications are held in very high regard and often pay off well in terms of earnings and social position. The result has been a marked absence in Germany of the familiar pattern in so many other countries, in which vocational education is the mark of a scholastic "loser."

Sweden may have gone further than other nations we have studied in being willing to change examination policy to tailor curricula to suit individual choices and to relate it to employment as well as to study options. It now possesses a highly differentiated upper, post-compulsory, secondary school system. Many of the 27 tracks defined as alternative programs of study at upper secondary school level are avowedly vocational. All, in theory, are of equal status and, with continuous testing, lead to equal rights to enter higher education and further training. In practice, a hierarchy of prestige and opportunity continues to exist. However, by abolishing the final examination for academic graduates and replacing it with a nationally provided but locally administered system of regular assessment of individual student achievement, Sweden has somewhat attenuated the role of simple academic success in distributing future opportunity, and has improved the relative standing of vocational education.

France has a long tradition of in-school preparation for employment. But vocational education was nevertheless clearly perceived as of lower worth. However, as noted above, the French have widened and differentiated the formerly purely academic *baccalauréat* by adding to the number of technical and vocational options available now, and likely to come along in the near future. As evidence of their popularity, 140,493 candidates took the technical options in 1987 (of whom 65.31 percent were successful), and newly introduced vocational options attracted 1,160 candidates in 1987, 8,850 in 1988, and are expected rapidly to draw greater numbers.

England has just combined its GCE "O" level examination (older, more academic, and university-based) with the CSE (newer, more diversified, and school-based) into a single multilayered examination (the GCSE) for 16 year-olds, which contains elements of both. The intention is also to improve the relative standing of "nonacademic" students and subjects by using differentiated criteria, and by recommending that academic subjects be examined (and therefore taught) in ways that emphasize applications of knowledge, stressing practice rather than theory. (There is of course a contradiction here between the government's attempt to use the examination system to raise academic standards and reduce curricular diversity, while at the same time encouraging vocationalization of those very academic subjects as well as increasing vocational subject options.)

Apart from the changes involved in the GCSE, the Department of Education and Science (DES) established a specific program to encourage local authorities to develop programs to enable students to enter the world of work better equipped (the Technical and Vocational Education Initiative, 1983). Another vocationally oriented scheme, developed directly by the DES, was the new credential, the Certificate of Pre-Vocational Education (CPVE), incorporating general education and specific vocational studies. However, it is difficult to assess its impact: it is awarded on the basis of performance in prescribed courses, not on any set of external examinations, per se. So far, at any rate, it has not established itself as a popular credential.

In the Soviet Union, the rhetoric has been highly supportive of vocational education in the context of universal polytechnical schooling. However, the Soviet Union has not chosen to influence the reality of the curriculum by weighting the secondary school leaving examination more heavily toward vocational subjects and work practice.

Instead, a curiously traditional and academic type of secondary curriculum has persisted amidst the vocational rhetoric.

The pattern in the PRC is very similar. Despite the government's announced policy of achieving 50 percent secondary enrollment in each sector (vocational and academic general education), the examinations remain oriented to the traditional academic subjects, with no move to assign extra weight to "practical" subjects.

Japan has largely avoided both the rhetoric and the reality of vocational education in the nation's secondary schools. The regular secondary schools are relentlessly academic in orientation. The small vocational school sector is run by a separate ministry, the Ministry of Labor, and has had little influence on the mainstream of secondary education. The Japanese approach relies on the schools to provide a high level of general education, and on the future employers to provide the directly job-related skills. To that end, for most Japanese youngsters, both the curriculum and the examinations at the end of schooling contain relatively little choice, and few if any vocational elements.

These goals of examination policy (to change the curriculum; to shift standards; to elevate the status of nonacademic education) all reflect a growing human capital development approach to educational choices. Japan stands out in this respect, with its use of a highly competitive examination policy at both the beginning and end of upper secondary school, to serve qualitative and quantitative human-capital goals. Shared by socialist and capitalist nations alike, this orientation is as marked in the already developed nations as it is among the newcomers to development, and it may be observed as well in nations that have inherited quite different educational philosophies. Examinations are regarded as ways not only to increase the quantity and improve the quality of desirable human capital, but the results are seen as indispensable indexes of educational performance and achievement.

Examination Policies and Control

Changes in end-of-secondary-school examination policies and practices will affect two basic aspects of control of education: which level of government authority (central, regional, or local) exercises effective control over the operation of the schools; and how the transfer of graduating secondary school students to further study or to employment is directed.

China's experience with respect to examinations and control of the schools has probably been the most volatile of the eight countries studied, with swings of policy occurring at roughly 10-year intervals since the beginning of the People's Republic. Examination policies have been changed to conform to the swings in the control of educational policies in general. Especially under the influence of the Soviet Union, and in an effort to repair the damage done to education during war and civil war, control of the schools and the transfer of students was initially centralized in Beijing's hands. A national system of examinations was introduced in 1952, reinforcing the power over the schools of those authorities who "owned" and administered the examinations. The departure of the Soviet advisers in 1960, the political rupture with the Soviet Union, and the announcement of the Great Leap Forward marked the beginning of change in concentrating power in Beijing.

Policy swung decisively with the onset of the Great Proletarian Cultural Revolution in 1966. The basic theme of the GPCR was to challenge and destroy the power of the central bureaucracy, especially in education. In the course of this Mao-inspired "second revolution" (this time against the general governmental bureaucracy, and particularly against the educational establishment), examinations were abolished. Students were no longer expected to prepare themselves for academic tests; transfer at the end of secondary school depended on evidence of appropriate social class origin and demonstrated enthusiasm for the new radically populist policies.

In 1976 the overthrow of the Gang of Four brought a restoration of central control over education and a marked shift of emphasis on "expertness" in place of "redness," predictably reinforced by the return in 1977 to highly selective examinations organized on a nationwide basis at the end of upper secondary school.

During the 1980s substantial administrative authority over the examinations was devolved to the provinces and to a few of the larger cities, Beijing and Shanghai in particular. General directions were issued by the State Education Commission, but implementation was in the hands of the provinces. In like manner, secondary school graduation examinations were to be instituted by provincial authorities, beginning with Shanghai and Beijing.

In the last year or two, yet another swing of policy back toward greater central control of the examinations has become evident: devolution and decentralization of the examination system allegedly has become too costly. Construction and validation of examinations by each of the provinces is said to impose undue financial burdens on the educational system. Chinese educational authorities have recently introduced new forms of examinations such as short-answer questions and multiple-choice, machine-scorable tests, in order to reduce costs and improve comparability and objectivity. Such measures are likely to increase national uniformity at the expense of provincial autonomy.

There have been times in China when examinations were seen primarily as obstacles to desirable changes, as instruments assisting in the defense of the status quo – the period leading up to the Great Proletarian Cultural Revolution, for example. But in the period following that upheaval, examinations have been once again regarded as very useful instruments to help change attitudes and behavior.

However, one of the enduring aspects of education in China has been the tiny fraction of the age-group admitted to higher education (for every 100 children enrolled in grade 1 in a given year, only about 3 students are accepted into higher education). Maintenance of this policy has been facilitated by the highly selective examination system. Thus far the Chinese people have been willing to accept the legitimacy of the "selecting-out" process that the examination system represents.

Few other countries have experienced the alternating swings of examination policy and control of education that we have described in China. At the other end of the spectrum in this respect is the Federal Republic of Germany, in which control of education overall and of the *Abitur* in particular has been consistently a responsibility of the Länder. The *Abitur* has undergone some important changes in the last 20 years, but it remains a fixed element in German education. The Federal Government has, with the agreement of the Ministers of Education of the Länder, established a central mechanism for university admission nationwide, and broad agreement on the scope and standards of the *Abitur*. This has helped deal with the allocation process, in large part through agreement on the numbers to be admitted to certain programs and institutions in especially great demand *(*the *numerus clausus)*. But control of the examination by Land authorities has reinforced Land prerogatives in education, and has added to the already significant obstacles facing Federal governments that have tried to extend the power of Bonn to influence educational policies and practice.

In France, the examination system has changed sufficiently to help achieve some larger targets of control, but as in Germany, it is more generally seen as a bulwark against any fundamental change in education. On the other hand, quite unlike Germany, French government administration in general, and the control of education and examinations in particular, have been highly centralized in Paris. Beginning in the early 1980s, a policy of modest devolution has been introduced, to give more authority to *départements* and the larger cities. An accompanying devolution of responsibility for the *baccalauréat* has meant yielding some authority to the 23 *académies,* to choose from among the list of topics for each subject issued by the Ministry of Education in Paris, to construct the specific questions, and to organize and set the standards for grading the answers. In this way, examination policies have helped support some significant changes in France's general style of public administration.

As the expansion of secondary education proceeded, the number of young people with formal *baccalauréat* qualifications, entitling them to enter higher education grew rapidly. In order to control access to the more desirable institutions and programs of study, a second set of examinations assumed greater importance. These were highly competitive examinations (the so-called *concours),* channelling about 10 percent of the successful *baccalauréat* graduates to the *Grandes Ecoles* and to special programs in the regular universities. The *concours* has acted in effect as a kind of pressure relief valve, siphoning off the most academically able students (who are then provided with superior facilities and instruction for the completion of their higher education). Successive French governments have thus been able to promise the universities more resources, while in practice leaving them to struggle on, trying to cope with the lion's share of higher education enrollment on budgets that have remained severely constrained. There is a certain parallel here with China in the use of highly competitive examinations to legitimize extreme economy in the use of public resources for higher education.

Sweden, like France, has been seeking to decentralize in modest fashion a system of governmental and educational control that has traditionally been highly centralized. Formal responsibility for education was devolved to the county and municipal authorities at about the same time that the end-of-secondary-school examinations were abolished. However, the Swedish central authorities were not about to relinquish all oversight of education, and a system of continuous testing, under the general direction of Stockholm, but administered locally, has been in place for over a decade. The data on student achievement are used not only for counselling individual students, but also to check on the performance of each school within its district, and of each district compared to others.

The Swedes saw the traditional *studentexamen* as a major obstacle in the way of democratizing the schools and individualizing instruction. In 1977, Sweden widened eligibility to apply for admission to higher education, to include many groups beyond graduates from the traditional 3- and 4-year upper secondary schools. Anyone with a minimum of two years of secondary education, or the equivalent, or who was over 25 years old and had at least four years of work experience, could apply. Places in higher education were then supposed to be allocated roughly in proportion to the numbers in each of these categories of applicants. In those areas of study for which applications exceeded places available, school marks became very important (or, for adults applying under the 25:4 rules, scores on a SAT-style test). Thus, abolition of the end-of-high-school (university entrance) examination has not done away with the need to allocate scarce places in higher education in a manner that could be defended as objective and fair.

Recent events in Britain provide another illustration of the two faces of examinations as potential instruments of change in education, but equally likely to be reinforcers of the status quo. In voicing profound dissatisfaction with the record of educational professionals and the local educational authorities in managing the schools, the Thatcher government was also reflecting its wider doubts about the performance of local government authorities (especially those in the hands of the Labour Party) in managing local services as a whole. The common thread that runs through the entire set of changes embodied in the Education Act of 1988 is the desire to curtail the educational prerogatives of the local authorities: to reduce their curriculum discretion; to subject their pupils to regular testing and publication of school-by-school results; to put them at risk of losing control of their schools should a majority of parents so desire with their votes; to limit their financial powers; and to divest them of their tertiary level institutions. To help achieve these goals, and to give the central government more control over the external secondary school examinations, the number of examination boards has been sharply reduced (to five regional groups, each comprising former GCE and CSE boards), and their work subjected to close oversight by the newly created School Examination and Assessment Council (SEAC), the members of which are appointed by and report to the Secretary of the DES. In future, all external examinations at the secondary level will be required to receive SEAC's imprimatur. These changes represent a decisive expression of faith in the power of examinations to shift the locus of control of education away from the periphery (individual school principals and local education authorities) toward the central authorities, and thus to unravel what has been the stuff of educational administration in England and Wales since the beginning of public education over one hundred years ago.

In the United States, the absence of a Federal government presence in secondary school examinations has, as in Britain until the recent reforms, severely limited the power of the national authorities to influence, let alone control, what goes on in the schools and in the school systems of the 50 states. On occasion the Federal government has been able to exercise considerable influence by offering Federal funds for specific educational programs (for example, to upgrade curricula in mathematics, the sciences, and foreign languages), but budget constraints have blocked extension of that approach. However, as we have already noted, what is absent on the Federal level is very much present at the state level. There the introduction of new curricular requirements has been reinforced by the establishment of regular testing programs during the course of schooling, and the introduction of final tests and examinations to ensure some minimum level of competence before the award of the high school diploma. State governments have become increasingly assertive in relation to the local jurisdictions which have traditionally exercised considerable autonomy in how, or even whether, they assessed student achievement at the end of secondary school.

Finally, we should cite Japan's well-advertised use of the examination system to control access to higher education. Examination results have become far more than the basis for simple admit/reject decisions; they serve to locate each student on a finely divided scale of achievement, validating his/her selection into a college or university that is ranked on an equally finely calibrated scale of reputation.

Conflict over the direction of educational change will often be centered on control of the examinations, reflecting sharp tension between national and provincial authorities. Indeed, the fate of school reform often depends on who controls the external examination system, and to what end. In Britain, the central authorities have exerted control over the examinations, in order to use them as a lever for change. In China and France, likewise. In the Federal Republic of Germany, the noncentral authorities have used the *Abitur* for the opposite purpose, to moderate the extent of change. While the Soviet Union has presented itself as highly centralized in control, in practice local discretion is nowadays quite large, especially in the matter of the content and standards of the final secondary school examination. This has added to the already substantial difficulties in the path of using central government power to reform Soviet education. In the United States, ownership and control of the examinations is split between states and the private testing agencies, making for a highly complex and not at all clear relationship between changes in the examinations and the reform of education.

Examinations and Political Goals

Beyond their effects on education, changes in examinations may help achieve particular political goals. The political use of examinations is especially evident when an existing system of external examination is abandoned, or an abandoned system is reinstated. The experience of many of the eight countries studied exemplifies this phenomenon.

In Russia, in 1918 soon after the Bolshevik revolution, examinations, school tests, and marks (including examinations for university entrance) were all abolished, as symbols of Czarist elitism and discrimination. Admission to higher education was instead determined on the basis of social class origin and political activism. The abandonment of examinations and marks signalled the end of an era of highly formalized instruction and school organization. However, by the end of the 1920s progressive practices had come under severe attack. Stalin's political and economic program called for "building socialism in one country," and doing so in the shortest possible time, no matter what the cost. Rapid industrialization demanded less relaxed methods of education than those practiced by the so-called pedologists, most of whom were dismissed from their posts (and worse) in the period 1929-33.

The pedagogical approach of the pedologists called for a "child-centered, student-governed" school. Teacher authority was supposed to take second place to students' collective decision making. The practice was always much less in evidence than the rhetoric, but in any case the pedologists' theories were at odds with the authoritarian political and social system that Stalin was intent on building. Tests of academic achievement were reinstated in the early 1930s. A resolution of the Central Committee of the Communist Party, dated 25 August, 1932, mandated end-of-year examinations in the schools, as a quality control measure, and in the same year examinations for university entrance were established. These changes sent an unmistakable signal to the schools and to Soviet society at large: a relatively unstructured period in Soviet schooling was at an end, and a more uniform, formal and traditional system was to be instituted to prepare youth for an effective role in the building of socialism. Objections that this meant a recreation of elitism were overridden on grounds of national interest, just as in China fifty years later when a similar reversal of policy took place with the announcement of the Four Modernizations. In 1944, a Soviet government order established a secondary school leaving examination for all would-be graduates.

The restoration of examinations announced a new direction in the national political order. It represented not only a means of bringing order and national cohesion to the school system, but it also signalled that the period of experimentation with school governance by student collectives was at an end. The existence of examinations helped teachers reassume their traditional position of authority. Today, the secondary school leaving certificate, or certificate of maturity *(attestat zrelosti),* is firmly entrenched as the nationwide credential all Soviet students must gain in order to graduate from complete secondary schooling. The credential is uniform throughout the Soviet Union and is based on the results of written and oral examinations given in schools during May and June in all major subjects, as well as on grades received during the final (tenth) school year.

The *attestat zrelosti* serves ostensibly to ensure that the Ministry determined curricula are followed and that achievement standards are regularized. In practice, however, wide discretion is left to local districts and schools in the actual administration of the *attestat* examinations. While the broad themes and topics of study are prescribed in each republic's syllabus, the actual questions asked in the examination are formulated by the local examining board, composed of teachers and administrators of the very schools examinees attend. Oral questions and answers are widely used. Moreover, the criteria by which candidates are evaluated are also very much in the hands of the local examining boards. Widespread uncertainty about the meaning of *attestat* results and concern about the uneven quality of education from school to school, district to district, and republic to republic, have impelled institutions of higher education *(VUZY)* to require that applicants sit for special, institutionally arranged entrance examinations, many of which are extremely competitive.

The high degree of local discretion and the variability in both the content of examinations and standards of achievement is part of a larger delegation of the particulars of educational practice to the localities. It may also be seen as a concession to the rights of the nationalities, a source of constant tension and unresolved conflict in the Soviet Union. While the common view in the West of Soviet education is that it is a rather monolithic system tightly run from Moscow, the reality is very different, and nowhere more so than in the realm of examinations. Moreover, because both the secondary school graduation examinations and the university entrance examinations are highly decentralized and wholly in the hands of the secondary schools and the individual *VUZY*, they have become exceptionally weak potential instruments of change.

Soviet educational policy claims to use the schools to identify, nurture, and promote talent in standard meritocratic fashion. On the other hand, socialist ideals of equality are also strongly voiced. There is persistent tension between these two objectives, and although the late 1920s and the early 1930s marked the time when the rhetoric of the Soviet school swung decisively away from equality, it did not go all the way to pure meritocracy. Instead, parental position, connections, influence, political correctness, and even place of residence all have come to play a large part in settling how far and in which direction a youngster will go in higher education and career. Precisely because their standards are exceptionally malleable at the local level, the school and university entrance examinations admirably support the compromise that has been established between meritocracy and equality. It is not difficult for a Soviet tenth-grader to gain the *attestat zrelosti:* the demands of equality can thus be seen to be decently met. However, securing a place in a good quality *VUZY* is quite difficult: selection via competitive entrance examinations appears to satisfy the meritocratic ideal, however tarnished that ideal may be by increasing evidence of social class bias, favoritism, and even outright bribery in the acceptance decisions.

In this connection, it should be noted that in the USA where testing is widely used, efforts to make more systematic use of external examinations are blocked by objections that they discriminate against minorities, females, recent immigrants, and so on. Although examinations are supported by many as a neutral, objective means of identifying superior achievement or talent, they are regarded by others as contraventions of the nation's egalitarian philosophy, even to the extent of offending provisions of the United States Constitution by denying equal protection under the Fourteenth Amendment. In like manner, the *baccalauréat* has been criticized in France as likely to exclude potential students from working- and lower-class families, and thus as an undemocratic and discriminatory mechanism. Indeed, the conflict between meritocratic and egalitarian principles appears to be fundamental to the use of examinations by nations, regardless of whether they are socialist or capitalist. Sweden has sought to resolve the conflict by abolishing the traditional academic school graduation/university entrance examination, thus advertising and reinforcing the overall social welfare and egalitarian policies of its social democratic government.

Other nations, too, have used changes in the examination system to signify political changes and to help achieve a particular political result.

In Britain, the package of changes represented by the Education Act of 1988 underlined Prime Minister Thatcher's determination to instill a "value for money" accountability mentality in the schools and universities, as she had tried to do in the wider economic sphere. Hence the prominent place given in the Act to the establishment of a system of continuous assessment of student achievement via tests and to revamped secondary school examinations that are expected to emphasize the practical, applied aspects of subject matter.

The 1987 "reform of the reforms" in the Federal Republic of Germany represented a reversal of the more liberal social and educational policies of the preceding era. The call for restricted choice of subjects and more uniform and demanding standards of achievement in the *Abitur,* as in Britain, followed a swing to the political right. Ministers of Education of those Länder won by Christian Democrat and Christian Socialist majorities designed measures to prevent pupils dropping "difficult" subjects and gaining the *Abitur* in "easy" subjects, and incorporated these changes in the national standards. Trends in both English and German examination policies reflect the power of an electorate demanding return to more traditional content and standards of performance.

Yet another dimension of the political significance of examinations may be noted. Examinations are a means whereby nations can assert and maintain a sense of national identity. For example, in France, one response to changes and diversification in the curriculum has been growing fear of the loss of French cultural *patrimoine.* The requirements for a common core of subject matter embedded in the *baccalauréat* are seen as a bastion of defense against erosion of the foundation of knowledge on which a secure sense of national identity is based. In parallel fashion, voices in the US are raised in favor of a common core of studies (particularly in literature and history) to be systematically examined at the end of high school, as a means of remedying what many consider to be a major failing of the system. Thus, whether as protection against erosion or as means of revival, examinations can play an important part in the politics of nationalism.

Conclusion

In spite of the many criticisms levelled against them, examinations remain very much in fashion, and are increasingly relied upon to help move educational systems in desired directions.

At the outset of this inquiry our view of examinations was that they would be revealed as instruments that could *either* reinforce *or* obstruct educational change. The evidence, however, clearly points to their serving *both* functions, sometimes sequentially, but frequently at one and the same time. Thus the changes introduced in the *baccalauréat* over the past thirty years have clearly helped implement some basic changes in French secondary education, for example, the elevation of mathematics and the natural sciences to a higher level of subject prestige, over philosophy and literature. At the same time, the structure and content of the *baccalauréat* has continued to reinforce many long-standing elements of the French system of secondary education. France is, however, not alone in this. Other nations, for example, Germany, England, and China, provide instances of the paradox that changes in examination policy may also sustain traditional features of a nation's educational system.

Examination systems present two faces to the world in another way: they are both embraced and excoriated, often by the same people for different reasons; sometimes by different people for the same reason. As the experience of Germany indicates, on the one hand the demands of the *Abitur* are cited as the cause of student overload, and on the other hand they are defended as the necessary protection against dilution of standards. In Japan the examinations are constantly castigated for the damage they cause to young people's mental and physical health ("examination hell" is the term employed to indicate the week or more of concentrated examinations at both the beginning and the end of Japanese upper secondary education), yet the Japanese are immensely proud of the test prowess of their young people in international comparisons of scholastic achievement. The French can, and do, regard the *baccalauréat* as both a lever for effecting change in education, and at the same time, as an obstacle to further change. In England, the GCSE is criticized for being a tool of the Conservative government used to achieve national uniformity and reduce optionality, while others welcome the new examination for its legitimization of such progressive measures as school-based assessment. And (paradox again) teachers everywhere are inclined to view external examinations as restricting their professional autonomy, but at the same time enhancing the perceived importance of their indispensable work in preparing the candidates.

Although there are numerous examples of examinations being supported and changes in examinations being proposed in expectation of the changes in education and society they can help bring about, once "modernized" or "reformed," the examinations do not necessarily continue as dynamic elements in the educational system. The Soviet Union provides a classic example of this dialectic process at work. Since the early years of the Stalin period, social and political conditions have changed markedly. In addition, a set of entrenched interests has grown up around the examinations for the *attestat* and for entrance into higher education. Ironically, Soviet education has proved extra-ordinarily difficult to change. partly no doubt because of the examination policies that were introduced over fifty years ago as part of a program of vigorous reform. On the other hand, England's fundamentally new GCSE, in combination with the creation of a national curriculum and assessment system, serves as a means of reshaping English education, replacing an examination system that, despite additions made over recent years, had for long served as an obstacle to change.

Present Soviet and past English examples may be striking, but they are not unique. In most countries, after some time (perhaps a decade or two, perhaps longer) what was devised and implemented as a solution becomes in its turn the problem. What began as a lever to effect and reinforce change, then ends as an obstacle in the way of further change.

The changes in examination policies that we have identified conform well to the human capital development approach to the purposes of education. First of all, if education is in fact an investment made by society in its citizens, it is appropriate to figure out what return is being obtained. Hence, the results of examinations and tests come to be used not only to rank individual students, but to estimate what has been learned by the aggregate of students. The United States is a leader in this respect, especially now that the National Assessment of Education Progress has been given more funds and a fresh mandate. Britain and Sweden have also moved strongly in this direction.

Second, insofar as education can raise workers' productivity and earnings, it is argued that the proportion of the total curriculum devoted to material of direct vocational use should be expanded, and that the examination system should be changed to encourage this shift. France and Germany lead in this respect, and Britain is following their example. Curiously, China and the Soviet Union, two socialist countries who have voiced the rhetoric of vocational and polytechnical education most strongly, have not altered the predominantly academic content of their end-of-secondary-school examinations. Nor has Japan "vocationalized" the examinations, preferring instead to provide employers with a large supply of academically proficient graduates, whose subsequent employment-based training can go forward thoroughly and efficiently.

Third, the human capital development approach implies that potential talent should be developed as much as possible. It follows that the examination system should be geared toward "selecting-in," rather than "selecting-out." We might expect to see examination policies change to enhance the potential guidance and counselling functions of examinations, and we do indeed observe this in Sweden, and to a lesser extent, in Britain and the United States.

Finally, emphasis on the economic value of schooling also supports the more traditional view of examinations as devices to identify and nurture high-level talent. Each nation argues that it is in direct competition with other countries, and therefore needs to develop higher levels of knowledge and skills in many more young people. Curricula must be made more demanding, and standards and requirements must be raised. Of all the eight countries we have considered, it is probably Japan that has pursued this goal most vigorously, but the same rationales and goals are now widely cited in the United States, Britain, and France.

But the prominence given to the human capital development uses of schooling need not mean abandoning the more conventional humanistic goals of education: a broad and general approach to personal development, self-discovery, individual growth. With all the emphasis on preparing the young for productive contributions to their nation's economy, examinations continue to be dominated by the traditional subjects of the liberal arts curriculum: language and literature, history, cultural and civic knowledge, as well as mathematics and science. Examinations are thus a means of strengthening both sets of educational aims.

However, what may be even more important at this time is "the other face" that examinations show as stimuli to effort, and as quality controls in education. Whether directed at human capital development or at personal growth, or at both, examinations are opening up to larger numbers and a greater variety of students. While more and more succeed, it is inevitable that more become clearly labelled as failures. Cynicism envelops the student devoted to mastering the skills and acquiring the knowledge to pass the critical examination at the end of secondary school; discouragement and even burnout accompany failure or follow success. As a recent letter-writer to *Le Monde de l'Education* (June 1989) observes, the problem with making the *baccalauréat* the target for 80 percent of youth by the year 2000 is that it will create growing numbers who will have failed the examination and as many more who will be turned off school and even all future self-education by excessive emphasis on preparation for the examination. As Mathews observed, in introducing his study of examinations (1985):

On an historical scale examinations are a recent phenomenon, at least in their application to the mass of people. Perhaps not quite so inescapable as death, they form, none the less, part of the experience of most people in the developed countries and increasingly in the developing countries. Seen in their early days as means of liberation from the inequities of advancement through privilege, patronage and wealth, they now appear to some as a distorting influence on education and careers. It could well be that the next decade will be a critical period for examinations. In some countries there are signs of a decline in their use; indeed, there are instances of outright rejection; in others their use and influence increase. Precipitate rejection of them could be as unwise as slavish reliance on them. In any event, a period of appraisal is called for.

NOTES

* Harold J. Noah and Max A. Eckstein (1992). "The Two Faces of Examinations: A Comparative and International Perspective," in Noah and Eckstein (eds.), *Examinations: Comparative and International Studies*. Oxford: Pergamon Press: pp.147-170. Reprinted by permission of Butterworth-Heinemann Ltd. This paper was part of a larger comparative and international study of secondary school completion examinations, undertaken by the authors with funds provided by The Spencer Foundation, Chicago, whose assistance is gratefully acknowledged. Valuable research help was given by Jeanne Weiler.
1. Criticism of this kind is not altogether new. See Emile Boutmy, *Baccalauréat et Enseignement secondaire, projets de reforme* (Armand Colin, 1899), described in *Le Monde de l'Education, No.* 157 (Feb. 1989).

REFERENCES

Boyson, Rhodes (1975). *Crisis in Education.* London: Woburn Press.
College Entrance Examination Board (1983). *Academic Preparation for College: What Students Need to Know and to Be Able to Do.* New York: CEEB.
Le Monde de l'Education. No. 161 (June 1989), p. 7.
Mathews, J.C. *(1985). Examinations: A Commentary.* London: Allen & Unwin.
National Commission on Excellence in Education (1983). A *Nation at Risk: The Imperative for Educational Reform.* Washington D.C: US Government Printing Office.
Valentine, John A. (1987). *The College Board and the School Curriculum.* New York: CEEB.

23

Tradeoffs in Examination Policies:
An International Comparative Perspective*

Controversy over examination policies is commonplace in the contemporary world. It has been exemplified in China's abandonment of secondary school and university entrance examinations during the Cultural Revolution, and their reinstatement 10 years ago; in the disputes over the form and purposes of the *Bac* in France, disputes that from time to time threaten to undermine the very continuance of government; in the concerns expressed in Japan that whatever the benefits its 'examination hell' may bring in the way of stimulating student and teacher efforts, they are being bought at the price of severe tension placed on young people and their families; and in the current vigorous discussions in England over the institution of the GCSE, the changes proposed for the GCE Advanced Level examinations, and the introduction of periodic national assessments of pupils' progress throughout their school careers.

Argument ranges over the entire spectrum of matters associated with examinations – from narrowly technical problems of examination procedures, through questions of broad educational significance, all the way to issues that touch fundamental ideological concerns and political preferences. Not that any particular question about examinations can be neatly categorised under a single such heading. Even the most arcane technical question can, and not infrequently does, carry with it implications for education as a whole, and even political choices; and these, in turn, can quickly involve specialised psychometric problems.

The specific terms of debate vary significantly from nation to nation and from decade to decade, but some recur. None of the policy problems are easy to solve, and some are so difficult that they can well be called dilemmas. In consequence, each nation's system of examinations may be regarded as representing a set of provisional compromises among competing values. While seeking to increase perceived benefits in one direction, a nation almost inevitably gives up some benefit or exacerbates some problem in another direction. It is in that sense, therefore, that we view extant examination systems as configurations of tradeoffs, arising out of the dilemmas of evaluation policy.

For example, consider the characteristic of *examination uniformity*. Uniform examinations across the entire nation facilitate comparability and evenhandedness of treatment between different groups. But uniformity exacts its price: regional and local interests may feel slighted, the centre's purposes are likely to be served at the expense of the peripheries', and opportunities to adjust the examination to recognise the different needs of regions or groups at different stages of school development are inevitably reduced.

Or, consider the extent to which *options* are permitted. A large measure of optionality brings the clear benefit of adapting the examination to the subject preferences and aptitudes of individual candidates. But optionality inevitably weakens the sense of a national curriculum and a national culture. A credential based on a familiar standard set of compulsory subjects is easy for employers and admissions officers to interpret; they can be puzzled indeed by the complex regulations and weighting schemes used to equate the essentially non-equatable assortments of examination subjects offered by candidates.

Or, consider the choices for the *format* of the examination. Oral examinations were once quite common at the end of secondary school, because they offered an opportunity for assessment based on interaction between the examiners and the candidate, and thus permitted examiners to shape standard questions to individual candidates. Nowadays, oral examinations are rare, mostly because the cost is considered too high, but also for fear of loss of objectivity and comparability across candidates. Precisely in order to gain such objectivity, a few nations have turned to multiple-choice, machine-scorable examinations, which also have the significant benefit of costing very little per additional candidate, once the substantial initial expenses of constructing and pretesting have been met. Yet many believe that in the end these benefits come at too high a price, encouraging styles of teaching and learning that they would prefer to avoid.

These and other tradeoffs can be illustrated from the experience of the eight countries in our study.

The United States

More than most countries, the United States has embraced the device of machine-scorable examinations, usually in the form of collections of multiple-choice items. This has been done largely because the commitment to widening the clientele served by examinations has been so strong, and the resulting numbers of candidates so large. Large numbers of candidates in turn made it economical to invest considerable resources in formulating, pre-testing and revising a very large bank of items, from which actual question papers could be constructed. The option of retaining the traditional extended-answer type of examination was rejected, for reasons of cost and complexity of organising a grading system that would be seen to be equitable. The choice has exacted some substantial educational costs: the development of written language skills among the student population is not a high priority; careful construction of an answer gives way to learning test-taking tricks and the tactics of guessing; in practice, short-item questions tend to emphasise recall-type learning, rather than analysis and problem-solving. These drawbacks are widely conceded, but the price has been paid and the tradeoff has been made relatively willingly and uncomplainingly in order to secure the important political value of a more accessible and objective examination system, as well as the ability to deal reasonably inexpensively with the consequent flood of candidates.

A second noteworthy feature of the United States examination scene has been the rejection of the slightest hint of a centralised system of examinations in the hands of the national government. Nor, indeed, do most of the 50 states offer a secondary school leaving examination or university selection/entrance examination. Instead, the job is left to what are essentially private organisations, such as the Educational Testing Service (which provides the Scholastic Aptitude Test on behalf of the College Entrance

Examination Board), and the American College Testing Program.[1]   Though the provision of examinations by these organisations has introduced a certain element of coherence to an educational system that would otherwise be exceptionally fragmented, their non-public status has nevertheless helped maintain the states' rights and even parochial bases of American education and they have done little to help raise general educational standards in less advantaged parts of the country.

However, some change may be in the offing. The Educational Testing Service has recently (1987) been handed responsibility for conducting the National Assessment of Educational Progress (NAEP), and for publishing and analysing the results. At the same time, NAEP procedures are to break with past practice, and in future are to make possible the publication of interstate comparisons of cognitive achievement of students at ages 9, 14 and 17 years. In consequence, some observers are forecasting that the United States is, perhaps unwittingly, veering toward establishing a *de facto* national achievement test that will eventually drive the adoption of a *de facto* national curriculum.[2]

Japan

At the other end of the spectrum of control and coherence of education in general and examinations in particular, Japan until 1954 operated a very economical system of selection for higher education entrance, on the basis of a single, nationwide, standardised examination. In view of the extreme importance of the decisions that were being made on the basis of this single examination, the quantity of resources spent on providing it was remarkably low. Between 1954 and 1976 various other programmes of selection were tried, and in 1976 the present two-stage system was introduced, primarily in order to improve control by colleges and universities over the make-up of their entering classes.[3] The first stage, the Joint First-stage Achievement Test (JFSAT) is retrospective and seeks to test mastery of the secondary school curriculum; the second stage examination is constructed, offered and graded separately by each higher education institution. These second-stage examinations are partly retrospective, but in many cases they also attempt to be prospective, trying to forecast candidates' potential fit to the future course of study. One effect of the two-stage plan has been to transform the JFSAT into a preliminary qualifying examination, and although the plan has enabled the institutes of higher education in Japan to retain a good measure of control over their student recruitment, the tradeoff has been the significantly higher resource costs that are now involved in selection for post-secondary education in Japan. A large share of these resource costs is borne by candidates and their families, who invest time and funds in one-on-one coaching, after-school schools (the famous *juku*), and the expenses of travel to distant cities to sit for the second-level examinations. Nor is the total of these costs negligible: they can run to the equivalent of many thousands of US dollars for one family.

Of the eight countries in our study, Japan and the United States are the only two to have adopted a virtually exclusive multiple-choice, machine-scorable format for the university entrance examinations. The Japanese appear to have been persuaded, along with the Americans, that such tests are more objective, provide higher levels of comparability across candidates, and are generally more efficient to administer by examiners who are facing hundreds of thousands, if not millions, of candidates. Perhaps more than in the United States, the Japanese have paid a heavy price for these benefits, producing tests that require candidates to memorise vast quantities of 'facts', thus downplaying originality and flexibility of thought.

In addition, there are important intangible costs arising from intense competition for places in the best universities and the resulting academic and psychological pressure on candidates. Indeed, the competition is so intense and the pressures are so great during the secondary school period that the universities complain that students arrive burned-out, determined to make up for their lost youth, and unwilling to continue to study hard. The contrast with the United States is sharp. There, the complaint is about the lack of challenge that many high schools offer to their students, and the shock that college freshmen can receive when confronted for the first time with major demands upon their time and intellect.

France

Over the past four decades, France has placed increasing reliance on the school system (as distinct from employers) to provide its generally buoyant economy with trained labour. As a consequence, more young people are carried further in school to a degree that would have been very difficult to predict from the France of the 1950s. Moreover, as youth unemployment has become ever more worrisome, the schools have been pressed to tailor their curricula and organisation to the desires of employers, a development seen in many other countries, too.[4] One consequence of the vastly increased numbers and new types of candidates finishing a full secondary education has been a recognition of the limitations of the academically oriented *Bac* examination of, say, 1950, in the changed circumstances.[5]

The French solution to this problem has been to retain the *Bac* in form, but to furnish it with substantial new content. In a major effort of educational adaptation, a *Bac* that had been organised on a narrow humanities- and mathematics-oriented basis and was easy to comprehend, has become an extraordinarily differentiated and complex examination system, with a host of *séries, lignes,* and options (38 in 1988, compared to just four before 1950). Although in some respects the French system has now moved some distance towards the English specialised model, this should not be exaggerated, as the *Bac* retains a large core of general education subjects required of all candidates. Nevertheless, one can no longer speak of a single nationally comparable examination administered to all candidates. Instead, a strongly demarcated hierarchy of prestige has emerged, with the mathematical options at the head, and the vocational options forming the tail. We should also note that, in spite of the persistence of a common core of subjects, the highly differentiated *Bac* has provoked fear that France is dissipating her intellectual *patrimoine*. Whether this is a benefit or a loss is, we suppose, a matter of taste, but taken simply as a matter of fact rather than of values, French *culture générale* has become a little less *générale*. The changes made in the *Bac* represent bold and on the whole successful moves, but they have been achieved at some price.

The most obvious has been a loss of comparability across candidates, who take widely different assortments of subjects, different papers in nominally the same subject, with different weights given to the results, depending on the particular option.

In addition, the limited devolution of administrative authority from Paris also extends to the administration of the *Bac*. Each of the 23 *académies* selects its own assortment of questions from the centrally approved list, and has some latitude to set its own standards of grading. Some *académies* have even acquired reputations for their relatively lenient standards. An examination system that began with strong commitment to strict comparability across the entire country (including even overseas departments and dependencies) has had to yield up that important value.

Last, as has occurred in so many other countries, the opening of broader access to the *Bac* has produced a flood of students for the French universities. Yet the university system has been held on an exceptionally tight budget rein by successive administrations. The result has been the development of scandalously poor conditions of study for many students, especially those in the universities situated in and around Paris. Competition for entrance into the better provided areas of the universities and particularly into the *grandes écoles* has intensified to the point that the *Bac* has become a kind of first-level qualifying examination, with the decisive examination being either the *concours,* or the examination for admission to a *grande école.* This represents a devaluation of the *Bac,* perhaps an inevitable cost of its democratisation and of its extension to the vocational tracks.

Federal Republic of Germany

The expansion of secondary education in the FRG took place a full 15 years later than in France, and, as with the *Bac,* the *Abitur* examination has been significantly altered to cope with the increased numbers and the changes in the kinds of candidates.[6] However, the *Abitur* was less radically altered than the *Bac*, perhaps because the need in the FRG to secure some measure of agreement among 11 quite differently oriented *Länder* governments always tends to put a brake on change. In addition, while the *Bac* is marked by a generally high degree of central direction, a determining characteristic of the *Abitur* is its school-based control. In matters of format, both France and the FRG (in distinct contrast to the United States and Japan) have retained a traditional approach, relying on extended answers to questions, even to the extent of maintaining a certain reliance on oral examinations. Especially in the FRG, the combination of local control and written and oral examinations raises questions about the extent to which grading standards are kept consistent even within a given *Land,* let alone across the *Länder*. Because the FRG makes less effort compared even with France to ensure such standardisation, an important element of chance and arbitrariness has developed.

Since 1979, the demands made on candidates for the *Abitur* have been reduced. In particular, they have been permitted to offer selected subjects at lower levels of difficulty. The changes have encouraged a vast expansion of the number of young people completing their secondary education with the Abitur, but again, as in France, certain costs have been paid for this advance.

First, and most dramatic, has been the need to introduce restrictions on the right of the *Abitur* holder to enrol in any university faculty of his/her choice, the so-called *numerus clausus.* The lines of study affected are those that carry high social prestige and/or offer the opportunity of high earnings in the future (and which are also extremely expensive for the state to provide), for example, medicine and dentistry. Since the legal entitlement to a university place was probably the most cherished aspect of the *Abitur* credential, the price paid for expansion has been high.

In addition, admission to the faculties and departments under *numerus clausus* is determined via a highly complex points system, that takes into account not only the marks received in the *Abitur* (with differential weightings for different subjects for candidates choosing different sets of major and minor subjects), but also school grades. Even so, because competition is so intense for admission to some faculties, tiny fractions of a percentage point in the final placement can become critical in the admissions process. Another cost of the changed system and the introduction of *numerus clausus* is that some candidates with the highest scores are entering the most favoured and prestigious faculties, even though their interests, aptitude or previous educational specialisation may lie in other directions. They are simply reluctant to 'waste' high standing in the admissions ranking on a place in a less prestigious line of study. This clearly is not a welcome development, especially in such fields as medicine.

These problems have caused the Council of Ministers of Education to reconsider the changes made in the *Abitur*. In the autumn of 1987 decisions were taken that amounted to restoring some of the older standards and regulations, especially limiting candidates' freedom to select subjects at lower levels of difficulty.

People's Republic of China

Examinations for entrance to higher education and higher level technical training in the Secondary Technical Schools serve primarily to control access to severely limited resources, already strained by a shortage of well-prepared teachers, inadequate buildings and equipment and out-of-date libraries. In the current drive to modernise the Chinese economy and the armed forces, the pendulum of Chinese higher education admission policy has once again swung to an extreme position. Ideological faith and socialist 'good works' now count for little; nor is peasant origin any longer so helpful. Instead, admission depends on success in the examinations at the end of senior secondary school. 'Expertness' is valued more highly than 'redness', at least for the time being. This policy of placing student ability above political orthodoxy as the major criterion for advancement is a political risk the current administration has chosen to run.[7]

More even than in France, the basic stance of the examination system in China is one of rigid central control and uniformity of administration and content, although some devolution of authority has been made to Beijing, Shanghai and Tientsin. Partly this characteristic builds upon traditional state practices, but partly too it is based upon a desire to select on a strictly equitable basis the best and the brightest of Chinese youth for university education. The number of candidates is exceptionally large (in 1988 2.7 million prepared for the national college admission tests), of whom only a quarter will be accepted for study.[8] Overall, about 2% of first graders go on to higher education. The combination of intense competition and virtually nationwide uniformity of the examination leads to pressures on students that are every bit as severe as in Japan.

The Chinese authorities have introduced substantial elements of multiple-choice and short-answer questions into what had previously been a traditional extended-answer type of examination. They have not yet moved to machine-scorable formats. Given the large numbers they are presently dealing with, the costs of grading and administration must be burdensome. As the number of candidates increases in future years, the temptation to move to machine-scorable tests and the attraction of the low marginal costs associated with such formats must grow ever greater. At least one student of examination policy in China has predicted that the time is not far off when the pressure of numbers on the examiners will become irresistible, and a vast school population of multiple-choice, machine-scored examinees will be added to those of the United States and Japan.[9] If so, there is a distinct danger that the changed format will reinforce the already strong emphasis in Chinese schools on rote learning and the recall of 'facts'.

Soviet Union

As in so many other respects, the Soviet Union provides a sharp contrast to China. Though there is significant influence exerted from Moscow, each of the 15 republics is responsible for setting the content and standards of the secondary school examinations for the leaving certificate, the *attestat zrelosti*. Schools work within the Republic guidelines, but in turn enjoy a good deal of local discretion. The teachers who have prepared the students dominate the process of setting the questions and evaluating the responses. Paradoxically, in a society and a school system that are in most respects characterised by substantial central direction, the school completion examination is not. Thus, the Soviet Union has settled for a curious compromise between the rhetoric of centralised planning and the practice of local discretion.[10]

The tradeoff for such local discretion is a substantial loss of comparability of marks, and this has led the VUZY (universities and technical institutes) to insist on applicants sitting for special, institutionally set and graded entrance examinations, very much along Japanese lines. As in Japan, the examinations are highly competitive and can impose substantial travel costs on students. There is virtually no coordination among the VUZY concerning the dates on which they will hold their examinations, examination syllabi are idiosyncratic, and grading formulas, cut-off points, and so forth, confidential. *Glasnost* has much work yet to do in this corner of Soviet life!

A consequence for many Soviet youngsters has been to turn higher education admission into a process incorporating large elements of game-theory, almost textbook examples of decision-making under conditions of imperfect knowledge and uncertainty. Apart from the persistent reports of discrimination against certain ethnic and religious groups, influence peddling and corruption, the system appears to lack important elements of overall fairness and objectivity.

Sweden

In 1971 Sweden introduced a new form of upper secondary school, designed to continue the education of a very large fraction of the post-compulsory age-group, and integrating three formerly separate types of schools (gymnasium, vocational and continuation school). The various study courses of those schools were largely imported unchanged into the new integrated school, represented by 27 so-called 'lines' of two or three years duration. Some of these lines are highly academic (especially the natural sciences line); others are more vocationally oriented; yet others are 'general'. In the mid-1970s, Sweden discarded a limited but usable final secondary school examination system in order to reduce the strain on pupils, produce more valid and reliable predictors of university success, and (it was hoped) correct socio-educational inequities in assessment. In place of the final examination, the Swedes installed a combination of marks gained during regular classroom and home work and in nationally set tests administered at intervals during the school career. Meanwhile, in 1977 a major reform of the higher education system revamped admissions criteria. Work experience and age (maturity) were given strong weight in the admission decision, and completing less demanding upper secondary school lines was not by itself sufficient for consideration for admission to higher education. Additional study and credentials were demanded.

Abandonment of final examinations was also motivated by the desire to improve the diagnostic and predictive value of tests of individual student achievement and to give teachers national benchmarks against which to set their own pedagogical efforts.

The Swedes have been willing (and able) to incur rather heavy costs to achieve these goals. The new system requires time-consuming collaboration among teachers in a given school, and across schools in a region. Exceptionally detailed record-keeping is required, and the Swedish National Board of Education is charged with the responsibility of preparing and standardising the tests given in the basic school subjects at various points along the school ladder. Although Sweden may have abandoned its final secondary school examinations, there has been no abandonment of tests and examinations in general. Indeed, one might well argue that there is now more examining and evaluation based on tests and examinations than ever before.

In 1987, it was announced that examinations and testing in the upper secondary school will be complemented by an assessment programme for the compulsory school years, to begin with the 1988-89 school year and to take in successive grades. All grades will be covered and reported on at three-year intervals. This so-called 'National Evaluation to Give a Holistic Picture of School Activities' will not confine itself to the academic side of the school, but will include data on the social and home environments of the pupils, their health, their social and emotional development, and their attitudes.[11] What is being proposed is a massive national enterprise, carried out to an exceptionally thorough degree, and demanding the expenditure of very significant resources, both human and material.

External examinations have thus been replaced by continuous assessment, nationally planned but locally executed. In all of this, the authorities are seeking to ensure that the decentralisation of school administration in Sweden will not lead to unacceptable degrees of inequality of provision. Regular evaluation of the entire Swedish school system is supposed to provide the data on which any necessary remedial actions can be based.

Such a thorough-going system of sustained scrutiny raises a question for Sweden which has current relevance in many of the states of the United States, and which soon may become important in England: How much attention by way of tests and examination can a school system stand before it becomes over-routinised and over-preoccupied with frequent, probing testing? Is there a danger of turning education into mere instruction? Our own view is that the Swedes are indeed risking the payment of a very high price for their commitment to constructing a comprehensively detailed data base of the performance of their schools, their teachers, and their school children.

England and Wales

Recent developments in English secondary school examinations, the GCSE, A and AS levels and the introduction of plans for regular in-school assessments have been very contentious. Parallels with Sweden are striking, though the two countries have arrived at their present policies starting from distinctly different traditions of educational administration.

Without going into the details, the events of the last couple of years represent an abrupt acceleration of what has otherwise been a glacially slow process of transferring authority over the schools from local to central government. In the interest of establishing national standards, voluntarism and localism are being forced to give way.

Ever since Robert Lowe, Kay Shuttleworth and Payment-By-Results in the mid-nineteenth century, it has been clear that examinations and testing could be used effectively in England as a lever to change the way in which the schools operate. Since the demise of the General School Certificate and its associated London Matric regulations, it has not been necessary for a given student to take any particular subject or to follow any particular syllabus within that subject, except in so far as he or she wanted to take an examination, or the school demanded it. The cost in terms of lack of coherence in school curricula and indefiniteness of expectations of what the schools should be doing has now been judged by the government to be too great to be supported any longer. The new structure of examinations is intended to help implement what amounts to a national curriculum, though that new structure is not likely to be accompanied by any change from the traditional extended-answer format. Perhaps it is worthwhile noting that a much greater effort has been made in England (both within and across the examining boards) than in either France or the FRG to ensure standardisation of grading criteria. For this reason, some of the more serious doubts about the fairness of marking that are voiced in these last two countries have been absent here.

The changes already implemented or foreseen for the end-of-secondary school examinations in England should be seen as part of a proposed comprehensive assessment procedure throughout the nation and for the mass of the school population.[12] This last will be a major innovation in the English context, and will be one that is likely to come, at least initially, with a high price tag attached in terms of professional morale. Morale among teachers and head teachers in England has already fallen to levels not seen in the entire period since 1870, when the state-supported education system was established. Some will argue that comprehensive assessment procedures are necessary, because only if it can be publicly demonstrated that the schools are returning value for money will the teaching profession be accorded the respect, appreciation and material rewards that it deserves. And, it is argued, a recovery of such respect is the precondition for a major upturn of morale in the profession. This justification for what has become known as 'accountability' is heard on all sides in the United States, and is very strongly sounded in Sweden. However, it fails to explain how more intense scrutiny of the work of teachers is going to help them achieve that essential characteristic of respected professional status, a large degree of personal autonomy in deciding how professional practice shall be carried out. For this reason, it will be advisable in England to take careful note of Swedish experience. Because they are very far ahead along the road of examining, testing and evaluation that is currently being charted in England, any drawbacks (or remedies) the Swedes discover *en route* should be quite instructive here, too.

Conclusion

In this paper, we have sought to show how important characteristics of examination policies and practices in each of eight countries can be usefully viewed as compromises, or tradeoffs, between desirable alternatives. Such tradeoffs are inherent in trying to negotiate four contemporary and well-nigh universal dilemmas of examinations policy. Each dilemma has been created in large part by the pressures of universal secondary education, and the consequent expansion of higher education.

Dilemma 1. A traditional examination that was used in many countries to select from a small secondary school élite an even smaller élite to enter higher education has been recognised to be inadequate to cope with vastly greater numbers and different types of candidates. Yet it has proved difficult to widen access to the examination without some devaluation of the credential gained.

Dilemma 2. Examination uniformity is desired in order to promote comparability of marks, as well as to help create or conserve a common national culture. Yet, reconciliation of these desiderata with demands for diversity to meet special subnational needs and with the increasing diversity of the secondary school curriculum has not been easy to accomplish.

Dilemma 3. Because of the powerful influence that examinations have on the way teachers teach and students learn, it has been difficult to make use of the new technology of testing without adversely affecting the purposes and styles of schooling.

Dilemma 4. As secondary school coverage has grown, education becomes an ever more critical national concern and its costs come to represent a significant charge on tax revenues. Governments see the schools as part of the struggle for international competitiveness, and they are sensitive to demands that taxpayers should receive 'value for money'. Hence the emphasis on 'accountability'. But governments' readiness to use examinations as a device to monitor and change education tends to undermine the professional autonomy and status of school personnel. Yet strengthening professional autonomy and status may well be a necessary condition for successful operation of an effective school system in the contemporary world.

While not every one of the eight countries examined here represents these dilemmas and the consequential tradeoffs with equal force, taken together they demonstrate their importance in any comparative consideration of examination policies and practices.

NOTES

* Harold J. Noah and Max A. Eckstein, "Tradeoffs in Examination Policies: an international comparative perspective," *Oxford Review of Education,* 15 (1989), pp. 17-27. Reprinted by permission.

1. John A. Valentine (1987) *The College Board and the School Curriculum* (New York, College Entrance Examination Board).

2. "...although NAEP claims not to be in the curriculum business, it may enter if NAEP assessments are used for interstate comparisons. Subject matter that is assessed on these 'national achievement tests' is critical because it is likely to represent a 'national curriculum'." Steven F. Ferrara & Stephen J. Thornton (1988) Using NAEP for interstate comparisons: the beginnings of a 'national achievement test' and 'national curriculum', *Education Evaluation and Policy Analysis,* 10, p. 209. See also: Alice J. Irby (1987) "Administration and management of examinations: practices in the United States", paper presented at a World Bank seminar, Lisbon, Portugal (mimeo.).

3. Tadashi Hidano (1987) "Admission to higher education in Japan," in: Stephen P. Heyneman & Ingemar Fägerlind (Eds) *University Admissions and Standardized Testing: principles, experience, and policy options* (Washington, D.C., The World Bank), pp. 9-25. Also: Japan, Ministry of Education, Science and Culture (1988) "A new entrance examination system," *Monthly Journal of Ministry of Education, Science and Culture.*

4. Harold J. Noah and Max A. Eckstein (1988) "Business and industry involvement with education in Britain, France and Germany," in: Jon Lauglo & Kevin Lillis (Eds) *Vocationalizing Education: an international perspective* (New York, Pergamon), pp. 45-68.

5. "Ministry tackles tough exam with pleasing results," *The Times Educational Supplement* 22 April 1988, p. 14; Jacques Colomb (1987) "Examinations and selection for higher education" (Washington, D.C., World Bank) (mimeo.);

Ministère de l'Education Nationale (1988) *Baccalauréat de l'enseignement du second degré* (Paris, Centre National de Documentation Pédagogique).

6. Andreas Flitner (1987) *Für das Leben, oder für die Schule?*, pp. 140-163 (Weinheim, Beltz). See also: Hartmut von Hentig (1980) *Die Krise des Abiturs und eine Alternative* (Stuttgart, Klett-Cotta).

7. People's Republic of China (1986) *A Brief Introduction to Higher Education Enrolment Examinations in China* (Beijing, The State Education Commission of the People's Republic of China); Keith Lewin and Wang Lu (1988) "University Entrance Examinations in China: the Quiet Revolution," paper presented at the annual conference of the British Comparative and International Education Society, Bristol (mimeo.).

8. "Beijing Journal," *The New York Times,* 12 July 1988.

9. S. Heyneman, Remarks at the conference of the Comparative and International Education Society, Atlanta, Georgia, April 1988.

10. Wolfgang Mitter (1976) *Secondary School Graduation: university entrance qualification in socialist countries: a comparative study* (New York, Pergamon).

11. Swedish National Board of Education (1987) *National Evaluation To Give a Holistic Picture of School Activities* (Stockholm, Author).

12. Jo Mortimore & Peter Mortimore (1984) *Secondary School Examinations,* Bedford Way Papers 18 (London, Institute of Education, University of London); Caroline Gipps *et al. (1986) The GCSE: an uncommon examination,* Bedford Way Papers 29 (London, Institute of Education, University of London); Michael Kingdon & Gordon Stobart (1988) *GCSE Examined* (London, Falmer).

24

Secondary School Examinations: International Perspectives on Policies and Practice*

[From Chapters 2 and 3: The Candidates and their Schools]

Sweden

Sixten and Ingrid live in the northern outskirts of Stockholm, close to a lake in the suburb of Stocksund, where almost everyone seems to have a boat of some kind. Both students are in the final year of their upper secondary school courses, though Sixten's has been a long (four-year) course, while Ingrid is finishing a two-year program.

They entered school at age seven (after two years spent in kindergarten) and completed the compulsory, comprehensive, "basic" nine-year school attended by all young Swedes. They then transferred to their present school, a *Gymnasieskolan* (an integrated upper secondary school). Admission was virtually automatic, taking place without entrance examinations or other formalities. In the country as a whole, very few (only about 10 percent) of the graduates from the basic school decide not to continue their education into upper secondary school. In Stocksund the percentage of noncontinuing students is minuscule. This is the point at which specialization begins in the Swedish school system. There are twenty-five different upper secondary school "lines" to choose from, some academic and some vocational. Courses last for two, three, or four years, according to the type of course.

Ingrid is eighteen years old. Even though her parents had higher hopes for her career, she chose a relatively undemanding two-year line, nursing. Her father, an official in the central government's National Board of Education, died when she was eight years old, leaving her mother to finish her qualifications as a general medical practitioner while raising their only child. In her early teenage years, Ingrid became very beauty- and fashion-conscious and spent long hours immersed in glossy magazines – Swedish, American, German, and French. Although this has given her a certain facility in foreign languages, she was left with little spare time for formal school study, and her grades suffered. If she had wanted to follow her mother's path into medicine, she would have needed to enroll in one of the three-year lines: natural sciences or perhaps liberal arts (classical variant). But with her interests and undistinguished school record, this did not seem realistic.

Ingrid is not especially interested in much of her schoolwork. She quite enjoys some of the romantic literature she has to read in Swedish and English language classes, as well as parts of her studies in biology, since she sees its relationship to her future in nursing. Other work in the standard common curriculum for all students includes continuing study in Swedish language and literature, English, history, mathematics, and physical education. The directly vocational portion of her course comprises theoretical courses in nursing and a practicum in the Karolinska hospital, which she thoroughly enjoys, except for the more mundane housekeeping chores she is asked to perform.

In contrast, Sixten is an academic high-flyer. Neither of his parents was ambitious for advanced education or social status for themselves – his mother drives a taxi and his father is a maintenance worker in Svenska Handelsbank – but both have marked his lively intelligence and encouraged him in his schoolwork. His grades in the basic school were superlative, and his ambition is large. On entry into the Gymnasieskolan he was undecided whether to apply for the four-year natural sciences line or the four-year technology line. In the end he opted for technology. By the end of his second year, he knew that he would specialize in the final two years in one of the most prestigious and difficult of all lines: chemical engineering.

For the first three years, Sixten continued with Swedish, English, mathematics, and physical education. He also took civics in the first year, and studied a second foreign language (German), history, basic chemistry, and technology for the first two years. In the third and fourth years, he added an array of chemistry courses (physical, organic, electrical engineering, biochemistry, chemical technology, technical chemistry), either for one year or both.[1] In addition, now, in his final year, he is preparing his special project paper on some of the chemical engineering problems to be faced as Sweden proceeds to deactivate its nuclear power reactors.

There are no final leaving examinations at the end of secondary school for either Sixten or Ingrid. Instead, they have taken tests and examinations throughout their courses of study. For example, Ingrid has already taken tests set by the National Board of Education in Swedish language and literature in her final (second) year. The English-language achievement test is scheduled for March 15. Sixten took similar tests in English, German, and chemistry in his second year and in Swedish, mathematics, and physics during his third year. The tests are typically composed of a mixture of multiple-choice and extended-answer items, three hours for each subject. The dates for these tests are set for the entire country by the National Board of Education[2] and are spread over the academic year. This is done in order to make the testing process part of the ordinary school routine and to reduce the tension usually associated with a marathon period of testing crowded into one or two weeks at the end of the school career.

In addition to these "national" tests, a minimum number of other written tests in subjects is required, usually two or three a year. These may be set by the individual subject teacher alone or by all the teachers of that subject in a school, or occasionally for an entire school district. Grades are assigned on a five-point scale from a low of one to a high of five.

In this, the final year of school, all that remains is to complete the course of study. The award of a leaving certificate is made on the basis of satisfactory achievement over the entire course of study taken as a whole. Ingrid is making the grade, though not easily. She has improved her work since basic school and now has good hopes of finishing school with a respectable leaving certificate. This requires at least a three in all major subjects. Sixten, even with all his talent for study and exposition, is having a hard time keeping up with the enormous amount of work that is expected of him. He will soon be twenty, and he has been stretched academically for the past four years, ever since he left the relatively relaxed basic school. There he had grown used to getting fives without too much trouble. It was an effort to keep up his general education subjects for the first three years. If anything, his study load in this final year is even heavier, especially as he aims to submit an outstanding special-project report. But he is devoting all of his time to technical subjects where hoped-for high grades will be important for his application to a university. His parents are justifiably proud of the grades their son is bringing home, a mixture of fours and fives.

Swedish government policy in education aims at equalizing access to post-secondary education, irrespective of the location of students' homes and schools. While parts of Sweden, especially in and around Stockholm, are highly urbanized and suburbanized, the country is large (one thousand miles from north to south) and mostly quite sparsely populated. Both students feel that living as they do in Stocksund, with its generally higher standards of income and education, they probably have to try harder in order to achieve the best marks in their schoolwork and their examinations than students from less favored parts of the country.

With all the undoubted importance of the tests, examinations, and marks, neither Sixten nor Ingrid feels the competitive urgency experienced by the Chinese and Japanese students we shall meet later. Their records have been accumulated over several years and include an exhaustive record of their experiences and accomplishments, grades on school, district, and national tests, and comments by teachers. They also include notes on periodic discussions about career preferences. Although Sixten particularly feels some anxiety about his immediate future, compared with typical secondary school completers in most other countries he and Ingrid are able to take matters very much in stride. The final year of school is important, but not absolutely critical to their futures.

They are confident that they will be able to pursue whatever careers they choose without too many hurdles placed in their way. They can always try a second time, and even a third, if their application for higher education or further training is turned down. There are ways of entering alternative career paths if they should change their minds later on.

Most important, perhaps, Ingrid and Sixten are not moved by much fear of unemployment after school. Ingrid is well aware that there is a severe shortage of nurses in Sweden and knows she will find a warm and ready welcome in a hospital once she graduates. She has had enough of being a full-time student, she feels, and has no intention of going on to a university, which is just as well, as her grades make it unlikely that she could be offered a place. Entry into hospital nursing will provide further training and a salary, outstanding working conditions, and a job she likes. However, if she changes her mind later in life, the door to higher education is not closed. Since autumn 1991, students who graduate from the upper secondary school with low grades have had an opportunity to take a proficiency test for university entrance to demonstrate their improved academic aptitude.

Sixten has his sights set on continuing his studies in chemical engineering at the university. But his leaving certificate will also confer on him the title of Certified Upper Secondary School Engineer. So if by remote chance he does not get a university place immediately, he expects to be able find employment without difficulty (after doing his military service). In any event, as soon as he is twenty-five, he can apply again to enter the university under the 25-4 rule (minimum age twenty-five; minimum work/military service of four years), which reserves a number of places for people like himself. His prospects, he has every reason to believe, are very good.

These two young Swedes have been educated in a system that strives to provide wide educational opportunities to all. Tests and examinations continue to exist, but a deliberate effort is made to ease the psychological strain on students and to make the tests as nonthreatening as possible. The central government and the localities (municipalities) collaborate in providing the examinations, with the close involvement of teachers. A student who at first does not succeed can try again. The examination results are important, but do not virtually control an individual's future, as we shall see is only too frequent elsewhere.

Japan

Kohji and Miyoko's teachers and parents have consistently held them to high standards of comportment, study, and work, and have encouraged them in an impressively competitive spirit of academic achievement. They live and go to school in Kyoto, one of Japan's most important cities. Kohji's father is an investment manager in Sumitomo, a Japanese bank. He has worked there ever since he graduated from his university twenty-five years ago, and he expects to remain with the firm till he retires. Miyoko's father runs a small automobile repair garage, employing four mechanics. In both families, the mothers are at home, even though Kohji's mother had completed four years of college in foreign languages (English and German). The two youngsters are
now in the final year of the *kotogakko* (senior high school, grades ten to twelve) in company with students much like themselves, with excellent school records and success in examinations. Each day, Kohji and Miyoko travel over an hour to the other side of town to get to their school, but they feel that the privilege of attending this institution is well worth the effort. Their school has an outstanding reputation based on its record of student success in the university entrance examinations.

Transfer from junior to senior high school is, as a rule, based in part on the results of achievement tests at the end of grade nine, and in part on high school entrance examinations. Miyoko and Kohji were admitted on the basis of their superior marks after three years in junior high school. Local educational authorities follow slightly different practices, but for some years now, most have tried to steer a middle course, trying to avoid the elitism that comes with strict selectivity when transferring students to senior high school and at the same time placing a limit on the extent of student heterogeneity within a school. Local policies thus make use of several criteria for transfer: examination results, parents' preferences, and the desired range and mix of student abilities in each school.

School attendance is not mandatory beyond grade nine and parents of high school students must pay fees. Nevertheless, the majority of sixteen-to-eighteen-year-olds are enrolled in the general, academic full-time course of study in a senior high school, and about 95 percent of the age group complete secondary schooling through grade twelve. A small number are part-time students and some are in technical schools.

If Kohji had not done well enough in the entrance examination to gain entrance to this more selective public school, his father would undoubtedly have made the effort to pay the substantial fees at a private school. There he would receive better preparation for the university entrance examinations than the other public secondary schools in town would provide. Miyoko's parents, however, would have given this a lower priority in the family budget, reasoning that girls do not need to have the same educational opportunities as boys.

The public school system in Japan is directed from Tokyo by the central Ministry of Education (popularly known as "Mombusho"), but which delegates administrative responsibilities to prefectures and towns. But major educational policies, such as curriculum structure and content, textbook approval, school organization and schedules, teachers' credentials and pay, are all determined and controlled by the ministry and are uniform across the nation. General policies are determined by national committees, discussed and voted upon by the Diet, and often questioned and vigorously opposed by the national teachers' union.

Kohji and Miyoko's curriculum for the first two years in senior high school differed little from everyone else's: Japanese, social studies (history, geography, and civics), mathematics, science, health and physical education, arts (music, art, calligraphy), and a foreign language (English). Miyoko, like all the girls, also takes home economics. Only in the final year have a few options become available, providing some opportunity for additional, more advanced work in either science and mathematics or the humanities, related perhaps to their target for the future. Miyoko chooses an elective social studies course, and Kohji takes additional mathematics at a more advanced level. These choices account for only 10 to 15 percent of their school timetable, however, and most of their classes are the same as all other students', using the standard textbooks and following the ministry's prescribed syllabi.

Kohji and Miyoko's memories of the more relaxed primary years, when school was fun, have faded. Junior high school had been something of a shock, with its increased pressure to perform, regular formal tests, and emphasis on preparation for the third-year examination. Some of their peers became demoralized by the change of climate, some even taking to such antisocial behavior as bullying their weaker classmates *(ijime)*. Senior high school has intensified the pressure.

The thirty-five-week school year opens at the beginning of April, with classes running from eight to three, five days per week, plus a four-hour day on Saturdays. With six periods in a complete day, this provides for thirty-two classes a week of fifty minutes each, plus school clubs and activities. After school closes, Kohji and Miyoko, like more than half of their class, go directly to a juku. This is a private school where students may choose from an array of craft, aesthetic, and enriched study classes. But a major focus of this extracurricular system is intense instruction to reinforce what was taught in school and training in the techniques of taking the public examinations. The fees are high, but their parents do not begrudge the expense. Kohji arranges through his juku for his scores on practice tests to be sent to a company that specializes in predicting examination success. The company will also advise him about which universities he should apply to, given his scores and other personal details. Kohji attends the juku three afternoons during the week, Miyoko on Saturday afternoon. Only when they get home will there be time to sit down to their homework. They do not find this routine unusual since they have been attending such after-school classes since sixth grade: Miyoko attending music lessons, and Kohji classes in general school subjects. It is simply a part of the daily program and duties and the normal expectation among friends and family. Indeed, if they were not enrolled in juku, they would feel rather left out of things.

Much of the final year in high school has been directed at preparing for the entrance examinations for higher education. By now Kohji and Miyoko are accustomed to the daily grind, and they have become most efficient at the memorization and rote learning that characterize their schooling. The pace of work and intensity of study, which have been heavy all along, have become even greater – about sixteen hours a day[3] – and there is less time for relaxation, for meals, and even for sleep. There has been no time for social activities for quite a while; now even chatting for a few minutes after school is seen as wasting time and provokes feelings of anxiety and guilt. They hear stories about classmates who have succumbed to physical and mental illness due to the pressures. The press adds to the stress by reports of student suicides – but they have no personal knowledge of anyone who has been that despairing.[4]

Kohji has been advised by the company that has analyzed his juku scores that he stands a chance of gaining admission to Tokyo University (Todai), a national, public university and one of the most highly regarded in the country. Miyoko also hopes to attend a public institution, though she recognizes that given her family's unwillingness to send a girl to a four-year degree-granting institution, she cannot aim very high. The first step is to register to sit for the Joint First Stage Achievement Test (JFSAT), organized by a special department of the Ministry of Education. The JFSAT is not needed for graduation from high school, nor do most private colleges and universities require it of applicants. But it is necessary as the first stage of application to the public institutions. So, halfway through the school year, in October, the two students submitted their application forms to sit for the JFSAT. Now, at the end of January, in common with about four hundred thousand of their peers across the nation, Miyoko and Kohji are taking the JFSAT at their school. Candidates take tests in six or seven subjects. There are some variations: for example, Kohji sits for a more advanced paper in mathematics, while Miyoko chooses a European History option.

The results of the JFSAT and the dates of the entrance examinations set by the universities are announced. Many of Kohji and Miyoko's contemporaries have obtained good results on the national examination. The Todai entrance examination will be conducted by the university in two months. Kohji signs up with a travel agency that is assembling a group of high school seniors to travel to Tokyo for the examinations and a few additional days in the capital. The tour package includes rail fare, hotel accommodation, meals, transportation from the hotel to the university's examination halls, and a sightseeing trip before the return home. The entrance examination will last two days, and applicants may choose to be tested in two or more subjects – some choose as many as five. Kohji will be examined in four subjects, including an advanced test in mathematics. Todai usually has about four applicants for every place offered, so this will be an exceptionally competitive examination, much harder than the JFSAT.

Miyoko takes only the JFSAT, for she does not expect to be able to apply to a college or university that requires a special entrance examination. For those who apply and are accepted, there is the prospect of four relatively relaxed years, beginning the social life they had little time for during the demanding years of secondary school. Now there should be time for dating, joining clubs, going to movies, and having fun, since the demands of college work are nothing compared with what they have endured in high school preparing for the entrance examinations. Moreover, for those who have been admitted to their chosen department in their chosen university, the future is already secure: they will have little difficulty obtaining a job that will earn them security and a good income.

Although Kohji did well in the JFSAT, he does not secure a place at Todai. He is utterly disappointed and ashamed. He feels he has let down his teachers, his school, and his family even though everyone knows how intense the competition is. Despite the hard work and late nights of study, he can only conclude that he did not make a sufficient effort. He resolves to try again and to study even harder. About a quarter of all candidates in the examination repeat it. To join the ranks of the repeating candidates (so-called *ronin)* is not dishonorable, and Kohji has been told, too, that almost half the applicants admitted to Todai and to medical colleges across the nation, which are in especially great demand, are ronin.[5] The chances of getting into a good university program are certainly enhanced by an improved second set of results. Driven by the desire to erase his failure and motivated by his interest in a math/computer science career, Kohji immediately enrols in the *yobiko* (a crammer solely for university entrance examinations) to prepare for another attempt a year hence.

The yobiko fees and the cost of the study materials will be high, but Kohji's parents consider it well worthwhile. Good results mean entry to a top national university, where fees are low, quality of staff, facilities, and education are superior, prestige is high, and career opportunities are outstanding. Provincial universities do not offer these advantages, and set a clear limit on what careers will be available and the extent of advancement that may be expected in the future. Although some private universities have high status and thus offer better opportunities, they are very expensive; some of the others are viewed as second-rank or below.

If worst comes to worst and the results are not good enough for Kohji to be accepted in the course he wants, he may even take the examinations yet again, for there is no limit on repeating and students on a waiting list may apply for admission to a university as often as they wish until they succeed. However, though first-time repeaters are frequent, and second-time repeaters are common, few persist beyond that point.

For a young man, every effort must be expended to enhance the chances of entrance to the best university possible, for his whole future depends on it. But this is not so for daughters. In Miyoko's family, discussions over the examination results and her future are much briefer and take a different turn. While not outstanding, her marks are quite good and she has earned the praise of her family and friends. Though it is no longer rare for girls to continue their education, most still do so in junior colleges and in programs traditionally considered suitable for females: primary school teaching, nursing, business skills (secretarial work), and the "softer" subjects like the arts, humanities, and social sciences. Secretly, Miyoko had hoped to take a humanities degree in the provincial four-year college, and her marks are more than adequate for this. But her father insists that she attend the nearby junior college and study business skills, so that is where she will go for the next two years. If her marks are good, if her ambition and intentions remain strong, and if she can persuade her parents to give their permission, she may yet be able to attend the provincial university and obtain the degree.

The pressure exerted by examinations in Japan is extraordinarily high. They control the lives of students (and their parents) to a degree that is very rare in the other countries of this study. Indeed, it is not too much to say that education in Japan, particularly after sixth grade, is defined as preparation to take examinations. Secondary school students are provided with a very clear set of objectives, and they are expected to make the effort necessary to achieve them. Only lack of effort, not lack of ability, it is commonly accepted, stands in the way of their success. So, it is to study, more study, and yet more study for tests and examinations that Kohji and Miyoko have devoted themselves for more years than they can remember.

[From Chapter 10: Findings, Options, Trade-offs, and Dilemmas]

Findings

Our study shows that in a number of respects, national examination systems are converging toward common forms and practices. Examination systems that have traditionally been decentralized give strong indications of greater centralization, and those that have been centralized in their control appear to be becoming less so. In every country the secondary school examination system has expanded to embrace a far greater proportion of the population of senior secondary school students. Expansion has been part consequence, but also part cause, of the ongoing differentiation of examinations that traditionally have been quite limited in their range of subjects. The changes have provided candidates with an increased range of choices among subjects and levels of difficulty. Often this has taken the form of including a greatly increased number of employment-related options. Convergence is evident, too, in trends among systems that have relied exclusively on open-ended, extended-answer formats to introduce multiple-choice, machine-scorable items and among those that have emphasized objective tests to introduce more elements of extended answers.

Last, the study highlights the two faces of examination systems. Examinations play a dual role in broader educational change. They can serve both as levers and obstacles to educational change, even within a given country. Although governments are prone to seize upon examination systems as handy instruments for pushing schools and teachers in desired directions, equally common is the resistance mounted to such initiatives by school administrators, teachers, employers, and even parents, using the examination systems to defend the status quo.

Impact and Reach of Examinations   In none of the countries studied does every student coming to the end of secondary education sit for an external examination. Large groups are often unaffected. Some have been selected out of the examination-preparatory tracks. Others attend a school that is simply not engaged in the business of preparing students for the examination. Nevertheless, the influence of an examination system permeates a nation's education system. It affects performance expectations, curriculum content, and definitions of scholastic success and failure. Especially for those who prepare for the examination, the impact on school and personal life is likely to be profound, as in Japan, France, Germany and England/Wales, where successive years of upper secondary schooling are characterized by a crescendo of concentration and effort. But even in other countries, students' lives in and out of school focus upon examinations. There are exceptions, however. Sweden makes a deliberate attempt to minimize the impact of the tests, and in the United States preparing for and taking the SAT and the ACT is far from the defining experience of the typical student's high school career.

Controlling the Examinations   We have observed many variations in the distribution of authority and responsibilities for national examinations. No nation has a single, centrally determined examination for all possible purposes. Control and ownership of the examinations can be in the hands of the central government, or shared among subnational units, or in a "quango," or even, as in the United States, in a private not-for-profit corporation. In France, China, Japan, and Sweden, the end-of-secondary-school examination systems are controlled mainly from the center by a special agency of each country's ministry of education. But even in these formally centralized arrangements, there are strong elements of devolution to regional or local authorities. Conversely, even when the system is formally decentralized, usually some oversight is entrusted to a central authority. Thus, in the Soviet Union each republic has formal authority over the attestat zrelosti, but took its cue from Moscow. In England/Wales, several largely autonomous regional examining boards are in control, but they collaborate on administrative matters and examination content, and they are increasingly subject to supervision by the central government's Department of Education and Science through the School Examination and Assessment Council. In Germany, though the Länder retain formal sovereign powers over their Abitur examination systems, they enter into voluntary agreements that in practice limit their discretion. In all these countries, control and ownership of the examinations are in the hands of public bodies, either a government department or semi-independent public agency.

The situation is quite different in the United States. Here, although a few states arrange for end-of-secondary-school achievement examinations, none has national currency, nor does the federal government provide a national examination system for the schools. The United States is exceptional in its reliance on private organizations like the Educational Testing Service and the American College Testing Program to provide end-of-secondary-school external tests and examinations, free of federal direction or control.[6]

Apart from who "owns" the examinations, there is the question of the role of teachers – mainly, though not exclusively, secondary school teachers – in performing such specific tasks as constructing test papers, proctoring the examination sessions, evaluating responses, and monitoring the whole process. The latter function can influence teacher-student relationships profoundly. When, as in Japan, China, England/Wales, the United States, and France, all grading of external examination answers is done anonymously, without teacher participation in grading their own students' answer papers, students and teachers can become allies in the business of outsmarting examiners. This is more difficult in Germany and the Soviet Union, where a student's own teachers play a large, overt role in evaluating his or her examination work. In addition, the German and Soviet practice indicates the presence of considerable trust, whether justified or not, in the skill and judgment of teachers, a positive reflection on their professional status. Swedish practice contains elements of all of the above.

The Examinations   Examination systems strongly influence the school curriculum, to the extent that in England/Wales, France, China, and Japan the subjects examined and the syllabi for the examinations virtually determine the school curriculum and the objectives of teaching. The format and content of examinations reflect what an educational system considers to be the knowledge and skills of most worth. They also reflect and stimulate curriculum changes. New curriculum elements tend gradually to find their way into examination papers, usually at the expense of traditional ones.

Tests incorporating significant practical work, such as laboratory exercises or artistic work – so-called performance examinations – are common in some places, rare or absent elsewhere. Multiple-choice formats are becoming more common, but still remain the exception rather than the rule in the eight nations of this study. Although all examinations test recall and comprehension, more advanced intellectual activities like problem-solving, critical analysis, and creative expression may also be assessed. New forms of evaluation are emerging that involve more than a timed paper-and-pen test. Rather, the new forms take into account an accumulated corpus of the candidate's work in the subject. Some advocate reporting results in more detailed ways, beyond traditional letter or number grades, to reflect fuller "profiles" of achievement.

The Demands Examinations Place on Candidates, Compared   Examination systems define a nation's expectations of students and its standards for educational success. Although all systems impose requirements upon candidates, these vary considerably. Some, like France and Germany, call for many subjects, an extensive syllabus, and long examination papers; others are less burdensome, for example, the United States. All systems offer certain options to candidates in choice of subjects and in level of difficulty, some of them very limited, others more numerous. In France scores for a subject examination are weighted differently in the final overall grade according to the candidate's specialization. In Germany and recently in England/Wales, candidates may take a subject as a major or a minor, with different examination papers based on different syllabi.

Comparing the relative difficulty of examination systems involves evaluating their general requirements, the content and the format of examination papers, timing and time limits, and the available options. Although such an exercise includes some objective data, like the number of examination hours, much rests on subjective judgments. We confined our analysis to the two most frequently tested subjects, national language/literature and mathematics. We conclude that end-of-secondary-school examinations are very burdensome in Germany and France, especially when they are compared with the relatively undemanding tests in Sweden and the United States. The content of the tests in Germany and France places high cognitive demands on candidates, extended answers are always required, and the time allotment is prolonged. In all respects, the examinations in Sweden and the United States are much less burdensome. Examinations in England/Wales and Japan lie between these extremes, but toward the more difficult end of the scale; China and the Soviet Union toward the less difficult end. Our conclusions refer only to the national external examinations and not to the university entrance examinations given as a second stage in Japan and the Soviet Union.

Success Rates Compared   Some examination systems, like Japan's JFSAT and the United States' SAT and ACT, provide results simply in the form of a numerical score, with no indication whether the score means pass or fail. Other systems, for example, France, England/Wales, and the Soviet Union, provide certification of passing or failing as well as a numerical or letter score. In those countries where the examination serves primarily as a selection instrument for post-secondary education, success is defined in practice as gaining entrance to higher education. In China the score is made known to the candidate, but it is meaningful only as it relates to the cutoff point for admission to college. Therefore, comparative and international study of success rates presents some difficulty.

Differences of organization and practice in secondary school systems, in admission standards to higher education, and in the announcement of results must be taken into account, and complicate comparison even more. Our broad conclusion is not just that success is defined differently but that success rates differ quite markedly across nations and that each nation appears to regard its own rates as somehow part of the natural order of things. Difficult examinations help reduce the percentage of the age group passing, but preselection tends to ensure that success rates with respect to the number of candidates are kept high. The gap between success rates in the United States and Sweden at one end of the scale and China at the other might better be termed a gulf. In the United States and Sweden the doors to post-secondary education are wide open. A high school diploma is not difficult to achieve and there are ways of getting admitted to some college, somewhere, without even completing the standard high school course of studies. This stands in stark contrast to China, where the percentage of the age group entering universities is very small. Our estimate is as low as 2 percent of the age group. We conclude that success rates reflect both national resource levels and the willingness to make them available for secondary and post-secondary education. In this way, success rates can be regarded as artifacts of national policies, for they go far beyond the narrow business of determining how much candidates know and how well they can demonstrate knowledge.

The Politics of Examinations   Because we know them to be powerful instruments of control, examination systems can become a focus of attention, even of political debate and struggle. This has been particularly evident in China, England/Wales, and Germany, and the political temperature surrounding examinations is rising sharply in the United States. On the other hand, even though the Swedes have made the greatest change of all by abandoning the traditional end-of-secondary-school examination and moving to a system of periodic local and national assessments, they have engaged in little dispute over examinations. In the Soviet Union, too, although many educational topics have been vigorously discussed, the examination system has generated little if any attention.

Possibly the most important cause of political engagement with examinations in recent years has been the very large increase in the number of students completing secondary education. Examinations that once involved only a tiny fraction of the population now interest a much wider public. Disputes over structure, format, and content of examinations often reflect differences in basic educational philosophy, even standard political ideology. As the number of stakeholders is growing, so are the voices of groups focusing attention on their particular interests and points of view. One important result is an increasing demand for examining bodies to be accountable for decisions and to follow full-disclosure principles as part of normal practice. They are only too frequently caught in a crossfire of charge and countercharge. In the United States the examination authorities, ETS in particular, are criticized for constructing "unfair" tests that are systematically biased against ethnic minorities and women. In some instances, the examiners are accused of overemphasizing the traditional aspects of the examined subjects; in others, the charge is that the examinations have thrown out too much of the traditional canon in favor of faddish approaches and material. In history and language and literature, particularly, the "modernization" of curricula and examination syllabi has been accompanied in the United States, France, and England/Wales by expressions of concern that national identity, national pride, and knowledge of the national heritage have been undermined by the introduction of world history, multicultural history, non-Western literature, language for communication, and the like.

The Persistence of Examinations   In spite of the conflicts surrounding them, examinations appear to have great survival capacity. Indeed, they have done more than persist, they have positively flourished. Why? First, they fulfill a number of essential functions for the school system and for society at large, namely (a) assessing student achievement, (b) controlling curriculum and instruction, (c) allocating rewards in education and employment, (d) motivating students and teachers, and (e) validating/legitimating knowledge and educational activity.

In addition, social changes have forced the bureaucratization of relationships that once could be satisfactorily maintained on a personal basis. When only a small proportion of the population stayed in school long enough to become candidates for the end-of-secondary-school examinations, everyone knew everyone else, and attendance at a particular school or the recommendation of a teacher could be relied upon to communicate to university professors or prospective employers a comprehensible and reliable evaluation of a student's preparation and performance. In contemporary society, schooling has become a mega-enterprise, public and complex, touching virtually every citizen and, most important of all, widely regarded as critical for individual and national prosperity. Examinations are expected to provide objective, reliable measures of accomplishment on which rational and efficient decisions about the future of individuals can be based, along with national benchmarks that enable citizens to assess the contribution made by the schools to the total national economic effort.

Finally, examination systems have demonstrated great adaptability in the face of changing circumstances. As the content of work has demanded more specifically technical knowledge and skills, so school curricula and examinations have moved to incorporate more applied and vocational elements into subject matter that was once almost exclusively academic and abstract. To meet accusations of subjectivity and unfairness in grading, examination systems have developed tests that lay claim to objectivity. And, reinforcing the trend from norm-referenced to criterion-referenced assessment, there are now signs of movement away from reliance on one-shot, time-limited tests toward the incorporation of such nonexamination criteria as portfolios, profiles, and school records in the final evaluation of candidates. Sweden is furthest along this road, using both continuous assessment (a mix of centrally and locally set examinations, required and optional) and grades from course work done during regular school activities.

Options and Trade-offs

Comparative and international observation can go beyond the obvious "good points versus bad points" approach. A series of "What if?" possibilities can be phrased in terms of the trade-offs implicit in specific examination arrangements in particular countries. This should appeal particularly to policymakers and administrators, who are required to negotiate an acceptable path between opposing, even contradictory, goals as they try to achieve one set of objectives without paying too high a price in terms of other desirable outcomes. As in other aspects of a country's social life, examination policies and practices reflect compromises among such competing values and goals. While seeking to increase perceived benefits in one direction, a nation almost inevitably gives up some benefit or exacerbates some problem in another direction. It is in that sense, therefore, that we can view extant examination systems as configurations of trade-offs. Here, for example, are three such sets of trade-offs evident in many countries:

> Administering a uniform examination to all, rather than allowing candidates to choose which examinations and subjects to take, and at what level of difficulty, facilitates comparability of scores, but shortchanges individual, regional, ethnic, cultural, and other differences.

> Machine-scorable formats are economical, but their use risks neglecting the development of those skills that are difficult to test using these formats.

> Moving away from one-shot, time-bound examinations to assessments based on the results of work done over extended periods of time is likely to provide more authentic evidence of a student's capacities, but raises problems of grading standards, fairness, and comparability that are very difficult to solve.

Uniformity versus optionality represents one of the most critical sets of trade-offs in the realm of examinations. Some nations, for example, Japan, China, the Soviet Union, and the United States, in the SAT and ACT, offer limited options in what is essentially the same examination for all candidates, whereas other countries, particularly England/Wales, France, Germany, and Sweden, offer candidates a large measure of choice among subjects, syllabi, kinds or degrees of specialization, and levels of difficulty.

Uniform national examinations facilitate comparability and evenhandedness of treatment for different groups. But uniformity exacts its price: opportunities to adjust the examination to recognize the different needs of regions or groups at different stages of school development are inevitably reduced; regional and local interests may feel slighted; and the center's purposes are likely to be served at the expense of the periphery's. These are the educational and social costs of a single examination, of special concern in countries covering a varied territory or comprising a large and heterogeneous population. By the same token, a large measure of optionality brings the clear benefit of adapting the examination to the subject preferences and aptitudes of individual candidates. Examinations can in this way also be tailored to different educational and occupational prospects and to the broad requirements of society and the economy.

But optionality inevitably weakens the prospects for a national curriculum and the sense of a national culture. It raises problems of comparability and may even provoke concerns about equity. A credential based on a familiar standard set of compulsory subjects is easy for employers and admissions officers to interpret; they can be puzzled indeed by the complex regulations and weighting schemes used to equate the essentially nonequatable assortments of examination subjects offered by candidates.

The retreat from uniformity to diversity is well illustrated by changes in examination policy in France and Germany. The changes made in the baccalauréat represent bold and on the whole successful moves, but they have been achieved at some price. The most obvious has been a loss of comparability of candidates, who take widely different assortments of subjects and different tests in nominally the same subject, with different weights given to the results, depending on the particular option. Only in name, certainly not in practice, is there a single national end-of-secondary-school examination administered to all candidates in France. Instead, a strongly demarcated hierarchy of prestige has emerged, with the mathematical options at the head and the vocational options at the tail. Furthermore, devolution of some limited responsibilities for selecting examination questions and awarding marks has led to the view that standards are not the same across all académies. An examination system that began with a strong commitment to strict uniformity and comparability across the entire country, including even overseas departments and dependencies, has yielded to the need to accommodate a wider spectrum of the student population and broadened definitions of what should be learned at school and assessed.

In addition, despite the persistence of a common core of subjects, the differentiation of the baccalauréat has provoked fear that France is dissipating its intellectual *patrimoine*. Whether this is a benefit or a loss is, we suppose, a matter of taste, but taken simply as a matter of fact rather than of values, French culture générale has become a little less générale.

As with the baccalauréat, the Abitur has been significantly altered to cope with the increased numbers and heterogeneity of candidates. It has changed less radically than the baccalauréat, however, perhaps because the need in Germany to secure some measure of agreement among eleven quite differently oriented Länder sets limits on the possibilities of change. In addition, whereas the baccalauréat is marked by a generally high degree of central direction, a determining characteristic of the Abitur is its school-based control. Especially in Germany, the combination of local control and written and oral examinations raises questions about the extent to which grading standards are kept consistent even within a given Land, let alone across the eleven Länder. Because Germany makes less effort compared even with France to ensure such standardization, an important element of chance and arbitrariness has developed.

Even more than in most centralized countries, the basic stance of the examination systems in both Japan and China is one of strict central control and uniformity of content, characteristics that build upon traditional state practices. Few options are extended to Japanese candidates. They may choose mathematics tests of different levels of difficulty, additional tests in social studies, and a particular foreign language. In China, although the detailed administration of the examinations and the final selection process are delegated to the provincial authorities, they are required to operate within narrowly drawn guidelines. The intent is to ensure a strictly meritocratic selection of candidates for entry into higher education. Although criteria other than examination scores are taken into account, especially evidence of political reliability, work experience, and good health, performance on the National Unified College Entrance Examination remains the major criterion for selection. Considering that the number of candidates is exceptionally large – in 1988, 2.7 million prepared for the national college admission tests, of whom only a fifth were accepted for study – the Chinese system has produced a truly impressive degree of comparability among candidates. But this insistence on a uniform examination has severely limited the range of studies in the secondary schools, as well as the freedom of Chinese teachers to experiment with new materials and methods. To that extent, educational development has been held back in China.

The Soviet Union provides a sharp contrast to China in practice, though not in formal terms. On paper, the center, Moscow, is dominant and only token variations from standard uniform syllabi and examinations are permitted; in practice the republics and the localities enjoy considerable latitude. Each of the fifteen republics has responsibility for setting the content and standards of the examinations for the *attestat zrelosti*. Schools work within the republic guidelines, but in turn enjoy a good deal of local discretion. The teachers who prepare the students dominate the process of setting the questions and evaluating the responses. Even though many teachers are members of the Communist party, this degree of autonomy presents a curious disjuncture with the tight control the party and the central government exert over school curricula and textbooks. Paradoxically, in a society and a school system that are in most respects characterized by substantial central direction, the school-completion examination is not. Thus, the Soviet Union has settled for a curious compromise between the rhetoric of centralized planning and the practice of local discretion.

Once again, the trade-off for such local discretion is a substantial loss of comparability of marks, and this led the universities and higher technical institutes (the VUZy) to insist on applicants sitting for special, institutionally set and graded entrance examinations, a second stage very much along Japanese lines. In the final years of Soviet power, the universities have received formal encouragement to establish their own entrance criteria and examinations.[7] Diversity and optionality achieved in this manner entail significant costs and aberrations. The location of the examinations can impose substantial travel costs on students. There is virtually no coordination among the VUZy concerning the dates on which they will hold their examinations; examination syllabi are idiosyncratic; and grading formulas, cutoff points, and so forth are confidential. Admission into higher education has consequently become something of an exercise in game theory, requiring candidates to exercise decision-making skills in conditions of imperfect knowledge and uncertainty. The system appears to be lacking important elements of overall fairness and objectivity, to say nothing of the persistent reports of discrimination against particular ethnic and religious groups, influence-peddling, and corruption.

In Sweden the changes in the examination system since the mid-1970s have gone hand-in-hand with changes in the upper secondary school curriculum. These offered students a much wider choice of courses and devolved administrative authority over the schools from the center to the municipalities. Sweden discarded a fairly uniform national end-of-secondary-school examination, replacing it with a combination of marks gained during regular classroom and home work and in nationally set tests administered at intervals during the upper secondary school career. The goals were to reduce the strain on pupils, produce more valid and reliable predictors of university success, and correct socioeducational inequities in assessment. These were judged to be as important as insisting on a high degree of comparability via a uniform examination.

The new system by no means abandons attempts at comparability across candidates. Teachers keep detailed records of their students' achievements, and much time is given to moderating grading standards, so that variations are minimized within both schools and regions. All of this makes important demands on educational resources, but so far the Swedes have been willing and able to incur the necessary costs in order to try to reconcile the respective demands of individual diversity and national comparability.

There is some evidence that the system may not be working to provide a wholly satisfactory degree of comparability. Beginning in September 1991, high school seniors could choose to take the Swedish Scholastic Aptitude Test (SSAT), a day-long assessment of verbal, quantitative, analytic and problem-solving abilities, and offer their scores in place of the usual high school records when applying for admission to higher education.[8] Previously this route had been open to mature-age students only.

If the trend in Sweden has been to devolve authority from the center to the local government units, events in England/Wales since 1987 represent an abrupt acceleration of what had been a slow transfer of authority over the schools from local to central government. In the interest of establishing uniform national curricular standards, voluntarism and localism have been forced to give way.

Since the demise of the General School Certificate and its associated London University Matriculation regulations, it has not been necessary for a given student to take any particular subject or to follow any particular syllabus within that subject, except insofar as he or she wanted to take an examination or the school demanded it. The former GCE O level and CSE offered, and the present GCSE and A level examinations all continue to offer, a truly startling array of options. The government decided that this laissez-faire policy had produced such incoherence in school curricula and such indefiniteness in expectations of what the schools should be doing that it had to go. Hence the quite revolutionary decision to introduce regular national assessment of each student's knowledge and skills, which together with the new GCSE examinations is intended to help implement a national core curriculum.

So far, the government has declined to interfere with the GCE A-level examination system, which continues to offer a rich variety of subjects and examination syllabi to schools and candidates. However, problems occasioned by lack of comparability have been reduced by cooperation among the examining boards to identify core topics in syllabi in such basic subjects as mathematics and literature. In addition, a much greater effort has been made in England/Wales than in either France or Germany, for example, to ensure standardization of grading criteria, both within and between examining boards. For this reason, some of the more serious doubts about the fairness and comparability of marking that are voiced in the latter countries have been restrained in England/Wales, though by no means absent.

In the United States the benefits of local control and optionality have been secured, but only at the price of absence of widely recognized achievement standards. State and local control of the schools in the United States has produced a bewildering array of instructional practices, far exceeding even the variety formerly available in England/Wales. In addition, very few of the fifty states offer an external secondary-school-leaving examination or university selection/entrance examination. A high school graduate's academic achievement is thus reported on the basis of school-based, teacher-awarded course grades, with little or no effort made, as in Sweden, to ensure comparability of grading standards among schools or even in many instances within a school.

To compensate for the resulting extreme lack of comparability, the "national" examinations of the Educational Testing Service and the American College Testing Program have deliberately provided few options to the individual candidate. In this way a limited amount of comparable information about college applicants is provided. On the other hand, employers hiring the non-college-bound usually have only the applicant's high school diploma as evidence of academic achievement. Sometimes, but by no means commonly, an employer will have a copy of the applicant's high school transcript, but even then may be hard-pressed to divine what a particular grade means with respect to academic ability. Most employers have responded to this uncertainty by ignoring transcripts altogether. So far, the United States has steered away from instituting an officially sanctioned, uniform system of examinations, though recently, as a result of rising concern about achievement standards, the possibility of some form of national school-leaving examination has come under consideration.[9]

The Persistent Dilemmas of Examination Policy

While the example offered by other countries gives strong support to the notion that a national, external, end-of-secondary-school examination is useful, and even necessary, its introduction into the United States should not be regarded as a panacea for the country's educational ills. In addition, although there are clear advantages accruing to Germany from its Abitur, to France from its baccalauréat, and to Japan from its JFSAT, the critical policy question when trying to adapt foreign institutions to domestic purposes is: How can the United States secure these advantages, while avoiding, or at least minimizing, the disadvantages that may accompany them?

Entirely satisfactory solutions for such policy problems are rare indeed. Moreover, as the circumstances of an examination system change, so a new set of compromises among the competing goals is likely to be required. For these reasons, the choices that must be made are best regarded as persistent dilemmas that examination authorities have to learn to live with, leaning sometimes to one side, sometimes to the other. Among such dilemmas are the following:

Dilemma 1. How to retain the function of the examination as a stabilizing element in the educational and social systems, while:
(a) providing flexibility and opportunities for change in content and format of the examination;
(b) introducing new, nonexamination criteria of assessment, for example, course work and portfolios;
(c) expanding the number of candidates.

Dilemma 2. How to promote examination results that are comparable and understandable, while:

(a) introducing new, more sophisticated ways of reporting results;
(b) introducing nonexamination criteria of assessment;
(c) introducing new subjects and differentiated levels of subjects.

Dilemma 3. How to maintain the value of the credential earned by examination success, while:
(a) increasing the number of successful candidates;
(b) introducing nonexamination criteria of assessment;
(c) reducing the burdens and pressure on students;
(d) controlling examination costs.

Dilemma 4. How to ensure a sufficient degree of regional authority and school or individual autonomy, while:
(a) implementing national standards of content and quality;
(b) recognizing the claims of internationalism;
(c) using examination results to monitor school system performance.

Dilemma 5. How to use the examination to select for subsequent education, training, and jobs, while:
(a) also certifying satisfactory completion of secondary education;
(b) not discouraging too many candidates, that is, picking winners without creating too many losers;
(c) providing flexibility of examination content, in particular, access to new subjects.

Dilemma 6. How to incorporate the new information technologies in the examination system and secure the promised benefits of greater efficiency and cost savings, while safeguarding teaching and learning from undesirable side effects.

Dilemma 7. How to maintain and increase the professional autonomy of teachers, while:
(a) using examination results to monitor school system performance;
(b) strengthening national curricula and national standards.

Dilemma 8. How to raise standards of performance, while:
(a) increasing the number of successful candidates;
(b) using nonexamination criteria of assessment;
(c) reducing the burden and pressure on students;
(d) reducing examination costs;
(e) not discouraging too many candidates.

Each of these dilemmas represents a potential problem associated with use of the examination system to control either individual destinies or what occurs in schools. In consequence, as the United States quite properly considers reform of the testing and examination system as a way to lever education to a higher level of performance, policymakers need to be constantly mindful of the likelihood of unintended, undesirable consequences of their decisions. Other countries have often "been there before," and the consequences of going in this or that direction are available for inspection.[10] If for no other reason, the record of other countries' examination experience repays attention.

NOTES

* Excerpted from Max A. Eckstein and Harold J. Noah, *Secondary School Examinations: International Perspectives on Policies and Practice* (Yale University Press, 1993): 36-40, 68-74, 218-224, 226-232, 243-245. Reprinted by permission of Yale University Press.

1. All students in upper secondary school continue the common curriculum-Swedish language and literature, English, history, mathematics, and physical education. The particulars of the curriculum will differ, however, depending on the course chosen. The longer programs allow for more advanced work and some specialization in the third and fourth years.

2. As the decentralization of the Swedish school system continues, the authority of municipalities has increased while that of the board has been sharply reduced, though it retains an important coordination role. New arrangements for implementation of the new policy are currently under way.

3. John Greenlees, "Pupils Go Crackers over Study Aid," *Times Educational Supplement* (June 17, 1988): 15.

4. Thomas Rohlen notes that suicide rates are not higher for Japanese high school seniors facing examinations than for their counterparts in other nations, but that examination pressure as a *cause* of suicide is probably higher. Some of the yobiko (cram schools for repeaters) have their own clinics. Thomas P. Rohlen. *Japan's High Schools* (Berkeley: University of Berkeley Press, 1983): 327-334.

5. U.S. Department of Education, *Japanese Education Today* (Washington, D.C.: U.S. Government Printing Office, 1987).

6. Some states do limit the otherwise unfettered discretion of the testing organizations. For example, New York State requires ETS to provide each SAT candidate with an item-by-item printout of the grading of his or her responses.

7. *Bulletin of the State Committee of the USSR on Public Education. Professional education series. 1/1991; Poisk 6/91.*

8. Kenny Bränberg et al., "The Influence of Sex, Education and Age on Test Scores on the Swedish Scholastic Aptitude Test," *Scandinavian Journal of Educational Research* 34, no. 3 (1990): 189.

9. See, for example, the work of the New Standards Project, developed jointly by the National Center on Education and the Economy, Washington D.C., and the University of Pittsburgh's Learning Research and Development Center. In addition, the National Council on Education Standards and Testing, created by the U.S. Congress in early 1991, is likely to have a major impact on the debate over standards of achievement and modes of assessment in the United States. The preferred solution seems at the moment to be the establishment of a set of nationally recognized standards, identifying a core of subjects and their content, which state educational authorities could adopt, while adding whatever they wish to the state's own examination to meet local preferences.

10. Albert Shanker, president of the American Federation of Teachers, calls attention to the experience of other countries, as follows: "People who predict disaster [if the United States were to adopt national standards and assessments] should look at how systems work in other industrialized countries. Some of these systems are better than others, but none is a disaster, and there's no reason to believe we'd have one here. In fact, there's every reason to believe we could make such a system work." "National Standards and Exams," *The New York Times* (March 1, 1992): 4.7.

25

An International Perspective
on National Standards*

Let me will start with a short quiz. Does anybody know who said:

> In modern times people's views about education differ. There is no general
> agreement about what the young should learn, either in relation to moral virtue
> or to success in life. Nor is it clear whether education should be more
> concerned with training the intellect or the character. Contemporary events
> have made the problem more difficult, and there is no certainty whether
> education should be primarily vocational, moral, or cultural. People have
> recommended all three.[1]

Who said that? Although it sounds exceedingly contemporary and relevant to our
symposium today, it was said by Aristotle over two thousand years ago. These basic
questions about the nature of the curriculum and appropriate standards in education
have been with us for a very long time. I have been asked to speak on the topic from an
economist's point of view, as well as to consider the issue of national standards from an
international perspective.

My basic position is straightforward. I believe that we in America need to steer
away from our present antipathy toward nationally recognized standards in education. I
believe we have gone overboard in the direction of local and state autonomy. In
consequence, we have permitted de facto national standards to be set by private
agencies such as textbook publishers and the Educational Testing Service. It is
important, however, as we move toward the establishment of nationally recognized
standards, to avoid the rigidities that have been associated with them in many other
countries.

Economists, as you know, are accustomed to view the world through cost-benefit
lenses. Every social arrangement embodies a particular set of choices among costs and
benefits and the issue of national standards in education is no exception. In what
follows, I will point to three categories of costs that are increased by our not having
national standards in the United States. Then I will point to some of the problems other
nations have had in devising national standards and operating with them.

The first cost of not having national standards is the cost of non-comparability.
Life becomes more complicated and therefore more expensive when each state and
local school district issues its own high school diploma based on state or even local
criteria. In the monetary world, we do have a common national standard. It is called

the dollar. Its existence helps us to carry on our daily life and business affairs with much greater dispatch and at lower cost than if we were saddled with fifty different currencies. In education, however, we are in just that position. We have myriad different educational standards. College admissions officers and employers develop some rules of thumb to guide them and over time they accumulate experience about the worth of some high school diplomas compared with others, but it remains exceedingly difficult to make equivalency assessments. It is a hit-and-miss procedure, affording no great degree of reliability. Decisions to admit or to hire, based on the evidence of high school diplomas or high school grade averages, will say yes to many who should have been told no. Worse still, decisions will say no to many who should have received a yes answer.

Second, there are costs of information. National standards help to lower the costs of acquiring valid and reliable information about the characteristics of candidates needed to make judgments. Without high-quality information about the further educability and trainability of applicants, admissions officers and employers resort to ad hoc screening devices. The costs of acquiring and administering ad hoc tests, and interpreting the results, are far from negligible. They could be markedly reduced, given national standards of scholastic achievement.

Third, there are the costs of private substitutes. Because the regular educational system does not provide credentials based on a recognized national standard, a system of private substitutes has developed. The Scholastic Aptitude Test (SAT) and the American College Test (ACT) were invented precisely in order to fill the gap left by the educational system. There are a number of costs associated with the use of parallel and privately organized testing. I am not referring to the entrance fees that must be paid either by taxpayers or parents, for I have no evidence that they are exorbitant. Indeed, given what the testing organizations set out to do, they appear to do it in an adequately cost-effective manner. Rather, it is the cost in terms of a loss of confidence in the tests themselves that is worrisome, and especially the many challenges to the tests that are mounted on the ground that they are biased against groups defined by sex, race, residence, culture, and so on. A nationally approved set of standards could be and probably would be subject to similar charges, but at least they could be defended on the important ground that the standards were the creation of an elected government and not of a private, unelected group.

A further cost is in terms of the type of teaching and learning that substitutes for national standards have promoted. The establishment of a multiple-choice mentality in education was never intended by the testing organizations, but that is the way it has turned out. Any tendency already present in our school system to view education as primarily a progression through a series of highly specific multiple-choice and short-answer questions has been strongly reinforced by the testing organizations' adherence to the multiple-choice and associated formats. This in turn leads to another cost in terms of lowered public confidence in the tests. The testing organizations have been most reluctant to make public the contents of each test after it is administered. They claim with justification that this would raise expenses significantly by making it much more difficult to reuse test items that already cost hundreds if not thousands of dollars to construct and validate. Still, in modern society accountability is a golden word, and in these matters of the private establishment of standards, accountability means public accountability. Without it, costs in terms of distrust, dispute, and litigation are certain to increase.

Nevertheless, even though the absence of national standards involves us in heavy costs, we must realize that their adoption is far from being without problems. To identify some of these problems, we can turn to the experience of three or four major countries that actually have national standards. We shall see that the call to national standards in education should be answered with caution.

What should be the substance of educational standards? Sometimes this is put as the classic curriculum question: What knowledge is of most worth? This is never an easy question to answer. In countries such as France, Japan, and the Soviet Union, for example, it has been somewhat easier to answer than in the United States. In a way, these countries have advantages that we do not. The French, for example, have a very clear sense of their French culture. The Japanese have an even stronger sense of their culture, plus an ethnically homogeneous population. The people of the Soviet Union have an exceptionally powerful state apparatus to help implement a comprehensive political ideology.

Yet the French continue to debate and criticize what they teach in their schools and what they include in their examinations. At times the debate gets so heated that it spills over onto the streets in demonstrations. The Japanese have just been through a period of soul-searching concerning their school curriculum. The former prime minister, Mr. Nakasone, is in the vanguard of those who assert that the schools need radical change if Japan is to maintain its position in the world. The current prime minister, Mr. Takashita, on the other hand, seems to be quite certain that the current curriculum serves Japan well. He has adopted the Japanese equivalent of the attitude, "If it ain't broke, don't fix it." In the Soviet Union, *glasnost* has revealed, among other things, the deep divisions within the country about the nature of communism, the events of the Leninist and Stalinist past, and the meaning of these things for education.

If these countries have serious disputes and unsettled fundamental questions about the curriculum, what chance is there that this country, with its cross-cutting social, economic, political, and ethnic divisions, can reach a national consensus on the substance of the curriculum – which is, after all, the basis for educational standards? Moreover, in setting standards, we have to decide whether there should be one set for all students finishing high school, or an array of standards for different desirable outcomes, reflecting different types and levels of student ability. Two different answers to this question are exemplified by practices in Japan and Sweden.

Japan is at one end of the spectrum, with very narrowly drawn standards focused on academic achievement that most students are expected to reach and set at levels that we tend to regard as rather high. This approach has undoubtedly contributed to Japan's ability to secure unusually good achievement in math and science. Even in Japan, however, it has proved impossible to establish a single high standard for all children and some differentiation continues to exist. Sweden, like Japan, sets its standards centrally and runs a unified curriculum for all students during the initial nine years of compulsory education. It has taken an opposite tack to Japan on examination and selection, as well as in the degree to which it is ready to recognize variation in the talents and interests of young people. Sweden, with no final end-of-school examinations, has established a centrally monitored system of continuous assessment of students' performance on a very broad basis. It has also developed a host of differentiated programs of study for the senior high schools.

Thus Japan and Sweden exemplify a linked pair of questions for our own policy considerations. At what point might a unified standard become a most unwelcome and uncomfortable straitjacket? And at what point do differentiated standards become no standards at all?

We may note, too, that standards that begin their life as uniform and high level maxima tend over time to become differentiated and in part, at least, lowered.

Germany's *Abitur* and France's *baccalauréat* have exhibited these trends during the past fifteen years. The *bac,* which as late as 1950 had only four variants, now has no fewer than thirty-eight. One has to be very well informed indeed to understand exactly what a brand new holder of the *baccalauréat* has been studying, let alone what standards she or he has attained.

In England, long-standing tradition has excluded the government from setting school curriculum and establishing standards. Curricula have been in the hands of local educational authorities and even school principals. During the postwar years, an array of parallel standards and examinations grew up alongside the Ordinary and Advanced Level General Certificate of Education to meet the needs of students who are not in the academic tracks of the secondary school system. Last year the Thatcher government announced that the differentiation of curricula, standards, and examinations had gone too far. This year the government is in the process of establishing a national curriculum, instituting procedures for continuous assessment of student achievement in that curriculum, and sweeping together the variety of school-leaving examinations under the wider umbrella of a new exam, the General Certificate of Secondary Education. Nevertheless, under the new Thatcher dispensation, while national standards will be established for seven-, eleven-, and fourteen-year-olds, differentiated standards will remain for those sixteen years of age and above. Indeed, they will be extended. Thus, although the British government has announced that it wants to break with past practice in which only a minority of children left school with a marketable credential in hand, differentiation of credentials by level of achievement will continue to be a characteristic of the British system of making and implementing standards.

Let us return to the United States. Many American observers have charged the schools here with being too conservative, teaching outdated material and obsolete skills. Yet foreigners looking at U.S. schools and comparing them with their own tend to see something quite different. Instead of inertia, they see an extraordinary readiness in American education to establish new goals, to try out new materials and procedures, and even to adapt new ideas imported from abroad – at least as compared with what they see in their own countries. If such flexibility does exist here, it is highly likely that one reason is the very absence of the national standards that are the norm abroad. Compare our situation with that in France, the Soviet Union, or Japan. There the national standards established by the ministries of education and enshrined in the centrally administered end-of-school examinations lock teachers and students into curricula and methods that are very difficult to change. However skillfully a nation chooses the standards it wishes to enforce today, it is quite difficult to prevent those standards from becoming solid obstacles to the changes that may be needed tomorrow.

The conclusion I draw from all this is that simply to say we need standards does not even begin to solve the tough issues that lie in wait. Indeed, if the political disputes surrounding the *bac* in France or the arguments engendered by the introduction of a national curriculum and continuous assessment in England, or even the charges leveled at the Regents Examinations in New York State, are anything to go by, the imposition of standards can engender as many problems as it helps remedy. In particular, it is not easy to get agreement on what the aims of education should be – that was Aristotle's point twenty-three centuries ago and it is still true. It is not easy to decide what kinds of standards to adopt, and it is not easy to keep standards intact once you have them – but to paraphrase a favorite question of the rabbis, Where is it written that it should be easy?

In any event, my sense is that national standards are no panacea. Long-lasting improvement in education will come only from securing and retaining knowledgeable, skilled, and caring teachers in the nation's classrooms – teachers who are supported and whose work is respected by parents and society at large. National standards may be useful in helping teachers lead youngsters to learn, but here as in other countries, they are neither the necessary nor a sufficient condition for generating the quality schooling students deserve.

NOTES

* Harold J. Noah, "An International Perspective on National Standards," *Teachers College Record*, 91:1 (Fall 1989): 17-22. Delivered at a Symposium on National Standards for Education, held at Teachers College, Columbia University, November 29, 1988, as part of the College's centennial celebrations. Reprinted by permission.
1. Aristotle, *Politics,* VIII.2.

26

A Comparative Assessment of Assessment*

The impact of examination systems on curriculum development: an international study.
Christine De Luca, 1994. Paris: UNESCO.
National examinations: design, procedures and reporting. John P. Keeves, 1994.
Paris: UNESCO – International Institute for Educational Planning (Fundamentals
of Educational Planning No. 50)
*A Comparative Study of Current Theories and Practices in assessing students'
achievements at primary and secondary level.* Henry G. Macintosh, 1994.
Geneva: International Bureau of Education (IBE Documents Series, Number 4).

Why have some countries become so exercised about national assessment and
examinations over the past decade or so? In England and Wales, the GCE has been
substantially restructured, examinations for a new vocational qualification were
introduced, and pressure is great to reform A-levels; in the United States, local
administrations and the several States have been introducing new high school
graduation requirements, some for the first time, and the idea of some kind of national
school-leaving standard has again been raised; Sweden, which had virtually replaced its
traditional university entrance examination with a more elastic set of tests and reports is
having second thoughts; and Israel last year cancelled a part of its stringent academic
requirements for the traditional Abitur-like *Bagrut*. And why has so much interest been
sparked in what is going on in foreign parts? Only a few years ago, it would have
seemed most unlikely that national examinations "in other countries" would generate
such intense interest and scrutiny.

Over half a century ago, Paul Monroe and I.L. Kandel of Teachers College,
Columbia University conducted a major international inquiry on the subject in
collaboration with scholars from several other nations. But it was not until the 1950s,
with the groundbreaking comparative achievement studies of the IEA (International
Association for the Evaluation of Educational Achievement) that comparative interest in
examinations revived. It was clear that these were important administrative devices
used for selection within national school systems, but they might also explain
significant differences in student achievement among those countries. Then, in the late
1980s, World Bank efforts to reform teaching methods and curriculum in developing
nations pointed to the instrumental value of national examinations for reforming
curriculum and teaching. Since that time, study and discussion within individual
countries as well as comparative investigations have repeatedly pointed to the critical
importance of examination systems not only for student selection but also for setting
and even raising educational standards.

Simply stated, assessment is important in a variety of ways to a variety of interested parties. It serves at one time as incentive and as yardstick for schools and school systems; it is a means of accounting as well as an instrument for individual advancement; and, increasingly, it provides a measure for nations to compare themselves with others. Thus, to examine examinations is no simple academic enterprise: it reaches into many corners of a country's total social context.

The three studies under review testify to the increasing attention given to the various roles and forms of national examinations: how they work, what they stand for, what is changing in some places, and what can be learned through comparative, international scrutiny of their practices. In particular, attention is increasingly directed at the question of how examination systems affect and are affected by school curriculum and achievement standards, and the vexing questions of how best to assess students and monitor school systems. Each of these works informs us on social and educational policy and practice in contemporary societies and makes an enlightening and useful contribution to the subject.

The three reports differ, however, in purpose, scope, methods and provenance. Their very differences suggest a number of criteria one might employ to assess them, including the number and range of countries described and discussed and the levels of schooling considered; the methodology employed; the sponsors of the respective works; the purposes of the studies; and the special academic interests they address.

The comparative study by de Luca, Research Officer of the Scottish Examination Board, was sponsored by Unesco, and conducted on behalf of the International Association for Educational Assessment. It seeks to assess the influence of examination systems upon curriculum development in seven countries, four of them in the developed world: Colombia, Egypt, France, Japan, Scotland, the U.S.A. and Zimbabwe. Data and conclusions are derived from extensive literature search including reports from professional and other publications, and responses by informed persons to a questionnaire. De Luca concludes that examination systems do indeed have considerable effects on curriculum development. But whether these are positive or negative depends on a number of factors such as: the articulation between examinations and curriculum, the relationship between the agencies responsible for each of these activities, the degree to which teachers are involved in policy and the actual practice of curriculum and examination formulation, the availability of in-service training, and the degree of importance attached to the results. The author concludes that exams can have positive effects upon curriculum reform but that the effects on pupils are generally negative. Nevertheless, she observes, measurement of attainment and maintaining standards remain the major functions of examination systems and provide powerful justification for their continued existence.

Macintosh conducted his investigation for the IAEA on behalf of the International Bureau of Education in Geneva. The goal of this study was somewhat different from de Luca's: to compare how current thinking on assessment relates to practices in ten countries, half of them in the developed world: Australia, Bahrain, England and Wales, Guatemala, Israel, Malaysia, Namibia, Poland, Scotland and Slovenia. It points to recent changes in assessment in each country and overall, gives examples of gaps that appear between theory and practice and identifies some factors explaining these, and suggests ways of linking theory and practice more closely. The title is somewhat misleading, however, since it is more about the *uses* of assessment than anything else, and on the relation of assessment to educational change, rather than on assessment theories *per se*. Macintosh concludes from his survey that, across the countries reviewed, selection continues to be the major purpose of assessment, rather than monitoring or diagnosis. He concludes that there is little pressure for change, that current practices on the whole do little to help prepare students for adult life or to address the many social and educational problems that beset societies.   The author agrees that assessment may serve as a vehicle for curriculum change and that this requires increasing involvement of teachers, but he regards most current assessment practices as obstacles to reform.   Macintosh is all in favor of educational change. But the higher the examination stakes, the greater the pressure on examination-makers to maintain reliability and neutrality, and, hence, standards. The result, he asserts, is that examinations are less and less likely to encourage innovative and progressive curricula, which are called for as the school populations involved grow larger and more diverse. He ends with a call for more systematic and comprehensive training for teachers in the uses of assessment.

Keeves's contribution differs from both the previous two in several important respects. It is one of a Unesco series explicitly directed towards educational planners and administrators as well as those generally interested in how educational planning may relate to national development. It, too, provides information on how countries select and certify their students, and discusses the various roles of central examinations, the influence they exert in their nation's school system, and their purported benefits and disadvantages. Keeves's sources of data on national examinations derive from the 24 countries which participated in the IEA 2nd Science Study in the mid-1980s. This is the largest sample represented among the three studies, and therefore allows the author to make general, more global statements with greater authority. From the outset, this work is more truly comparative and more than a set of country studies. Keeves assumes that his readers have much of the necessary background knowledge about the countries he refers to, or at least that they have access to it and acknowledge the importance of context. He can therefore more easily move from a few selected themes to particular instances, rather than from a congeries of information to points of similarity or differences as de Luca and Macintosh tend to do. Thus, for example, he puts together in one table in succinct but comprehensible form such variables as school attendance at different stages of national education systems, grades at which the several stages end, points at which national examinations take place, and participation rates in tertiary and terminal secondary schooling.

Keeves's contribution differs from the other two reports in another important respect. Like the other two authors, he distinguishes between the different roles of national examinations. But he also analyses a number of practical and technical aspects of comparative achievement testing in considerable depth, raising the question, what are the consequences for national examination systems of advances in measurement and statistical analysis.   For these exercises, the author is eminently well-qualified, given his considerable involvement with educational research in Australia and with the gargantuan international work of the IEA projects. In conclusion, Keeves suggests that the functions of national examination systems develop from a stage of selection and certification, to monitoring and deliberate policy influence upon curriculum and teaching – an intriguing historical model that deserves attention.

The national case study approach taken by both de Luca and Macintosh presents considerable background information on each country, somewhat more generous in the de Luca work.   Generalizations about trends and their causes often appear in the national profiles, but only in Keeves's contribution do we gain a sense of what these signify historically and from a more global perspective.

In addition to the factual information, the questionnaires distributed by Macintosh and de Luca respectively invited comments and informed opinion from respondents. Macintosh directs attention to current assessment theories and practices and on changes that specialists consider necessary. He reports views on how far existing arrangements were adequate to "meet the needs of contemporary society" and to prepare young people for adult life in it. In respect of her seven countries, de Luca's study of the influence of examination systems on curriculum development is based on a literature search, including press cuttings from "reputable education authorities," as well as responses by experts to a questionnaire. However, though only de Luca uses the term in reference to her respondents, each study makes use of an 'opportunity sample' of countries, an oxymoronic term if ever there was one!

Each work pays attention to the different forms of assessment and the characteristic practices in each of the countries they surveyed. Across the countries surveyed, essay, shorter answers and multiple choice are the main forms, with some oral examinations, depending on the national traditions. But it is not easy for the reader to track how prevalent a given form of practice is across countries, nor are the answers very evident as to why one style is more common in some places than others. For example, why do Japan and the U.S.A. depend so heavily on multiple choice, England and others upon essay answers, while some European countries, Poland and Slovenia, trust their teachers enough to rely on oral examinations. Still, internationally viewed, educators and administrators appear as very traditional and conservative. Only de Luca points to the relatively innovative practice of profiles of achievement as envisaged in the State of Vermont, U.S.A. An unfortunate example as it turns out. The State Education Dept. recently cancelled its plans for such a system for budget reasons.

However, as Macintosh observes (p.26):

> ...there are in reality only a limited number of modes of assessments which can be used. How they are used is what matters. An individual can be asked to do something either in writing or orally or pictorially or through first hand or simulated demonstration. He or she can respond in writing, orally, pictorially or by demonstration – all common modes of assessment in wide general use and referred to frequently in these responses. There is, therefore, no new mode of assessment awaiting around the corner to be discovered... Furthermore, this shared narrow assessment framework operates in an equally narrow curriculum framework...

All agree that teacher involvement in assessment is a significant variable, whether in setting the tasks, grading the students' responses, or evaluating and amending the examinations themselves. Considerations differ according to the stage or level (primary, secondary, college entrance), and whether one is looking at these specific jobs or participating in overall national or regional policies discussions. Profiles of achievement obviously require considerable teacher input, as do teacher-graded, independent student examination assignments ("course work"). These may call for a teacher role that differs from a country's precedents, and for new skills and attitudes that require training and development. While attaching or even including students' scores from classroom assignments and periodic tests to marks gained in external examinations is common, preparing teachers explicitly to be involved, knowledgeable, and skilled in overall assessment practices is not. And it seems that when innovations are introduced, adequate investment in in-service teacher training is often lacking. To involve teachers more extensively and effectively in assessment is expensive and often calls for classroom teachers to adopt roles previously reserved for inspectors or administrators, a challenge to the teaching corps and many school administrators as well as to conventional thinking.

Data about the effectiveness of school practices used to be an internal matter for schools and school systems.   But in many countries nowadays, such information has special significance beyond the realms of schools and educators as ways of demonstrating public accountability. 'League tables', currently in fashion in England as they have been elsewhere, serve as a means of such monitoring.   The importance of external examination results on such balance sheets cannot be understated.   Like national attempts at data collection for the purposes of school assessment (e.g. the former efforts of the APU in England and Wales and of NAEP in the U.S.A.), they may have broad ramifications for school funding and administrative autonomy, or for parents seeking the best education for their children in an open market.   The results of assessment, accompanied by other data, are also critical for comparisons across regions, and for the kind of monitoring that takes place when countries decentralize aspects of their educational administration.   In short, the results as well as the forms of assessment are important not merely to students and teachers, but also in an increasingly consumer-oriented society, and have themselves become a market force in education.

Together, the three studies confirm that there is more to the study of examinations than statistics and psychometrics, and far more than merely comparisons of their academic content, to which, incidentally, none of the authors pay much attention. All three works demonstrate the broad instrumental uses of large-scale assessment practices and indicate the national policy implications.   As a group, however, they inform the reader less than they might have done on a number of pertinent dimensions.   For example, as already indicated, despite the considerable detail provided on a country-by-country basis in the de Luca and Macintosh studies, the authors do not generally venture into generalizations about the direction of national trends, let alone international ones. But more fundamentally, they do not point to many of the   political aspects of examination practices. Political here refers to the participation of interest groups in the struggle to institute or to prevent changes. Depending on the country and its changing circumstances, the interplay of various interested parties may be critical in affecting the outcome of debates over many kinds of assessment issues. The pressures emanate from local and national government, school administrators, teachers, parents, students, university professors, employers and unions. In certain countries on occasion these may also include political parties.   The issues affected include examination format, requirements, and management.   Should the examinations be harder or easier? Unitary and uniform for all or multiple assessments, variable by some criteria or other? To what extent should they be internal to the school, or external, centrally or regionally determined?

Given the various uses of examinations identified by the three authors – student, school and educational system evaluation, selection, monitoring, instituting and maintaining standards, improving curriculum and teaching – it is difficult to see a world without some systematic use of assessment devices in schools. Despite rising and strident criticism, indications are that assessment, examinations, and credentialling are becoming more rather than less pervasive and more important on all fronts. Two of the three studies are rather negative toward national examinations, because of their impact upon curriculum development and the lack of articulation between examination theory and practice. Their authors are sympathetic towards the ideas of reform and change and regard national assessment as on the whole obstacles to it. Keeves takes a more neutral line and is less judgemental on the subject.

To return to the question posed at the beginning of this essay, why are nations now so interested in the instruments of assessment and in the management of examinations? Because, apart from pedagogical considerations such as student learning and school management, examinations are a means of exerting power over individuals and groups. The owners of examinations, whether Ministries of Education, Boards of Examiners, private agencies, or whatever, possess power over important resources and decisions. Moreover, the results have value, economic as well as social. While they are by no means the only factor, poor examination results deny students access to certain levels and forms of advanced schooling and thus may close the doors to social, political, and economic advancement. In some countries, too, poor examination results are a reason for parents to choose another school for their children, or even cause an administrative authority to exert stricter control over a school. It cannot be sufficiently stressed that this is not just an individual, personal matter, or a domestic issue. Nations are more aware than ever before that their fortunes in the world depend on the educational levels of their populations. Average national school achievement is no longer merely a status symbol but, though crude, stands as one outstanding indicator of a nation's economic and social health.

Which brings us finally to the many dilemmas confronting those who look beyond the merely technical aspects of assessment. As Keeves observes (citing Eckstein and Noah on the subject[1]), policy options abound. This reviewer would have welcomed more attention to some systematic, comparative analysis of these dimensions, for example, the relation of policies and practices to such indicators as the level of development of educational systems, and the diversity of students that they service. The mix of more and less developed countries in each of these works should suggest some observations on the first of these topics, if only tentative. The overall expansion of schooling to include larger proportions of youth and thus a vastly more varied population than in the past, is an obvious and dramatic development but one treated only in passing by these authors. One of the purposes of international study is to gather relevant information, which all of these works do. But a second purpose is comparison, and only Keeves demonstrates much more than simple juxtaposition of the timely and interesting data gathered in these works.

In theory, the options are many, as we think of what may be the most desirable and efficient devices for assessing progress toward the educational and national priorities that nations determine are important for them. But it is hardly likely that even the most enlightened and energetic comparative investigation will come upon the one best system, even in theory. As some comparativists used to say, each country gets the system it wants (or deserves). It cannot divest itself of its historical context or of the effects of its own changing conditions. But is it too deterministic to conclude, then, that the 'best system' is the one best suited to the particular context?

The three works in their several ways demonstrate the great value of such comparative scrutiny to shed light on a set of problems that are common to all educational systems. Each is informative and thought-provoking to anyone interested in the forms and processes of assessment and in education in general. None of these works could have been accomplished without large-scale collaboration among people and institutions and demonstrates the value, indeed the necessity of such international cooperation. The effort and energy that went into each of these three works was considerable. Parenthetically, could the work not have been more efficiently done if the authors and their sources of information had communicated more closely?

We now have a body of literature on the subject of educational assessment that extends well beyond histories of examinations in Imperial China and 19th century Europe. Just as there are fashions in consumer tastes, so there are fashions in educational research. One hopes that the topic these works deal with is not a passing fad. We still have much to learn on the subject and it is far too important to be neglected. Comparative study of examinations has made us increasingly aware of the complex and multiple effects and causes of particular assessment practices. Educational planners and examination reformers ignore these at their peril and at the risk of having their plans fail or produce unanticipated outcomes.

As we have noted, policy dilemmas abound. They will not disappear. But these three works remind us that when considering examinations, or for that matter any educational issue, we must from time to time return to first principles: certainly, what and how do we wish to assess, but more fundamentally, what are the goals and functions of education in modern society that are to be the targets of our examinations?

NOTES

* Max A. Eckstein, "A Comparative Assessment of Assessment," *Assessment in Education* 3.2 (1996): 233-240.
1. Max A. Eckstein and Harold J. Noah (1993). *Secondary School Examinations: International Perspectives on Policies and Practice.* New Haven and London: Yale University Press. Pp. 243-45.

27

Great Expectations: An International Comparison of End-of-Secondary School Examinations*

Introduction

National examinations represent general expectations for student achievement, reflect standards, and provide both a stimulus to establishing overall quality in education and a yardstick to measure it. This paper reports on end-of-secondary school external examinations in four countries of particular interest to the United States. Common and divergent features of practice are described in their respective contexts, including examination content and format, the burdens placed on candidates, and the organization and management of external examinations. The different patterns provide policy makers in the United States and elsewhere with a range of possible options for improving school performance in their own systems, but also present them with numerous dilemmas. These revolve around such issues as how uniform or diversified an external examination should be, what level(s) of difficulty should be targetted, and how the respective claims of national and regional authority can be reconciled.

The Functions of National Examinations

Before presenting the data and comparisons from international study, one question needs to be raised: what are the functions of a national, external examination?

Historically, examinations such as the *Abitur*, the *bac*, the Japanese (Joint First Stage) university entrance examination, and the General Certificate of Education in England/Wales were instituted to serve two linked functions. Taken at the end of upper secondary school studies, they certified completion at a satisfactory level of achievement, and they selected young persons for higher education, professional training, and thus, ultimately, for high office and status in society. In doing this, they were instruments whereby valuable rewards were distributed to a limited number of recipients going on to advanced studies. These are the traditional gatekeeper functions of national examinations.

But such examination systems also serve additional purposes. They are in several important ways a means of *quality control* within education systems. The prospect of the examination affects a student's motivation to achieve, influencing the quality of his/her work; the test paper itself legitimizes the school's course of study and shapes what teachers do in the classroom; and the results form part of parents' evaluation of their children's schooling.

In addition, however, national examinations fulfil a third group of functions relating to their broader *social, economic, and political* implications. We are all well aware that examinations, while not always conclusive, are powerful influences on individual success in adult life. But they also serve as a gauge of the quality of a nation's educational efforts and its work force. Taxpayers and politicians use the results to estimate how well national resources have been spent, to measure the status and relative progress of a given regional, social, or ethnic group relative to another, and to compare their nation's educational level with that of other nations. All in all, a national examination system produces results that are used in many ways, some directly associated with teaching and learning in schools, others more general. But whether they act as gatekeepers, means of quality control, or as instruments with social, economic and political implications, a common denominator of national examination systems everywhere is the powerful influence they exert over schooling and over people and their futures.

As a consequence, such examinations receive close attention in both educational and political circles, particularly as circumstances change and problems emerge that are common to many countries. Though some of these have only recently become matters of great concern abroad, the following concerns are certainly prevalent at this time in the United States: a sense of decline in the overall quality of educational practice and school outcomes, mounting evidence of inadequate and inconsistent achievement standards across the nation, and a growing suspicion that student potential at all levels of ability is neglected and insufficiently challenged. Students whether of average or higher potential are unchallenged, and their performance suffers due to the absence of generally accepted and consistent high expectations. Hence the accelerating move in the United States toward setting national goals, defining national standards, and creating ways to assess progress toward achieving them.

Some Findings of Comparative Research

One of the conclusions revealed in comparative, international study of examination systems[1] is that the traditional gatekeeper functions of national examinations, certification and selection, are remarkably persistent. But no less significant are the additional functions mentioned above: quality assessment and control within school systems[2], and broad social, political and economic objectives outside them. Several countries have made significant changes in their examination systems, some of them highly controversial, in order to meet new circumstances and objectives. The growth in size and diversity of the secondary school population in most of the countries we studied is without doubt a major factor in accounting for this. But it is by no means the only one. Changes in educational philosophy and teaching objectives and techniques, changing labour market demands, and changing social and political conditions all contribute to the ferment about national examinations.

This paper focusses on examination systems in England/Wales, France, Germany, and Japan, and upon those comparative findings of most interest to policy-makers in this country. All the nations are highly industrialized, all are committed to open access to post-compulsory education, and all have been successful in this policy, having provided some form of schooling for all up to age 16 and for the majority of 17-18 year olds. It will be concerned primarily with two of the three sets of functions outlined above: national examinations as gatekeepers and as instruments of quality control.

Amidst current efforts to upgrade educational standards in the United States there is wide agreement that students are a precious resource whose gifts and talents remain sadly undeveloped.[3] The following observations clearly have important ramifications for all students, the broad range considered "average" as well as potentially high achievers in the school population.

Examination content and format   Everywhere, national examinations at the end of secondary schooling represent academic expectations. [See Table 27.1] The sheer physical and mental effort required to sit the external examinations is generally great[4] and the subject requirements are also considerable, indicating the amount of preparatory work necessary.   Youngsters in France and Japan, as in most of the countries we studied, are required to obtain passing marks in at least 6 or 7 subjects in their final examinations, and possibly more, depending on their course of studies and plans for subsequent study.   In Germany, Federal requirements for graduation ensure that all study a broader curriculum through the final year of secondary school, though only four subjects are required in the *Abitur*.   In England/Wales, where specialization begins far earlier than elsewhere, students usually submit only two or three subjects for the GCE[5], though they usually take more than one paper in each subject.

Both the quantity and quality of content demanded by the examination papers is very high compared with the United States.   External examinations in all countries require a good amount of information recall, but to various extents they all also test higher order cognitive skills, such as comprehension and interpretation, application and analysis of new and old material.   Questions asked of eighteen-year-olds in England/Wales, France, Germany, and Japan in their respective national language and literature papers illustrate the differences.   With the exception of Japan (and the United States), extended responses are usually required.   All require recall and some demonstration of comprehension.   But the most demanding questions, those requiring analysis and synthesis, are in fact characteristic of the papers in the first three countries. In Japan, questions testing comprehension are more common, since the Japanese reliance on multiple-choice does not easily allow for the kind of performance that an open-ended essay requires.

We observed similar characteristics in the history/social studies examinations.   All require a large amount of factual recall, but the questions also call for discrimination in presenting data, interpretations, judgements, and analyses.   Conventional GCE questions are often quite brief but the essay answers demand specific facts in an historical context to explain, verify, or justify a particular position, such as: explain how Prussia benefited from Frederick the Great, or, why were the French defeated in the Franco-Prussian wars?   Newer types of questions may present students with data and archival materials to interpret and from which they are to draw inferences or justify a generalization.

French students must interpret and comment on a set of documents such as texts, maps, diagrams and statistical facts or write an extended essay: e.g. using your own examples, analyze how liberal democracy works in the Western world, or, based on a set of documents on, for example, Soviet society, write on daily life, ethnic diversity, and tensions in society.   Examinations in Germany differ from *Land* to *Land*, but usually consist of two or more essays on a period, theme, or event.   Often, the questions are introduced through a short text or contain pointers on aspects of the topic that should be addressed.   Japanese students, again in multiple choice format, must show knowledge of historical periods and where people and events fit into these, but they are also asked to select the correct explanation for an event from several options and identify the correct or incorrect generalization from a number of statements offered.

Comparison of the scope, form, and content of examinations in mathematics reveals similar characteristics, though there are differences between those required of all candidates (as in Japan) and the more advanced papers chosen by specialists (in all countries including Japan). All cover a range of mathematics areas though they differ in the amount of attention given to each. All call for repetition of standard items and procedures learned from textbooks and teachers. But to different extents, they also contain more difficult questions requiring problem-solving, selection of the most appropriate means of solution, and their correct application.[6] Problem-solving (analysis and synthesis) is in fact the major part of mathematics examinations in England/Wales, France, and Germany, whereas examinations in Japan and the United States tend to stress applications of mathematical skills and concepts.

The burden on candidates and their success rates   We were overwhelmed at times by what students can do if expected to do so[7]. Like many other observers, we were sometimes adversely impressed by the heavy burden placed upon them. Concern over excessive pressure on students is widespread in several countries: reduction in the number of subjects required for the *Abitur* in Germany and the addition of new program options in France, and persistent disquiet over what Japanese students must endure, all attest to awareness of the possible negative effects of too heavy a load of work. But these criticisms and changes occur predominantly in the countries where the demands have been exceptionally great and where few students were permitted to pass. Not surprisingly, the reforms prompted cries that standards were being lowered, a result for which we found no firm support.

A majority of those sitting for such exams pass. Furthermore, as larger numbers sit for them, the ratio of passes to candidates has remained fairly constant or even risen somewhat. This may of course be in part a result of pre-selection through specialized schools and classes, or the practice of "redoublement" (repetition). It is also clearly due to the fact that teachers, notwithstanding reservations they may have concerning syllabus, testing devices, and pressure to achieve, have a clear idea of what their students need in order to do well and generally see their responsibility as helping them to do so. But the inescapable conclusion is that the examinations do in fact represent standards of achievement that are not merely attainable but are actually achieved by large proportions of the candidates. The examples cited are not exceptional instances and provide only a glimpse of the high expectations placed on candidates in England, Germany, Japan, and France.

Organization and management of national external examinations   National examination systems are managed in a variety of ways, usually reflecting the different administrative traditions of each country. In France and Japan, the examinations belong to the Ministry of Education, in England/Wales to a number of quasi-autonomous regional examination boards, in Germany to the examining authorities of the several *Länder*. France, for example, with its relatively centralized and uniform educational system, issues a mark and a credential that has nationally currency and, with some exceptions, provides entry to any university in the country. The *Abitur* in Germany, where education is a responsibility of the *Land* (province), carries similar legal authority, though a *numerus clausus* limits access to some institutions and programs. Yet in both cases, to a far greater extent in decentralized Germany than in France, the actual formulation of the examination papers, their content, and the grading are all variously delegated to sub-national levels.

In France, the *académie* (regional education authority) makes its own choices from subject topics listed by the Ministry of Education and is responsible also for administering and grading the examinations (though according to national guidelines). Federal policy in decentralized Germany is based on consensus reached by the Ministers of the several *Länder*. The Standing Conference of Ministers of Education of the several *Länder* maintains unity and a degree of uniformity by constant review of the process, issues guidelines that regulate many aspects of the examinations, and periodically revises them. Each *Land* has its own arrangements so that differences may be quite marked among the regions (Bavaria, for example, has a centrally set uniform examination for all candidates, others allow localities and schools within their *Land* a larger role in determining the process and the outcomes). However, consensus on general guidelines and a high degree of reciprocity ensures nation-wide credibility and reliance on the results.

In what has been the notably decentralized case of England, examinations at the end of secondary school have been in the hands of university-influenced regional examination boards, traditionally autonomous of the Ministry and local education authorities. This has changed considerably and rapidly in the past decade due to concern for excessive variability in the school curricula across the nation, decline of comparability among regions and schools, and the desire of Government to limit local and independent authority in educational matters.[8] The several examining bodies maintain close communication among themselves to keep a common core of examination content, and compare standards and grades in order to remain sufficiently comparable. In sharp contrast, uniformity of content and comparability of the results in the national common (first stage) university entrance examination in Japan comes from a central agency of the Ministry of Education which devises, administers, and grades the common examination.

Two-stage examination systems   Countries often provide pre- or post-selection via a second round of examinations. The GCSE taken in several subjects in England/Wales is followed two years later by the specialized GCE A-level; France's *bac* is followed by the *grand concours*, taken by the more ambitious and able students; Japan's national achievement test is followed by entrance examinations set by universities. But all the countries we have mentioned, whether formally or informally, pre-select within the school system, sorting youngsters at least two or three years earlier into different programs or classes, not all of which prepare for the examinations.

The various roles of teachers   In all the examination systems we studied, teachers are involved in different phases of the process, from formulating the questions to deciding the marks.   Subject specialists do this together with school administrators and university-based subject experts.   In Japan, as in the United States, psychometricians are an additional influential cadre of participants, though experts in test construction and analysis of the results are becoming more evident in England and other countries.   In Germany, teachers serve as examiners in the still common practice of orals, as they do in France, where, together with administrators, they are members of juries that determine the final grades of candidates, resolve inconsistencies in marks, as well as adjudicate any infractions in the procedures.[9]   Even in Japan, where a specialised unit of the Ministry is responsible for all aspects of the national examination, teacher committees formulate questions, review the results, and prepare revisions for the next years.

Some of the newer practices (e.g. school-based examination assignments) inevitably involve teachers as judges and raise new problems of willingness and trust. Concerns are expressed over subjectivity and loss of comparability when teachers grade school-based assignments that are parts of the examination or assemble and assess profiles of achievement.[10]

Some comparative observations   The contrast between the foreign examination systems we have described and the external examinations commonly taken in the U.S. is quite startling.[11]   These are all exceptionally undemanding with respect to content, format, and other requirements.   Only the Advanced Placement examinations contain comparable challenging material (though there are no required subjects).   But only a small, though nowadays growing, proportion of students take these.[12]   Teachers, psychometricians, and subject specialists have considerable input into these examinations, but the only controls on their activities are "in-house" governance and, more recently, public opinion.

However, nowhere are all interested parties totally satisfied; both the means and the ends of the external examination systems are frequently under fire, often resulting in important changes.   Moreover, few nations rely solely on the results of external examinations for graduation and admission decisions.   In most countries, professionals are divided on the subject but there is considerable movement towards including standard school assignments and records of work in a dossier for the final assessment, together with the examination results.   Grades for at least the final school year are conventionally included in the results in both France and Germany, and the school-based assignment is becoming more common as part of the total examination grade in England/Wales.

In all examinations, excellence is recognized by high marks or grades that differentiate outstanding from merely passing performance.   In addition, examination systems usually make provision for advanced papers chosen by students who have specialized in given subjects.   These differ in breadth and depth from the basic papers and are therefore subject to higher standards of evaluation.[13]   However, subject requirements ensure that breadth is not sacrificed to depth (except in the case of the GCE in England/Wales).

From an international comparative perspective, we also observed some convergence in examination practices.   In more centralized France, many responsibilities and choices are being delegated to regions and we observed efforts to respond to regional interests and local languages;   on the other hand, other more decentralized countries (England/Wales for example) sought to obtain a greater degree of uniformity and comparability of results through a national core of common subject matter and regular assessments of student achievement.   In countries that have relied mainly on a one-shot, often uniform examination at the end of secondary school, alternatives have been introduced in the form of subject options and additional kinds of evidence of student performance.   Such convergence extends also to the format of examination papers themselves: multiple choice, machine scorable, so-called "objective" tests, formerly common only in Japan and the United States, are being introduced elsewhere, primarily as an efficiency measure, while extended answers that permit better judgement of quality (sometimes referred to as "authentic" tests), are again being promoted in Japan and the U.S.   Movement of this kind usually represents an effort to improve a perceived deficiency within the country.

Dilemmas and Options for Policy-makers

Examples drawn from foreign practice are interesting and instructive, for although they obviously cannot simply be transplanted to a new setting, they represent a range of practical and often provocative possibilities. However, policy-makers cannot endorse them simply on their own educational merits. They must question the possibilities of adaptation to their own domestic circumstances, and their suitability both as to ends and means.[14]

Most important, however, policy-makers are required to negotiate an acceptable path between alternative goals that may all have great merit but are sometimes opposing if not totally contradictory. They must determine the tradeoffs among alternative policies and weigh the costs and benefits of reform measures. Thus in educational as in other policy decisions, they try to achieve one set of objectives without paying too high a price in terms of other desirable outcomes. The variety of national examination policies we have observed in different countries illustrate this.

The policy options can be grouped around a number of persistent dilemmas. We select only two foci for discussion here, both central to current concerns in the United States: uniformity vs. diversity, and the levels of expectation embodied in examination papers and their grading practices.

Uniformity vs. diversity   Japan and the United States both offer limited choices to students in standardized, uniform national examinations, in contrast to England/Wales, Germany, and France which give candidates many options among subjects, syllabi, kinds and degrees of specialization, and levels of difficulty. The first policy sets limits on diversity in school curriculum and standards of achievement, but facilitates comparability, and is, supposedly, more evenhanded. However, there are serious costs: differences among regions, groups, and individuals are glossed over, often leading to accusations of cultural and ethnic bias; examinations cannot easily be adapted to the preferences and aptitudes of candidates, and to the varied requirements of society and the economy.

These criticisms are particularly intense in the United States. But by the same token, there are also costs to diversity and optionality. The prospects of a common core of national curriculum and a sense of national culture may be reduced; questions will still be raised about social equity and comparability; admissions officers in higher education and prospective employers may be puzzled by what a credential stands for. The changes introduced into the *Abitur* and the *bac* over the past two decades have made them more responsive to national and to students' needs, but the costs in terms of comparability, fear of loss of standards, and more, are apparent. The slow transfer of authority over examinations in England/Wales from local to central authority is intended to do away with what many have regarded as too great a variety of options and a laissez-faire approach to programs of study. Together with regular nation-wide assessments and a national curriculum, the reformed examination system is intended to increase student participation and curriculum uniformity.

The common dilemmas include: how to retain a common core of curriculum while responding to the various demands of regions, the economy, and social differences; how to supplement examination results with non-examination assessment criteria; and how far to differentiate examination papers for different groups and individuals. Many of these same issues also impinge on the vexing problem of expectations.

Levels of expectation   Expectations influence performance levels. So much is clearly known through experience and research, and teachers ignore this principle at their peril. However, specifying the kinds and levels of expectations to be held of students is a more complex matter. It is faced by all countries committed to open access in education: how many subjects, which ones, and at what levels of competence; what mechanisms should be employed to monitor this. All the foreign countries we have cited face similar dilemmas: how to set demanding standards of achievement without discouraging too many students, that is, picking winners without making too many losers; and how to maintain high standards of performance, while increasing the number of successful candidates.

In the countries we have cited, standards are established and maintained in a variety of ways, based on their respective precedents.[15] In all of them, a demanding national examination carrying substantial rewards such as admission to higher education and professional status continues to be a major means of doing this, though complemented by other mutually reinforcing mechanisms. Germany and France have traditionally used a system of in-school selection culminating in a rigorous external examination to maintain high educational standards. Japan's external examination, in an ostensibly less selective school structure, serves to set high standards to strive for and, not incidentally, ensures close adherence to the national curriculum (as in France). It may be supplemented for some students, as in France and Japan, by a second round of examinations set by universities. A central or regional authority specifies a required curriculum in France, Germany, Japan, and in recent years in England/Wales. An inspectorate may be an additional controlling factor, as in France and until recently England/Wales, while new assessment systems also serve to define and monitor national standards as in England/Wales and the United States (APU and NAEP, noted above). Thus national examinations do not stand alone as guarantees of quality standards, but are a major feature in a set of mechanisms to set and implement expectations for student achievement. They act as powerful incentives to learn.[16]

From their main traditional role as gatekeepers allowing only a small number of a selected minority to advance, national examination systems have been adapted to open doors to greater numbers of students and to meet changing socio-economic demands.[17] But everywhere they have retained their commitment to maintain high standards and are concerned with levelling up, without cost to average or poorer students.

The fact is, however, that the United States is an exception among the nations we have observed in lacking the precedent of a national, public examination system which sets high expectations for subject-matter achievement and through which successful candidates can obtain a credential having national currency.[18] Thus a critical link leading to high quality performance is missing, that is, the connection between curriculum and student achievement: external assessment according to broadly accepted, demanding criteria of learning. Other systems are able from time to time to reform their examinations in order to meet changing circumstances and policies, but the U.S. has no such recourse and thus deprives students of an important if not critical source of motivation.   In recognition of this lack, it has recently begun the reform process by setting national goals and seeking consensus on standards of achievement in specific subject areas. This accommodates traditions of local State control in education and follows its own national precedents for school reform.[19] Federal initatives are now combining with State collaboration and professional input to encourage reforms in curriculum, teaching, and assessment as ways to lever education to a higher level of performance.[20]

Conclusion

What are some of the lessons to be learned from these examples of how countries assess students at the end of secondary school? The first broad conclusion is that there is no perfect system for all purposes, all circumstances, and all places, and that as new considerations come into play, changes are introduced in one direction or another.[21] There are many ways of organizing, managing, and forming a national examination system, but none serves all necessary purposes to the satisfaction of all involved. [See Table 27.2]

Comparative research shows that in no country, do all youngsters take the national examination [see Table 27.2]. Nor is the national examination necessarily totally uniform and the same for all candidates, nor limited to one type of assessment. In fact, it is rare for all candidates in a given country to take the identical examination, though there will be common ingredients. Nor need a national examination be governed by a distant and arbitrary central authority. Even in the most centralized countries, some authority is delegated to sub-national units, yet in the more decentralized system, mechanisms exist to ensure a considerable degree of similarity in form and content of examinations across the country. And, most significantly, though the debates over national examinations and standards persist in many countries, the high achievement standards that those examinations represent are no longer held to be only for a narrowly selected few but are rather targets for the many to aim for.

Current efforts to upgrade educational outcomes in the United States are currently focussing on establishing common content standards in various subjects. The debates over how to implement such standards and assess the results are under way. Of course, no single reform measure will disarm all the critics or solve all the problems of American education. But whatever local and national reforms are envisaged in American education, it is first and last on the shoulders of teachers that responsibility falls, even though their capacity to perform their tasks effectively is constrained by circumstances largely beyond their control: public attitudes, local and central government involvement (or sometimes apathy), parental cooperation in their efforts, and appropriate pre- and in-service education. Teachers everywhere are responsible for assessing the results of their teaching, but in other countries they may also be assigned heavy responsibility for setting, administering, and grading the most critical examinations in their students' lives. This requires faith in their professional competence and involvement at various levels of policy determination and practice.[22]

However, the levels of student work which can be achieved depend on the values and expectations that teachers internalize and express in their daily work. Without an emphasis on superior achievement in their own education, strong moral and actual support from within their own school systems, and reinforcement by those around them, they are unlikely to succeed in affecting the direction of educational improvement.

In all the developed countries considered here, a majority of students now attends upper secondary school. Participation in national examinations has greatly increased (even in England/Wales, where growth has so far been relatively slow), and student choices and alternative methods of assessment have also increased, resulting in greater diversification. What were once exclusive and highly selective traditional examination systems continue to serve their certification and selection purposes, though they have been changing towards selecting in rather than only to selecting out. But beyond selection, they remain as standard setters representing high expectations and stimulating high achievement.

Evidently, U.S. emphasis on ability and aptitude testing has not been a sufficient means of ensuring high standards of student performance.[23] Instead, one outcome appears to have been to set limits on expectations for achievement and impose minimum levels of achievement for graduation. But incorporating high expectations in the form of end-of-secondary school assessments and holding all students to them would go a long way toward removing those obstacles. As evidence at home and abroad indicates, challenging standards and demonstrated success are powerful motivational devices, have a positive effect upon average students, and enhance the performance of high achievers.[24] [See Table 27.3]

A concluding note: the following observations bear on the use of comparative data about examinations to inform current moves to improve education in the United States. Firstly, any system of assessment reflects the goals and expectations of a country's educational system; examination syllabi and questions embody society's views of what knowledge is of most worth; and the practices derive from national precedents and concerns for excellence. Secondly, while the motivational power of high expectations is indubitable, information about the relative difficulty of national examinations, how they are governed, and how teachers participate, can be seriously misleading unless informed by appreciation of the school and social context in which these practices take place. To attempt merely to make "easy" examinations harder or "harder" ones easier will inevitably have consequences for the entire educational system. Some will be quite unexpected, and policymakers are advised to study the various experiences of other countries if they wish to minimize surprises.

Table 27.1
National Examinations: Country Profiles

England/Wales (General Cert. of Education, Advanced Level)
  Governed by regional, university-associated Boards
  Distant teacher involvement
  Important for university admission and employment
  No subjects required, but usually 2-3 taken
  Est. pass rate: 70% of candidates
  Approx. 16% of age cohort receive passing grades
Examination content: very difficult

France (*Baccalauréat*)
  Ministry control through regional administrations
  Close teacher involvement
  Critical for university admission/important for employment
  Minimum of 6-7 subjects required
  Est. pass rate: 66+% of candidates
  Approx. 33% of age cohort pass
Examination content: very difficult

Germany (*Abitur*)
  Governed by Minister of each province
  Close teacher involvement
  Critical for university admission/important for employment
  Four subjects required (incl. one oral)
  Est. pass rate: 95% of candidates
  Approx. 30% of age cohort pass
Examination content: very difficult

Japan (Joint First Stage Achievement Test)
  Governed by Ministry
  Distant teacher involvement
  Important for university admission and employment
  Minimum of 6-7 subjects required
  No pass/fail; approx. 66% of HS grads. enter college
  Approx. 36% of age cohort enter college
Examination content: somewhat difficult

United States (Scholastic Aptitude Test, American College Test, Achievement Tests, Advanced Placement Tests)
  Governed by private, commercial companies
  Distant teacher involvement
  Variously important for university admission
  No subject reqs.; usually taken in English/Mathematics
  No pass/fail; approx. 66% of HS grads. enter college
  Approx. 60% of age cohort enter college
Examination content: AP Tests only, difficult

Table 27.2
Foreign External Examinations: Some Comparative Features

Participation: nowhere do *all* students take the end-of-secondary school exam, though the numbers are rising in most countries.

Choices: while a common core of subjects and of content within subjects is usually required, students in many countries have broad choices among and within subjects.

Control: national examinations are controlled by both central government and regional authorities; the balance of shared authority/responsibility depends on national precedents in educational administration. In the more decentralized systems, examination practices may differ considerably, though regulated by a national authority.

Teachers: teachers and subject specialists are everywhere involved in the examinations, though in different capacities and ways, including examining and grading their own students.

Content and format: except for Japan, all countries rely mainly if not exclusively, on extended answers to questions; they give considerable attention to questions requiring higher order skills such as analysis and problem-solving; in some cases, examination papers include school-based assignments.

Difficulty: the burdens placed on students and the difficulty of the question papers differ among systems, making comparison especially complex. However, the standards exemplified in the national exams are uniformly high compared with those most commonly taken in the U.S. (SAT, ACT).

Success: the majority of candidates pass (60+% to 90+%). This is due to a combination of factors including pre-selection, nationally determined standards, the motivational effect of the examination, its tangible and status rewards.

Uses of external examinations: nowhere do the results of external examinations serve as the sole criteria for graduation and admission; school records and teacher recommendations supplement them. In some countries, a second round of examinations selects students for university admission and/or special programs or institutions.

Table 27.3
Examination Systems and Quality Control

What are the uses of national external examinations at the end of secondary schooling?

– They embody educational standards and achievement criteria.

– They draw attention to educational requirements, general and specific, and to the need to revise them from time to time.

– They set curriculum goals for school systems and teachers.

– They provide a means for assessing how far these goals are met.

– They give students targets to aim for.

– They motivate students toward achievement.

– They offer rewards for accomplishment.

NOTES

*   Max A. Eckstein, *Great Expectations: an International Comparison of End-of-Secondary School Examinations.* Background paper prepared for a Conference of the Office of Educational Research and Innovation, Department of Education, Washington, D.C., submitted February 3, 1994.
1. Max A. Eckstein and Harold J. Noah. *Secondary School Examinations: International Perspectives on Policies and Practices.* New Haven and London: Yale University Press, 1993; and Eckstein and Noah (eds.). *Examinations: Comparative and International Studies.* Oxford and New York: Pergamon Press, 1992.
2. Note specifically, the National Assessment of Educational Progress (NAEP) in the U.S. and the Assessment of Performance Unit (APU) in Britain. See, Caroline Gipps, "National Assessment: a comparison of English and American trends," in Patricia Broadfoot, Roger Murphy and Harry Torrance (eds.). *Changing educational assessment: International perspectives and trends.* London: Routledge, 1990, pp.53-64.
3. Expressions of concern are now legion, from the National Commission on Excellence in Education. *A Nation at Risk* (1983) to a more recent publication concerned particularly with gifted and talented students, *National Excellence: A Case for Developing America's Talent.* Washington, D.C.: U.S. Department of Education, Office of Educational Research and Improvement, Oct. 1993. Comparative data and insights, added to domestic criticism, have raised national awareness of serious educational problems to a new high.
4. We calculated that German, English, and Japanese candidates must spend a minimum of 10-15 hours in the examination room on their required subjects alone, while the bac demands something like 20-24 hours. SAT and ACT exams, covering the two subjects of language and mathematics, call for 3 hours; achievement tests in a subject are one hour.

5. The General Certificate of Secondary Education, taken at about age 16, represents the end of a broad general secondary schooling and is taken in four or five or as many as 8-9 subjects. The General Certificate of Education (Advanced Level) comes after two or more additional years of more specialized study of three or four subjects.

6. See Eckstein and Noah, *Secondary School Examinations:...*, pp. 132-140, 155-169, and Appendix.

7. See Eckstein and Noah, op. cit, especially chapter 7 and Appendix. See also, National Endowment for the Humanities. *National Tests: What Other Countries Expect Their Students to Know.* Washington, D.C.: National Endowment for the Humanities, 1991. We also examined British, French, and German publications that offered students model answers and guidelines on how to prepare them.

8. The move to bring the examination boards under Ministry supervision if not total authority was the resolution, under the Thatcher government, of a long-standing struggle between powers (Education Reform Act, 1988). Additional factors, educational and others, were also involved in a complex and still persistent conflict over national standards and a national curriculum, periodic national assessment, financing schools, and the powers of local educational authorities.

9. In Germany, too, teachers are members of the committees that perform similar duties, often in respect of students they have taught themselves.

10. Evaluation of their students' performance has always been a critical responsibility for teachers. However, when there are potentially far-reaching consequences as in external examinations, trust in their authority, that is, their competence, reliability, and objectivity, depends on several factors, including their professional status and their training. Nowhere is this as high as it once was.

11. These are the Achievement Tests, S.A.T., and A.C.T. Like Japan, the U.S. is exceptional in relying heavily on multiple-choice, standardized tests.

12. The same might be said of the examinations for the International Baccalaureat. As its name indicates, it was inspired by European practice and represents high standards of academic achievement. Though, like the AP, it is taken by relatively few students, it has gained some popularity in recent years and some schools in the U.S. have adopted it for selected students who follow special programs of studies. Schools that have adopted the IB, are impressed by its "quality control" effects upon curriculum, teaching, and student performance.

13. For example, German students must take four subjects in the Abitur, two of them at an advanced level. French students take advanced papers in their chosen series (set of subjects including required, optional required, and optional); Japanese students may select advanced papers in mathematics.

14. The U.S., in common with many countries, has a long and rich history of importing educational ideas and practices from abroad. But for a century and more, comparativists have reiterated the hazards of thoughtless and uninformed educational borrowing that ignored cultural differences as well as contextual similarities. Nowadays, for example, opposition to the formulation of national educational policies and their implementation continues to be grounded in fears of government "interference" and the diminution of States' rights, views that are deeply embedded in the nation's historical precedents and common consciousness. However, this ignores two facts: the strong record of the Federal Government's welcome contribution to educational progress at various critical times, and the examples of countries that guard local autonomy in education as jealously as does the U.S. but nevertheless subscribe to common national goals and procedures. As

our study reveals, Germany and England/Wales are among the nations that have reconciled traditional local or other control with national goals in such matters as educational standards, curriculum, and end-of-school examinations, though not without difficulties.

15. Harold J. Noah, "Setting Standards in Other Countries," in *Promises to Keep: Creating High Standards for American Students (Report to the National Education Goals Panel, Nov. 15, 1993)*. Pp. 44-53.

16. Recent comparative work provides further evidence along these lines. See John Bishop. *Impacts of School Organization & Signalling on Incentives to Learn.* Ithaca, N.Y.: Center for Advanced Human Resource Studies, Cornell University, Nov. 1993 (Working Paper 93-21).

17. Those resisting efforts to change the GCE A-level examinations in E/W often refer to it as "the gold standard" which, if altered will inevitably result in educational devaluation.

18. Of the countries we studied, only two have abolished well-established national end-of-secondary school/university entrance examinations: the U.S.S.R., soon after the 1917 Revolution, and China, at the Great Proletarian Cultural Revolution (1966). In both cases, they were regarded as symbols and means of old elitist educational and social practice. Access to higher education became based on personal recommendations and records of service. In both countries, national examinations were reinstated after a few years.

19. The U.S. leaves it to the States (and to communities, schools, and teachers within them) to perform such tasks. One or two State education authorities use examinations explicitly for selection and many more have begun to define and assess standards for credentialling purposes in order to improve student performance. But these are often stated in terms of minimum standards for high school graduation and represent average or less than average competencies.

20. See, *Testing in American Schools: Asking the Right Questions.* Washington, D.C.: Congress of the United States, Office of Technology Assessment, 1992, pp. 29ff.

21. We do not mean to gloss over the complex ramifications of efforts to change a nation's examination system, which are not limited to education alone but closely tied to many aspects of society, political as well as social and economic. For example, in Germany, the success of the Social Democratic Party in 1969 was followed by important reforms in the Abitur, partly rolled back after 1982, when the Christian Democrats were returned to power. In Britain, as already noted, reforms under the Education Act of 1988 reflected Conservative Party policy on educational control generally, including powers over local authorities as well as external examinations. See also note 18 above on communist rejection of what was seen as elitist practice.

22. *Testing in American Schools: Asking the Right Questions.* Washington, D.C., especially p. 148 comparing the responsibilities and the role of teachers in examinations. See also, Eckstein and Noah. *Secondary School Examinations*, pp. 91-92.

23. An informed critic described U.S. students as the most tested and the least examined in the world!

24. Substantial evidence at home and abroad supports the view that all students are likely to benefit from a high quality system of standards and rigorous assessment representing high expectations. As access to public examinations increases, more students of all backgrounds participate and more succeed, showing that fears that the poor or ethnic minorities would suffer are exaggerated if not entirely

unfounded. Educational disparities among sub-groups, it is submitted, cannot be ended by continued low expectations and second class standards. See, for example, Albert Shanker, "Goals 2000", *The New York Times*, May 23, 1992, p. E7.

PART IV: EDUCATIONAL POLICY

28

Trends in Public Secondary Education in Western Europe*

During the past fifteen years, educational development in the various countries of Europe has passed through several stages. The conclusion of World War II left a series of emergencies for which immediate answers had to be found. There were shortages of staff, equipment and buildings, and often a backlog of six or more years' neglect of necessary improvements and extensions. Such a measure as the Emergency Training Scheme for Teachers in England is an example of a stop-gap plan to cope with one particular shortage. However, concurrent with such short-term programs, concerned with the most basic educational provisions, there were also varied plans for more long-range reconstruction. The famous Conference in Algiers in 1943 is an example of preparatory discussion by those concerned with French education; in that same year, the White Paper on Educational Reconstruction was being discussed in the British Parliament. The fruits of these activities were the later proposals of the Langevin Commission in France, and the Education Act of 1944 in Britain. The latter included both immediate and long-term planning and a fairly radical reconstruction of the educational scheme. Soon after, in Occupied Europe, the Allied Forces in Italy and Germany were similarly concerned with both emergency and reconstruction.

With the easing of the most pressing concerns comes the opportunity to co-ordinate and evaluate, not only the efforts which have been made, but also the broad plans which have been proposed. Post-war legislation has generally been characterized by radical thinking and optimism. However, the euphoria brought by the end of a war is so often soon dissipated in the exhausting battle of the peace. At such a time, the ambitiously optimistic spirit of reconstruction may also be lessened. A more cautious planned expansion replaces the scheme for extensive reconstruction, ideas of reform have once again to vie with practices which are entrenched in the typical ways of thinking of a people. The educational legislation of the last five years or so has been characterized by such an approach, by plans for reform and expansion which reflect the changes in the spirit of nations since 1945. The particular economic situation of a country, its current philosophical outlook and social thinking, specifically define the educational scene in each area which is to be considered here.

In England, no single item of educational legislation has had the comprehensiveness and far-reaching implications of the Butler Education Act. Significantly enough, however, the major educational document in England during recent months has been a report issued by a ministerial committee and briefly discussed in Parliament.[1] It deals with that age group which lies beyond the scope of compulsory education, sixteen to eighteen years. The Crowther Report, so called after the name of the committee chairman, is concerned with the extension of education upwards. It recommends raising the school-leaving age to sixteen, proposes a plan for part-time education beyond this, and also considers the expansion of curriculum offerings for students of this age. In particular, the report criticizes the excessive concentration upon a small grouping of academic subjects which has been characteristic of education in the upper forms of the Grammar School. In fact, the report is basically concerned with a general broadening of the base of secondary education, with making it more general and more varied. Inadequate expansion in scientific and technological areas is also criticized.

However, the recommendations of this document are not simply directed towards the expansion of the scope of secondary education in England, and a lessening of its degree of specialization. They are responses to a number of irresistible pressures from outside the educational system as well as from within it. They are also admissions that the existing system has not kept pace with developments in society and in the world at large. Thus, for example, the increase in the numbers of those students voluntarily remaining in school beyond fifteen years of age has changed the exclusive quality of upper secondary schooling (the Sixth Form). In social representation, and therefore also in aspiration, there is a considerable change. But British society has changed too since the days in which the grammar school achieved its form. There have been far-reaching developments in the organization of society, in economic organization, and in Britain's role in world society. To complete the picture of change, mention must also be made of the vast increases in Man's knowledge about science and technology and his greater power over his environment. The Crowther Report is a response to these influences which must affect all aspects of life. It recognizes as essential a number of real alternatives to the still prestigeful academic secondary schools. Other forms are not only respectable and legitimate, they must be helped to achieve such recognition.

This point raises a problem which has been central to English education for several decades, "parity of esteem" between different types of secondary schools. In giving official approval to the tripartite system of modern (general), technical and grammar (academic) schooling, the Education Act of 1944 introduced a great degree of order into a patchwork array of schools of all kinds, and made articulation between primary and secondary levels more realistic. But this definition, though sensible and not unprecedented, has still to achieve acceptance in the face of social realities. The fact remains even today, that one type of school retains its former prestige and exclusivity, the grammar school. It is the prime avenue to university education or to a white-collar job, and though entrance to it is on the whole by merit, it represents more than anything else the essential goal for the middle-class parent. Because of this social fact, one can hardly claim that the ideal of truly equal opportunity has been achieved. Modern schools, and even technical schools do not have comparable status with grammar schools; a disproportionate number of middle-class children obtain places in grammar schools; too many children of less well-endowed families fail to obtain grammar school places even though they may have the ability.

One way in which educators have attempted to do justice to this problem is by devoting much attention to the selection devices used at the end of primary schooling (11 years of age). The merits of different types of examination, of interviews, of record cards, and so on, have been, and still are, the subject of interminable debate. But they are all variations on the same theme, and based upon the assumption that the tripartite system is to continue as it exists now.

There is, on the other hand, a more radical approach to this problem, which is one of both social injustice and brainpower wastage. This is represented by those who seek a more basic reorganization of the very structure of secondary education. A prime example of such a scheme is the Comprehensive School. Like the American comprehensive high school, such an institution accepts students with different kinds and degrees of ability; unlike its American counterpart, it retains a process of "streaming" (homogeneous ability grouping) within the school. This institution is seen by its protagonists as the answer to the inequities of the present system, as the efficient use of resources, and a means of ending entrenched and self-propagating class disparities.

Comprehensive schools are not, however, the only way of introducing the comprehensive principle into secondary education. Several local authorities in England have introduced their own variations on the pattern of tripartitism in the secondary system. A notable example is the County of Leicestershire, whose plan for reorganization, at first experimental and limited, has now been extended and also copied to some extent by a number of other educational authorities.[2] In this scheme, all children in a district are transferred together to the same school (the "high school") for the three years following primary education. Here they all follow more or less the same syllabus until they are about fourteen, when all those whose parents undertake to keep them at school until at least sixteen are transferred to the local grammar school. The others remain at the high school for one more year of work-oriented and general terminal education.

It is apparent that such developments represent a departure from the direction set by the tripartite reorganization of 1944. The basic principle remains the same, but the anomalies of the system are being considered and perhaps will eventually be dealt with. Though the Ministry of Education has increased in scope and influence since 1944, its role is still primarily an advisory and a permissive one, while local authorities take the initiative. Thus the government approach is the traditional British one of cautious empiricism, accepting change when it is there, rather than moving towards it with any speed. Yet as one looks at the various developments in English secondary education in the last decade, a certain pattern does emerge. Attempts are being made to deal with injustice and inequality of opportunity, there is a response to the new needs of a speedily increasing school population, and to a new social philosophy.[3] Educational thinking is responding to such factors as changes in social mobility, lessening of social distance, influence of mass media, and certain aspects of the idea of the Welfare State. But traditional characteristics of English education are not being abandoned.

Like the Crowther Report in Britain, the *Rahmenplan* (master plan) for West German School Reform published in April 1959 attempts to synthesize present educational thought and trends and provide direction for the future.[4] It is basically a design for reform proposed by a committee of varied interests and specialties in a country where education is the responsibility of large local administrative units. The document aims at the unification of schools in the 11 *Länder* by closer collaboration of Federal and local power, and of citizens' committees representing a variety of national interests.

Here, as in most of Europe, the sequel to World War II is not far off. The Occupation forces were concerned with eradicating the education system which was one important means of inculcating the Nazi ideology. Decentralization was one means of breaking the uniform cast of German education. But once this had apparently been accomplished, there came into prominence a number of problems, some of them long-standing, others emerging in the contemporary society. The old traditions of state paternalism, of class consciousness, of the humanistic-classical intellectual tradition embodied in the education of the *Gymnasium* are the important background facts. The new phenomena are the revolutionary social and political changes of the last fifty years. The problem today is to improve access to secondary education, and to make it more appropriate for those who move on, that is, the total population. The dominant voices in the debates on education today in West Germany are those of various groups among the population, in itself a good sign in a country where hitherto vested interests (state or professional) used to have the only say.

In 1959, the Conference of Ministers of Education which was responsible for the *Rahmenplan* agreed to concentrate on three major points: extension of the *Volkschule* generally to nine years, improvement of secondary school selection procedures, and reforms in the narrow specialization of the last years of study at the Gymnasium. At the same time, however, experiments consistent with the recommendations of the total plan are to be encouraged. Thus the direction of future developments has been pointed, and includes a period of observation and "trying-out" for students completing their primary education (the *Förderstufe* of two years) followed by selection of one of several tracks. There is no wholesale abandonment of the traditional structure, but a serious attempt to provide opportunity for future white-collar or technical workers by expanding the *Realschule*. On the one hand, the most specialized and selective path of secondary education is to be "modernized," on the other, the opportunity of the student is to be increased in a number of alternative ways.

In many respects of course, the situation in Germany is comparable with that of England. The *Gymnasium*, somewhat like the English grammar school, is subject to question for its academic bias and its prestige; then there is the problem of equity for aspirants to such a desired avenue to advancement. There is also the problem of making the alternatives to an academic secondary education real ones. In society at large, there are also comparable phenomena: an increase in economic well-being, the emergence as voices to be reckoned with of larger masses of the population, the blurring (if not complete dissolution) of former class lines and all that goes with it.

Though it does propose expansion, the *Rahmenplan* does not move far from the traditional form of German education. In France, however, the post-war reform in education proposed by the Langevin Commission was a plan for radical change. The Reforms in Public Education of January 1959 are the end to a chapter of French educational history which covered thirteen years of argument over these proposals.[5] In brief, the main provisions are as follows: the age limit for compulsory education was raised to sixteen years, provision was made for a two-year period of observation for eleven-year-olds ending primary education, followed by one of five different programs appropriate to the student as well as to the needs of French society.

In its acceptance of the two-year *cycle d'observation*, the French reform has telescoped the Langevin proposal of a five-year cycle of orientation. It not only recognizes the principle that a child is entitled to an educational environment which encourages the full development of his potential in all respects, but also establishes a system which should facilitate this. The alternatives which a child has after the age of thirteen, give him greater opportunity than ever before to obtain manual and technical education and to obtain a less onesidedly academic education.

One reason why such legislation was so long in being passed (it is a more modest variant of the Langevin proposals) is quite apparent: the weakness of successive post-war French governments. But the critical evaluation of French education implied in preparation for this measure is very significant. There is a deep concern for French national unity and sense of purpose dating back to the self-criticism and analysis which followed the capitulation of France in 1940, and which persisted through the post-war struggle to establish a sound economy, a stable government and a healthy society.

There is also the realization that the traditional French education was no longer altogether adequate. Change in society, and changes in knowledge rendered the classical-humanistic instruction of the *Lycée*, and the Napoleonic system within which it operated, unjustly restricting, outdated and inadequate.

Once again, parallels may be drawn between these developments and those in other European countries. Though the war left different residues in each country, though developments since then have varied in each society, there have been similar criticisms of the nature of academic secondary education, of selection for it and of the absence of adequate alternatives. All three countries so far referred to plan in their respective ways to do justice to these problems.

Lest it be assumed that there are only similarities among the educational problems of European nations, mention must be made of Italy, which has recently entered upon its most ambitious educational plan.[6] Large sums of money are to be spent over the next ten years to help schools from the kindergarten to the university. Yet the focus of this major legislation is quite different from that of educational activity in England, Germany and France. The main points are as follows: free education for all until fourteen years of age, and beyond this for those in professional schools; the provision of additional school places and teachers to cope with the increase.

The urgent need for these measures, unambitious as they may seem, is revealed by the fact that even today, illiteracy in some parts of Southern Italy is as high as 30 per cent, and approximately 40 per cent of Italian children between eleven and fourteen are not attending school at all. In Italy the problem is still, therefore, one of the basis of education, the total population. Much of the money will be devoted to implementing the principle of compulsory universal primary education, and what is to be spent for post-primary and university education will be for the increase of what exists in these areas. Thus the Government is strengthening a secondary structure which has little reference to the democratic aims implied in the total ten-year plan. Undoubtedly, when the effect of this present effort is felt, the secondary system will have to respond to pressures from below, and an example of such a response might be in terms of the new Medici proposals.[7] This law would extend the common ladder upwards for one year in the lower secondary schools, and then establish a four-track system (humanistic, technical, artistic or general) into which students would be guided. But Italy, with all its long history of secondary and higher education, its wealth of tradition in learning, the arts, and technology, is in this respect far behind those countries already mentioned. She has still to find her way out of the vicious circle in which lack of money prevents educational expansion, and lack of trained personnel prevent economic expansion. Suffice it to say that in Italy, a multi-track secondary education for all has yet to be established, whereas in the other countries equity has to be injected and increased.

In attempting a comparison of educational trends in Western Europe, the problems are not only those of limitation of space. There is a multiplicity of terms of reference which must be defined, albeit briefly, for the achievements attained in education can only be evaluated with respect to the aims of education and the society under consideration. Former traditions and past progress in education are of course also relevant to such an examination. Even though the countries mentioned have all undergone similar historical and spiritual influences, such as Christianity, the Renaissance, the Reformation, and the Industrial Revolution, nevertheless the outcomes were varied. Language, cultural tradition, "national character" are all very different, as are national aims and aspirations, and characteristic ways of doing things. Whereas England is in the main an industrial society, France is still predominantly rural and agricultural; Germany is extensively involved in the latest technological and industrial progress, Italy is much less so. France and Italy are traditionally committed to an "elitist" approach to education, though they reveal their peculiar differences. Church-State relations in education, and the role of private schooling are both topics which would help to complete the total picture.

These examples of variations could be multiplied in the areas of economic and social organization, politics, philosophy, history, to say the least. They are mentioned here as a reminder that any generalizations which might be made are subject to the characteristic qualities of a given country.

Much of the effort in education in Europe is still directed toward making good deficiencies for which World War II was responsible. The post-war rise in the birth-rate, now affecting the secondary schools, aggravated the difficulties. Success in coping with such problems is then at the lowest level a matter of money and numbers. The following figures illustrate growth in numbers alone:

*Total no. of children in secondary
Education of all kinds*[8]

England & Wales	1948	1,875,997	1956	2,475,000
France	1950	794,070	1956	1,157,000
W. Germany	1950	828,631	1956	1,218,000
Italy	1950	503,943	1955	659,000

While these figures do not show the age groups covered and the percentages of those in attendance, it does show one of the dimensions of the problem. But numerical expansion alone (or lack of it) is not the only concern. Reform and expansion in kind have been the main topic of this paper, and in this respect the major trends in Europe must now be reviewed.

In some respects, the countries which have been reviewed seem to be at different points along a road towards somewhat similar and allied goals. The traditional exclusivity and selectivity of secondary education in Europe is being dissipated as its more comprehensive function develops. Intense specialization is being lessened with the concern for a more general education. With more and more numbers being involved, standards of all kinds are being changed, and in the eyes of many, quality is giving way to quantity. So far as curriculum is concerned, the humanities withdraw somewhat and the sciences and technology advance. These trends, in some cases obvious, in others becoming more perceptible, are occurring in a context of flux in social class organization and of the response of industry to the impact of a new technological age.

All these countries have under consideration the problem of widening opportunity, both as an aspect of social justice, and as a part of national well-being and development. However, the American observer should be warned against assuming that talk of equality of opportunity means the same thing on both sides of the Atlantic Ocean. Democratic thinking in Europe has not on the whole accepted the principle that the solution is to offer to all students the identical educational nourishment. The idea is rather that each should have the appropriate selections from the menu, and that some are more likely than others to appreciate and benefit from the more exotic dishes. It is only fair to point out that in the recent re-appraisal of education in the United States, the latter point of view is once again becoming respectable. It is debatable which outlook is philosophically more tenable and which in the long run more efficient. It is enough here merely to observe that they are rather different concepts of democracy, and that the extension of educational opportunity in European countries need not necessarily have the same ends as in the United States.

Of paramount importance too, is the role of administrative tradition in each country. The French plan, for example, is a blueprint which has yet to be implemented. Like the Italian measures, it has been devised by thinkers and is being implemented from above by planners. The *Rahmenplan,* and the structural changes emerging in English education seem to be more the result of protest from emergent groups in society demanding opportunity and parity. It is the latter which seem more spontaneous, more likely to be acceptable and effective, more in tune with the social movements of our time. The respective traditions of change in each country are to some extent also revealed by their plans. Yet the similarities in spirit and in the final goals which are stated, and the comparability of many of the measures, seem to suggest that educational change is moving in the same direction though from different points.

The specific ways in which proposals have been voiced and plans made are, of course, functions of conditions in that particular country. France, with its strong classical tradition of learning, is now seeking real alternatives to what was one narrow path to advancement. At the same time, a change is implied in the distance between social groups employed in different life activities, in the pre-eminence given to intellectual and literary skills. The nation, too, might be expected to benefit from development in its scientific, industrial and technological areas. That this process is one which will take considerable time is obvious. The example of England, further ahead on a similar path, reveals some of the brakes on progress that ingrained attitudes provide. While in England these emanate from traditional class attitudes (the whole area of the grammar school, and feelings associated with it) and a suspicion of speedy, imposed change, in France it is a result of a characteristic tradition of learning on one side, and on the other, an outlook deriving from the rural life of many of the population.

The problems raised by the offering of several different paths in secondary education are at the moment crucial in Europe. At some point or another, the school must make a decision on a student, and the student must be helped to choose. Ability, aspiration, prejudice – all these play a part. A trend common to progressive thinking in England, France and Germany is apparent: there is less and less reliance on a selection test, and more time spent on sifting, selecting, guiding, directing. The "high school" in the Leicestershire Plan, the *Förderstufe* (*Mittelschule* or intermediary school) in the *Rahmenplan,* the *cycle d'observation* in the French reforms, all have this in common. What is unique in Europe then, is that as the single track is being extended upwards, the break between primary and secondary schooling which was so crucial (at about 11 years of age) is becoming a little less final, and a new division is emerging at about 13 or 14 years, after which the traditional specialization again emerges. Undoubtedly therefore, in structure, and in the aims of education for this intermediary level, parallels can be seen with the American junior High School, and a movement can be discerned in this direction.

Does this mean that in education, as well as in popular music and consumption of soft drinks, Western Europe is being Americanized? That the Soviet Union is correct in pointing out this voluntary (or involuntary) acceptance of cultural imperialism, and the danger to "Western" and "uncommitted" nations? In some respects, undoubtedly yes, though the phenomenon is not limited to countries outside the Soviet bloc. These, like the nations of Western Europe and North America, are all in varying degrees affected by the growing power of mass media of communication, and by the growth of administrative bureaucracy. With regional variations, the era of mass society is being achieved with all that is implied in this. Sociologically speaking, the older class divisions are gradually turning into a multiplicity of slightly differentiated strata. Leadership is moving away from the traditional elite into the hands of new groups, the managerial class, or "the diploma elite". In the United States, one notes this trend as a concomitant of the breaking-down of hereditary class privilege and the extension of equal opportunity to more and more people. In the Soviet Union it is associated with similar ideals, but more specifically with the efforts of a powerful oligarchy to achieve a classless society and a powerful industrial, economic and military unit in a short space of time. But the crucial similarity is surely that in all cases, the characteristics of a mass society are functions of industrialization and urbanization, as well as some form of egalitarian philosophy. Under both Soviet totalitarianism and Western democracy (French, English or American exemplars), similar trends are accounted for by similar objective facts of national development. The differences are seen to be functions of social organization and cultural tradition peculiar to the particular nation.

In secondary education, Europe is in varying degrees much aware of the fact that complete reliance upon the procedures and outlook of the nineteenth century (and earlier) is no longer adequate. Education for national development is important, but the memory of Nazi education is still strong. However, the older perspective, which includes the classical humanistic tradition in learning and an elitist organization of education, has by no means disappeared. It is still a part of educational thinking, and will continue to operate as a conservative influence upon the powerful pressures of government, industry and mass society. In this, it may even turn into a creative and dynamic influence in our present era, as the "New Conservatives" in both Europe and the United States claim. With all the criticism which may be levelled at it, the strong conservative educational precedents of Europe may yet be the antidote to the tendentious pressures of mass society.

Western European countries are faced with the problem of making secondary education multi-purpose. They are also confronted with the problems of their own changing societies, in which it is hoped the education system can play both a constructive role and one which will ease the tensions engendered by change. Those systems of secondary education which formerly trained leaders only, must continue to do so, but must recognize the need for more and different attributes and skills. At the same time, secondary education is now grappling with the task of mass education. In this, its greatest obligations are the maintenance of an educated citizenry, and the creation of defences against the evils of mediocrity, complacency and alienation, which are implicit in modern mass society.

NOTES

* M.A. Eckstein, "Present Trends in Public Secondary Education in Western Europe," *The High School Journal*, 44 (October, 1960): 8-19. Reprinted by permission of the University of North Carolina Press.
1. Ministry of Education, *15 to 18; Report of the Central Advisory Committee for Education (England)*. Vol. 1 (Report). London; H.M.S.O., 1959.
2. Stewart C. Mason, *The Leicestershire Experiment*. London; Councils and Education Press Ltd., 1957.
3. Ministry of Education, *Secondary Education for All – A New Drive*. Comnd. 604. London; H.M.S.O., Dec. 1958.
   Max Eckstein, "Britain's White Paper on Education and Its Implications," *Comparative Education Review*. Vol. 3, No. 1, June 1959.

Edmund J. King, "Comprehensive Schools in England," *Comparative Education Review*, Vol. 3, Nos. 2 and 3, Oct. 1959 and Feb. 1960.

4. Ursula Kirkpatrick, "The Rahmenplan for West German School Reform," *Comparative Education Review*, Vol. 4, No. 1, June 1960.

5. Cultural Services of the French Embassy, "Reforms in Public Education," *Education in France*. No. 5, Feb. 1959.

Charles H. Dobinson, "French Educational Reform," *Comparative Education Review*, Vol. 3, No. 1, June 1959.

6. Lamberto Borghi and Anthony Scarangello, "Italy's Ten-Year Education Plan," *Comparative Education Review*, Vol. 4, No. 1, June 1960.

7. Joseph Justman, "Character and Quality of Italian Education," *Information on Education Around the World*. Bulletin No. 39WE, U.S. Dept. of Health, Education and Welfare, Feb. 1960.

8. U.S. Bureau of Census, *Statistical Abstract of the United States*. Government Printing Office, Washington, D.C.; 1953, 1959.

29

Education, Credentialling, and the Labor Market in the European Community: An Agenda for Research*

Introduction

Until the end of World War II, it was virtually impossible to contemplate a functioning association of the countries of Western Europe. However, since that time, following a growing sense of interdependence and the tempering of nationalistic attitudes and practices, the European Community (EC) has evolved. The integration of the West European labour market, formally completed on January 1, 1993, promises an eventual removal in practice of obstacles to the free movement of educated, trained, and credentialled labour within Europe. Abolition of the legal and bureaucratic barriers to the movement of labour will not mean an abrupt flood of professionals and skilled workers across national frontiers. Indeed, all signs to date point to only modest growth in such migration. Nevertheless, given time, an integrated labour market is likely to become a standard feature of life in Europe. The number of EC citizens working in Member States other than their own will surely grow. In turn we can expect far-reaching changes to occur in the content and structure of technical, vocational and higher education, together with their associated credentials. These developments offer a unique opportunity to study the relationships among the labour market, education, and credentialling. This paper outlines an agenda for research as these changes go forward.

In the course of their establishment, the educational systems of the European countries diverged from broadly common, church-defined models, to reflect strongly-held nationalistic ideologies. In addition, professions and specializations proliferated, each with a distinct and complex body of knowledge, path of preparation, and structure of credentials, designed to serve industrialized and, more recently, information-based economies. Governments erected a formidable array of administrative controls, designed partly to protect the jobs and living space of their own nationals from the competition of immigrants. Employment in the public services was normally open to citizens only. Both the higher professions of medicine and law and the skilled and semi-skilled trades were hedged about with an array of training and credentialling requirements. Completion of compulsory education (and even complete general secondary education), certified by possession of the associated credential, came to be the standard prerequisite for further education and training. Thus, while it was not impossible for a qualified person trained and credentialled in one country to move abroad to practice, s/he would have to surmount a barricade of retraining and reexamination requirements in order to do so.

Together with the natural barriers to the movement of persons from country to country (language and cultural differences, costs of travel, and loss of the support afforded by one's native community), these artificial requirements raised formidable obstacles to the free movement of qualified persons among the countries of Western Europe. Now, across the entire area of the twelve member states of the EC, the artificial barriers to movement are in the course of being swept away, and even the natural barriers are substantially weaker.

Considerable efforts have been made to identify and remove the barriers that prevent persons qualified in one nation from practicing in another. Some of the problems associated with the international equivalence of credentials have already been addressed, mostly by arranging for the mutual recognition of credentials among the members of the Community. Educational and training programs are being changed so that graduates will become better equipped to take advantage of the new conditions of the Western Europe of 1993 and beyond. Younger persons, particularly, are likely to take advantage of the opportunities for greater international mobility. Their perceived costs of migration are lower than for older, more established persons, and their expected benefits are collectible over a longer period.

Within countries, "European" elements are being introduced, albeit slowly, into school and university curricula, foreign language teaching extended and improved, study abroad facilitated, and international cooperation in vocational training encouraged.[1] Though they have proceeded unevenly from member State to member State, taken together these developments have begun to lower the natural barriers to the movement of persons by reducing the foreignness of other European countries. Across the EC, new Europe-wide agencies and programmes have been created to initiate and support these efforts.

Public education in the European countries developed, as elsewhere, to serve two major functions: to nurture a sense of patriotism and national community; and to equip young people to contribute more effectively to the economy, thus raising both national production of wealth and personal incomes. As the concept of patriotism enlarges to embrace the European Community, and as the labour market widens from national to Europe-wide dimensions, the older content and structures of education are likely to be markedly affected.

Although the formal objectives of the Treaty of Rome included improvement of the educational, cultural, and social condition of the population, no provision was made for a comprehensive set of programmes that might achieve that objective. The promoters of the Treaty acted as though they believed that no special provisions would be necessary, assuming that improvements in these non-economic spheres would automatically follow the accomplishing of their primary objective, the establishment of unfettered markets allowing the free movement of capital, goods, services, and labour across the Community.

This assumption underwent a slow modification over the next 30 years. By the end of the 1970s agreements had been made which accorded recognition across the EC of each member State's credentials, but for a strictly limited number of occupations only. Indeed, one might have assumed that progress on the educational, cultural, and social fronts of the EC would continue to be piecemeal and slow for the indefinite future. The high enthusiasm of the founding fathers of the EC had long evaporated and the Community appeared, if anything, to have regressed since the mid-1960s.

However, the arrival in Brussels on January 1, 1985, of a new President of the

European Commission, Jacques Delors, marked the beginning of a decisive rejuvenation of EC policies and acceleration of the pace of change. His assumption of office provided a powerful impetus to the development of Community institutions, including, but by no means limited to, those concerned with the educational, cultural, and social condition of the population.

Under the general rubric of a "social Europe," the EC countries are developing an extensive *formal* framework for the improvement of educational and training provision, facilitation of cooperation among and between educational institutions, employers, and trade unions, reform of credentials and the process of credentialling, and access to employment.

The so-called European Single Act was signed by all 12 member States before the end of February 1986, and entered into force on July 1, 1987. It is this Single Act, embodying substantial modifications to the 1957 Treaty of Rome, which currently forms the constitutional and political basis of the present European Community. Among other provisions, the Single Act required the mutual recognition of member States' technical standards and credentials, beginning January 1, 1993, and authorized a substantial delegation of powers to the European Commission in Brussels to make and enforce regulations in connection with the acts adopted by the Council of Ministers.

A series of European Council meetings since 1987 has widened still further the ambit of EC policy making and practical cooperation. Agricultural and financial policies have been substantially restructured. In particular, a Council meeting in Hanover in June 1988 emphasized the social and human goals of the Community. But that meeting also revealed large divergences of view among the member States in the matter of permitting the free movement of persons across national boundaries. Council meetings in Strasbourg and Madrid in 1989 began the march toward a future union of the monetary systems of the Twelve (not without protest from the British government), but they also sought to place emphasis on the social dimensions of the Common Market. Later meetings in 1990 and 1991 looking toward further steps on the monetary front and the creation of a more integrated political system and common social policies across the Community have raised questions that have proved to be exceptionally difficult to solve to the satisfaction of all member States. The differences were evident at the Council summit in Maastricht; they were made even clearer in the negotiations over the Maastricht treaty; and they came fully into the open during the hesitant process of eventual ratification. Despite these fits and starts on the political front, what continues to go ahead is the central subject of this agenda for research: the opening of labour markets to the nationals of other EC countries and the need to consider in timely fashion the adjustment of educational and training systems and their associated credentials to the reality of a more integrated Europe.

Educational and Social Programmes of the EC

The view that European capacity to compete in international markets and to prosper economically depends on improvements in its systems of education and training is widely held both within member States and at the Community level.[2] Educational policy in the EC forms part of a wider programme of social amelioration, dealing with common problems as varied as youth unemployment and equity in the employment of females, immigrants, and disabled workers.

New agencies have been established to provide forums for discussion, to act as centers for data collection and analysis, and to coordinate demonstration projects. In turn, this activity is intended to inform the drafting of common policies and their implementation. For example, CEDEFOP (European Centre for Development of Vocational Training, Berlin) was created in 1975 "to assist the [European] Commission in encouraging the promotion and development of vocational training and of in-service training". Its activities include: study visits for vocational trainers and specialists; compiling and maintaining a data base; carrying out comparative studies; and supporting research. A number of projects are specifically directed at assisting the transition of young people from education to employment.[3]

In addition, a host of varied Europe-wide educational and training programmes, targeted toward particular populations and educational needs has been established.[4] The purpose of these programmes is to promote education and training in all of the EC member States, via opening access, innovating curricula, improving teaching and encouraging links to industry and employment.[5] However, while all of this is being done within a context of Europeanization, the activities are carried out within each member State choosing to participate. Differences in education and training practices among member States highlight the need to ensure that differences in credentials do not hinder mobility across national frontiers. At the same time that the Community has developed these programmes, it has sought to arrange for a common currency of qualifications. As Clark Kerr observed: "The EC endeavour is the greatest of all intentionally planned experiments with the internationalisation (or at least regionalisation) of learning ever undertaken. This development implies greater similarity of degrees and of instructional content for students, . . ."[6]

Mutual Recognition of Credentials

The movement toward a more integrated Europe has generated new approaches to the differences among its members in education and training, and among entry and retention qualifications for various careers.[7]

The Treaty of Rome established the principle that members of the independent professions have the right to practice in any member State, either on a permanent or a temporary basis, under the same conditions that would apply to a national of that country. But this right was often limited in practice by the need to hold a professional qualification, certified by a diploma, certificate, or other credential issued in the receiving country, or recognized by it as equivalent.

Efforts at harmonization and mutual recognition proceeded at first on the basis of directives concerning individual occupations.[8] But the process of reaching occupational agreements involved lengthy discussions among practitioners and government officials, and raised different problems, according to the occupation under consideration. For instance, in the case of veterinarians, the directive was seen as relatively non-contentious in Britain, Germany, Ireland, and Luxembourg. However, in Belgium and France some political significance was attached to the agreements, due to competition between these nations regarding the right of Belgian veterinary surgeons to practice in France. The French State examinations were said to be more demanding than examinations in other member States, and French university training for veterinary surgeons is based upon rigorous admission standards. The French professional association was opposed to any liberalization of its standards in order to facilitate free movement.

By the middle of the 1980s, it was apparent that the piecemeal, occupation-by-occupation approach was proceeding too slowly, and in May 1986 the European

Commission issued a directive adopting the principle of the mutual recognition of diplomas, as recommended in *The White Book*.[9] The directive was approved by the European Council in 1988. Henceforth, a receiving country would not be permitted to deny an applicant who possessed the higher education diploma(s) required in another member State permission to practice that profession. The same prohibition applied in the case of an applicant from another member State which did not require any diploma at all, but who had completed at least two years of full-time practice. However, knowledge of the host country language continued to be a requirement, and a course of professional retraining could be required in addition, if great differences existed in the training of the two countries.

So far, member States' responses to the Europeanization of education and training are fragmentary. and differ considerably from country to country. However, the integration of the European labour market is proceeding, accompanied by innovations in education and training and mutual recognition of qualifications. A major research task in this area is to describe, analyse, assess, and explain these diverse responses.

The concept, "Europeanization," extends well beyond the idea of an integrated labour market and encompasses more than merely the prospects for increased mobility of qualified persons within the EC. It includes such tangible elements as a more open market for capital and technology, and the growth of new institutions, regulations, and arrangements. But it also incorporates fundamental changes in attitudes and knowledge, ways of thinking and behaving. Europeanization means the growth of a new consciousness that transcends national identity, an "esprit" that no longer regards other cultures and languages as obstacles but rather as enriching elements on the European scene, providing opportunities for individual and social advancement.

In this process, education is a prime force. It is therefore the focus of the first of the several research questions we propose.

Research Questions

1. *How are curricula, standards, and requirements at different levels of the educational system changing in connection with the Europeanization of the labour market? In which countries, in what respects, and through which agents/agencies? In particular, how are the processes of assessment and credentialling changing as opportunities for mobility increase?*

We suggest a focus on two levels, upper secondary and post-secondary schooling and training, and on general academic and vocational/ professional programmes at each level. Changes in curriculum, standards, and requirements refer to the increasing emphasis on vocationally-relevant courses, "European" studies, convergence of assessment standards, techniques, and structures, performance-based assessment, greater access to post-compulsory education and training, and retraining opportunities.[10]

One issue of special interest is the external pressure on education and training requirements generated by the opportunities for greater mobility of labour. Some nations are conscious that their requirements for certain occupations are more demanding than those of their neighbours. For example, Germany is currently having to consider the inconsistency between its own rigorous requirement of 13 years of education prior to university and the standard 12 years common in the other EC member States. Other member States are becoming conscious that the standards they expect high school graduates or entrants to professional training programmes to reach are relatively low.

As labour mobility in Europe increases, interest is likely to focus on what candidates for a particular qualification or position can do, rather than on what knowledge they have acquired as a result of their education and training. We direct attention to the extent to which the European nations are turning from the traditional written examinations and interviews to reliance upon work experience, performance testing, and profiles of achievement.

2. How open in practice is the labour market to individuals wishing to live and work in another member State?

Whereas in formal terms legislation and regulations have opened doors to greater mobility, the extent to which this has in fact occurred remains uncertain. Community policies toward the "Europeanization" of credentials have changed in the past and may be further reformulated in the years following 1993. Additional formal measures may be necessary to facilitate the movement of individuals in specific credentialled occupations. We suggest monitoring current developments with respect to setting European standards for education and training, international equivalence, and mutual recognition of qualifications. This will enable us to identify some of the problems, the obstacles to agreement, and the solutions that become acceptable to the participants.

Data could also be gathered on the migration patterns of qualified persons among the EC countries in the past ten years, and over the first three years of the Single Market (1993-96). These patterns can be compared with the numbers of qualified persons from non-EEC countries entering the Community countries for work. This will indicate which occupations in which countries have proved to be most attractive to migrants, and whether such migration is greater among the EC countries.

Finally, gathering anecdotal information concerning the experience of individuals in a few selected occupations will provide a valuable supplement for determining what barriers remain to the free movement of qualified personnel.

3. How are the educational opportunities, qualification levels, and employment of women and girls being affected by the wider European labour market? To what extent is the commitment to equality for women being met?

While most western European nations, both EC and non-EC, have in some form forbidden discrimination, the labour market continues to reflect past discrimination against women. In most European countries, the proportion of females in total enrollment in general secondary and higher education stands at 50 per cent or higher, yet females are still typically underrepresented in those lines of professional and vocational education and training with most prestige and status.

The EC has issued several directives on equal opportunities for females, having important implications for schooling, qualifications, and social and labour policies. For example, Council Directive 75/117/EEC addressed the issue of equal pay while 76/207/EEC dealt with equal treatment. The 1976 Directive specified that: "Vocational guidance, vocational training, advanced vocational training and retraining should be accessible on the basis of the same criteria and at the same levels without any discrimination on the basis of sex".

Two EC action programmes (in 1985-87 and 1986-1990) were prompted by fears that unemployment among young females might rise and by the needs of special groups, such as older women, requiring special assistance in training or retraining. The overall objective was to integrate women in employment and in professional and social life. Yet a wide gap remains between principle and implementation. For example, despite repeated calls for more training provisions for females in the new technologies, much of the existing training is still associated with traditionally female occupations. And even when training is provided in new areas, it is often so narrow that women are quickly left with obsolete skills.[11]

In the course of addressing Questions 1 and 2 above, comparisons should be made between male and female participation in education, training, and employment, and in mobility across selected European borders.

4.   *What is the nature of the political debate on these changes of education and credentials in each country? Who are the participants in the debates and what are the obstacles to and catalysts of change?*

Each major step toward changing national credentials to better fit a European norm provokes opposition from some quarter or other. Responses to these changes often reflect attitudes to the extension of the powers of the Community in general. Some in the educating professions are very enthusiastic about Europeanization, while others complain that they are being asked to make changes without being consulted and without being given the necessary resources, and that the demands are diversions from the 'proper' ends of education. Leaders of national organizations often express fears of loss of national autonomy and national control of curriculum content. Professional organizations object to loss of control over the structure and content of qualifications leading to entry into their respective occupations.

The usual pattern has been for the EC to set up a commission for a particular task, invite countries to participate, study and then make recommendations for member States to amend and adopt in the form of a treaty or convention. This procedure permits countries to move toward a set of stated targets more or less at their own pace. Over time, the discretion of countries has tended to become more limited as the European Commission has issued directives based on those treaties and as the European Court of Justice has issued rulings in response to questions brought before it. We propose to document the growing role of the European Commission and the Court of Justice and the challenge they present to national authorities and their autonomy in matters of education and credentialling.

Over time, changes have occurred in the Community's approach toward the internationalization of credentials. Up to the mid-1980s, most of the discussions and action on international equivalency of credentials had been directed toward harmonization of credentials, occupation by occupation. However, beginning in the 1980s, the emphasis changed from "harmonization" to "mutual recognition" of credentials. What are the reasons behind this change of overall strategy, and the significance for the future with respect to policy and procedures? Are European credentials likely to develop? If so, for which credentials, and in what form? Are they likely to supplant or complement national credentials?

Over the past 15 years, bi- and multi-lateral agreements have been made with respect to the setting of European standards for education and training and, in particular, with respect to the international equivalency and mutual recognition of qualifications. Tracing these agreements and, more importantly, analyzing the substance of the discussions and reports leading up to them, will identify the participants in the process and their roles, their (changing) relationships and powers, the solutions that became acceptable to them, and the obstacles that stood (and stand) in the way of agreement.

Differing and often opposing views are expressed in the normal way in the mass media and specialist publications, and in parliamentary debates. We propose an examination of these sources, to report on the major participants in the debate, the roles they perform, the nature of the arguments, and the extent to which they influence the outcomes.

5. *What are the major parallels (and differences) in the experience of the United States and Europe with respect to the relation between the degree of openness of the labor market and education and credentialling?*

North America offers two units of potentially illuminating comparison with Europe: the United States and the prospective North American Free Trade Area. While it is too early to assess the effect of NAFTA upon the matters under consideration, the United States provides a long established model for comparison. In both the US and the EC, formal sovereignty in educational matters lies with the "second-tier" of constitutional authorities – the 50 states and the 12 member States, respectively. The US already has its well-developed, exceptionally stable federal system; the EC is in the midst of creating a tighter confederation, some individuals and member States even working toward an eventual United States of Europe. On each side of the Atlantic, therefore, we find separate systems of education, training, and credentialling coexisting with labor markets that are in one case (the US) exceptionally open, and in the other (the EC) opening more and more as time passes. To compare the development of agreements about harmonization, equivalence, and transferability between the European nations and the United States offers an expanded opportunity to analyse interactions among education, qualifications and the labour market.

In the United States, local and state control of general secondary education has contributed to the absence of a common national path to higher and professional qualifications, and indeed little consensus on what such a path might look like. Each state has enjoyed the right to set its own standards, resulting in widely differing requirements and qualifications. The common school ideal and the long-established principle of open access through comprehensive schooling provided some nation-wide basis of educational goals and experience. But this stopped far short of a common curriculum of knowledge and skills, uniform standards of achievement, or a nation-wide credential related to subsequent education, training, and entry to the labor market. Private testing agencies, such as the Educational Testing Service and the American College Test Program, developed in response to the need for yardsticks that could be used to select candidates for higher education and professional training. Independent accrediting agencies comprising representatives of professional organizations and State government were established to set standards for higher education institutions and professional schools. In some occupations (for example, in medical education), the power and status of a national professional organization were sufficient to establish common standards. However, a license to practice a particular profession usually requires passing a state examinations in the particular state in which it is desired to practice, in addition to obtaining a relevant higher education diploma. And the US continues to struggle with such issues as national standards in education, national assessment procedures, and qualifications for teachers.[12]

As the EC has progressively extended the scope of its activities, the Twelve, like the US, have also had to deal with the problems of arranging that a qualification obtained in one jurisdiction is acceptable in another. The process began with negotiations intended to achieve harmonization, occupation by occupation, and is presently governed by the principle of mutual recognition, embodied in the Single Act. In many ways, Europe faces much more difficult problems in adapting education and credentials to the demands of an open labor market than has the United States. The educational traditions, customs, and structures of the European countries are substantially more different from one another than the educational histories and current arrangements of the states of the US. The European nations lack the unifying framework that is provided by a long-standing common school ideal, though this has emerged quite strongly in Europe since mid-century. Also, all-European professional organizations are still much weaker than their national counterparts in the United States. Moreover, the United States has had two centuries to work out the form of the relationship between a national labour market and educational and credentialling structures that are largely state-based, while the European nations must face the problems of adjustment in a much shorter time frame.

Given these differences, we believe that there would be merit in a comparison of the responses of the two political units, the United States and the European Community, to the economic pressures to change educational arrangements and credentialling characteristics. In particular, we expect to be able to show how different circumstances in the two polities have shaped their different approaches to the rights of access to employment, assessment practices, credentialling, and the establishment of the mutual recognition and/or equivalence of credentials.

Conjectures

Research on the preceding questions will offer an opportunity to document the complex interactions among education, qualifications, and the economy. We here offer a number of conjectures about what we expect to discover with respect to several relevant themes and relationships.

1.   *On the Europeanization of credentials*   The pressures that have moved policy from an emphasis on harmonization to the principle of mutual recognition are likely to continue, and will in time, we believe, lead to all-European credentials and to coordination and confluence of the roads leading to them. Such all-European credentials will most probably remain complementary to existing national credentials, rather than become substitutes for them.

As between vocational-professional qualifications and academic qualifications, the former are closer to employment and the labour market than the latter. Hence, given also the Community's high interest in fuller employment policies and enhanced internal mobility of labour, we expect that the movement to create and adopt European credentials will be faster in the vocational/professional than in the academic areas.

2. *On ways of assessment and credentialling*   We expect to see a continuing trend away from primary reliance on one type of assessment, written examinations of the traditional type, toward assessment with multiple characteristics – the traditional written examination no doubt remaining, but augmented by submission of portfolios of work done, records of achievement and experience, and extended external- and self-critiques of the materials submitted for assessment. In addition, we expect to see movement toward so-called *bilans* or dossiers of study and experience.

We conjecture that this trend away from primary reliance on formal written examinations will be most evident in assessment for entry into and graduation from professional training programmes. In particular, we believe that mutual recognition of professional/technical qualifications will increasingly be based on comparison of training and work experiences as related to tasks to be performed on the job, rather than on equivalence of formal qualifications.

While we expect also to see continuing debate over and innovation in the form of end-of-secondary school general education qualifications, we expect to find that admission to higher education will continue to rely primarily on credentials acquired through written achievement examinations.

3. *On the effects of freer movement of highly educated professionals upon agencies that certify and control membership in specific occupations, in particular, the traditionally self-governing professions, such as medicine* Professional and craft organizations have been very effective in limiting entry to their respective occupations, thus "maintaining standards" – and (not incidentally) the incomes of their members. For many of these organizations, limiting entry by imposing high standards of training and experience and lengthy periods of apprenticeship has been their primary and best defended function. Most of them enjoy legislative and regulatory arrangements arming them with power to license new entrants, restrict competition among their members, establish fee schedules, and the like.

We expect that these professional and craft organizations will perceive serious threats in the pressure of the European Commission to permit more competition in matters of entry and pricing of services and, in particular, to open their occupations to foreigners. We expect to report a record of footdragging and downright obstructionism to EC initiatives from these quarters.

4. *On the relative pace of change in education/credentialling and the labour market* It is normal for changes in education, training, qualifications, and the labour market to proceed unevenly. This has certainly been so in the EC, where, despite the rhetoric promoting changes in education and training as the key to enhanced productivity and international competitiveness, Europeanization to date has proceeded much further in the trade, monetary, and political areas, than in education, training, and their associated credentials. We expect that this difference in pace will continue, as increasing attention to the development of "social Europe" is more than matched by developments on the economic and political fronts.

Thus, we expect to conclude that changes in the EC labour markets have driven changes in education, training, and qualifications, and not vice-versa.

5. *On the effects of increasing Europeanization of labour markets on the training activities of employers* The EC and its member governments have encouraged employers and unions to enter into various kinds of working arrangements with the education system as "social partners". Moreover, the EC's "active employment policy" in an integrated Europe calls for training and employment policies that encourage movement of workers to another firm, another occupation, even another nation, especially when technological advances are transforming and even making obsolete entire occupations and industries. Meanwhile, firms have always worried that they may train their employees and apprentices so well that their competitors will hire them away. Large firms seem to be less concerned over this than small firms.

We expect to find that this difference according to size will persist; that large employers will probably increase the amount of training they provide; that small employers will continue to be reluctant to offer much training; and that the specific effects of an integrated labour market on employers' willingness to provide training will not be distinguishable from the secular trend for all employers to provide more training as the technologies used in production become more complex.

6.   *On the relationship between political attitudes toward the EC and educational restructuring*   The governments of the Twelve have very different views of the benefits and costs of the EC as presently constituted, and as proposed for the future. Spain, for example, has been very enthusiastic about the Community and plans for its further development; Britain has been a determined opponent of all projects that look "visionary," wanting to make sure that the country is not being pushed into programmes leading to further loss of British sovereignty. These are differences of general political attitude toward the EC. In addition, there are many differences of view over particulars. For example, the French are strong defenders of the Community's costly agricultural support policies, against the opposition of Spain, Italy, and Britain. The Germans (at least until recently) have wanted to move faster toward a European equivalent of the US Federal Reserve Bank than do most of the other member States, particularly the British and the French. The smaller member States, Belgium, the Netherlands, Denmark, and Luxembourg take a much more favorable view of plans for a closer political and financial union than do the larger countries, which have more real sovereignty to lose. The British government is particularly hostile to assorted plans for an eventual United States of Europe, an all-European currency, or a European Reserve Bank – especially if it is located in Frankfurt! The British government has also voiced strong criticism of the idea of a "social Europe," arguing that the Community should stick closer to the original, narrower concept of creating a wider economic space in Europe, leaving social policies (including education) to the individual member States.

Each member State's record of adapting its systems of education, training, and credentialling to fit the new European realities will be strongly associated, we conjecture, with these differences in viewpoint and attitude. More specifically, we believe that the countries with a more pro-Europe stance, such as Spain and Italy, are likely to take more extensive steps to Europeanize than, say, the British, going even beyond the France and Germany.

7.   *On alternative paths toward integration of education, qualifications, and the labour market*   The final item on this proposed research agenda affords an opportunity to compare the well-established federal system of the United States with a European one that is in the process of integrating, without having yet achieved a cohesive political union. It is highly probable that within, say, 15 years the EC will have moved quite far and fast along the road to labour market integration. The EC and the US are then likely to present two quite different models of adapting distinct education and training systems to the existence of a single labour market. The EC approach will be based on deliberate measures embodied in Community-wide legislation, to Europeanize curricula and to implement mutual recognition of credentials and qualifications; the US model is likely to exhibit a far smaller degree of deliberate, country-wide organization. Our final conjecture is, paradoxically, that the EC with a confederal structure still far from completely realized will be then more "coordinated" in its educational arrangements than the US, despite the latter's time-tested, solid political federation.

Conclusions

Relationships among the labour market, education, and credentialling are never easy to pin down. Analysts and policy makers are well aware that, in general, these relationships are interactive, but they are less clear about how they are affected by specific and deliberate policies. This outline of some key items for research study offers an opportunity to take advantage of the distinctive way in which change is being accomplished in Europe – via a complex mixture of treaty provisions setting overall goals and frameworks, regulations issuing from a "central" authority (the European Commission), specific occupational agreements, Community-wide programmes, and member States' individual initiatives proceeding toward commonly agreed upon goals, even though at different speeds. This agenda focuses on the changes occurring in European education and credentialling, consequent upon the opening of labour markets to the free movement of persons.

A distinctive characteristic of the current European situation is that a very large labour market is being suddenly opened after centuries of fragmentation and extreme segmentation. This is a kind of "natural experiment". The effects of such a rapidly opening labour market are likely to be exceptionally strong, and consequently reveal more than is typically possible about the effect of the labour market changes on education, training, and credentials.

NOTES

* Max A. Eckstein and Harold J. Noah, "Education, Credentialling, and the Labour Market in the European Community: an Agenda for Research". *Revista de Educacion* 301 (May-August 1993), pp.91-106.
1. On the pace of introduction of "European" elements into school curricula, see Raymond Ryba, "Toward a European Dimension in Education: Intention and Reality in European Community Policy and Practice". *Comparative Education Review* 36:1 (1992), pp. 10-24.
2. *Oxford Review of Economic Policy* 4:3 (1988). Special Issue on "Education, Training and Economic Performance".
3. For a description and analysis of pilot projects in the EC second program on young people's transition from schooling to working life, see: John Banks, *Transition of Young People from Education to Adult and Working Life*. Brussels: IFAPLAN, June 1987 (European Community Action Program, School-Industry Links, Working Document); and Michael Bolle *et al., Vocational Training and Job Creation Schemes in the Countries of the European Community*. Berlin: CEDEFOP, 1987.
4. See Appendix for a selection of EC education and training programmes.
5. Ladislav Cerych, "Higher Education and Europe after 1992: the framework;" and Guy Neave, "On Articulating Secondary School, Higher Education and 1992" *European Journal of Education* 24:4 (1989), pp. 321-332 and 351-363.
6. Clark Kerr, "The Internationalisation of Learning and the Nationalisation of the Purposes of Higher Education: two 'laws of motion' in conflict?" *European Journal of Education* 25:1 (1990), p. 16.
7. Louis H. Orzak, *International Authority and Professions: The State Beyond the Nation-State*. San Domenico, Italy: European University Institute, 1992; and Louis H. Orzack, "The General Systems Directive: Education and the Liberal

Professions," in L. Hurwitz and C. Lequesne, editors, *The State of the European Community: Politics, Institutions, and Debates in the Transition Years, 1989-1990*. Boulder, Colorado: Lynne Rienner, 1991.

8. See *Guide des professions dans l'optique du Grand Marché*. Brussels: European Commission, 1988, for a complete listing of these directives.

9. *L'achèvement du marché intérieur: Livre blanc de la Commission à l'intention du Conseil européen*. Milan, 28-29 June, 1985.   This called for completion by December 31, 1992 of a total and irreversible fusion of the twelve member States' markets into a single common market of over 320 million consumers and producers. The White Book also commended the principle of *the mutual recognition* of member States' technical standards (including credentials) in place of attempts to *harmonize* these standards and credentials along common lines.

10. Guy Neave, "On Articulating Secondary School, Higher Education and 1992"; Franco Carinci, "The Impact of Post-1992 Europe on Law Studies"; Angel Luis Gonzalo and Jorge Peres, "1992 and Changes in the Content and Structure of Engineering Studies"; Hans Karle and Thomas Kennedy, "Medical Education in the European Communities: moving toward 1993 and beyond" *European Journal of Education* 24:4 (1989), pp. 351-363; 381-387; 389-398; and 399-410.

11. In a 1985 report, CEDEFOP stated: "... Of the new training measures designed specifically for women, only a few are intended to qualify the trainees for the production or application of new technologies". Moreover, in vocational courses specifically designed for women, CEDEFOP concluded that the nature and rate of employment after training were below standard. Programs providing for equal access often lacked provision for women to enter the labour market, thus were unlikely to improve the outcomes of their education or training.

12. Under the auspices of the federal government, an effort to promote the establishment of national standards in the major school subject areas is now underway in the US. See, *Raising Standards for American Education*. A Report to Congress, the Secretary of Education, the National Education Goals Panel, and the American People. Washington, D.C.: The National Council on Education Standards and Testing, January 24, 1992.

30

Academia in Anarchy*

In recent years the economics of education has been one of academe's outstanding growth industries, its rise signaled by an outpouring of books, studies, monographs, and articles, and its legitimacy attested by the appearance of courses entitled "Economics of Education," "Education and Economic Growth," and "Education and Economic Planning" in universities across the land. Now that we routinely admit half of our young people to post-secondary education, and even graduate one-third of them with bachelors' degrees, hardly anyone questions the right of economists to apply their conventional tools and concepts to higher education. After all, some very valuable social resources are being consumed in this business of education, and it cannot be altogether illegitimate to ask if the best use is being made of them.

This is precisely what *Academia in Anarchy* attempts to do, and the ensuing condemnation is virtually total. The modern university is a house of straw, held together precariously, if at all, only by the inertia of ancient traditions observed still by faculty and administration but increasingly and overwhelmingly rejected by students. In this book the university appears as an economic freak literally asking for and deserving its current fundamental turmoil.

For those of us who work in higher education, the past decade has brought as profound a revolution in expectations and attitudes as it is possible to imagine. The Sixties opened (in the United States, at least) to a passive, almost somnolent student body whose torpor on political and social questions and whose cultural "squareness" had attained international notoriety. They were presided over by a complacent, confident faculty that looked forward to rapidly increasing demand for its services, as higher education grew in number of institutions, enrollment, and complexity. Administrators, too, saw only a golden future ahead, with money pouring in from government and foundations to expand building programs, research, and teaching. These were the fat years.

Now the Sixties have closed with a student body that has decisively abandoned privatism while embracing ideals and life-styles that were simply unthinkable ten years ago; with a faculty, much battered and bruised, whose confidence in itself and its capacity to manage university and extramural affairs has largely evaporated; and with university administrators gloomily surveying a prospect that holds only more of the same turmoil that has plagued most of them to their wits' end, and some even beyond. How could it all have happened? In particular, why has student militancy enjoyed such easy victory? Was it just the sheer power of revolting students' frenzied indignation, the pusillanimity of faculty, or the havering and uncertainties of deans, presidents, and governing boards? The authors of this irritating, yet very important, book say, in effect: "Yes, it was all this, and more". For, they argue, student revolt, faculty and administrative indecisiveness – all are merely predictable consequences of the weirdly irrational patterns we have adopted to organize our universities:

> ...*university education is not a free good.* It does not abound in nature and considerable scarcity value attaches to it. Resources that could be used to produce other things that are valued by men and women have to be employed to produce university education. Education is, in other words, an economic good. For this reason, the economic aspects of its demand and its supply cannot be wholly neglected. But if people will so curiously insist on arguing that university education is a free good, those who demand, supply, and finance it will begin to act as if it were, in fact, free! Increasing numbers of students will demand more and more university places, better and better physical facilities, and increasingly attentive devotion to their "special needs". Regardless of the supply of faculties and facilities, demands will invariably be excessive. When nominal (below cost) or zero prices are fixed on so expensive a good, it becomes inevitable that nonprice *rationing*, in some form or other, must be adopted. In addition, suppliers become increasingly immune to consumer desires, being allowed as it were, to "give away" an expensive good for which demand is excessive. Worse still, the product predictably deteriorates as suppliers begin to take on the arrogance of despots. But suppliers are not donors. They do not personally bear the costs of charity. Again, the delusion that university education is a free good leads to disregard both for cost reduction and for efficiency in large or small matters. This is first day economics. Yet its truth is widely denied, and institutions reflect this denial.

The argument is, therefore, essentially simple. Universities are peculiar places where the consumers (the students) do not pay the full economic cost of the services they receive, the producers (the faculty) do not sell the services they give, and those who pay for all this largesse (the taxpayers) are carefully denied control over the institutions they finance. What, the authors ask, would an industry producing automobiles look like under similar arrangements? Because consumers are getting their automobiles cheaply, or even free, the demand grows by leaps and bounds. In order to maintain "order" in the market, the producers establish rules for the allocation of scarce automobiles, perhaps (in elitist spirit) awarding them only to those who have demonstrated objectively that they can drive superbly or, following a compensatory philosophy, giving priority to citizens who never had the opportunity to learn to drive. Producers have little or no incentive to meet the variety of demands in the market place; instead they assert that they know better than consumers what constitutes a "good" automobile and refuse to produce anything else. The caricature is too painfully close to current reality in higher education to be funny.

Students who find themselves unable to affect the characteristics of the education they receive through normal market mechanisms turn to non-market behavior – petition, demonstration, strike, and ultimately violence. Faculty and administrations behave perversely, rewarding violence with concession, thus reinforcing the already built-in tendency to student direct action. Because university faculties do not regard their institutions as property for which they should care, they are tolerant of student action that threatens free and open use by other members of the university community. One is reminded that rare indeed is the tenor of the response made by the fellows of a certain Oxford college to a formal notice from students that they intended to occupy the main college building the next day if their demands were not met immediately. The fellows' reply rejected the students' ultimatum, and went on to remind them that the fellows counted in their number three men with World War II sabotage experience, plus two frogmen, five commandos, four marksmen, and a *franc-tireur*. The demonstration did not materialize – but then Oxford college fellows still perversely persist in regarding their colleges as their own!

The authors argue that attention to a few elementary economic. principles is a minimum requirement for the restoration of organizational health to the universities. First, and most important, if we must subsidize higher education, we should cease making payments directly to the colleges and universities, for this only perpetuates the insulation of higher education from the pressures of changing demand; instead we should pay the subsidies (preferably as loans) directly to the students. Second, when the faculty of any one college yields to violence or threat of violence, it ought to be made to recognize that its action forces the entire system of higher education to pay a price for the errors and weakness that have brought it to that plight – and that that price is exacted in terms of diminished public respect and hence reduced taxpayer and donor support. How are these external costs to be internalized for college faculties? The authors make an ingenious and novel proposal:

> Imagine the trade association of university professors, the AAUP in the United States or its equivalent elsewhere, collecting extraordinary dues from its members to finance a set of university Peace Prizes. These would be awarded personally to those university and college presidents who succeed in maintaining peace with dignity. This scheme may not be so farfetched after all, especially if the AAUP be replaced by some wealthy donor. And, if we may offer a bit of advice to donors here, there might be worse ways of giving a dime. University Peace Prizes would, at the very least, exert their effects in the proper direction. Much current donor support does just the opposite.

Salvation, Professors Buchanan and Devletoglou surmise, could come from two directions: from legislators who firmly restore the principle that crimes are crimes even when they are committed on campus; and/or from bold innovators who, recognizing the obstacles to rational administration of higher education inherent in the present modes of supply and demand, determine to reestablish higher education institutions on full-cost, market force observing principles.

If either of these prophecies comes true, we are in for even more high spirited times in academe than we have seen yet.

NOTE

* Harold J. Noah, review of James M. Buchanan and Nicos E. Devletoglou, *Academia in Anarchy: An Economic Diagnosis* (New York: Basic Books, 1970), in *Saturday Review,* (February 21, 1970): 74-75.

31

Private Education*

This collection of papers produced under the auspices of the Program on Nonprofit Organizations, Yale University, makes an important contribution to the literature on alternatives for public policy toward private education in the United States. Contributors include Daniel Levy, the editor, who in an introductory essay provides an overview of the issues involved in establishing a public policy toward private education, as well as a closely argued chapter on the ambiguities inherent in the terms "public" and "private" applied to educational institutions; Donald Erickson, on the factors affecting the supply of and the demand for private schooling; Roger Geiger, who describes the complex diversity of American private higher education; Mary-Michelle Hirschoff, who builds the implications for public policy of assuming that the desire to enhance parental choice is the major justification for fostering private education; Estelle James, with a close analysis of the financing of schools in The Netherlands, and a second contribution analyzing the consequences of the subsidization of graduate education from the surpluses generated by undergraduate enrollments; Mark Kutner, Joel Sherman, and Mary Williams, who trace the history of Federal government financial assistance to private schooling since 1965; and Richard Murnane, who in two chapters critiques the methods and inferences of the Coleman, Hoffer, and Kilgore comparison of the academic effectiveness of public and nonpublic secondary schools in the United States.

The authors are authorities in their fields. They write clearly, document their claims well, and they are at pains to draw the implications for public policy of the stories they are telling. The volume is well edited, and is to be thoroughly recommended to all interested in the questions raised by the existence of private education alongside publicly financed and publicly provided schools, colleges, and universities, and in the intriguing questions for public policy raised by the fact that in many countries, not least the United States, public money finds its way to private institutions and private money goes to public ones.

Of special interest to readers of this journal will be the extensive use of data drawn from other countries to illuminate the choices open to government and educational institutions in the United States. School finance and educational policy studies in this country have very rarely looked beyond the borders of the United States. The reasons for this parochialism are not difficult to find. Fifty distinct state school systems within the border of the United States have offered a wide array of school policy and financing arrangements. No need therefore to look abroad for alternative ways of doing things. Important, too, is the conviction that each nation is sui generis in these matters; it is a widely held view (not without justification, either) that differences among the several

314

nations' history and governmental institutions make it very difficult to apply fruitfully any of the lessons to be learned from study of foreign examples. Admitting these problems, the editor nevertheless urges close attention to foreigners' ways of dealing with the public/private presence in education: "international policies can help raise ideas, debunk myths of either inevitable or impossible ramifications, and provide clues as to what to do – and what to avoid" (p. 11). In this spirit, much attention is paid to The Netherlands, which provides public money evenhandedly to private (which, in the Netherlands' context, as in other countries, means church related) and public schools. However, what the non-state schools gain in terms of equal treatment they pay for in detailed regulation and supervision by the public authorities of their curricula, teachers' qualifications, and financial affairs. There has been a good deal of discussion in the United States about the possibility that channeling tax dollars to private schools via tuition tax credits or vouchers might lead to substantial limitation of the present broad discretion of private schools in the United States to manage their own affairs. The evidence produced by James would seem to justify such apprehensions, and might well temper the enthusiasm of many in the private school lobby who are currently pressing for the introduction of public subsidies to private elementary and secondary schools.

Comparative study of higher education provides less clear guidance, it seems. Nevertheless, a most informative comparative chapter by Levy is entitled "Alternative Private-Public Blends in Higher-Education Finance: International Patterns". Levy identifies five major patterns of structure and funding of the higher education sector. The most common pattern provides for a single, homogeneous university sector, enjoying little institutional autonomy and with most of the money coming from the state. This pattern is found in the communist countries, Sweden, France (with a few exceptions), the former French colonies, the Federal Republic of Germany, Burma, Malaysia, and Sri Lanka. The second pattern is a variant of the first, providing significantly greater institutional autonomy, usually with some, now eroded, history of reliance on private funds. British universities are squarely of this pattern, over 90% of their receipts coming either directly or indirectly, via payments to students to cover their tuition fees, from the public purse. The general theme of this volume is that eventually he who pays the piper will call the tune in private education, so it is worth noting that even the Thatcher administration, rhetorically committed as it may be to shrinking the impact of government on British society, is now promoting very large inroads into the cherished traditional autonomy of the universities.

The third of Levy's patterns has two distinct university sectors, public and private, enjoying broadly similar funding opportunities. There are only a few examples of this pattern; he cites Chile, Belgium, The Netherlands and, marginally, Canada. Patterns IV and V cover those nations that have chosen distinctly dual systems: the public universities are supported by the taxpayer directly, and private institutions find their funds from a mixture of tuition fees, endowment income, contract work, and government funds. Pattern IV is typified by the dominance of the public sector. Examples are many of the Latin American countries, a number of whom have moved to pattern III as their private institutions could no longer survive without substantial public funding; pattern V is characterized by the dominance of the private sector, as in Japan, India, and The Philippines. The moral of this comparative excursus is that while the variety of structures and financing in higher education is exceptionally large, "lamentably, international analysis does not offer clear and attractive alternatives that could be neatly copied in U.S. higher education" (p. 210). This is a lesson that applies as much in comparative economic study as it does in comparative education.

NOTE

* Harold J. Noah, review of Daniel C. Levy, Ed., *Private Education: Studies in Choice and Public Policy.* Oxford/New York: Oxford University Press, 1986, in *Journal of Comparative Economics* 12 (1988): 129-131. Reprinted by permission of Academic Press, Inc.

32

OECD Reviews of Educational Policy*

I propose to examine the OECD reviews of national policies for education under eight headings: Some background on OECD as an organization, and some history of the programme of educational policy reviews. The five elements of a review. Who does the reviewing? Who wants to get what from the reviews? Who and what gets examined? Preparing for the review. Results of the reviews. Prospects for the review programme.

While I will do this with reference to all the reviews that have taken place so far, I'll be making particular reference to the German, Austrian and Canadian reviews, in which I had a direct role as examiner, and for two of which I acted as rapporteur.

General and historical background

One valued feature of comparative inquiry into educational phenomena is the opportunity to bring at least a fresh, and perhaps a more objective, perspective to bear on the educational affairs of another country. Recall that Marc-Antoine Jullien de Paris as far back as the second decade of the nineteenth century proposed that each European nation be required to supply answers to a lengthy annual questionnaire on its educational establishment. As the questions he suggested were many of them rather pointed, Jullien hoped that a proper sense of pride (and shame) would stimulate each nation to ever greater educational efforts. At least, the laggards would be exposed to international disapproval, and more progressively inclined nations could learn from the good example of others.

Jullien's notion of nations undertaking systematic, regular, self-administered examinations of their educational systems was ignored for the whole of the nineteenth century, but has been partially carried forward in this century by the work of the International Bureau of Education, Geneva, and by UNESCO. Examinations of member countries by the OECD are another strand in the process of international examination of educational policies.

The Organization for Economic Cooperation and Development is an international body with its headquarters in Paris. Its present membership of 25 countries includes the governments of Western Europe, Turkey and Yugoslavia, the United States and Canada, Japan, Australia and New Zealand. OECD had its origins in the consortium of countries that came together under the post-Second World War Marshall Plan. Originally named the OEEC (Organization for *European* Economic Co-operation), the name was changed to the non-regional appellation OECD in 1960. OECD's activities in industrial and agricultural policies, the commercial and monetary fields, education and science, and social policy are by now well developed.

The OECD seeks to be a locus for *intergovernmental* discussion, collaboration and co-ordination. In these activities, OECD is acting in much the same way as the more familiar UN agencies, ILO, WHO, UNESCO and so on. However, the OECD is unlike these UN agencies with respect to one thing it does *not* do, and one thing it *does* do. The OECD does *not* seek to incorporate non-governmental institutions or representation into its work, and it *does* conduct regular reviews of the economic (and lately) of the educational policies of member countries.

OECD *economic* policy reviews were established in the early 1950s. They are conducted by members of the OECD secretariat and attract considerable attention, as authoritative judgments about the means used by countries to achieve their stated economic and financial goals and the degree of success in attaining them.

OECD reviews of member countries' *educational* policy goals commenced somewhat later, but are already beginning to be seen as a series of considered evaluations of an important area of each government's social and administrative effort. While the OECD secretariat organizes and co-ordinates the educational policy reviews (in co-operation with officials of the host country), it does not undertake the review itself. This is done by a group of between three and six so-called examiners, appointed *ad hoc* by the OECD for a particular country review, with the approval of the government concerned. However, it would be fair to say that the educational policy reviews have not, as yet, attained the regularity, sustained achievement, and publicity achieved by the economic policy reviews, though, given time, this will perhaps develop.

The review process grew out of the OECD Conference on Economic Growth and Investment, held in Washington, D.C. in 1961. One conclusion of that Conference was that there should be regular national surveys of educational policies in member countries. The emphasis of the Conference, and of the proposal for reviews, was upon the manpower implications of educational policy and at least the first review, that of Ireland, was conducted in that spirit. In fact, the series of reviews began by being piggybacked on a three-year survey of education in Ireland, undertaken 1962-65, and published as an Irish government document, entitled *Investment in Education*. A team of OECD examiners visited Ireland for a week in June 1966, using this document as their background report. In October 1966 a so-called confrontation meeting was held in Paris at the OECD between the examiners and the Irish educational and political authorities, in the presence of the relevant OECD multi-government committee. The examiners' report and the proceedings of the confrontation meeting were then published by OECD. Thus was the pattern established that was used, with minor modification only, for subsequent reviews: a background report prepared by the country; an on-site examination and report by external assessors; an agenda of questions for discussion at a confrontation meeting; and a series of publications to conclude the process of review.

Sweden, Italy, Austria, France, Japan, the Netherlands, United States (educational research policy), Germany, England and Wales, Austria again (higher education), Norway, Canada, Australia, the Netherlands (again), and Austria (school policy) have since followed. Aspects of United States educational policy will be reviewed shortly (educational policies for the disadvantaged), and Yugoslavia, Sweden, and New Zealand are on the future schedule.

The five elements of a review

As I have mentioned, a complete country review has at least five important documentary stages:

1. A report, prepared by the educational authorities of the country under review. This document is usually known as a "background document". I will have something more to say about it later. For the moment suffice it to say that the background document provides examiners with a description of the relevant parts of the country's educational system, a statement of policy goals as seen by the country's authorities, and some reference at least to the major policy problems under discussion within the country. The background document is, in a sense, the examiners' primary source document for their review.

2. In a number of countries, and especially in Canada, a series of special research reports are prepared during the course of the writing of the background report. These are normally made available to the examiners, at their request, but are not intended for eventual publication as part of the OECD report. Other papers that are available to the examiners may come from special interest groups – particularly from teachers and school board associations, and from university groups.

3. After spending a period of time in the country, which may be as short as three to four days or as long as a month, the examiners produce their report on what they have seen and heard together with a list of questions which they wish to have discussed with the representatives of the country's educational authorities.

4. The examiners' report and the list of questions form the agenda for a session of the Education Committee of the OECD in Paris. Representatives from all of the OECD member countries are present and one or two whole days of discussion are devoted to the so-called "confrontation meeting". During the course of discussion based on the examiners' questions, it is expected that representatives from the other member countries will intervene, and over the years such interventions have become more and more the rule. In that sense, the confrontation meeting in Paris becomes a type of multi-national seminar on the problems of educational policy experienced by all the member countries, but with particular reference to the issues raised by the experience of the country under examination.

5. In at most a year from the date of the confrontation meeting, there will appear from the OECD a publication which includes the background report, or a summary thereof, the full text of the examiners' report and the questions they have raised for discussion, plus a summary of the discussion held at the confrontation meeting. From the point of view of the OECD, this publication marks the end of the country review process. Of course, this is by no means the end of the matter for the country concerned. Most often, a vigorous public discussion ensues at home that often continues for a number of years.

Who are the examiners?

The team of examiners consists of a minimum of three and a maximum of six persons, accompanied by an official from the OECD secretariat. Many of the examiners are university professors, especially those who have had some hand in the discussion and setting of educational policy in their own countries. In addition, examiners are drawn from the ranks of ex-ministers or deputy ministers of education, members of legislative committees concerned with education, and administrators (that is, civil servants) who have dealt with education at one stage or another of their careers.

Each team usually has an individual who has been on the receiving end of the examination in his own country. In addition, because of the number of reviews that have now taken place, the examining teams tend to include a rather large proportion of examiners who have taken part in examinations before.

As befits an international organization, the OECD attempts to achieve a good spread of examiners in terms of nationality. In no circumstances, may an examiner be a national of the country under examination. In Canada, for example, the examining team consisted of a Frenchman, a Belgian, a German, a Norwegian, and an Englishman, together with the requisite official of the OECD. One of the examiners, usually the member with the most diplomatic experience, is designated chairman, to make the formal speeches of introduction, and so forth. There is also a rapporteur (usually, though not always, not the same person as the chairman), who is responsible for coordinating the writing of the examiners' report. In the development of the work of the examiners, there is a great deal of collegial consultation, discussion, and group definition of outlines of the questions and conclusions. The schedule of interviews, and the itinerary within the country, usually provides for the examiners to stay together as a group for most of the time, so that there is a chance for an examiners' group consensus to emerge on important issues that must be dealt with in the examiners' report. However, a certain division of labour among the examiners also occurs, so that individual examiners tend to specialize in one or another aspect of education policy.

During the course of the country visit, and for a day or two at the end of the visit, the examiners engage in intensive periods of discussion and writing, in order that by the time they disperse, the rapporteur will have in hand a clear outline of basic arguments to be made in the final draft of the examiners' report.

In the intervening period between the end of the examiners' visit and the confrontation meeting in Paris, a three-way process of discussion of the draft examiners' report ensues among the examiners, the country authorities and the OECD secretariat. The goal now is to ensure that the final draft is free of errors of fact and gross misinterpretations of evidence that has been presented to the examiners. In addition, gaps in documentation and statistics are remedied as far as possible at this stage. My own experience demonstrates conclusively, I believe, that in no way is there censorship exercised on the examiners by either the country under review or the OECD secretariat. This is not to say that suggestions are not made for change in this or that aspect of the examiners' drafts, but the examiners are, in the final instance, free to render their own judgment in their own words.

Who wants to get what from the reviews?

It is, I believe, important to recognize that the reviews of country educational policies do not occur in a political vacuum. They are the result of a specific agreement between the authorities of the country concerned and the OECD secretariat, and are intended to serve a variety of interests.

The OECD secretariat has at least five interests in the review process. There is first the desire to have knowledge of the member country's experience, potentials, and problems in education shared as widely as possible internationally. On the basis of the review work, the secretariat hopes, too, to build an ever-increasing spirit of international co-operation.   Third, such work helps to cement further the particular elements of international cooperation that are represented by the OECD itself.   Fourth, any particular review is looked upon as an opportunity to improve the educational review process in general. It is hoped that practice makes perfect here as elsewhere. Last, the content of a review helps to test the validity of generally agreed OECD policies in educational affairs against experience of the member countries.   This has led to the considerable enrichment and modification of OECD educational policies over the years.

A country accepting a review also has a number of interests in mind.   There is stimulus provided to self-examination. Certainly that was a most important interest of the educational authorities of Canada, and the background documentation in Canada was the outcome of a coordinated effort among and between the provincial and federal authorities that represented a "first" for Canada.   Second, the review does provide a good platform from which a country can hope to inform the governments of many other countries concerning its achievements in the field of education, and its ambitions for the future. There is also an important plus in the opportunity to receive an external, and it is hoped objective, critique of the conduct of educational affairs that will be of value internally in the future construction of policy. Last, and this has often been of decisive importance for the timing of particular reviews, country authorities believe that a review and the surrounding publicity will help to mobilize support for a desired programme of innovation and change. There were strong elements of this motivation for the timing of the reviews that have taken place in Germany, Austria and Australia.

The examiners' interests tend to be somewhat more personal than the foregoing. Invariably, they have a vivid interest in learning more about the country they are visiting, and the process of visits and discussions makes for what amounts to a travelling seminar for the examiners.   Many of them tend to be interested in the comparative study of educational phenomena and are eager to test in practice the validity of Jullien de Paris' notion that international examination can help improve national educational policies.

In any case, there is an intrinsic attraction in the opportunity given the examiners to hold up a mirror, reflecting back to the country an image of its educational system as seen through the eyes of the examiners. The mirror is, no doubt, a distorting lens to some degree. Indeed, I would argue, it should not be a perfect mirror, merely giving back what was shown to it. There exists a strong, and properly strong, tension between the problems and "facts" as the representatives of a country see them and the way those same phenomena are viewed and evaluated by the examiners. It is precisely from these often unexpected, and not always welcome, reflections that the contribution of an examination will emerge, if it is to emerge at all.

Who and what undergoes these examinations?

I noted already that some twelve nations have had reviews of their policies for education, some more than once.   The OECD does not force itself upon a country. Rather, it is a matter of a member country finding it convenient or useful to request that a review be undertaken at a particular year.

Within each country, it is largely official governmental policies and the administrative and institutional apparatus for regular, formal education that is examined. In most countries relatively little engagement from the non-formal, non-public, and non-governmental sectors of education is sought, or achieved. The explanation for this is to be found in the emphasis upon official, governmental relationships which is the hallmark of the OECD.

An explanation is not, of course, a justification. Country examinations are regularly criticized for giving insufficient attention to the non-governmental sectors. In Canada, the so-called "interest groups" (representing teachers, school trustees, associations dealing with education of exceptional children, and so forth) were extremely critical of what they conceived to be a one-sided process of review. In Germany, too, there was little indication that the work of teachers' associations was considered worth devoting time to, so that whatever success the examiners had in meeting with representatives of teachers' associations was the result of *ad hoc* and informal arrangements. The review procedure in England and Wales formed a somewhat surprising set of arrangements. The examiners there met with Ministry officials only, and this caused something of a stir. In Austria, although the examiners did indeed meet with representatives of employers and trade union associations, they did so only in the presence of the officials responsible for education. However, the final judgment must be that, given the constraints on the time available, most countries do manage to have the examiners meet rather freely with an extraordinarily wide range of representative interest groups and individuals.

Preparing for the review

Some candidates for an examination are able to prepare for the Big Day methodically and in good time; others stay up all night, cramming together whatever they can in a helterskelter rush. So it is with country examinations.

The background reports for Canada and for Austria, to give just two examples, were assembled in the most thorough and painstaking way. They provided the examiners with comprehensive surveys of the educational systems and their operation. The background reports from some other countries have not been so thoroughly prepared (for example, in Germany), and they were in consequence of less use to the examiners.

The tasks facing a country preparing for an examination are basically threefold. It is necessary first to identify for examination a set of institutions, issues, policies, and plans. Some countries have taken a wide definition of their educational system for examination, including as much as possible in the survey. The reviews in France, Sweden, Germany and Canada were of this all-inclusive variety. In Austria and the United States segments of the educational system were identified, and there seems to be an increasing preference by countries and the OECD secretariat to structure reviews more narrowly within specified sectors of the educational system. This stage of preliminary definition and discussion can take upwards of a year. In Canada it took about four years to get from the initial idea of a review to the end of the process of definition of the structure.

The second and main stage of preparation is the work on the background report, which must summarize the system of education, describe its objectives and modes of policy making, and estimate the success and shortcomings of the system with respect to the stated objectives. Finally, in consultation with the OECD secretariat, the country authorities must establish a schedule of visits, discussions, mini-conferences, and appointments for the examiners, to occupy between a week and a month of full-time examiners' work.

In general, country authorities tended to be over-optimistic about the lead time that is necessary to get arrangements in final shape for an examination. Partly this is the result of delay that is inevitably associated with diplomatic protocol, but there is also a tendency to underestimate the complexities of the background report and the schedule of examiners' appointments. Both are fraught with potential political aspects. As the process of preparation for the review comes toward its end, more and more offices and non-official groups come to realize that a quite significant event is about to take place, and demand that they be granted some piece of the action, or some access to the background report before it is finally submitted. It is not therefore unusual to find that the date for the beginning of an examiners' visit is postponed, sometimes more than once.

Results of reviews

As a result of an educational policy review, the visibility of educational policy both nationally and internationally is quite definitely increased.

The immediate result takes the form of assessing "how we did" in an international scrutiny. Any and all elements of praise for the country and its educational system are, of course, seized upon with alacrity, and repeated in the press with many references to the examiners' objectivity and sagacity. At the same time, there is a marked tendency to rebut points of criticism (real or imagined) while underlining the ignorance of the examiners, stemming either from their lack of time or opportunity to acquaint themselves more thoroughly with conditions in the country, or from their sheer innate obtuseness. Such immediate reactions, while they generate a good deal of temporary heat, are not the most important.

In assessing the longer term effects of a country review, it is necessary to recognize that any given review cannot and should not be understood simply in terms of a single country report. The programme of reviews is essentially a serial process, in which there is a gradual accretion of a body of international audits, judgments, and identifications of trends of policy. Hence, the context in which a given country review takes place is extremely significant for understanding why the examiners have concentrated on this or that aspect of the educational system, or emphasized this or that approach to educational policy.

Thus, policy reviews have tended to concentrate on a fairly limited range of issues: equality of educational opportunity (both as a goal and in terms of actual achievement); curriculum structures (especially the fit between schooling and work); the aptness of government and school governance structures; the role, influence, skills, and training of teachers; policies and practices for the education of certain special groups of children (linguistic, ethnic, socially disadvantaged, learning disabled and so forth); and the fiscal implications of educational policy.

These particular perspectives arise from the major policy concerns of the OECD as an organization. The politicians and administrators who attend OECD meetings, and all who read OECD documents regularly, thus accumulate gradually a body of case-study and comparative information that helps them to set their own, more intimately known problems and achievements in a wider context of understanding.

Within the given country, ideas and judgments that at first shock and seem unpalatable often become assimilable in time. In Germany in particular, there was great resistance to the ideas in the examiners' report, especially in relationship to the overloaded curriculum, hours of schooling, and the tight relationship between particular educational qualifications and specific occupations. But over the years there has developed increasing willingness within Germany to consider ways in which some of the areas of examiners' criticism might be dealt with.

Prospects for the review programme

The future of the review programme must depend upon the continuing support for it provided by the OECD member countries. In a sense, they are continually gauging what the review programme costs them in time, money and energies deflected from other worthwhile enterprises *versus* what they judge they are deriving in terms of benefits. Regarded from this point of view, the prospects for the review programme seem to be good. One gets the impression that, although the immediate governmental reaction to a review is "never again," the disenchantment does not last long. One may suppose, moreover, that there is a certain automatic momentum built into the review programme. Having jumped across the review hurdles itself, a country may be quite enthusiastic about other countries doing the same.

There are certainly arguments for tightening up and tidying up some aspects of the review process. Some suggestions that have been frequently made point toward making much clearer and more specific the particular areas, topics and aspects of education to be reviewed. Also, it is claimed that the examiners could well use better briefing of the country that they are to visit, and that the nature of the examiners' reports should be less value-laden and more objective and "scientific". And hopes are continually expressed that the entire review process might be held to tighter time schedules than has usually been possible.

There may indeed be much of value in these, and other, suggestions. I would merely warn against trying to go too far in the direction of routinizing and bureaucratizing the review procedures. It is, I think, worth emphasizing that the review process is essentially a set of acts of "discovery" – often self-discovery by the country concerned, and creative discovery by the examiners and the Education Committee of the OECD in Paris. It is fashionable nowadays to ask of every investment of public funds "What will the product be?" With respect to the reviews of educational policy, it might be useful to tolerate a certain amount of untidiness, in return for many of the benefits flowing from this unusual international exercise.

The process of reviews helps to build an international community in a way that is positive, practical, and non-threatening. Nations go about their educational business in their own manner, according to their best lights. Their sovereignty in education is in no way impaired, but through the reviews they demonstrate their willingness to "pay a decent respect to the opinions of mankind," as Thomas Jefferson put it on another occasion. In that spirit the reviews of educational policy have deserved and earned attention and support.

NOTE

* Harold J. Noah, "The OECD Review and Higher Education," *Canadian Journal of Higher Education* 9 (1979): 5-12. Reprinted by permission of the journal.

33

Education for Development*

Education is big public business all over the world. Although substantial private resources are spent on education (especially on training), the private share of educational expenditures is very much smaller than the public in virtually all countries. The dominance of public funding is usually justified by reference to the large external benefits said to be generated by education. It is argued that, left to private financing, individuals and families would severely underinvest in education, from the point of view of a socially optimum level. Be that as it may, large-scale public expenditures on education are also capable of generating economic problems. For example, protected from the pressures of fee-paying clients, public school systems can (and do) continue quite happily for decades to offer curricula that have little current economic value. They can (and do) underwrite primary school structures that waste large sums of money on grade 1 entrants who will drop out of school after a year or two, well before basic literacy is attained. On each year of university education they can (and do) cheerfully spend 20, and even 30, times the money spent on a primary school place. They continue to do this in spite of the mountain of evidence that the social rate of return to higher education is often only a half or even a third of the rate of return to primary schooling. These are only some examples of the obstinately uneconomic public policies in education documented in this volume. In addition, the authors explain and illustrate the various techniques of economic analysis used by economists to diagnose the problems and form the basis for helping government agencies to mitigate or avoid them.

The book concentrates on the less industrialized nations and draws heavily on the results of research funded by the World Bank. The bank's interest in these matters springs from its increasing recognition that national economic development proceeds best when investment in physical capital is complemented by an appropriate development of the human capital stock, of which education and training form a large part. Hence, the bank has been willing to revise its earlier policy of restricting loans to programs of physical capital development. The first World Bank loan for educational development was made in 1962, and the authors note that since that date there has been commitment of "over $85 billion in about 260 projects in more than 90 countries" (p. 4).

Separate chapters are devoted to cost-benefit analysis, manpower demand and educational supply, private demand for education, computing the costs of education, estimating the efficiency of educational operations, considerations of equity, and links between education and other important human capital sectors (health, fertility, and agricultural productivity). The strength of the book lies not in any major new insights that are offered but in its provision of a comprehensive, excellently documented review of the relevant research and policy-oriented literature. The authors have produced a well-organized, authoritative volume that will serve well the needs of teachers, students, educational administrators, and policymakers. It is likely to be consulted frequently by all of these, as well as by scholars, with profit.

There are two large questions to be answered by a book with the title *Education for Development*. Are there important connections between investment in education and economic growth and development? And, if there are, how do they work? The authors cite evidence that education (especially in the poorer countries) contributes directly and indirectly to economic growth via higher levels of labor and capital productivity, higher incomes, improvements in health, lower fertility rates, and improvements in the "quality" of children.

In the heady days of the 1960s, economists and politicians joined in making highly optimistic forecasts of the benefits of educational expansion. Education was just one of the sectors that profited, along with international aid, the building of physical infrastructure, social services, and military expenditures, from the prevailing climate of public liberality. Just at this time, too, the concept of human capital was given theoretical and empirical content by a company of talented and prolific economists, among whom were Theodore Schultz, Gary Becker, Jacob Mincer, Mary Jean Bowman, Lee Hansen, and Burton Weisbrod in the United States and Mark Blaug and John Vaizey in England. Their work made it academically respectable to promote education as a good investment in the future earning power of today's students. In a world in which production is increasingly dominated by the impact of new technology, we have quite properly come to recognize education and training as necessary, though not sufficient, for economic advancement.

From the material presented by the authors, it becomes very clear that we have moved a long way from the fairly simplistic approaches that marked earlier thinking about the relationship between economic development and education. For one thing, the political climate for education has changed markedly. We live in a period of fiscal defensiveness, not least in the nonindustrialized economies. Just as education benefited from a previous period's liberality, it now suffers in today's tightfistedness. Even in the richer countries of the world, the cry is for a bigger and more certain return on money spent on education. The Thatcher government has brought British teachers in the maintained (i.e., state) schools to the brink of revolt, as the government continues to insist that even present levels of funding, let alone any increase, depend on the introduction of new structures and practices in the schools. Similarly, there is virtually open war between government and British universities on proposals to cut funding, reshape the pattern of higher education provision, and monitor performance. In France, the Socialist government elected with Mitterand soon beat a retreat from its initial promises of massive university growth, and the current Conservative administration of Chirac has introduced a budget for 1987's educational expenditures that is a monument of restraint. The same is true for the Federal Republic of Germany at both the federal and provincial levels, irrespective of political coloration.

In addition, in many countries governments have not been careful enough to arrange matters so that education avoids exacerbating social and economic inequalities. Urban dwellers too often are served at the expense of rural people; males study in the expensive technical branches of education more than females, thus getting more of the national resources for education spent on them, even if the overall enrollment ratios across the sexes are approximately equal; and, as in most other avenues of life, the rich enjoy a better deal than the poor. The authors cite evidence that modes of financing education, especially at the higher levels, may be perverse, with the poorer countries tending to pick up virtually all the private costs of education via outright grants to cover living expenses, travel, books, and so on, as well as charging either no tuition at all or fees set well below average costs. The result of such public generosity toward the relatively few who gain places in higher education is that private returns and social returns diverge markedly, with the latter well below the former. Demand for places in higher education expands well beyond the capacity of countries to provide it, and, as it is disproportionately the children of the well-to-do who succeed in the competition for university entrance, the student financing system ends by facilitating a politically (and even morally) undesirable transfer of tax resources from the relatively poor to the relatively rich. One of the strongest recommendations of the authors is that these systems of outright living grants and low tuition should be abandoned in favor of fuller-cost pricing and ample loan programs.

The authors are, however, properly cautious when it comes to most recommendations. The basic lesson they seem to want to convey is that there is no one recipe for successful educational investment, even if policy goals for education are clear and nonconflicting (which is rare, to say the least). Instead, the authors warn, "Because of the wide variety of benefits of educational investment and the diverse needs of different developing countries, no single formula can be applied to all countries or to all education projects" (p. 321).

Most of the economics of education proceeds on the basis of "macro" – level data and models. For example, attempts to relate forecasts of manpower requirements to educational and training supply programs, calculations of average national rates of return to different levels of schooling, and calculations of the impact and incidence of costs and benefits are all dealt with from a "macro" point of view. However, a substantial chapter of the present volume is devoted to an important "micro" aspect of the economics of education: the internal efficiency of the schools. Education consumes sizable fractions of GNP. In 1984, the figure given for the developing countries is 4.5%. Relative to the public budget, the share of education is even larger. The figure given is 16.1%, again for the developing countries. The importance of using resources for education efficiently is thus obvious – at the same time that there are few systematic pressures on the schools to improve their efficiency. Indeed, much of the pressure appears to move the schools in the opposite direction: each teacher teaches fewer children; the children stay in school more days per year and have more years before graduation; subject matter splits into ever more refined slices of knowledge; and equipment becomes more costly. There is a lot of conflicting evidence about the relationship between higher unit costs in education and the outputs of the schools, so we are by no means certain that value for money is rising, at least in the industrialized countries.

As usual, the story is somewhat different for the poorer nations. On the one hand, it is clear from the evidence cited in the book that expenditures for books, paper, desks, and the other basic paraphernalia of schools are pitifully inadequate. The overwhelming share of the education dollar goes to pay teachers' salaries. Classrooms in which even the teacher has no textbook, let alone the children, are only too common. Such conditions argue strongly in favor of not only a reallocation of resources within the school system but also an overall increase in resources. On the other hand, the data cited show clearly that, measuring their educational "effort" by computing expenditures as a fraction of GNP, the poorer nations are making as much of an educational effort as is reasonable to expect. The dilemma posed by the combination of expenditure levels far below a minimum threshold needed for effective schooling and a level of financial effort that cannot easily be expanded from the side of public funding has presumably only one solution: broad-scale efforts to diversify sources of finance for education by incorporating even larger elements of private funding.

These are just some of the crucial questions of investment policy for education treated in this book. Equally valuable are the sections dealing with techniques of project appraisal in education. These techniques have not, in general, reached any very high level of sophistication (which is probably a good thing, given our rather weak understanding of the way in which education works), and the techniques described should be comfortably accessible to most planners and administrators in government and education.

In sum, I forecast a justifiably strong demand and long desk (as distinct from shelf) life for this admirably produced and most reasonably priced volume.

NOTE

* Harold J Noah, review of George Psacharopoulos and Maureen Woodhall. *Education for Development: An Analysis of Investment Choices*.   New York: Oxford University Press (for the World Bank), 1986, in *Economic Development and Cultural Change* 36 (1988): 415-419. Reprinted by permission of the World Bank.

34

The Utility of Country Case Studies
for Educational Planning*

The set of activities called educational planning is a far from thoroughly defined branch of governmental activity. Not infrequently the best laid educational plans go awry, and many are not so well laid in the first place. Educational planning is an art that continues to need all the help it can get. What aid can it expect from country case studies?

Comparative education had its beginning in country case studies and nowadays, too, they dominate the comparative education scene, at least quantitatively. But there are notable differences between the early and the contemporary country case study contributions. We are seeing some rather sharply focussed analytic, replication studies, in contrast to the more discursive, descriptive and "one-shot" work of the past. Of late, we have had a number of outstanding sets of replication studies. Examples are the financing of education studies sponsored by the International Institute for Educational Planning, Paris; the country educational policy reviews, conducted by the Organisation for Economic Cooperation and Development, Paris; and the Mathematics Achievement and Six Subject studies of the International Association for the Evaluation of Educational Achievement (IEA), Stockholm.

In the past, authors and sponsors of case studies were openly optimistic about the direct, immediate value of studies of foreign educational systems for domestic policy-making and planning. Today, a properly much more cautious note is sounded. Moreover, in the long period up to the mid- and late 1960's, when the major emphasis was upon quantitative expansion of schooling, the tasks facing the educational planner looked reasonably manageable, his data needs seemed well definable, and evaluation criteria intuitively available. All this aided and abetted a fairly positive approach to the question of using studies of foreign school systems to improve the management of one's own education.

The goals of education planning have now become more complex and less easy to define, if only because the emphasis has shifted to qualitative improvements. In consequence, data needs are now more difficult to specify and success criteria have become less obvious and more arguable. In such a world, the contribution of country case studies to the work of the educational planner is less intuitively clear. Nonetheless, I believe they are useful.

First, case studies can help in the recognition of problems. Educational planners need to do more than react to the problems set them by policy-makers and administrators. Planners need to be aware of a wide range of crucial educational problems in other countries than their own. This is desirable, partly to give them perspective on what may otherwise seem to be problems uniquely their own and partly to forewarn them of problems that they may need to face before too long. Surely this must be one of the major benefits of perusal of the 8-10 OECD Country Educational Policy Studies, that have so far appeared. The range of problems touched on and discussed is so extensive that no educational planner could leave their reading without at once a sense of comfort that his country is not alone in having to deal with some very difficult situations, and a warning of difficulties perhaps not yet faced at home, but already presaged abroad. Thus, the strains produced in Japan by a highly competitive system of entry into the prestigious "best" universities; the problems occasioned in France by application of a legalistically defined principle of *égalité* to reform of secondary education; the missed educational opportunities in West Germany because of too rigid an insistence upon the maintenance of "academic standards" – all this and much more are valued fruits of the OECD country case studies series.

Equally with the widening of horizons on problems comes the benefit of a wider perspective on solutions. Nothing in educational planning and policy is more difficult than the transplanting of one country's procedures and institutions to another. Rigid, unenlightened copying is a sure prescription for failure. But this is no argument for the opposite viewpoint: that there is nothing to be learned from foreign example. On the contrary, a careful appraisal of the way other countries go about schooling their young is indispensable. Here, too, not only the OECD country studies, but also the 21-nation IEA work will repay close study. For, brought together in compact, systematized fashion is a wealth of information on the range of possibilities for ordering the institutions of schooling.

More valuable even than reviewing the finished product of other people's case studies is participation in an internationally directed case study of one's own system, or of a foreign system. The training and job-experience of an educational planner is likely to be incomplete without such an experience. The OECD studies and the IEA work have had one of their most valuable impacts in the very process of involving hundreds of individuals in consistent, systematic thought, discussion, inquiry and writing concerning educational practices, goals and values.

With these points in mind, it may be worth reviewing the specific use to educational planners of the National Case Studies that A. Harry Passow, Max A. Eckstein and I conducted, within the framework of the IEA Six Subject Study. (The final report is in press and will be published shortly under the title, *International Studies in Evaluation VII – The National Case Study – An Empirical Comparative Study of Twenty-One Educational Systems*. (Stockholm: Almqvist and Wiksell; New York: John Wiley and Sons.)

The IEA National Case Study

Work began in 1968, to identify those major aspects of each country's socioeconomic, political, cultural and school systems that can be regarded as having some prima facie anterior relationship to the levels of school achievement in the subjects tested by IEA. Over 50 aspects were so identified, and variables that would reflect these aspects were agreed. After a lengthy process of international discussion and refinement, a final questionnaire (the National Case Study Questionnaire, or NCSQ) was determined, accepted, and submitted to each of the national IEA centers for completion. The NCS analyses are based primarily upon the country data submitted in response to the NCSQ by 20 IEA National Technical Officers (no reply was received from Romania). The final report contains country-by-country "profiles" of the socioeconomic, political, cultural and school systems of 20 countries, as well as analyses of the relationships between each country's average level of school achievement and the factors described in the profiles.

In summary, the NCS reports on level of economic development, standards of health care and nutrition, national affluence, population size and urbanization, female participation in the labor force, financial effort for education, family size, parents' availability to the young child, extent of foreign contacts, linguistic and cultural diversity and religious affiliation. School system factors include: enrollment size and growth (both compulsory and postcompulsory), student-teacher ratios, ages of beginning and ending compulsory education, and arrangements for transfer from primary to secondary schooling and from secondary to higher education. Characteristics relating to the teaching cadre are: control over teacher personnel decisions, emphasis on pedagogy in teacher training programs, academic ability of recruits to teaching, teachers' pay, professional organizations, representation on public bodies dealing with education, and teachers' power over instructional decisions. Curricular and instructional matters are represented by degree of openness of the system to curriculum reform, centralization versus local/regional modes of implemented curriculum change, and number of hours of instruction.

The National Case Study report thus contains a vast amount of systematically organized information on national social and educational systems. The report does not, however, attempt to be comprehensively encyclopaedic; instead, each element of the information presented there is included only because it is used to test an hypothesis concerning the correlates of national achievement levels.

Throughout the NCS volume, cautions are expressed regarding imperfections of the data which severely limit the implications for policy and planning to be drawn from the findings. The indicators are often only gross estimates (sometimes hesitantly provided by IEA national technical officers) and these are related to achievement scores in science and reading comprehension only. Hypotheses could be tested only with a small number of cases, never exceeding 19 countries. While a number of the relationships are consistently in the same direction, the data do not lend themselves to sophisticated statistical treatment which would warrant drawing strong inferences. Some of the findings suggest support for hypotheses with respect to younger children (aged 10 years, or "Population I" according to IEA definitions), but not for somewhat older children (aged 14 years, or "Population II"), or vice-versa, thus raising additional questions about the nature of the relationships which might exist.

The levels of knowledge generated by the NCSQ are not adequate for providing the planner or policy-maker with information directly applicable to action. NCSQ data generally do not provide guarantees that taking action X with respect to some aspect of the educational system will yield increased achievement in the subject areas tested. Furthermore, the criterion used in the IEA studies is school achievement as measured by test scores, and not the entire complex range of outcomes that schools are intended to deliver. No planner will wish to concentrate the efforts of schooling entirely upon measured achievement in particular subject areas (even when the measures do include non-cognitive aspects), at the expense of everything else. Hence, an analysis which related an indicator or cluster of indicators to aggregate science and reading comprehension measures, without attempting to examine trade-offs (because the data do not warrant such analyses), is inevitably limited. However, it can sensitize planners to question what is the conventional wisdom and focus on qualitative as well as quantitative factors, and furthermore, when read in conjunction with the other IEA volumes, the NCS findings provide a basis for wide-ranging speculation about policy.

Educational planners need to give attention to the conditions and processes which affect the functioning of the institution called "school" in achieving its objectives, but in addition they must not neglect the other agencies and institutions affecting home and family background. While it is often argued that schools are not the primary institutions of economic and social reform, but more typically preservers of the status quo, democratization of the schooling process and extension of access to educational opportunities are trends in all IEA nations. The data, however, are not fine enough to provide definitive guidance for the policy maker about such issues as socioeconomic and/or racial balance of student populations, allocation of financial resources, or the desirability of investing in schooling rather than in other social welfare areas.

In addition to reporting the outcomes or achievement measures in specific subject areas, each of the other IEA volumes reports relationships between achievement and other pedagogical and sociocultural factors within the school and classroom context. These data analyses are consistent across nations in emphasizing the significance of home background on those aspects of cognitive achievement which were assessed. The policy implications of these findings of the Coleman and Plowden Reports are not unambiguous. The school system may not be in a position to have an immediate impact on the home and family (although there are educational programs which are designed to do just that, especially with respect to child-rearing patterns), yet in those areas within its domain – curriculum, instruction, resources, educational climate, student body composition, staff deployment, and so forth – reforms and reallocations may be possible which could affect both the cognitive and affective growth of students.

A sampling of some of the conclusions we advanced will illustrate the potential utility of these studies. A number of NCS hypotheses deal with the expansion of pupil enrollments for the system as a whole and for the primary and secondary levels. Generally, the notion that the greater the expansion in enrollments over the period 1950-1960-1969 the lower the achievement, is confirmed when all countries are taken together. However, the negative correlations are much smaller and sometimes become marginal when the developed countries only are considered. Rapid changes in enrollment naturally place burdens on school systems with respect to facilities, staff needs, and educational costs. While systems may be able to cope with these problems on a quantitative basis, the qualitative aspects are more difficult and it is to these aspects that planners must give attention.

The finding that there is a low correlation between growth of secondary enrollment and average Population II achievement for the developed countries lends additional support to the conviction that expansion of secondary school opportunities does not necessarily mean lower achievement. Certainly, the questions of retentivity and expansion of enrollment at the secondary and tertiary levels – among the most significant areas educational planners must deal with – should continue to be dealt with in terms of national priorities. Certainly, the concept that "more means worse" is generally not supported by NCS data nor by the several subject reports. However, if planners focus only on the physical aspects of growth instead of on qualitative dimensions such as quality of staffing, flexibility of instructional programs, and variety of curricular materials, some decline in achievement levels may be expected.

The large and regular differences between the developed and the developing countries necessitated treating the four developing and the fifteen developed nations separately in many instances. The findings suggest that the significance of certain indicators differs between the developed and developing countries. Some of the indicators may, in fact, be operating on a threshold basis, or, once having reached a certain level, major increases beyond this level may not have a discernible relationship to achievement. The inverse relationship between economic development and Population II achievement among the developed nations deserves attention: the higher the level of economic development, the lower the Population II achievement.

There is consensus that the quality of education is closely tied to the quality of teachers in a nation's schools. Certification, selection, hiring, and assignment of teachers can be made at the national, regional (or state), local, or school building level. There seems to be little difference in aggregate achievement between those nations which perform staffing functions on a centralized basis and those which are more decentralized. Policy makers who deal with issues of centralization and decentralization of educational processes will need to take into consideration other factors (e.g., local control and political power) in resolving these problems. There is little evidence in the NCS data to suggest that centralized or decentralized staffing policies are associated with achievement levels.

There are a number of factors which determine the range and level of academic ability of recruits into teaching, and various professions compete for the best in academic talent. Most of the IEA countries recruit their primary teachers from a lower stratum of academic ability than that from which they draw their secondary teachers. Eleven nations recruit their primary teachers from the lower half of the academic ability range. On the other hand, three IEA nations recruit secondary teachers from the top half of the academic ability range and six recruit from the second quarter of the academic ability range. Some positive relationship is shown between the average academic quality of teacher recruits and achievement scores, especially at the Population I level.

In ten of the 19 IEA nations, primary school teaching is viewed as a woman's job while in the remaining nine it is regarded as a career for either males or females. On the secondary school level, however, in all but one country teaching is perceived as a career for either men or women. Only in one is secondary teaching perceived as primarily a job for men. In many countries, there is considerable concern about the perceived "feminization" of the teaching profession and the consequences on affective development, particularly of boys. The NCS data provide some support for the hypothesis that the perception of primary teaching as a job for females is associated with lower achievement scores.

"Opportunity to learn" seemed to be one of the important aspects affecting achievement in Science and Reading Comprehension. Opportunity to learn is, of course, related to the number of hours of instruction available to pupils. When taken in conjunction with related findings concerning "opportunity to learn," the implication for the planner is that hours of instruction and exposure to particular areas of knowledge have substantial impact on levels of school achievement.

There are four distinct kinds of implications to be drawn from the NCS data. Some findings suggest that the policy makers might take "positive action" if increased achievement in Science and Reading Comprehension is desired. Some findings suggest that certain aspects of the so-called "conventional wisdom" are not borne out cross-nationally, and policy makers would do well to seriously query such wisdom. Some findings suggest that policy makers should look to make qualitative rather than quantitative changes and recognize that "more" alone may have little bearing on the question of "better" or "worse".

What we are left with insofar as the policy planner is concerned, are a number of hints and possible implications which need to be examined on both a within-country and a cross-national basis. The correlations of the indicators with achievement, it must be repeated, deal with achievement in Science and Reading Comprehension. An educational system has broader goals than achievement in these subjects, goals of both a cognitive and affective nature, goals dealing with individuals and the society. Those were not considered in the NCS analyses, and the policy maker and planner must perforce consider these other goals, and make decisions on a wider basis than that of measured school achievement alone.

NOTE

* Harold J. Noah, "The Utility of Country Case Studies for Educational Planning," *Notes on Education* (New York: Institute of Philosophy and Politics of Education, Teachers College, Columbia University, 1974) 5: 4-7.

35

Educational Financing and Policy Goals*

Summary

The preceding report is based on a series of studies of the arrangements used to finance primary schools in ten of the OECD member countries: Australia, Canada (province of Ontario), the Federal Republic of Germany, Italy, the Netherlands, Norway, Sweden, the United Kingdom (England and Wales), the United States of America (California and Florida), and Yugoslavia.

Chapter I describes in summary fashion the variety of approaches used within each of the ten countries to finance primary schools, and connects those approaches to certain key concerns of educational finance policy. Chapter II examines some of the relationships between types of financing instruments and key policy concerns across the ten countries.

In five of the countries (Italy, the Netherlands, Norway, Sweden, and England and Wales) primary school finance is a concern of two levels of government: the central and local (often municipal) authorities. In Australia, local (municipal) authorities for education do not exist, so that there also school finance is the responsibility of two levels of government – the state governments (with the lion's share of the responsibility) and the Commonwealth government, that provides both direct and indirect assistance. In the United States and in Yugoslavia three levels of government (federal, state/republic, and local) are all directly involved in primary school finance. In Canada (Ontario) and the Federal Republic of Germany, the two remaining countries, the prime direct agents of primary school finance are the provinces/Länder and the localities, but the federal level plays an indirect role via its various programmes of fiscal equalization among the provinces/Länder.

Full central funding at the state level is the hallmark of school finance in Australia. Yugoslavia represents the other pole, with a very high degree (70-80 per cent) of reliance on local sources of funds. The other countries are ranged between these extremes. In general, the Netherlands, Italy and Sweden present a picture of relatively high proportions of central funding for schools; the United States, rather low central funding. In Ontario, provincial (central) funding has become more and more important in the last decade, and in the German Länder, too, the Land authorities provide a very substantial (60 per cent or more) share of the total costs of running the primary schools. In England and Norway the sources of finance are, on average, about equally divided between the central and local governments.

School finance is an ordinary and regular part of general governmental finance in all of the countries, except Canada and the United States. In these latter countries local school jurisdictions are usually separate, politically and legally, from general local administration. Separate school taxes are the rule and the local school districts do not usually receive financial support from the local government units.

In most of the countries (Canada, Germany, Italy, the Netherlands, Norway, Sweden, the United States, and Yugoslavia) non-local funds are made available to help support the operations of local school authorities primarily through various education-specific channels. In England. the central government makes a general grant-in-aid to a local authority, which has substantial latitude in deciding how generously it wishes to support its schools, in competition with the claims made by other locally provided services on its revenues. Similar relationships exist between the federal and state/Land/provincial authorities in Australia, Canada and Germany.

Some countries move beyond education-specific taxation and intergovernmental transfers to systems of categorical aid. Thus, in Sweden, the central governments assist municipalities in their school finance on the basis of a set of tightly drawn provisions related to distinct aspects of school operation and, especially, to the costs of teachers' salaries. The Netherlands, too, has a complex set of categorical aid arrangements for calculating transfers from the central government to the local municipal authorities. In the United States, also, federal aid to the states for school purposes has been based on categorical grants, though within the states non-categorical, education-specific transfers have been the norm.

Chapter II of the report explores the relationships between funding arrangements and three major policy concerns: equalization, locus of control, and diversity of provision and parental choice of school.

Three principal approaches to equalization are identified:

- equalization of tax bases to support education
- equalization of per pupil or per capita expenditures
- equalization of physical inputs, particularly teacher services.

England and Wales exemplifies a system that focusses on the equalization of tax bases. In Florida and Ontario, too, there is substantial emphasis in that direction. The same is true at the federal-Land interface in Germany, at the federal-state interface in Australia, and at the federal-province interface in Canada.

Equalization of per pupil or per capita expenditures is a fundamental aim in Florida, and many United States and Canadian jurisdictions approach the aim in part by mandating minimum (foundation) levels of expenditure per child enrolled. Other countries approach the goal indirectly. For example, the effect of full state assumption of school costs in Australia seems to have as a by-product a high degree of equalization of per pupil expenditures.

Equalization of physical inputs, particularly of teacher services, is the hallmark of school finance arrangements in the Netherlands and in Sweden. There are also strong elements of this approach in Norway, where the system goes beyond mere equalization to achieve substantial compensatory effects for children in isolated, rural and poor communes.

Limitations and Potentials

In the field of school finance, this study breaks new ground by combining a focus upon policy concerns with a comparative approach via ten countries. As far as the present report is concerned, the authors are painfully aware of its limitations. Questions concerning the true comparability of formally equivalent arrangements that have developed in different national contexts remain worrisome.

Country study authors were not always able to fit their data gathering and analysis into the agreed common framework that best suited the ultimate comparative purpose. The authors of the comparative paper have, no doubt, been sometimes unaware of important nuances of meaning, misunderstanding the precise importance of a particular term, or phrase; and the sheer volume of data to be considered must have produced some error in the final instance.

But, in spite of these, and perhaps other shortcomings, the entire project demonstrates that a comparative study of this kind is indeed possible and that it can produce some results of value: description of what exists in ten countries by way of the many different financing arrangements for primary schools; classification of those arrangements and their association with certain major policy concerns; and the possibility of using the data assembled to test the validity crossnationally of a number of commonly accepted generalizations.

Conclusions

1. *In whatever particular terms it is formulated, equalization can be successfully approached via either full central funding or mixed central-local funding, given certain conditions.* Full or nearly full central funding is an obvious option, illustrated by the Australian and Netherlands systems. Mixed central-local funding using categorical grants is another, especially when the support is directed toward the financing of teacher costs, as in Germany, Norway and Sweden. And mixed central-local funding using block grants can be arranged so as to have marked equalization effects, especially where differences among localities in fiscal capacity are low and/or the proportion of central funding is high (for example, Florida, Ontario, and England).

2. *Many countries have improved outcomes in terms of equalization by instituting changes of emphasis and intensity of financial assistance and intergovernmental grants; they have not found it necessary to recast radically their school financing systems.* Rather, a continuous process of reappraisal and modification of financing arrangements, to take account of shifting demographic patterns and changing socioeconomic structures, is the norm. While it is clear that none of the countries has succeeded completely in attaining the goal of equalization in all its aspects, most of them have made considerable progress in their recent past, without having had recourse to measures that represent fundamental breaks with traditional modes of financing schools.

3. *A corollary conclusion is that search for a "perfect" or "ideal" system of school finance is likely to be not only unnecessary, but futile.* The very variety of school financing arrangements that is observed leads to a strong suspicion that there can be no one best way to organize these matters, and that each country has adopted its particular pattern of school financing as the result of a long process of adjustment and compromise to its particular national context and to the major policy goals it has favoured over the long term. This conclusion tends to be reinforced when we recognize that some of the important goals set for a school finance system are likely to be mutually inconsistent, at least over certain ranges. Thus, equalization goals may conflict with the goal of expanded parental choice; tax equalization and expenditure

equalization may also be difficult to achieve fully at the same time; and efforts to achieve satisfactory levels of service for those with special needs may encroach on desires for greater local autonomy. In such a situation, the "worth" of a particular set of school financing arrangements depends heavily on the relative values placed on each of the goals involved, as well as on the extent to which a particular financing mechanism is able to promote them.

4. *Unitary states do not, ipso facto, attempt or achieve more equalization than do federal countries.* Partly because school finance and equalization mechanisms are generally more complex in the federal countries (if only because of the presence of an intermediate level of government), and partly because federal countries generally exhibit wider ranges of socioeconomic differences within their borders than do the unitary states, it might seem reasonable to suppose that unitary states attempt, and even achieve, more equalization than do the federal states. The ten countries in the present study comprise five unitary states (England and Wales, Italy, the Netherlands, Norway, and Sweden) and five federal countries (Australia, Canada [Ontario], Germany, the United States [California and Florida], and Yugoslavia). Yet an examination of each set of countries does not reveal a relationship between type of political structure and equalization of school revenues or expenditures.

5. The concept of equalization has been broadened in many countries to recognize that certain categories of children have handicaps that justify compensatory, and not just arithmetically equal, treatment. In terms of the financial instruments used to satisfy this goal, two approaches were identified and discussed: the use of programmes of categorical aid, and the use of pupil-weighting systems. Both are in widespread use and each has its particular set of advantages and disadvantages. *Categorical programmes tend to reinforce standard, often centrally devised and regulated, approaches to special provision.* At some stages of educational development this may be considered an advantage, at other stages a drawback. *Pupil-weighting systems, on the other hand, tend to leave the school-providing authority with more freedom of action, but they also bring with them severe problems associated with the identification of children in need of special services.* Such systems are also open to abuse if school authorities seek to inflate the number of children for whom they will "earn" larger weightings.

6. *The proposition that a high degree of non-local funding produces a more standardized, uniform structure of schooling or is negatively associated with local autonomy was not supported by the evidence of the country studies.* The mere fact that more money is supplied by one level of government to another level does not guarantee that the grantor level will exercise more control over the activities of the grantee level.

7. *However, a corollary proposition, that the mode by which non-local funds are made available will influence the degree of local autonomy permitted, is substantiated.* For example, the greater the reliance on non-categorical modes of funding, such as the use of block grants or service-specific non-categorical grants (for schools, housing, or roads, for example), the greater the degree of overt discretion enjoyed by grantee authorities. Conversely, greater reliance on categorical grants (for teachers' salaries, school building construction, or school programmes for the disadvantaged), is associated with less local autonomy. This is explained by the need to build regulatory controls and limits into categorical funding programmes that would otherwise turn into blank cheques issued to the grantees.

The report concludes that *the erosion of local autonomy, where it has occurred, has not happened as the result of deliberate moves on the part of either the local or the non-local authorities. Rather, ever higher levels of service have been demanded, at all levels of government, and the costs of provision have tended to outrun the localities' financial powers.*

8. The study noted that, in most of the countries, some public funds are made available directly to some non-government schools. In particular, the financing arrangements used in Australia and the Netherlands to support nongovernment (mostly, church-related) schools are described, and are contrasted with arrangements in Ontario, where public money is not given to private schools, but is available to both the non-denominational public school system and to the predominantly Roman Catholic separate school system. It is probable that provisions for supplying public funds to non-government schools will support a greater degree of diversity of provision and effective parental choice than is the case in countries where such arrangements are absent. But, a concluding cross-national analysis shows that *there does not seem to be any systematic relationship between the "standardization" of schools provision (lack of opportunities for parental choice) and particular aspects of school financing, such as the proportion of non-local funding provided.*

9. Finally, some countries place a great deal more weight on financing instruments to "steer" primary school policy and administration than do others. For example, in Canada, the Netherlands, the United States, and Yugoslavia, financing mechanisms play quite a large role in school affairs. In Germany, Italy, and Sweden, less so. But there are no clear correlates of this choice: *greater reliance on financing instruments (as distinct from direct, detailed regulation) does not appear to affect systematically any important outcomes of school policy.*

Suggestions for Further Comparative Work

Further comparative work dealing with school finance would seem to be justified, and three main approaches, at least, are worth consideration.

First, there is the possibility or replicating the present project for another sector of the school system, for example, secondary schools, vocational schools, or pre-school institutions. Such a study might well be of value in its own right, as well as serve to validate the approach used here.

Second, the importance of teachers' salaries in school finance is obvious, and we have noted that in some countries the reimbursement (or assumption) of teacher costs plays a major role in the system of school finance. A comparative study that examined the consequences of basing school finance on teacher cost reimbursement or assumption might have quite substantial policy implications, as well as serving an important informative function.

Third, the present report deals in a somewhat summary manner with some aspects of financing schooling for children with special needs. This topic requires particular attention and comment here. The present report pursues at greater length three approaches to equalization – of the tax bases for education, of per capita expenditures and of physical inputs such as teacher services. However, such measures fall far short of the demand to provide an equally effective education for all the different and often greater needs of many groups of children. Thus, along with general measures, including financial ones, aimed at equalising opportunity, governments have also increasingly provided extra resources for children with special needs. A number of countries view the demand to continue in this direction as the current major challenge to national educational policy, and a comparative study that took this as its central theme could be of greatest utility at the present juncture.

However, the present report well illustrates that the value of an inter-country study lies in the opportunity it affords to deal with underlying principles. Thus, while a general notion of "handicapped" is often used to define children with special educational needs, this term should be recognised as an aspect of a more general differentiation among school populations. The general principle is that policies are being directed toward school populations which are differentially recognised for educational purposes and for whom higher levels and different modes of financing are required. A whole range of school populations, however they are delineated by country authorities, according to various social, cultural, linguistic, racial, ethnic, geographic, physical and mental characteristics, are the subjects of special educational attention. A new comparative study could usefully follow the precedent established in the present report to examine the general principles in this field in which policy is related to finance.

Finally, it has been recognised in this report that financing instruments may not of themselves be the major means for effectuating policy but that they may provide a key element along with other instruments in the larger organisational context. Therefore it is suggested that in future enquiries this organisational context be made more explicit.

NOTE

* Harold J. Noah and Joel D. Sherman, *Educational Financing and Policy Goals for Primary Schools: General Report.* Paris: Organisation for Economic Co-operation and Development, 1979: 64-69. Reprinted by permission of the Organisation for Economic Cooperation and Development.

36

Soviet Education's Unsolved Problems*

Perhaps no society places more trust in education to solve its important political, economic, and moral problems than does the Soviet Union. In this sense, of course, Soviet social philosophy peculiarly parallels our own. It is messianic and idealistic. Policy is based on the firm belief that man can radically improve society, and that in this task the school will play a leading role.

Despite fearful difficulties, some of their own making, others imposed on them from outside, Soviet social construction has brought the country a long way forward since 1917. This progress is especially evident in education, as the accompanying charts show. The Soviet government invests between one-seventh and one-eighth of its total budget in formal education, and perhaps 7 per cent of the Soviet national product goes into providing formal education (compared with 3 to 5 per cent spent by the Western, developed countries out of far greater incomes per head).

Yet, despite undoubted quantitative progress and continued massive investment in education, the Soviets face at least three sets of intractable problems when they come to weigh the achievements of their schools. They are problems of ideological training, problems of moral training, and problems in the area of the economics of education. Let us examine each of these in turn.

There can be no doubt that the Soviet system has generated deep political loyalty, particularly among the young people, and some of this, though not, indeed, all of it, may properly be ascribed to the operation of the schools. But the Soviet system demands more than vague, generalized loyalty to the State. Especially from its responsible citizens, it requires a firm Marxist-Leninist world outlook and enthusiastic participation in the building of Communism at home. The political training given in the schools and universities, as well as in the youth movement, is designed to foster these virtues among the young people.

Yet it is a commonplace that the formal political training given in compulsory lecture courses on Party history, historical materialism, and economics are met by only the supreme indifference of most students. They know that satisfactory examination results in these subjects are required for graduation, but they also know that even more important are good grades in their "subject" examinations. Lack of commitment by young people to the tasks of Communist construction is widely and frequently deplored in the Soviet press. Even a society that did not make the all-embracing Soviet claim to total individual commitment to group purposes might be legitimately concerned, but the Soviets feel compelled to regard it as a continuing challenge to do better with their youth.

The total result of the indoctrination effort is impossible to measure, but the observer of the Soviet scene is impressed by the fact that young people in the Soviet Union by no means speak with a single, undifferentiated voice. Many (and especially many of the better educated) are highly critical of Soviet society, and they are critical of it in non-Marxist-Leninist terms. Yet the total political impact of Soviet education has certainly not been a negative quantity. Many young students feel grateful to a system that has given them educational and employment opportunities vastly superior to those their parents and grandparents knew. But, as in the West, young people manage to serve the State and remain loyal to it, often without surrendering their total intellectual commitment to the official political creed, and seeking all the while to adapt its peculiar structures to their personal gain. How to secure total, unselfish political commitment remains one of the unsolved problems of Soviet education.

Paradoxically, the government is at the mercy of its own slogan of "bringing the schools closer to life." Soviet doctrine freely admits that the present society is riddled through and through with what it calls "traces of the bourgeois past." Some of these traces remain obstinately substantial, and the pupils' contact with them by no means helps the school to foster the desired political orthodoxy among the young. How to use the school to counteract the adverse political influence upon the pupils exerted by parents, acquaintances, and the workpeople met in the course of vocational training, while insisting all the time upon the closest contact between the school and the real world outside, is one of those long-wearing problems that provides pedagogical journals in the Soviet Union with topics for decades on end.

Moreover, "life" in the form of the practice of Soviet government itself teaches lessons that few students can entirely ignore. The spectacle last October of the ignominious dismissal of Chairman Khrushchev and the complete silence since imposed upon him confirm the average Soviet citizen in his political apathy. When the country not only is run by a cabal, but even appears to be so, none of the formal lessons given in the schools to promote political enthusiasm and to teach the paramount place in history of objective, material, nonpersonal factors makes much sense.

Consider now the allied set of problems for Soviet education that is to be found in the field of the moral training of Soviet youth. Great emphasis has been placed on the need to raise up a new Soviet citizen. Honesty, courtesy, sexual morality, vigorous intellectual and physical activity are all major elements in the character of these new men. Unfortunately there is little sign that they are emerging in Soviet schools and colleges in any greater number than was previously apparent. Again, it appears that formal instruction has failed to upgrade the general level of Soviet personal and social behavior, and in any case, the line between socially demanded virtue and what the English call "priggish" behavior (a holier-than-thou attitudinizing) is always very thin. However, the problem is not that Soviet moral education has been too successful and is creating wholesale a nation of prigs, but that significant groups of the young people remain immune or, even worse, react negatively.

Apart from the dishonesty indicated by reports of minor and major black-market activity, the persistence of juvenile delinquency worries the authorities. Official doctrine has taught that this phenomenon was merely temporary, occurring in Soviet society as a direct consequence of the wartime disruption of families. But that familiar phenomenon of modern urban life, the teen-age gang, has proved to be no respecter of state boundaries or different social systems. As in the West, in Africa, and in Asia, there are young people in the Soviet Union who see in their society nothing for themselves. They reject its goals, its values, its forms, its institutions, its dress, and even its conventional language; and they invent or borrow from abroad styles and interests that express that rejection.

Of course, as in the West, because these groups are themselves vocal and are loudly condemned by the organs of society, they receive more than their fair share of publicity, and one must guard against a tendency to exaggerate their typicality. Yet even if it is only a fringe of Soviet youth that attracts official attention because of its overt "antisocial" behavior, it is nevertheless a fringe that the Soviets count in increasing rather than declining numbers each year. The gap between the predictions of Marxist-Leninist social theory and what happens in the real world presents them with a challenge and a problem.

Paid production practice by pupils and students has raised problems connected with the proper Communist attitude to monetary reward for socially useful labor. It is generally agreed that the young students should be paid for their work, so that they learn the value of money and develop a proper pride in their ability to earn honest money in the service of society. The difficulty arises about how much the young people should be allowed to earn, and what to do if the desire for gain overshadows the real pedagogical and moral purposes of providing the opportunity to engage in productive labor.

Some schools have tried to avoid the dangers of fostering the selfish desire for personal gain by having the children work in groups or collectives, pooling their earnings in order to accumulate a specified sum for a collective project. The commonest types of collective project are excursions or school journeys, or some addition to the equipment of the school. However, the purists find something to object to even here. It is pointed out that the real purpose of the exercise in socially productive labor gets lost in the collective scramble to amass the sum necessary to meet the group target, just as much as it does in a system based on strictly individual rewards.

There are also the ethical problems posed by the occasional young member of the collective who does not pull his weight in the joint effort. What is to be done with him when it comes to spending the joint earnings? Should the collective follow the sound Communist principle: "He who does not work, neither shall he eat"; or should it recognize that it is, after all, dealing with a child who may not be fully responsible for his actions, and hope that the good example set by the rest of the group will gradually have its beneficial effect?

That the philosophical bases of Marxism-Leninism offer no guarantees of easy success in moral training is also shown by the history of atheist education and antireligious propaganda in the schools during the Soviet period. The crude anti-religious campaigns that marked the 1920s and much of the 1930s are now out of fashion. Instead, the main approach taken in the schools is to emphasize the superior quality of the answers which science, as opposed to religion, can give to the basic questions of human existence. Yet even those children who in the officially approved manner reject with open contempt the symbols of religion are by no means automatically to be counted as champions of the scientific, materialistic, and rationalist explanation of the great philosophical concerns of mankind. More than likely they are merely indifferent, or simply puzzled. It worries the Party authorities that nearly fifty years after the Revolution, lessons in atheism are needed as desperately as ever.

However impressive the quantitative figures and the rates of increase of schooling may be, the Soviet authorities are preoccupied by a number of intractable problems connected with the economic returns to their educational investment.

First, there is the difficult matter of quality. The headlong expansion of the Soviet period has often meant the establishment of new educational institutions and the growth of existing ones in circumstances that could only result in the graduation of students of below average skills. This is especially true in teacher training.

Second, there is abundant evidence (not least from Soviet sources) that curricula and methods of instruction too often foster old-fashioned ideas and useless formal knowledge, and serve only to develop unimaginative, routine-minded operatives.

Third, there is the problem of the internal distribution of the total resources devoted to education among the various branches of education. Large though the expansion of semiprofessional and vocational training has been, it has by no means met the needs of the economy. This means that while the Soviet economy still has plenty of unskilled labor and an increasingly sufficient supply of university-trained personnel, it lacks large enough cadres of semiprofessional and skilled middle-range personnel for the implementation of modern techniques throughout the whole range of industry trade, and agriculture. Consequently, while it is quite possible for Russia to startle the world with triumphs in Sputnik technology, to show significant achievements in some branches of basic science, and to undertake monumental projects in civil engineering and housing, the quality of work in many vital sectors of the economy is generally exceedingly low. Best Soviet theory is too often startlingly different from average Soviet practice, which gives rise to the suspicion that the "head" of Soviet education may be too large while the "tail," or perhaps, better, the "abdomen," is too small.

The fourth unsolved problem of Soviet education in the field of the economics of education has to do with the practice of "polytechnical education." The reform laws of 1958-59 marked the high point of polytechnical thinking in Soviet educational legislation. The most spectacular feature of the reforms was the requirement that all pupils in the three senior grades of the secondary school were to be occupied for one-third their school time (two whole days out of six) working in Soviet factories or on the farms. It was laid down that pupils would generally be expected to acquire qualifications in two different trades during the three-year period, and could not expect to obtain their school-leaving certificates without these qualifications. At the same time, it was emphasized that most young people of fifteen to sixteen years of age would be expected in any case to cease full-time schooling after finishing the eighth grade and complete their secondary education by part-time (evening or shift) studies after work was over each day. In order to accommodate the extra demands upon the curriculum made by practical labor-training, the period of complete secondary education was extended by one year to eleven years. This not only raised direct ruble costs of education for the State budget, but delayed for one year the entry of young people into full-time production. At first, Soviet enterprises had to bear the entire financial burden of providing the practical training and work experience for pupils, even to the extent of requiring the enterprises to pay the wages of the training staff, but this policy had to be abandoned. Nevertheless, the enterprises still have to provide and pay for special clothing, materials, tools, machine time, and space used to train pupils.

But the most serious burden on Soviet industry and agriculture is probably the disturbance of regular routines caused by the incessant invasions of factories and farms by young trainees. Luckless managers who react defensively and try to insulate the operations of their factories from the disruptive effects of polytechnical labor-training are roundly denounced for uncooperative attitudes and branded as unwilling to have the trainees do anything except routine and non-educational tasks around the factory. Conflicts of this type seem to be built into the system, making vocational training much more the responsibility of industry than of the schools. The factory manager will usually want either to use pupils in tasks where regular workers are hard to find, or to hold training costs down by keeping pupils working at a particular job once they have become reasonably proficient. The educational staff, on the contrary, will want the pupils to enjoy the highest level and the most varied assortment of work experience that it is possible to give. The pupils may well have an assortment of other ideas, shared neither by the factory management nor by their teachers. Some are bored by the whole affair and look for all kinds of easy assignments, especially those which involve them in just watching a skilled man at work. Others are interested in high pay for their two-days-a-week work, approve of any arrangement the factory can make for them to work steadily at one particular well-paying job, and regard with dismay their teachers' interest in moving them about the factory in search of new polytechnical experiences.

After five years of this experiment in work-study organization for the senior secondary schools, the 1964-65 school year opened with the abrupt announcement in mid-August by E.I. Afanasenko, Minister of Education of the RSFSR, that the senior secondary school course was to be cut back from three years to two years, and that the time allotted to production practice would also be cut. The official explanation was that the growing efficiency of Soviet pedagogy now enabled pupils to master in two years what had previously taken three. In fact, it has become increasingly evident that production training has turned out hundreds of thousands of rather poorly skilled young carpenters, lathe operators, and other relatively low grade, semi-skilled personnel whose training costs were completely wasted in the economic sense because very few of them would later in life be engaged in those trades in which they had been trained. Whatever may have been the ideological returns to practical vocational training of secondary school children, its economic returns have been slight. Vocational training of all Soviet youth has not yet been abandoned, but the writing is on the wall for another of N. S. Khrushchev's educational and economic panaceas.

The fifth problem is reflected in the view of the Soviet government that young men and women who have enjoyed a higher education at society's expense owe the State a few years' service in locations which may not be quite of their own choosing. The Soviet Union has a quite extraordinary number of somewhat unpleasant (or at least unpopular) and remote places to which young graduates may be assigned. The difficulties encountered by the authorities in persuading young graduates to take up jobs in these areas and to stay at them for the two or three years of the assignment are legion. But such difficulties are only part of the larger problem of the "correct," or "rational," allocation of the Soviet Union's reserves of skilled labor among all the alternative patterns of employment that are theoretically possible. However successful the schools and colleges may be in training millions of young people to work in the national economy, much of the profit to society is in jeopardy if there is widespread misallocation of trained personnel. Except for the armed forces, and for the post-graduation assignments just mentioned, the Soviets have rejected conscription of labor as a method of allocation. They prefer to rely upon a "managed-market" technique, in which the central planners are supposed to manipulate the relative monetary and non-monetary rewards and advantages of occupations and jobs to ensure that skilled labor goes where the planners want it to go, and stays there until the planners decree otherwise. But there is great dissatisfaction among Soviet planners and economists about the operation of the present system of labor allocation, and the suspicion is growing that there is significant waste of the trained manpower that has been produced at such great public cost.

Finally, a word about the costs of education. The Soviet state has a more than usual interest in these costs, for in the Soviet Union the State budget bears almost the full burden of the direct costs of teachers' salaries, building expenses, instructional materials, and so forth. Even insofar as Soviet enterprises or collective farms share the financial burden, the economic and financial planners must take these expenditures into account when drafting the all-important overall economic "balances" of the plan.

During the 1950s, enrollments in schools of general education fluctuated widely, yet throughout all the variations in enrollment, costs per pupil enrolled rose remorselessly. Indeed, between 1950 and 1961 money costs per pupil in the schools of general education rose by 56 per cent, and this at a time of generally falling ruble prices. In terms of constant rubles, expenditures per pupil in general education schools rose by no less than 79 per cent. Only in higher education was the financial picture brighter, because of the widespread introduction of correspondence and evening study. In higher education, in terms of constant rubles, costs per student actually declined by about 10 per cent during the decade.

The economies of scale that larger enrollments create (mainly by bringing down the teacher-pupil ratio) may help a little in restraining per pupil costs, but last November the underpaid Soviet teachers received their first general salary increase since 1948. The raises are considerable, amounting to between 20 and 25 per cent of most salaries in teaching. The Soviet school system is more "labor-intensive" than most (that is, the fraction of total costs spent on wages and salaries is still quite high), and increases in salaries have great and immediate impact on costs. Also, the main "cost-raisers" in the Soviet system are the small, so-called dwarf, rural schools with a dozen pupils or so. They are likely to remain a tough problem for any cost-conscious Soviet educational administrator, at least until the necessary billions of rubles are invested in construction of rural highways which alone will make rural school consolidations possible.

Another probable result of the cost problem in general education has been the apparent failure to reach the target of 2.5 million boarding-school places set by Khrushchev for the end of the current Seven-Year Plan in 1965. If ordinary general education has been somewhat expensive, boarding-school provision costs a fortune. In 1960, boarding-school costs per pupil were no less than seven times more than day-school costs, and average contributions from parents amounted to no more than 7 to 8 per cent of the total. Construction costs in boarding schools are generally about four times higher per place than in day schools. Little wonder that the expansion of boarding-school provision, so loudly proclaimed from 1956 to 1960, has since been less stridently advertised.

After all, the Soviet Union is not a country with resources to squander; in trying so hard to reach and overtake the West the planners have created a host of competing demands upon its wealth. Education secures a formidable slice of those scarce resources, and is therefore expected to make the best use of what it is given and help solve some of the pressing economic problems of Soviet society. The Soviets themselves seem to have come to a belated recognition of the existence of some of these problems. Last October it was announced that, for the first time in the Soviet Union, a research institute into the problems of the economics of education has been established at the Lenin Pedagogical Institute in Moscow. One can safely forecast that it will have much work to do, for despite the Soviet insistence on planning education and economic development, the study of the economics of education has been as neglected in the Soviet Union as it has been until recently in the West.

None of the problems of Soviet education reviewed here is new. Nor are they peculiar to Soviet society. In the West, too, we have our difficulties with juvenile delinquency, lack of commitment to high social and moral purposes, rising costs of education, and the inflexibility of the school system in the face of rapidly changing social and economic demands. But the Soviets have always claimed, and continue to claim, that their Marxist-Leninist approach to the problems of social institutions (including, of course, education) provides them swiftly and surely with the solutions to difficulties that continue to plague the West. At the very least, these hopes appear to be over-optimistic. Marxism-Leninism may have done much for the Soviet Union. What it has not done is to wipe away the intractable problems of education and Soviet society.

NOTE

* Harold J. Noah, "Soviet Education's Unsolved Problems," *Saturday Review,* August 21, 1965: 54-56, 64-65.

37

Communist Schooling*

JOHN I. THOMAS, *Education for Communism: School and State in the People's Republic of Albania.* Stanford, Calif., Hoover Institution Press, 1969. NIGEL GRANT, *Society, Schools and Progress in Eastern Europe.* Oxford, Pergamon Press, 1969. WASYL SHIMONIAK, *Communist Education: Its History, Philosophy and Politics.* Chicago, Rand McNally, 1970. SEYMOUR M. ROSEN, *Education and Modernization in the USSR.* Reading, Mass., Addison-Wesley, 1971.

There is now a substantial collection of books published outside the Communist countries discussing the origins, nature, structure and purpose of education under communism. The four volumes presently under review are valuable additions to that bibliography,

John I. Thomas' study is the narrowest in focus, dealing with educational developments in tiny Albania, with a population of only 2.1 million in 1970. Relying heavily upon Albanian and Soviet sources, and for the most part eschewing value judgements, Thomas provides a detailed view of how the present Albanian system of education rose on the ruins of Italian, French, Greek, and Turkish imports. He describes the familiar pattern of educational deprivation that still existed in Albania before World War II – a condition that spurred the Communists' subsequent commitment to extending educational opportunities, especially among women. In the space of less than 30 years, Albania has come a long way educationally – from a country that had not a single institution of higher education in 1945 to one that is now beginning to provide educational facilities on a par with those of its Greek and Yugoslav neighbors. Thomas' book is invaluable for its detailed account of this process.

Like the other Eastern European countries, Albania reconstructed its educational system in imitation of Soviet models, with only minor adjustments to adapt them to local conditions. Indeed, the strength of the Soviet example in Eastern Europe is nowhere evidenced more clearly than in Albania, notwithstanding the 1961 split with the Soviet Union. The transfer of Albania's allegiance to the Chinese branch of communism apparently did not mean that the usefulness and durability of Soviet models were at an end, at least in education. Although Thomas mentions these events, his book leaves the reader with a definite sense of incompleteness on this score. After all, the really interesting thing about Albania's educational development is that while the regime shifted its political allegiance from Yugoslavia to the Soviet Union, and then from the Soviet Union to China, its adherence to Soviet-based forms of education has endured. Why? That question Thomas does not raise.

Part of the answer is that the Soviet model has, in fact, proven very useful for countries, like Albania, which are seeking to effect extremely rapid transformations of their backward, predominantly agricultural societies, marked by traces of feudalism, into modern, industrialized, and mass-participatory states. This implies that it was not just a matter of the Soviet Union imposing its example by sheer force of military might and political power, but that the countries of Eastern Europe derived genuine assistance from the Soviet framework and philosophy of education. Is there justification for this belief? The conclusion offered by Nigel Grant's book is "Probably yes"; the answer from Wasyl Shimoniak is a resounding "No!"

Grant has written a shrewdly perceptive and on the whole sympathetic book about the countries of Eastern Europe, their turbulent history, their pre-Communist educational development, and the schooling patterns adopted under communism. While tracing the common pattern underlying the changes in education that have taken place in eight countries (Poland, East Germany, Czechoslovakia, Hungary, Romania, Yugoslavia, Bulgaria, and Albania), he also takes pains to explain how and why local variations have occurred. Writing a multinational, comparative book of this kind is a difficult task, and Grant has succeeded admirably.

The countries of Eastern Europe are in an interesting "love-hate" relationship with the Soviet Union. There is little in their histories (except perhaps for Bulgaria) to make them natural disciples of the Soviet Union; yet their military, economic, and perhaps ideological need for the Soviet Union is so great that, notwithstanding conflicts of varying gravity that arose on occasion in East Germany, Poland, Hungary and Czechoslovakia, the allegiance of the East European states to the Soviet bloc has not been seriously in doubt. Writing from the perspective of education, Grant is able to show that the Soviet model does have a genuine functional meaning for countries as diverse as East Germany and, say, Romania. Secularization of education; tying schools more closely to the requirements of planned economic development; widening educational opportunities, particularly for women, rural youth, and the poor; replacing a formal classics-oriented curriculum with one emphasizing mathematics and the natural sciences for all; and introducing strong elements of work-study and practical training into school programs – all these basic features of the Soviet educational model the Eastern European countries have found exceptionally useful to their own development.

Wasyl Shimoniak addresses an even wider canvas than does Grant, extending the scope of his study to include China, Cuba, the Mongolian People's Republic, North Korea and North Vietnam, although half of his long book is devoted to the development of education in Russia and the Soviet Union. For Shimoniak, the key to what has been going on in the Communist polities lies in the growth and consolidation of personal power in the hands of small groups of men, with education, too, being utilized to serve this purpose. Marxist-Leninist philosophy and sloganizing are seen as verbal cloaks for a powerful drive, both inside and outside the Soviet Union, to extend the sway of the Russian people and their culture and to extirpate (using violence, where necessary) the influence of organized religions. While Shimoniak is prepared to concede that some benefits have flowed from the establishment of Communist forms of government in and around the Soviet Union (emancipation of women, elimination of illiteracy, improvement in the material conditions of life), his judgment is that the price paid has been altogether too high. He also concedes that the Communist rulers of these nations have spent generously on education, but he views their motives as suspect. They needed schools to build economic power as a basis for military might, to facilitate the ideological indoctrination of the masses, and to establish the supremacy of Russian (or

Chinese) culture as the only true socialist culture, and all this primarily for the sake of consolidating their personal power. Shimoniak concludes:

> In brief, the language of communism cannot be trusted. Russian and Chinese communism are not the types of communism that were dreamed of for many centuries. As seen in every country where the Communists came to power, the individual lost his freedom not to the state, but to a few dictators, who were power-hungry individuals. There can be no two political parties, there can be no more than one representative in an "election," and there cannot be division of power between God and the ruler.

> At the same time the Communists realized that the only way to stay in power is to educate their own intelligentsia, their own leaders and their own children. For this reason, the number of schools has increased in every country they have occupied.

This interpretation of events and motivations takes the "devil-theory" of communism much too far. While self-serving political behavior, arbitrary rule, oppression of national groups, and the suppression of national and religious aspirations have certainly occurred under communism, they are unfortunately no monopoly of the Communist world. Moreover, the Communist system, especially in the fields of education and social services, does have its positive aspects from the standpoint of harnessing national energies for the tasks of modernization and economic development.

A distinguishing mark of Communist states is their commitment to reforming the ideals and philosophy of their citizens along so-called Marxist-Leninist lines. In this task, the schools, the higher educational institutions, and the youth movement are expected to play major roles. It is not surprising that this is so, for such institutions are ideally adapted to centralized, bureaucratic forms of control and to the inculcation of officially prescribed ideas and norms. Thus, education in the Soviet Union and other Communist states serves a much wider purpose than merely insuring the perpetuation in power of a small clique of rulers. It is intended to be the instrument for bringing into being a new type of citizen as the basis of a new social order. To see Communist education only in the light of the abuses of state power that have taken place, as Shimoniak tends to do, may lead us both to misunderstand the appeal of the Communist system and to underrate its potential for survival.

It is in this respect that Seymour Rosen's book needs to be read in conjunction with Shimoniak's. Though much of what Rosen has to say is not new, it is helpful to have collected in one place details on curriculum, enrollment, and educational structure updated to the end of the 1960's. Useful statistical tables on the economy and the educational system are given in an appendix. Moreover, the author is scrupulously accurate in his citations of sources and his transliterations (unfortunately something which cannot be said of Shimoniak), as well as in his facts. Like Grant, Rosen is clear about the distortions and defects of Communist sociocultural policies, but by looking at Soviet educational programs in the context of Russia's 250-year-old drive toward modernization, he achieves an objective analysis that serves as a counterweight to Shimoniak's one-sided interpretation.

Will mass education prove in time to be a Trojan horse in the Communist societies? That is to say, will not a highly educated population eventually become unwilling to tolerate the political and ideological authoritarianism that has characterized the Soviet and other Communist societies? This is perhaps one of the most important questions that confront analysts of the Communist system, but unfortunately it is one to which none of the authors whose works are reviewed here gives any attention.

The evidence to date is, of course, not encouraging. As in the Western countries, the elimination of illiteracy in the USSR did not automatically produce an independently thinking, politically sophisticated electorate. Rather, mass literacy was used to insure that the ideas of the dominant ideology received the widest publicity. Universal primary and near-universal secondary education under communism has proved to be a splendid instrument for the inculcation of an intensely narrow view of the world and the Soviet Union's place in it. Higher education has been developed in a framework of rigorous specialization and is designed not to open young minds but to train them to perform certain well-defined professional tasks. So far, it must be conceded, the Soviet state has been able to reap the economic benefits flowing from its educational system without paying any appreciable price in terms of the emergence of a more intellectually curious and ideologically obdurate citizenry.

What of the future? Here, I am inclined to be more sanguine. Soviet leaders might do well to remember Marx's insistence that the laws of motion of societies can be understood best in terms of men's relationship to the means of production. Everywhere, but especially in Communist states, the amount of public educational investment in the citizenry is becoming so vast that it begins to rival investment in conventional physical capital. Those who embody that educational investment cannot be treated simply as if they were animate tools. Indeed, they begin to assume many of the characteristics of an independent peasantry, seeking to exploit to the best advantage their individual holding of capital – in this case, education. If so, Communist states may eventually find that they have cast out their agricultural peasantry only to create a replacement class of independently thinking, small-scale "capitalists," the educated professionals.

The path to relaxed controls over intellectual inquiry and freedom of expression will no doubt be long and beset by many twists and turns, but the emergence of a highly educated population seems likely to present a growing challenge to the continuation of authoritarianism in politics as well as in culture.

NOTE

* Harold J. Noah, "Communist Schooling," in *Problems of Communism* XXII:5 (1973): 71-73

Notes on the authors

HAROLD J. NOAH is Gardner Cowles Professor Emeritus of Economics and Education, Teachers College, Columbia University, USA. He was Dean of Teachers College, 1976-81. For many years he was a member of the faculty of Columbia University's School of International and Public Affairs. He retired from Teachers College in 1987 and joined the faculty of the University at Buffalo, State University of New York, retiring in 1991. Born and educated in London (London School of Economics, and King's College) he has worked in the economics of education and in comparative education. He has been a consultant to OECD, UNESCO, and The World Bank. He is an Honorary Fellow of the Comparative and International Education Society (President of the Society, 1973-74), and a member of the National Academy of Education. He edited the *Comparative Education Review* from 1965-71. He currently divides his time between the mid-Hudson Valley in New York State and Cape Town, South Africa. His e-mail address is hjnoah@mohawk.net.

MAX A. ECKSTEIN is Professor Emeritus of Queens College, the City University of New York and a Senior Research Associate, Institute of Philosophy and Politics of Education, Teachers College, Columbia University. Born and educated in England, he received his first degree (B.A.Hons) and professional teaching qualification (P.G.C.E.) at King's College, University of London (1948-52), and taught English, French and German in London secondary schools (1952-1957). After joining the faculty of Queens College, C.U.N.Y. (1958), he obtained the Ph.D. from Teachers College, Columbia University (1964), specializing in Comparative Education. Former President and now Honorary Fellow of the Comparative and International Education Society, he has conducted research and lectured in many countries of Asia and Europe. He has served as a consultant on foreign education to the U.S. Dept. of Education and the American Federation of Teachers.

With this work, Eckstein and Noah celebrate over 30 years of collaboration in research and professional publication.

PHILIP FOSTER graduated from the London School of Economics with a degree in economics and sociology in 1948. After a period of military service he taught in East Africa (Uganda) for some years and then entered the United States in 1958. He gained his doctorate at the University of Chicago in 1962 and subsequently held professorships in the Departments of Education and Sociology at that institution. He was Associate Director of the Comparative Education Center in Chicago from 1964 until 1973 and Director from 1973 until 1978. Subsequently he was Professor and Head of School at Macquarie University, Australia from 1978 until 1981 and from then until his retirement in 1991 he was Professor in the Department of Educational Administration and Policy Studies at SUNY, Albany. Professor Foster has written extensively on problems of economic and social change in traditional societies with particular emphasis on the impact of formal systems of education on traditional social structures.

Index of authors